MW01098753

Selected Essays on China's Education: Research and Review, Volume 1

Selected Essays on China's Education: Research and Review, Volume 1

Written and Oral Narratives

Edited by

Gang DING

with an Introduction by

Ruth Hayhoe

BRILL

LEIDEN | BOSTON

ESPH Educational Science Publishing House

This book includes English translations of a collection of articles selected from 中国教育：研究与评论 (*Zhongguo jiaoyu: yanjiu yu pinglun*), edited by Ding Gang 丁钢 and published by Educational Science Publishing House, with financial support from Chinese Fund for the Humanities and Social Sciences.

Library of Congress Cataloging-in-Publication Data

Names: Ding, Gang, 1953- editor.
Title: Selected essays on China's education : research and review / edited by Gang Ding ; with an
    Introduction by Ruth Hayhoe.
Description: Leiden ; Boston : Brill, [2019] | Includes index. | Translated from Chinese. | Summary: "Selected
    Essays on China's Education: Research and Review (4 volumes) consists of 22 most influential theses
    on the history and tradition of Chinese Education. These essays, selected and translated from China's
    Education: Research and Review, a serial publication in Chinese, reflect the progress of qualitative
    research on Chinese education both within and outside China. Volume 1 focuses on Written and Oral
    Narratives, including six articles; Volume 2 focuses on History and Current Reality, including five articles;
    Volume 3 focuses on Knowledge and Tradition, including six articles; and Volume 4 focuses on Gender
    and Education, including five articles. Aiming to promote academic dialogues on Chinese culture and
    education, these essays explore important educational and cultural issues in China with a transcultural
    perspective"—Provided by publisher.
Identifiers: LCCN 2019023084 (print) | LCCN 2019023085 (ebook) | ISBN 9789004409798 (hardback) | ISBN
    9789004409804 (ebook)
Subjects: LCSH: Education—China. | Education—Research—China.
Classification: LCC LA1131 .S45 2019 (print) | LCC LA1131 (ebook) | DDC 370.951—dc23
LC record available at https://lccn.loc.gov/2019023084
LC ebook record available at https://lccn.loc.gov/2019023085

Typeface for the Latin, Greek, and Cyrillic scripts: "Brill". See and download: brill.com/brill-typeface.

ISBN 978-90-04-40959-0 (hardback)
ISBN 978-90-04-40960-6 (e-book)

Copyright by Educational Science Publishing House. All rights reserved.
English edition copyright 2019 by Koninklijke Brill NV, Leiden, The Netherlands.
Koninklijke Brill NV incorporates the imprints Brill, Brill Hes & De Graaf, Brill Nijhoff, Brill Rodopi,
Brill Sense, Hotei Publishing, mentis Verlag, Verlag Ferdinand Schöningh and Wilhelm Fink Verlag.
No part of this publication may be reproduced, translated, stored in a retrieval system, or transmitted in any
form or by any means, electronic, mechanical, photocopying, recording or otherwise, without prior written
permission from the publisher.
Authorization to photocopy items for internal or personal use is granted by Koninklijke Brill NV provided
that the appropriate fees are paid directly to The Copyright Clearance Center, 222 Rosewood Drive,
Suite 910, Danvers, MA 01923, USA. Fees are subject to change.

This book is printed on acid-free paper and produced in a sustainable manner.

Printed by Printforce, the Netherlands

Contents

Introduction

Ruth Hayhoe

It gives me pleasure to introduce these volumes with all of the chapters selected from the influential journal, *China's Education Research and Review*, initiated by Professor Ding Gang of the East China Normal University in 1999. Ding Gang personally selected this set of papers and organized them into four volumes: Volume 1 Written and Oral Narratives; Volume 2 History and Current Reality; Volume 3 Knowledge and Tradition; and Volume 4 Gender and Education. Through these broad themes one can immediately see the trajectory of Ding Gang's work as a scholar with degrees in philosophy, Chinese literature and education. On the one hand he is committed to explorations of China's unique knowledge traditions and the ways in which they continue to shape contemporary education and on the other hand he seeks to profile the actual experience of education on the ground through concrete and detailed explorations of such themes as the real life experience of women teachers being prepared for rural schools in a normal school, the education of white collar workers in Shanghai, the educational beliefs of teachers on the ground, and the consideration of such art forms as documentary film in education. In addition, there is a significant section on China's knowledge traditions, using sophisticated sociological theory to analyze and reflect on relations of knowledge, power and desire in China's long history. Finally the last volume is devoted to gender and education with essays that consider many angles of the lives of women students and women teachers, including the experience of students in missionary universities, how a gender culture is reproduced through textbook learning and interaction in the classroom, and how the life of one influential weaving artist enabled a generation of women to reflect in new ways on their education and work.

Interwoven with these thoughtfully crafted papers on the experience of education in practice and in the context of educational history are five papers by international scholars. These papers were translated into Chinese for publication in the Chinese journal in the years from 2001 to 2003 and reflect a particular commitment made by Ding Gang when he came to Canada as a visiting scholar in 1993 under a collaborative project sponsored by the Canadian International Development Agency. I was host for his time at the University of Toronto and was impressed by his determination to bring together two worlds that had barely talked to each other up until then—that of Sinology in North American and Western Europe and that of research into Chinese education in

China. Thus, he built relationships with a number of influential Sinologists in order to introduce their work to Chinese researchers. Professor Barry Keenan of Denison University in the United States was known for his book on the Dewey Experiment in China and his research on China's tradition of independent academies, known as *shuyuan*; Professor Paul Bailey at the University of Durham in the United Kingdom had done extensive research on the history of women's education in China; Professor Stig Thøgersen at the University of Aarhus in Denmark is a scholar who produced ground breaking historical research on education over a century in one unique county of Shandong province, using a wide range of local sources. Their contributions cover the response of US students to classes on Confucian humanism (Keenan's in Volume 3), to women's education in the early 20th century (Bailey's in Volume 4), and education in the radical years of 1957–1967 (Thøgersen's in Volume 2).

While I was focusing on the history of China's universities over the 20th century and their interactions with Western models at that time, I was deeply influenced by Ding Gang's commitment to the use of narrative and the different ways in which narrative method informed the research he was involved with. I felt the need to introduce unique dimensions of Chinese educational thought that had impressed me to the Western world. Suddenly it occurred to me that the best way of doing this would be by creating narrative portraits of the veteran Chinese educators I was working with on our collaborative project under CIDA. Thus six of the influential educators presented in *Portraits of Influential Chinese Educators* (Hayhoe 2006) made their first appearance in Ding Gang's journal in 2001 and are profiled in my essay in Volume 1, while the first chapter in Volume 2 outlines my broader motivation for studying Chinese education.

Ding Gang's vision for his journal and his choice of papers to include in this translation was to create the conditions for an encounter between China's education scholars and those in the West such that there could be mutual understanding and rich dialogue. In Ding Gang's paper in Volume 2, Perspectives on Globalization and Research on Education in China, co-authored with his talented colleague Zhou Yong, he defines globalization in the following way: the globalization process means the situation of "multiple cultures coexisting and interacting." He goes on to say that the fate of local societies is "not to choose between Westernization and extinction but rather to achieve a state of organic fusion in this multicultural context and at the same time to renew themselves in the age of globalization through this process of multicultural fusion."

These volumes reflect Ding Gang's vision and the rich collection of research papers he brought together through his journal. While the pieces by international scholars were translated into Chinese a long ago, the Chinese papers are now available in English, for the first time, through these volumes. I encourage readers to move among the different chapters and reflect on the possibilities of multicultural fusion that they offer.

References

Hayhoe, Ruth. 2006. *Portraits of Influential Chinese Educators*. Hong Kong: Comparative Education Research Centre, University of Hong Kong and Springer.

CHAPTER 1

A Teacher's Life under the Exercise of Imperial Power: Research on the Life History of a Private School Tutor

Liu Yunshan
Translated by Chad Meyers

Abstract

This paper reveals all the different kinds of power—cultural, state and social—experienced by a private school tutor after the abolishment of the imperial examination system through researching the written contribution of a private school tutor's diary that recorded over 40 years of growing up at the end of the Qing dynasty. With this diary, we penetrate and analyze the relationship between the scholar gentry and the state. The basic framework of this paper is an analysis of the imperial examination as hard institutional power and how it affected the life experience of teachers and molded relations between education and state, between teacher and education, teacher and state and so on; we furthermore point out how the habits that the scholar gentry accumulated over many years of practice instructed the spiritual world of the teacher as soft cultural power.

The[1,2] existing tradition of research on education usually refuses to call into account the political nature of education—while reproducing the ruling

---

1   This article was translated from its Chinese version, which was originally published in *China's Education: Research and Review*, 2002, volume 3, pp. 143–173.
2   The discovery of the case of Liu Dapeng has benefited from the series of articles from Mr. Luo Zhitian; I discussed this with the eminent Mr. Luo many times in the process of writing this paper and obtained many insights from him. This research is the introductory part of work undertaken after my PhD, entitled *Research on the Relationship between the Teacher and the Modern State* (2001: Beijing Normal University). The problem researched in said report was: at the conclusion of the imperial examination system and after the rise of modern Chinese education, how was the relationship between the teacher and the Chinese state molded? What was the influence back and forth between the developmental path of China's modernization and education? Why didn't the Chinese teacher shape up into the independent subject of the educational site in the modern school construction imitating Western forms? What kind of transition did the intention and role of the Chinese teacher undergo? This

ideology, it cleverly "de-politicizes" the language of education. The mainstream pedagogy insists that education transmits objective knowledge; the Parsonian school model shows schools to be a classical site of socialization that cultivate in students' loyalty towards "the common culture" and teaches students the necessary skills to gain a foothold in society. Its core purpose is to effectively acquire specific knowledge and cultivate a corresponding moral consciousness in order to rework the pre-existing social order. Inquiries into the nature of education largely defer to the technical objectives of managerial professionals, which are concerned with how a school can reach a pre-established goal. However it is very difficult to ask: why does this goal benefit one socio-economic group and not the other? This objective is concerned with such a technical question of "how to do [something]" but rarely investigates this deeper nexus of knowledge and power, culture and politics interwoven in education (Giroux 1988).

In opposition to tradition, progressive left-wing critics believe that a school is not at all a simple "factory," and that as soon as knowledge and power are linked together, culture and politics become inseparable, while school becomes a site of competition between culture and politics at the same time. School rarely presents the opportunity to promote children of the working class and other suppressed classes. On the contrary, it reproduces the relationships of capitalist production and the enforcement tools that legitimize the ideology of a ruling group (Freire 1968). Critical theory insists that school is no longer a site of education, but that school transmits and reproduces the culture of a ruling group and that the practices of power are pervasive in curricula and teaching. The ruling culture in schools hides itself behind a chosen set of rules, a legitimized specific form of language, and a model of reason. School not only cultivates students' approval and respect towards the culture of the ruling class, but at the same time continuously rejects the history, experience and dreams of suppressed groups. The state behind the school controls education practices with a specific ruling ideology through choosing commitments, diploma-granting policies and other powers of legitimization. Education is not only a construct within a social and historical context, but also a social and political practice. Education is originally a cultural politics.

When education is viewed as a field under the rule of political and cultural power, power—in earlier research on education as a continuous

---

research studies each, case by case, analyzing the relationship between the scholar gentry and the state shaped by the imperial examination system.

"absentee"—takes center stage. This article introduces the exercises of power into research. There are two kinds of active people in the Foucauldian "Panopticon": the educators (teachers) and the educated (students). In the network of power, teachers are discipliners and students are disciplined. The teachers' exercise of power is not at all simple, that is, teachers are not only the performers of the state exercise of power, but are rather the product of the exercise of power. The latter extricates the teacher in the concrete educational setting (the bearer of discipline) from the superficial field of power and inserts him/her into a broader social, cultural and historical context and explores multiple teachers, or the history of becoming an "abstract" teacher. In other words, the history of the effects of exercises of power show: the process of becoming a teacher is first of all "a process of being disciplined."

It is necessary to point out that regardless of whether it is "the disciplined" or "the discipliner," whether it is the teacher "being affected by" or "affecting" the exercise of power, the "exercise of power" transcends specific actors just like a structure, the actor can only adhere to this structure, and integrates him/herself into this structure. A teacher "reproduces" the logic of the exercise of power by using his/her practices of "being disciplined" and "disciplining" those receiving education. State power, cultural power and educational power are interwoven within this logic of power.

Methodologically speaking, this research obviously does not follow the path of positivism, but that of an empirical study, or rather, it is a narrative research. Post-positivistic instrumental reason is but "gliding on the surface of facts" (Giroux 1988); such research, whose toes never touch the ground, can only see "imaginary facts," "number fabricated facts," and "your desired facts." This article claims that to walk naturally onto "the scene" one does not only have "to be personally present on the scene," but also one's "mind has to be in it," one has to thoroughly analyze all of the relationships within the concrete, contingent, changing scene, and furthermore detail an accurate narrative, as if on a drawing board, in the attempt to preserve more of the "original flavor" of life. From those ambiguous slogans, trivial little events, and petty and even dramatic moods seize retained memories, these personal narratives that are becoming increasingly precious by the day, due to luckily having seeped out of those memories that are not worth remembering (but not at all unintentionally forgotten) or distorted (which is always an intentional construction); what this may help is to strip away another past, or to get in touch with the truth of the past. What this research needs to be vigilant about is not to reorganize this narrative into a small collection of evidence within a bigger narrative, a small footnote in a bigger history, but to try to leave a blank space for future interpretations.

Liu Dapeng (courtesy name You Feng, 1857–1942), who used the personal epithet "A man of Wohu mountain," and pseudonym Meng Xingzi (literally "the man awakened from dreams") came from the village of Chiqiao, the southern suburbs of the city of Taiyuan, Shanxi province. He resided in his ancestral home in Nan county, Chiqiao village, and was a man of humble character. At nine years old, he was taught under Liu Li, altogether for about ten years. Upon completing the study of the works of classics and history, in 1878, he passed the imperial examination at the county level (*xiucai* 秀才). In 1881, he entered the Tongfeng Institute of Taiyuan county, then again entered the Rongxiu Institute to study. In 1894 he passed the imperial examination on the provincial level (*juren* 举人); after that he participated three times in the metropolitan examination, in 1895, 1898 and 1903, none of which he passed. Beginning in 1886, he served as a tutor for nearly 20 years in the family school of the merchant, Wu Youqing, in the village of Nandu, Taigu county, Shanxi province. After 1914 he returned to his homeland, Taiyuan county, served as a principal of a small school, operated a small coal mine, cultivated a little piece of land, and led children to participate in field work and operations. He started his diary when he was 34-year-old and kept it from 1890 to 1942. While he recorded events in his diary for 51 years, today only 40 years of the diary remain. Later, Shanxi Peoples' Publishing House organized the collection into *Diaries in Meditative Purity* ("退想斋日记"). This article uses Liu Dapeng as a case study and the *Diaries* as a thread in order to dissect all of the powers of culture, state and society that affected a private tutor before and after the abolition of the imperial examination system.

Liu Dapeng was born in the 7th year of the Xianfeng Emperor (1857). As a child, he lived through the Tongzhi Restoration and as an adult he witnessed the gradual decline during the Guangxu period, and always had the feeling that the present was not as good as the past. In the 4th year of the Guangxu reign (1878), he completed the examination (where he passed as *xiucai* 秀才). In year 12 of the Guangxu reign (1894), he became a *juren* 举人, after which he participated three times in the metropolitan examination which he failed. By that time the abolition of the imperial examination system had begun. The time after the abolition we cannot help but compare to the "free" drifting of modern intellectuals in society (which in reality was a very "unfree" drifting in accordance with the waves of social change): from private tutor to school staff, school principal, and the head of county council, he later operated a long-term though small coal mine, but he lived the rest of his life always assuming the self-defined identity of a "farmer" in order to maintain the last bit of the symbolism of the studying/subsistence farming family.

The basic framework of this article is as follows: in the section titled "Disappointment," we analyze the distorted relationship between education and the state caused by the imperial examination system—the basic goal of education was to supply officials; not only were students taught by teachers in order to be prepared for the imperial examination, but the profession of a teacher itself was nothing but a resting place in the climb on the official career ladder or, upon failure, a temporary place to stay. In the sections titled "Upholding the Will" and "Reaching the Dead End," we will separately analyze the effect of duplicity in the Confucian ideal of education on teachers. In "Upholding the Will" we will show that Confucians emphasized the integrity of human character, and that there was even more of a need for teachers to serve as role models. Even on the verge of poverty one must not abandon Dao; but in "Reaching the Dead End," we will see that Confucian education lacked the skills to accept the new reality and to respond to the challenges of the new society. Even though, after the end of the imperial examination system, there had already emerged new social trades, and the old gentry started to break up, there were often those most-stubborn teachers of the Confucian *Dao* and also the most rigidly self-enclosed who were extremely pedantic; even though they were transferred to a new form of classroom in which to teach, they were absolutely incapable of turning over a new leaf, and [thus] in the end drove themselves into a dead end.

1   Disappointment

When I was young, I had the aspiration to become the duke of a large estate. When I came of age, I studied military books, but when I reached middle age I was trapped in the examination hall, continuously failing and stumbling, lamenting that my aspirations were greater than my meager talents, and could not bear to shoulder the great task. As I approached forty, although I had passed the examination, I ultimately had neither opportunities nor stable conditions, and could not help but to seek out a living by teaching.[3]

Here is a diary entry of one of the *juren* of the end of Qing dynasty, Liu Dapeng. At that time there were three career paths for scholars: high, middle and

---

3   Liu Dapeng, *Diaries in Meditative Purity* (Taiyuan: Shanxi Peoples' Publishing House, 1990), 198.

low. The high path was to pass the examination and become an official, that was the most desired ideal; the middle path was to serve as an assistant to an influential official, a position taken out of necessity; the dead end path was the setting up of a school teaching students and holding classes, all with a sigh of hoping for a talent but never running into one.[4]

---

4 Let us contrast again what kind of situation the highest career path among scholars was like. In 1865, 24-year-old Hu Chuan entered examinations at the county level and became licentiate (*xiucai*), but took the provincial examination several times in succession without succeeding as wished. From age 27 to age 30, he went to the "Dragon Gate Institute" presided over by the famous classics scholar from Yang Zhou, Liu Xizai, to submerge his mind in studies. From here onward till the age of 36, he busied himself spending money and effort whole-heartedly to erect an ancestral temple, work out the family genealogy and maintained an enduring interest in the geology of the frontiers [of the empire]. It wasn't until he put family affairs somewhat in order that he finally decided to leave the small world of his family's homeland, travel to the distant Beijing and try to develop. When he was 40 years old, he went to his rich merchant uncle and "received 200 in currency, left 100 to his family and carried 100 for his travel." He went from Shanghai to Tianjin, then turned to Beijing. In Beijing he relied on two recommendation letters, survived a rocky 42 days, went to the remote frontier city of Ninggu Ta [Hailin], where the traffic was congested, the climate was severely frigid, and criminals were banished to a "work camp." By the time Te-Kong Tong was recording the oral teachings of Hu Chuan's son, Hu Shi, his mind and pen could not help but to scratch the itch, sighing: "Hu Chuan, a 40 year old failed scholar from the South, his relatives are old, his family is poor, his wife had passed, his son was young, suddenly left his homeland and abandoned his well, took a loan and threw it into [his trip to] the frontier, where it took him longer than 40 days to get to the border to serve as an assistant to a little third rate official, Wu Dadeng!" Although this is a rare and commendable spirit, it perhaps was precisely because he couldn't find an opportunity worthy of ambition in the talent-rich southeast and Beijing that led to his resolve to go to a place where talent was most needed but where talent would be most unwilling to go. Wu Dadeng was most appreciative of Hu Chuan and would always bring Hu Chuan along in his expeditions at the frontier. He recommended him to the court saying, Hu Chuan "has both substance and function, he is full of capable and efficient material for the state [service], he is more than prepared to be selected as a provincial or county magistrate." Over the next 8–9 years Hu Chuan would continue to conscientiously follow Wu Dadeng to inspect sometimes the borders, sometimes the irrigation, sometimes to the north, sometimes to the south. In 1890, the already 49-year-old Hu Chuan went to Beijing to await dispatch to a new post, because at that time the selection of qualified officials was mostly by draft. Hu Chuan was drafted as a candidate for Jiangsu Province, that was truly the best opportunity. He brought his dependents to live in the provincial capital Suzhou, Houguan county, at 50 he was dispatched to Shanghai to undertake the inspection of "Shanghai *lika* 厘卡 tax," where he gained the reputation of "capable official." All the provinces and bureaus competed to enlist him. In 1892, the Beijing bureau selected the capable official Hu Chuan, and he headed to Taiwan to support the provincial government. The 51-year-old Hu Chuan, without a wife and having abandoned his child, headed to Taiwan alone. He managed the salt policies and military affairs all the way until defeat at the Battle of the Yalu River and the land partition reparations. When he was summoned back to the continent, he contracted beriberi and died a stranger in Xiamen. (See Tong Te-Kong, ed., *Oral Biography of Hu Shi* [Shanghai:

Beginning in 1886, Liu Dapeng served as tutor for nearly 20 years in the family school of the merchant, Wu Youqing, in the village of Nandu, Taigu county, Shanxi province; he became the typical example of a tutor, a *jiaoguan* 教馆 (or *zuoguan* 坐馆) who "spends his autumns and springs by peoples' households." Although Liu Dapeng took the lowest career path, he did not lack aspiration to climb to the highest path. When he became *juren* in 1894, Liu Dapeng was already 37. In year 1 of the *Xianfeng* reign, during the era of emperor Daoguang, the average age of *juren* was between 30–31 (Zhang Zhongli 1991, 124–125), so Liu Dapeng was a little bit old [for this title], but if he cultivated the right path and did things in the right way, and then ran into good luck, he might have the power to conquer the examination hall, and his future career would not be doomed. Unfortunately, he participated in the highest imperial examination three times, but had to return home without result. In his diary (that is, the state of mind and existential predicament behind the diary) he frequently vented a feeling of disappointment: "Working for more money (literally, *su xiu* 束脩 or dry pork meat) as a teacher is a dirty thing to do" (Liu 1990, 71); "my studies came to nothing but impotence, stranded on a path of teaching, feeling the anger of the landlord and the hatred of the students was really negative for my studies. Some say that teaching is enough to transmit Dao, but how many transmitters of Dao are there?" (Liu 1990, 72).

We cannot help but ask: why was Liu Dapeng disappointed to be a tutor? Because of the ideal: "motivating aspiration for high official position, promoting oneself to fill an official rank, devoted to the emperor above and helping the people below." Let us temporarily extricate ourselves from Liu Dapeng's "flourish of meaning" in "devotion to the emperor and helping the people." From the perspective of social stratification and social circulation, in the imperial era scholarship meant taking examinations, the purpose of which was to effectuate the upward flow between social classes, otherwise it couldn't be called beneficial and complete. This circulation affected two domains: in the four class system, it implied advancing from other strata into the scholarly stratum, whose members enjoyed all kinds of privileges; within the scholarly stratum [itself], it was the matter of becoming "official" by being a "scholar" and occupying an important position in the bureaucratic system.

So, what kind of privileges did the scholar gentry (*shishen* 士绅) enjoy in the "four class" society? Zhang Zhongli (1991, 29–39), in his research on the "privileges for literati (*shenshi* 绅士)," lists many of them in detail, for instance:

ECNU Publishing House, 1993], 9–25). Based on the traces, we can see from Hu Chuan's wandering life a fragment of the life of scholars who made official service their profession in imperial times so as to bring Liu Dapeng's career as a tutor into relief.

"the gentry is the hope of the city, the scholars are the head of the four classes,"
the county magistrate in their treatment of literati had to "interact [with them]
according to *Dao*, approach them in accordance with ritual propriety in order
to not allow power and influence to conspire"; the literati could freely visit
officials; the common people called the officials "the great grandfathers" and
referred to the *juren*, tribute scholars (*gongsheng* 贡生), county level graduates (*shengyuan* 生员), and Imperial Academy students (*jiansheng* 监生) as
"grandfathers"; the literati used valuable materials for their dresses in order to
differentiate themselves from the common public; the literati participated in
the courtesy ceremonies and also supported all kinds of sacrificial offerings;
even in the event of having committed a crime, the literati were not prosecuted,
if the crime was grave and required serious punishment the person was first
stripped of his title. The literati also enjoyed important economic privileges:
they were exempt from providing unpaid service for the government (they
held noble positions, were cultured, talented and refined, they also specialized
in the eight-legged essay writing style for the imperial examinations, and were
spiritual leaders of the society, how could they be subjected to crude "labor"?),
they could avoid taxes, pay reduced taxes or did not have to pay any excessive
taxes. Among them there were some (for instance, the silver and grain allowance scholars [*linsheng* 廪生]) and Imperial Academy students (*jiansheng*
监生) who could also receive a monthly cash allowance; aside from the government stipend, they could also get donations from their own families and other
non-governmental forces in order to stay focused on the study of sacred books.
Just as Gu Yanwu put it:

> Once having reached this point (that is *shengyuan*), they were exempt
> from the labor [requirements] of registered migrant households, were
> not messed with by village officers (*lixu* 里胥), were eligible for higher
> rank, had the right to visit higher officials and were not exposed to physi-
> cal punishment. Thus, today those desiring to become [like] *shengyuan*,
> need not yearn for official position, but only need to maintain oneself
> and one's family, and that is all.
>
> GU 1983, 21

Normally, such privileges for the scholar gentry (*shishen* 士绅) were already
enough to make people envious. However, within the scholar gentry class itself
there was a demarcation between lower level and higher level gentry (which
was drawn between whether or not one had received the rank of *juren*), and
the difference between the student gentry and the official gentry (which was
drawn between whether or not one had received an official post), and the most

highly regarded among scholars did not actually belong to the gentry but to officialdom. The Chinese imperial examination system often causes misunderstanding in people: as if traditional Chinese society highly valued learning and the heightened the status of scholars. In effect, the deeply-rooted tradition of Chinese society is an officialdom-based tradition. The regulations and design behind the imperial examination system were not so much made for the sake of heightening the status of the scholar as much as they were for resolving such problems as the narrowing source and degenerating qualification of the bureaucratic stratum brought about by the previous aristocratic class's hereditary system and "nine rank enfeoffment institution." Only by being granted a position with real power and responsibility a *juzi* [i.e. *juren*] could appropriate and accumulate rich political and economic capital, with the scholar gentry no more than a substitute, reserve and local assistance for the aristocratic class that had really attained officialdom. From this viewpoint, we can understand why Liu Dapeng was disappointed: although he had gained the honorable scholarly and official rank of *juren*, he was not able to attain access to the rank of *jinshi* (进士) [that is, the rank of a candidate for the highest imperial examination]. Only by entering the social stratum of *jinshi* could one secure the probability of becoming an official. After the middle period of the Qing dynasty, the *juren* were but a standby position for official rank—and, with many *juren* and few officials, the probability of being appointed was not large. Liu Dapeng was really just one of those left to wait, deserted in a long line outside the door to administrative service.

Why was Liu Dapeng's "dream of *jinshi*" or "dream of officialdom" not realized? We can obviously follow Liu Dapeng's logic of "self-reproach" to "reproach him": with his big aspiration and lacking in talent he could not shoulder such a large responsibility; we may skip his logic, and through "fate" and other outside forces, help ease his anxiety of self-accusation: the remoteness of the location, the clogging of the flow of information, and the fact that he did not dwell for any length of time at the place of great and glorified people in the native place of the Renaissance of education and culture.[5] However, if we place Liu

---

5 Only after his arrival in Beijing, did Liu Dapeng realize the importance of practicing the small regular script (*xiaokai* 小楷), yet the scholars of the south began receiving standard training in calligraphy from a young age, they also had to be significantly familiar with the structure of the imperial examinations. Chen Dongyuan's research point out that the northern scholars, from the beginning, produced political treatises following the form of examination questions, southern scholars, though, definitely did not begin with the political treatises at the first stroke, but rather did much reading and training from the outside and from the depths, and only then became capable of freely grappling with and learning [the art] with comprehensive consistency. Only when they reached the examination hall, did they express a

Dapeng's defeat in the context of the concrete operating mechanism of the imperial education system and its history, we will be able to see a more universal phenomenon.

The system and design of the imperial examinations were extremely intricate, for instance, they were equal and open in form—the commoners mingled with ministers, the farm-hands rubbed elbows with the Imperial Court, and the highest positions were open to the lowest stratum. Such a move guaranteed that every stratum, to a great extent, could be brought into the exercise of power in the imperial examination hall. Liu Dapengs were that sort of mobilized participant, who on the precondition of loyalty and by means of disciplinary mindset, advanced for the purpose of joining the ranks of power (decentralized power) and retreated also for the purpose of seeking the approval of power (co-prosperity), and began developing practices of their lives.[6] But, regardless of the examinations, the admission quota and frequency, the content of the examinations as well as the criteria of [candidate] selection was still meticulously designed and controlled by the state. This stratum of "literati" (shi 士), forged through the selection of imperial examination tests and education practices that were support for and subordinate to the tests—who enjoyed both privileges coming from above (given by central political authority) and great influence below (common society)—was a group of people indispensable and extremely useful to state governance. Maintaining the scale and numbers of this conglomerate was constrained by the two forces above and below: below, a number of privileges the literati enjoyed were established on the exploitation of the people, supporting such a conglomerate was a burden for the common people; and above, constantly setting up an elaborate space for the literati did assist in cultivating a sense of loyalty, but the growing force of the literati was a hidden threat for the power of the central government. Thus, the government always controlled the total number of literati and the proportion of their distribution within various locations and various strata. The imperial examinations were not for the sake of indiscriminately selecting talent of all kinds, but for the sake of exerting pressure on the two forces above and below, allowing them to strike a subtle balance between gentry (shen 绅) power, royal power and the

---

distinct style and not follow the conventional pattern. See Chen Dongyuan, *Zhongguo Jiaoyu Shi* 《中国教育史》 [*History of Chinese Education*] (Shanghai: Commercial Press, 1934).

6   The author here is citing Foucault's concept of biopower, referring to the governmental and institutional practices of controlling and developing biological aspects of a population through disciplinary hierarchies. The first biological aspect of control Foucault looks at for the sake of tracing the source of such practices is the controlling of viral infections, the "quarantine" solution to the plague and other sicknesses wiping out the European population before the so-called modern age of sanitation. (Trans.)

people's power. On the stage of the imperial examination hall, the Liu Dapengs were truly and passionately invested actors—what seemed like an individual's free choice, in reality, each joy and each sorrow—every given move—was the dispassionate manipulation of a director, and the director was the central government behind the curtain. Under the guise of the imperial examinations, the central government's control over the common people and individuals was just like a human body using the arms, and the arms using the fingers: force went wherever they intended. The imperial civil examinations were not so much a political and economic science of selecting talent, but rather a political science of maintaining rule and a science of disciplinary power over minds.

The main means of the government's control over the imperial examinations raised their cost.

First, the economic cost. Poor people could not bear the fees for long term studies and exams, for impoverished families an honorary scholarly title was an excessively luxurious adornment. Formally equal examinations—with economic discrimination—gradually weakened and even wiped out [the presence of] youth from poor families. Liu Dapeng's "family was poor, and only had a skinny field of ten or so *mu* 亩, not enough to feed a family of ten, [we were] entirely relying on father to do business work outside and on mother to do housework inside."[7] That was also the normal economic condition of scholars' families. They praised themselves as being "families both farming and studying Confucianism," for whom, "with the occupation of farming while studying, without farming you won't be able to provide for a meager existence, without studying you will be ignorant of the ritual order." Thus, "farming" became the last economic line of defense of a meager living and "studying" was the developmental direction of "establishing a life (*liming* 立命)." But Liu Dapeng's family, "after all did not know much about having a surplus." Liu Dapeng himself, after reaching his senior years, could not help but join the ranks of those "making a living by teaching," and had to take the path of teaching just like the majority of scholars (读书人) who failed to become officials. Feeding scholarship by teaching was precisely feeding the examination system by teaching. "The business of teaching was not what I desired, but I now venture out into the world to teach propelled by poverty."[8] "My initial aspiration was originally not the desire to teach, but now I venture out into the world as teacher to compute a meager living without the hope or prospect of blooming fortune. If I had

---

7   Liu Dapeng, *Diaries in Meditative Purity*, 44.
8   Ibid., 70.

the hope of prosperity, I would have sought another path of business to seek it, and were I to have aspirations, how would I allow prosperity to cloud my will!"[9]

Second, the cost to one's life. Taking examinations was managed in a way that became a process of slowly consuming mental power and life, and Zhang Zhongli has listed numerous examples as evidence in his *Chinese Gentry*. There was one candidate who waged eight wars to enter the autumn examinations (Zhang 1991, 190). He participated in the triennial provincial civil service examinations 8 times, which means he had to spend 20 years on it. For instance, in the realistic novel *The Scholars* (Wu Jingzi 1980), Fan Jin from Guangdong participated in the basic examinations [for the first time] at the age of 20, after which he took them more than 20 times without passing, and at 54 he finally got a passing score, but in the registry of candidates he wrote in his age as 30. One candidate passed as a licentiate (*xiucai*) at the age of 24, but when he took the provincial imperial examinations he was already 41, and his father had been a licentiate for 30 years. Another unlucky private tutor failed even the first round of county examination in the three rounds of basic examinations and for the sake of keeping his position as a private tutor took the county examination repeatedly for 30 years. Research on the average age of the candidates who were listed in the imperial examinations indicates that the age of county level graduates (*shengyuan* 生员) was around 24, for *juren* it was 30, for *jinshi* 35. For a lucky one, it would take more than 10 years of examinations to advance from *shengyuan* to *jinshi*. The ranks of those hungrier to break out of the lower level gentry repeatedly failed and tried again, working tirelessly all their lives. The literati spent a great deal of their time studying and taking examinations; their career was indeed one of taking examinations. Zhang Jian, who succeeded in climbing to the higher-level gentry spent 35 years on studying and examination taking; at the examination hall alone he spent 160 days. One candidate by the name of Yang Enpei "received training from a young age, studied *The Great Learning, The Doctrine of the Mean, The Analects*.... At the age of nine, he left home to receive training outside (*waifu* 外傅); studied Mengzi and also *The Book of Songs, The Book of Documents, The Book of Changes* and *The Book of Rites*, also studied *The Spring and Autumn Annals, The Zuo Commentary* and *The Guwen Guanzhi*, and after turning fifteen, began to compose eight-legged essays." At the age of nineteen he became a *shengyuan*, at thirty-two a *linsheng* (silver and grain allowance scholar 廪生), later to keep the position of *linsheng* he had no alternative but to continually take the annual political

---

9 Ibid., 55.

achievement exam (*suikao* 岁考) and political imperial exam (*kekao* 科考). All the way until the abolition of the imperial examination system, a career at the imperial examinations was about 30 years long (Zhang Zhongli 1991, 167–176).

Third, the discipline of the intellect. Zhang Zhongli's research on the content of the examinations indicates that in the 19th century the examinations all along consisted of three rounds. The topics were mainly chosen from the discussion topics of the Confucian classics. What was emphasized was the form of the composition, not the content. There were many constraints on writing a composition; it had to follow the predetermined form of an eight-legged essay. Even the number of characters in the composition was restricted, the candidates had to strictly comply with the stipulations because the examiners usually focused on the form. The reason why candidates succeeded was due to knowing how to write a composition in accordance with the strict format, its stipulations, and meter and rhyme and wording. Moreover, the text had to be ornate and the answers had to be set out neatly. And the thorough understanding of this "cultural capital" distantly separated from everyday language and everyday labor, obviously gave a significant advantage to those born in an official's family in comparison with those of humble origin.

Forth, the discipline of the body. Wang Yangming said that the art of examinations lies in:

> ... having to get up promptly to the rooster's call every day, washing and combing oneself, tidying up one's garments and sitting up straight, pulling oneself together and not allowing oneself to slack around. Day after day putting it into practice, when it comes to the moment one does not feel oneself overworked. Nowadays, for the sake of conserving their vital powers they eat rich meals with thick taste, drink unrestrainedly and loosely banter around or lay down all day long, thus they weaken their energy flow and muddle their spirits, and thereby invite sickness by prolonged arrogance—is this what nourishing of the spirit means? One has to restrict eating and drinking and stick to light taste, and then the energy flow will purify itself; contemplate less and discard the desire to please the senses, and then the spirit will enlighten itself, calm one's ambitions and sleep less, and then the mind will clarify itself. Among superior men there are none who do not devote themselves to learning in this way.
>
> WANG in He Huaihong 1998, 229

The exercise of power in the examination hall thus disciplined the bodies and life habits of the literati.

Although the examinations were declared equal, those who did not possess considerable economic and cultural capital were pushed outside of the ranks of competitors from the very beginning. Even inside the examination hall, the relationship between the candidates and the examiners revolved around cultural capital—organized through the legitimate authority in this examination field, one was the holder and distributor of cultural capital, and the other was the seeker and accumulator of cultural capital. But the inequality of capital that candidates possessed in the economic field and field of power outside of the sphere of the examination hall ordinarily resulted in inequality in the "structure of opportunities" that cultural capital distributed to them in the sphere of the examination hall.

Besides that, the late Qing society in which Liu Dapeng was immersed also had another significant characteristic, that is, rapid population growth. Such growth had an extremely serious impact on the entire society, one of the consequences of which was: the mechanism of bottom-up social circulation was falling increasingly behind population growth, the surplus personnel flooded every organization in every class, the upward path of official careers was blocked, and the opportunities of earning an official position by means of normal participation in the imperial examinations and attaining an honorary scholarly title were increasingly scarce. The congestion of the normal road to promotion to higher office inevitably made people resort to illegal paths, the prevalence of illegal paths also gradually narrowed down the normal road to promotion (Kong Feili 1993, 113–174).

Why didn't Liu Dapeng refuse this game and then open up a new path of life? We could perhaps help Liu Dapeng's disappointment by positioning him freely outside of the examination hall to do a rational regrouping: Putting talk of destiny to rest when beside [one's library] window, and not disputing the language in the [examination] hall—this is the ancient irrefutable truth of the path to honorary title, that is both following destiny and yet escaping destiny, what we call fully exercising one's powers to accomplish serious affairs. It is not hard to make a guess that Liu Dapeng in his era might often encounter this type of aforementioned encouragement from himself or others, it is not that such encouragement was not a kind of discipline; such clearly rational accounts were precisely the basis of the examination hall's legitimacy. It continuously disciplined Liu Dapeng who resided by Lushan Mountain but whose mind was in the mist of mountain clouds, just like a gambler who makes bigger and bigger bets, but, despite incurring greater and greater losses, becomes increasingly less willing to leave the gambling house—never taking no for an answer until squeezed dry.

The basic precondition of all of the disciplinary discourses constructed by the examination hall was to view the examination hall as a "black box"—everything inside the black box is justified and beyond all doubt.[10] The goal of the imperial examinations being open to the public was to select talents to take up official posts, when the ancient classics describe the significance of the imperial examinations they cite the proud words of [emperor] Tang Taizong upon witnessing the new successful graduates of the examinations: "The young heroes in the world under Heaven, enter into my snare." Is the profound mechanism behind Tang Taizong's pride the natural disclosure of the positive mindset of open-mindedness, recruitment of talent, and constructive engagement? Or is it rather in the sigh of flattening potential rivals with a superb institutional design such as the examination system?—this group inherits cultural capital, and to a certain degree plays the role of spiritual leader of

---

10   When M. Young, in 1998, looks back upon the rise of the new educational sociology he discusses how the curriculum may become the focus of research in the field of educational sociology, which seems similar in this spirit. People's expectations of the rational system of education stimulate a more fair and free society, and this is the origin of the research on the problem of equality in educational opportunities; following the interest in the equality in educational opportunities the "educational failure" begins to become a question that attracts the attention of educational researchers and strategists, but research on "failed students," however, from the beginning, focuses on the [question] "How to" help them in terms of effective studies, and does not question closely "Why?"—why is this group of people an educational failure? What is the standard, the curriculum content and even the organizational system of a school which cause this group of people to fail? Researchers "reveal" from different perspectives the characteristics of those who the lack the educational skills—the research consciously (or unconsciously) "defends traditional moral principles": from the standpoint of the education or a school, they [themselves] assist, criticize, or compensate the unlucky ones. A school's curriculum, their standards, and knowledge are all in a "black box," and the researchers "ignore" that the precondition of this problem domain lies precisely in its "approval" and "recognition"—where this line of investigation does not delve is precisely the exclusive domain of the rule of power. Until the new educational sociology begins to stir up this hornet's nest, and this neutral, objective, and legitimate place of curriculum and schools starts to appear as a place of contention over cultural power, all kinds of political bodies of knowledge will continue fighting for the hegemony of discourse, and "legislate" for play. This power is already no longer that (state) apparatus Althusser described, but rather a Foucauldian power dispersed throughout networks of social relations, it "produces" and "reproduces" successes and failures, the highest knowledge along with the basest common sense, refined and pure tastes along with crude and mediocre habits. The power here is no more a repressive but a productive practice. Our research of the power of the examination hall still first positions it within Althusser's framework, [but] how was imperial power embodied in the practices of the examination hall?

common society outside of the central political power; they naturally seize the symbolic power of constructing and explaining meaning, and this is precisely the crux of integrating the fragmented human mind and shaping the cohesive binding force of society.

Although continuously suffering setbacks, why did so many people still so passionately cling to the examination hall? This was because there was something in common that bound the exam-takers together, which determined their addictive pleasure in this action. This something was the "air of the scholar gentry" collectively assembled by all kinds of tangible and intangible things, from the Confucian classics and official literary language, calligraphy and poetics to the long robes and hats of rank. The air of the scholar gentry was slowly sculpted, consciously and unconsciously, in accordance with the norms of the examination hall, norms which accumulated over long years and countless months of preparing for and taking the examinations; they were the internalizations of the attributes intrinsic to the site of the examination hall in the very bodies of the constituents of the site. At the same time, it was due to such internalizations constructing this site into a world filled with meaning, a world endowed with radiant color, a world worthy of them investing into. Although the examination hall could not in any way provide the majority with honorary scholarly titles, and although officialdom was even less capable of imparting the majority with official posts, the examination hall did, however, become the site of what Collins called "status culture" which every exam-taker to different degrees wanted to have a share of.[11] The state power behind the examination hall not only manifested in the meticulous workings of the institution, but also became embodied in the sculpting of the Liu Dapengs' minds. In *The Scholars* there is a passage that elegantly illustrates the air of the scholar gentry: "Aside from this affair of human life in the world there is no second affair that presents itself. There is no need to say that fortune-telling and fortune reading are at the bottom of the barrel; it is that neither acting as a tutor nor a private secretary were end games. Nothing short of this engagement of advancing in study and attaining the title of *juren* and *jinshi* could count as bringing glory to the [scholars'] ancestors."

---

11   Ying Xing has a spectacular study on the "site of the examination hall" and the "air of the scholar gentry." See Ying Xing, "The Transformation of Social Relations of Control and the Site of the Examination Hall: Hunan Society from 1895 to 1913," *Chinese Social Science Periodical* (1997 Spring and Summer Issue), No 18–19; and Yang Nianqun, ed., *Space, Memory and Social Transformation* (Shanghai: Shanghai People's Publishing House, 2001).

How did Liu Dapeng look at being a tutor? Before attaining *juren*, Liu Dapeng already worked as a tutor. But after attaining *juren* his status changed, his position relative to this identity as tutor was not at all relieving to him. Always bemoaning his lack of alternative to this "meager bread-winning" enterprise, he once thought of quitting tutoring and returning home as "bending to the plow and serving the family."

Chinese scholars originally had the tradition of "studying to put it to use (*yong* 用)" which resulted in the absence of the orientation toward "studying for studying's sake." The original meaning of *yong* is having the capacity of state-craft and managing the world, and is also modifiable into "what is used" (*beiyong* 被用), namely "instruments." There is distinction between "small use" and "great use," as well as one between "suitable to use" and "unsuitable to use." Should we ask, for a second, how the desire of scholars for honorary official ranks was produced? And how did the "minister in common clothing" become the core complex of Chinese scholars? The function of the imperial examination hall was such that the site of education—or more precisely, the students' logic of studying and seeking learning—as nothing but the process of desire for official rank continuously growing, surging and inflating inside themselves— was far from extrinsic to the means of livelihood, but rather internalized as a practice of life. Scattered throughout the materials of private primary lecture halls that Chen Dongyuan researched are many encouragements and exhortations to study, poems about how, with the help of an official rank, one can become rich and powerful, for instance in the *Miscellaneous Copy from the Street Stall Engraving of the Thousand Poets* we find:

> Emperors value outstanding figures, and educate you with various writings.
> The worth of all other pursuits is small, book reading excels all other careers.
> You must study hard at an early age, writing can help you live well in the world.
> All high officials under the emperor are, without exception, scholars, indeed.
> A country boy, early in the morning, can be a high official in the evening.
> Success is not determined by birth, real men should be dependent on nothing.
> If a young man is able and well-read, he can be ambitious throughout his life.
> Others become officials with swordplay, I do so with a pen as sharp as knife.

A white stallion with a purple and gold saddle catches everyone's eye as
   it leaves the stable. It doesn't matter which family you are from, those
   who study enter officialdom.
Learning is the treasure of life, the scholar becomes the gem adorning
   the highest chair. He whom the emperor sees as the ruling minister
   must be a man of learned taste.
Don't say, he with the scholar's cap is prone to fall, poems and books do
   not put anybody down. Far away, and yet he rules the world, poor and
   yet he refines himself though learning.
Take the county exam one time, the prized writing will ascend in kind.
   The ripest fruit in written word, the emperor quickly picks first.
The joy in picking the most valuable coin is nothing to that of picking
   the most outstanding writer. Read by the light of a firefly and break
   free, and your name will be inscribed on the board of *jinshi* at the
   highest temple.
When the Palace transmits the board with the names of successful candidates, the Prince honors the number one scholar. Three hundred
   heroes [*jinshi*] follow me into the celestial world!
When the day comes that you pass the exam, your mother and father
   will feel ageless. The one who returns home rich and powerful, is, as
   expected, a boy.
Attaining a *jinshi* early at a young age, the emperor always proudly
   responds. Passing to each next level, a sound of thunder strikes the
   earth.
   WANG ZHU, 1975

Even though what teachers and students recited most was not necessarily
poems providing encouragement for learning and seeking honorary titles,
what they did recite most fluently and remembered most deeply was indeed
such content. One of the teaching methods the private tutors of China left
behind that we can emphasize is the "three presences"—the mind is present,
the eyes are present, and the mouth is present, and while training the students'
memory and patience the famous adages and aphorisms memorized most fluently would seed the schoolchildren's earliest or perhaps most elementary
experience of social life. What is interesting, under crude observation, was that
this was not only the private tutor's "hidden curriculum" outside of the goals
of education, but, under closer inspection, the empire's goal with respect to
education, whether in the design of the system, in the controls over the examinations or in the transmission of the conventional air was perhaps precisely
this. Jiang Menglin once noticed that a man who reached adulthood often

could find in all those memorized ancient classics the compass to [show him] the way to get on in a world.[12] The process of learning was really that of hoping to be constantly mobilized, it not only encouraged those like Jiang Menglin to be a student, but also definitely encouraged those like Liu Dapeng to be a teacher, encouraged all those students and teachers in the sites of education within and behind the examinations halls of China.

"Studying to put it to use" led the students to very seldom consider "studying" as their own duty. "Studying" only had "great use" by departing from "studies," the "transmission of learning," "teaching of learning" was rather the "small use" or even "useless." Those who "studied" and failed to "have use" but who stubbornly stuck to the way of "studying" were namely those walled in and cornered. Similarly, bureaucracy could be seen as a profession, but scholar gentry (*shi* 士) was not at all one. During the candidacy of, intervals between, and leisure time outside of the scholar gentry's continuous taking of examinations and enlisting for official posts, they often chose teaching. Thus, although teachers had their job posts they did not, however, identify with them. Liu Dapengs never approved of fixing their identity to the role of teacher which was only a necessary place to lodge oneself while preparing for the examinations. Students with their minds set on upward progression very seldom pinned their lofty ambitions down here; the scholar gentry who retired and returned home or the disempowered government officials who retired to weave a network [of influence] also never saw teaching as their profession, the wildly ambitious saw it as the effective preparation of recruiting forces and building up connections with the aim of mounting a comeback. Those among the scholar gentry holding wildly ambitious political aims were still ultimately very few, the majority undertook teaching, and to a smaller extent, killing time and enriching life; and to a greater extent, condescended to teaching offspring

---

12   Jiang Menglin recalled the life of private tutoring in the following way—in the first several years the life of private tutoring was for me directly analogous to prison, the only difference was: the criminals in real prisons were truly hopeless, while the students doing private tutoring all had infinite hope of future prospects. Did not all of the big scholars and aristocrats with official titles undergo the sufferings of tireless studies by cold windows? "A human being only becomes a higher human being by biting into the bitterest toil." "Emperors value outstanding figures, and educate you with various writings." "The worth of all other pursuits is small, book reading excels all other careers." "Others become officials with swordplay, I do so with a pen as sharp as knife." These proverbs spurred me to advance along the path of learning, just as a luxuriant fragrance in the early spring air invites a weary horse to green pastures. Otherwise I fear that I would have much earlier dropped the books and headed to Shanghai to do business. See Qu Shipei, ed., *Selected Writings on the Education of Jiang Menglin* (Beijing: People's Education Publishing House, 1995), 303.

of the same clan, and to benefiting their own native towns. In the traditional farming society, they farmed, while studying, to support their families—if students advanced they claimed the post, consolidated power, and protected their own family's interests; if they retreated they still had their own land and passed their days well-off and intact. Teaching was only a supplementary occupation, and students could *do* teaching, but could not claim teaching as a profession. Those who "made a living by teaching" lived in the gap between the "land" and the "political stratum" and became circulating particles of the social fabric, or in other words they were circulators without any secure place for themselves. If there was social upheaval the most prone to being hurt were indeed circulating individuals living outside of all of the protections of power; they directly interacted in their individual lives with the network woven out of the strongly powerful and all other powers, they didn't have any "protective belt" to hide and conceal them.

Chapter 33 of *The Story of a Marital Fate to Awaken the World* (Xi 1981) provides several prescriptions for the livelihood of *xiucai* in poverty: one is opening a book store, the second opening a satin shop, cloth shop, silk shop, or pawnshop, the third collecting manure, the forth is opening a casket shop, the fifth being a scholar gentry in and out of official posts. But all these were still no good, not because there was no money in them, but because either the taxes were too heavy, or one wasn't free, or was unable to do the task. Thus, "Considering thousands of paths late at night, only cultivating several acres of ink stone, plowing by brush and hoeing by tongue, farming oneself and chiseling oneself to excess, but if rain is scarce there is no fear of drought and if rain is plentiful there is no fear of flood, not only does one feed a family of eight and one's mind still broadens and body still fattens, dancing with joy, but even more, one outdoes so many of the average, becoming a god and Buddha too; that aside, one also enlightens the mind and illuminates the Buddha nature within, rendering that money beneficial and harmless [...] this is the essence of the *xiucai*'s way of life" (Xi 1981, 478).

From this satire of making a life from teaching for *xiucai* we can make out the general picture of the social predicament of the Liu Dapengs.[13]

---

13   The hierarchical division in common society of three religions and nine schools was delineated thus—the higher nine schools: first was Gautama Buddha, second was Daoist deities, third was emperors, fourth was officials, fifth was military officials, sixth was ministers, seventh was engineers, eighth was merchants, ninth was farmers. The middle nine schools: first was *juren*, second was doctors, third was *fengshui* diviners [...] fifth was painters, sixth was calligraphers, seventh was Buddhist monks, eighth was Daoist monks, ninth was lute and chess masters. Lower nine schools: first school was dog trainers, second was oil sellers, third was foot massagers, fourth was head shavers, fifth was

2   Upholding the Will

"From a young age those who study the path of Confucius and Mencius up to now strictly follow it and dare not depart from it. At this moment the state has changed the norms, they have set up the new study hall and have stopped the imperial examinations, scholars all have given up the study of Confucius and Mencius, and instead study the learning from the West. With trifling thoughts, different feelings are enough to put them at unease, and the result is rising and falling according to the tides of custom, is it not rotten to follow the tides of fashion? Others abandon [the path], but I do not abandon it. This is my will."[14]

What is the "will" that Liu Dapeng claims others have abandoned but he himself has not, and that he instead diligently upholds? It is the customary air of the scholar gentry shaped though many years in sites of examination and study. What is the intention of this customary air or "higher will"? We can cite some classics to peer into its general makeup. For example, a couplet composed by Zhu Xi for the White Deer Cave Academy "Sun and moon, two orbiting wheels, the eyes of the heavens and the earth; reading and writing, ten thousand scrolls, the hearts of the aspirant and the sage"; and another one composed by Gu Xiancheng for Donglin Academy "The sound of wind, the sound of rain, the sound of leafing [through] books, all these sounds enter the ears; family affairs, state affairs, the affairs of the world under heaven, all these affairs capture the heart;" and another couplet composed by Zhang Zhidong for the Guangya Academy entrance "Although rich and born high it does not affect one's mind, although poor and born low it does not divert one's path; with the root of connecting the classics and studying the ancients, with the aspiration of saving the world and walking the Way." Through this most important living practice of "upholding the higher will" the Liu Dapengs made contact with the customary air of the scholar gentry, the site of the examination hall, and even the site of teaching scholarship, and the power behind the examination hall was not only embodied in the meticulous workings of the institution, but also in the mind of the Liu Dapengs (the customary air was seen as the "higher will" that should be defended with one's life!); it was embodied both outside of Liu Dapeng's physical body and within Liu Dapeng's affective mind. Although Liu Dapeng continuously suffered setbacks at such sites and experienced being suppressed, in the world of meaning that these

---

dish carriers, sixth was tailors, seventh was actors, eighth was singers, ninth was flute players. Among all of these different kinds of trades and ways of making a living "teaching" never entered into any set.

14   Liu, *Diaries in Meditative Purity*, 152.

sites narrated, Liu Dapeng never felt any sense of alienation and his spirit grew up in this, his life was sometimes enriched, sometimes built up, and sometimes expanded in this. Liu Dapeng as an actor and the constraints of these external sites here were truly compatible in the ontological sense (Bourdieu 1998, 172). Liu Dapeng felt like he was at home here, like fish in water, like a natural. All of his efforts went toward changing the powerless awkwardness in this home.

Why did Liu Dapeng have to uphold the higher will? Posed otherwise, this is to ask what resources Liu Dapeng had to uphold the customary air of the scholar gentry. Ye Qizheng[15] once distinguished the intellectuals from the other two classes of social elites, believing that the social resource that the "intellectuals" held was "knowledge," and the resource of the "possessors of political power" was "power," and the resource of the economic elites was stuff with "material interest." The "knowledge" of the intellectuals, namely "refined culture," always encapsulated two aspects, "technical knowledge" and "literary learning" or "spiritual knowledge," that is natural knowledge of probing "what is" and normative knowledge of clarifying "what ought to be." In Chinese academic sites these two types of knowledge were always unequal, the latter was considered to be the higher knowledge that those "with knowledge" ought to deeply embody, and the former was only the rare or common sense that all the different agricultural and gardening trades depended upon for livelihood. The knowledge that the Chinese scholar gentry held in high regard was normative knowledge. Let us look at how Confucius makes a "small man" out of Fan Chi asking about husbandry:

> Fan Chi asked about learning husbandry, the Master said: 'You had better asked an old hand at husbandry rather than me.' He asked about learning gardening, the Master said: 'You had better asked an old hand at gardening rather than me.' Fan Chi left.
>
> The Master said: 'A small man Fan Xu is indeed! If a higher man were devoted to ritual propriety, none of the people would dare withhold reverence; if a higher man were devoted to what is righteous, none of the people would dare insubordination; if a higher man were devoted to trustworthiness, none of the people would dare not put sincerity into effect. If he is thus [devoted], people from all quarters will come to him carrying their children on their backs, and what use of husbandry would he have?'
>
> *The Analects*, 13.4

---

15   Se Ye Qizheng (1984) *Society, Culture and Intellectuals*, Taibei Dongda Book Company; "And who is an 'Intellectual' after all?," *Foreign Sociology*, 1998, No. 1.

Mencius makes the distinction even more clear, human beings are divided into greater human beings and lesser human beings, and labor is divided into mental labor and physical labor, some govern people and the others govern things, some feed people and others are fed by people:

> Affairs of all forms of craftsmanship cannot be undertaken alongside farming. Then, is the governing the world under heaven alone that which can be undertaken along with farming? There are the affairs of greater human beings and the affairs of lesser human beings. Moreover, in the case of any single individual, he may be equipped with what the various craftsmen make—[but] if everyone had to make everything one uses, this way of doing things would lead the people of the world to run all day long trying to make ends meet. Thus, it is said that some do mental labor, some do physical labor; those who do mental labor govern people, those who do physical labor are governed by people: those who are governed by people provide for people, those who govern people are provided for by people. This is the principle universally recognized.
>
> *Mencius*, 5.4

Let's look at it again. How is the *Dao* produced? *Dao* is by no means a transcendental, spiritual Being. *Dao* is the construction of human interests. The earliest form of *Dao* was knowledge, and a consultative knowledge at that. Those with the power to speak sat together and collectively discussed what set of norms should be made—this was very probably a single digit set of people, choosing rules for use in several conflicting predicaments. Once the rules were ratified they became the contract of this community, what Kant refers to as "men legislating for Nature." Contract means binding, and the meaning of "should" becomes "cannot but" and "do not dare not to" which is the core out of which the community is established and maintained; it could be a spiritual foundation and also an institutional foundation. After common sense knowledge is ratified, when knowledge needs to move toward practice for the sake of disciplining oneself and others, it is necessary that such knowledge is deified and becomes the awe inspiring *Dao* or Heaven (in modern society this could be "science" or "fairness" in other signifying systems). Moreover, there is the distinction of two series—the series of exercising political control (the political tradition) and the series of explaining how the world should be ruled (the tradition of *Dao*) (Wu Han, Fei Xiaotong, et al. 1988). In Confucius, the tradition of *Dao* and the political tradition were parallel and did not conflict with one another, each manages its own affairs; but by the time of Dong Zhongshu who brought up "Heaven" to suppress political power such that political power should induce fear and the emperor should sacrifice to Heaven. If political power does not sit right with *Dao* then it is the way of hegemony. And the most important support that rebels had to legitimize their actions was the idea of "carrying out *Dao* on behalf of Heaven." Dong Zhongshu proposed four hierarchical levels: the highest was Heaven, the middle the emperor, next was the scholar, and at the bottom was the people. So, who had the perspicacity to know the will of Heaven and comprehend *Dao*? *Dao* was found in the teaching of scholar officials, the teachers of scholar officials who carried on the tradition of *Dao*—which was the pure crown of Confucius. Every generation of teachers representing Confucius was constructed by the conspiring of scholars with emperors. The Confucian students of later generations had to remind the emperor to respect their own status or rectify their own name and give themselves power with the aid of Confucius (whether it was embodied in the Confucian temple or sacrificing to Confucius). Confucius, whose "Virtue aligns Heaven and Earth," whose "*Dao* carries the crown from the past into the present," who "compiled the six canons, and cast the model for all generations to come"[16] became the spiritual totem for Confucian students of scholarship, the "image of the first teacher, Confucius, instructing" up till now still remains the hallmark construct in some schools.[17]

---

16   Mao Lirui & Shen Guanqun (eds.). 1985. *General History of Chinese Education*, vol. 1 (Jinan: Shandong Education Press), 205.

17   While rambling about the education he received at his hometown Hu Shi says: "My mother yearned that I make a name for myself by studying, so often she urged me to worship Confucius every day. On the walls of the class of Mr. Yu Chen was hanging an ink lithograph of Confucius by Wu Daozi and we every evening after classes would have to bow in front of him. I went to my elder sister's house for the New Year celebrations and saw her son Zhang Yanxiang (who was a few years older than me) making offerings to an [improvised] Confucius ancestral tablet shrine; he made it out of a big red case, he used red paper to cut out the spirit tablet and a matchbox for a sacrifice table; on the table he glued an incense burner cut out of gold paper together with his offerings, outside of the shrine were glued many banners and couplets proper to the Confucius temple made of red and gold paper with such saying as 'Virtue aligns Heaven and Earth, *Dao* carries the crown from the past into the present.' When I saw this shrine I felt very envious and when I got back home I also made myself a little Confucius temple. [...] When my mother saw me in my reverence to Confucius she was extremely happy and gave me a little table so I could, too, make offerings to the shrine and also gave me a copper incense burner, every first and fifteenth day of [the month of] the lunar calendar she would always teach me how to burn incense and pay worship. This little Confucius temple, because my mother made it a point to preserve it, was still intact when I returned home from abroad at the age of 27 ...". See Hu, Shi *Forty Autobiographical Notes* (Haikou: Hainan Publishing House, 1997).

Xunzi first of all elevated teachers to the same level as that of Heaven, Earth, lord, and parents: "Heaven and Earth are the root of human nature, fore-fathers and ancestors are the root of one's kind; lords and teachers are the root of order" (*Xunzi* 2014, 55). A "teacher" becomes the embodiment and personal incarnation of Confucian ethical code, in Xunzi's view: "Ritual is that by which to correct your person; the teacher is that by which to correct your practice of ritual. If you are without ritual, then how will you correct your person? If you are without a teacher, then how will you know that your practice of ritual is right?" (*Xunzi* 2014, 175). Ritual is the highest standard, ethics is defined by ritual and a teacher is the comprehender, transmitter and executor of ritual. A teacher is the one who reflects the personal incarnation of the enlightened ritual propriety and students, by learning the short cut to the ritual propriety, are approaching the virtuous teacher. A teacher here becomes a prototype of "ritual propriety" for the society, if we were to use a verb to convert it into a predicate this "ritual propriety" here would gain the meaning of "to discipline"; and if we were to use "ritual propriety" as an adjective to convert it into an attribute, it would mark the unique characteristic of Chinese society. A teacher stands at the forefront of ritually proper society; his chief duty is to cultivate himself with ritual propriety. In his explanation of "model pedagogy" Yang Xiong said "One must first act and only then the people credit it; one must first demand and only then the people supply it." And also: "First regulate one-self and then regulate the people; this is what is called the Great Vessel [for a talent]," A teacher "first" "establishes himself," because "the government only stands insofar as oneself first stands," the teacher himself must master "speak-ing without regret and acting without shame," that is "by speaking without disobeying principle, one's physical form is therefore not shamed; acting with-out dodging the wicked [but rather taking them on], one's affective mindset therefore is unashamed" (Mao Lirui and Shen Guanqun 1985b, 125). Only by elevating the status of a teacher of ritual propriety, can the disciplinary mean-ing of ritual propriety not only gain legitimacy, but it can also win the highest status and respect. Thus we have such Xunzi's formulation: "A state that is going to flourish is sure to honor teachers and give great way to instructors. If one honors teachers and gives great way to instructors, then proper models and measures (*fa* 法) will be preserved A state that is going to decline is sure to belittle teachers and regard instructors lightly. If one belittles teachers and regards instructors lightly, then people will be careless. If people are careless, then proper models and measures will be wrecked" (*Xunzi* 2014, 595). In *On Learning* it is said even more straightforwardly: "When a teacher commands reverence, the *Dao* is respected, and when the *Dao* is respected, the people know to honor learning." In Xunzi's chapter 27, *The Grand Digest* (2014), and in the *Xueji* (On Learning), the high status of a teacher also stipulated very strict requirements for teachers: "Among the skills for being a proper teacher there are four elements, but being broadly learned is not a part of them. If one is dignified, stern, and inspires awe, one can be a teacher. If at the age of fifty or sixty one has proven oneself trustworthy, one can be a teacher. If one can recite and explain things without ever violating them oneself, one can be a teacher. If one's understanding is subtle and properly ordered, one can be a teacher" (*Xunzi* 2014, 115).

However, whether it is Xunzi or Dong Zhongshu, when they say these words their position has already changed; they are saying these words from the standpoint of political power. The one who really adhered to the original standpoint of the scholars was still the Grand Master of the tradition of *Dao*—Confucius. Confucius and Yan Hui had the following discussion:

> Yan Hui asked: 'Master, your *Dao* is so grand, there is no state in the world under Heaven that can bear it. Even so, what harm would there be if no one could bear you putting it into practice? It is by no state bearing it that shows the character of lordship. Not being able to cultivate the *Dao*, this is my lowliness. Having already greatly cultivated the *Dao*, but not having effectuated it is the lowliness of the state. What harm is it that none bear it? It is in not bearing it that shows the character of lordship.'
>
> SIMA QIAN, 1993, "The Hereditary House of Confucius"

Dao should be cultivated apart from the affairs themselves. The relationship between the tradition of *Dao* and the political tradition is merely "putting it into practice by effectuating it, concealing it by abandoning it." Only as a result of this there would be:

> With sincere faith he unites the love of learning; holding firm to death, he is perfecting the excellence in the *Dao*. Such a one will not enter a tottering state, nor dwell in a disorganized one. When the *Dao* prevails in the kingdom, he will show himself; when they are prostrated, he will keep concealed. When the *Dao* prevails in your land, poverty and a mean condition are things to be ashamed of. When the *Dao* does not prevail in your land, riches and honor are things to be ashamed of.
>
> *The Analects*, "Tai Bo," 13

> ... When the *Dao* prevails in his state, he is to be found in office. When the *Dao* ceases to prevail, he can roll his talents [lit. jewels] up, and keep them in his breast.
>
> *The Analects*, "Wei Ling Gong," 7

The scholar of Confucianism is this kind of person who will never separate himself from the tradition of *Dao* even for a moment, when the imperial
power and *Dao* converge, one can emerge to fill the office; when the imperial power and *Dao* diverge; then one retreats and preserves.[18] The *Dao* of
Confucius that he advances to and retreats from finds in Yang Xiong a more
precise formulation: "when serving official office, one wishes to carry out one's
righteousness, when occupying office one wishes to display one's *Dao*, never
tiring of serving and never tiring of teaching" (Mao Lirui and Shen Guanqun
1985b, 214). As a scholar the pillar of Liu Dapeng's spirit stands on his "higher
will" manifested in the grand *Dao* of the ages, and upholding the higher will
was the very sense of his life, if teaching was a matter of him settling down at
home, then upholding his higher will would be the enterprise of recognizing
and developing his own being.

Let us abstract ourselves from the narrative of the ancient classics and
return to the everyday life of a lower level man—the private tutor Liu Dapeng.

How did Liu Dapeng uphold his higher will?

"Leading a simple and virtuous life." In Liu Dapeng's diaries there appear
such phrases as "eastern room [of the house]" and "western guest,"[19] this
east and west pairing very clearly reveals the power relations between the
teacher and his employer, and we can demonstrate why Liu "spending his
autumns and springs by peoples' households" was by no means a peaceful and
easy affair.[20] "Men who teach, men who hold their noble aspiration close to

---

18   Fei Xiaotong, "On Scholars of Confucianism," in Wu Han, Fei Xiaotong, eds. *Imperial Power
      and Gentry Power* (Tianjin: Tianjing People's Publishing House, 1988), 28–30.

19   The room to the east and western guest refer to the master of the house and the visiting
      teacher respectively, because, according to ritual, the master of the house occupies the
      east of the house upon the visit of the teacher, who occupies the west of the house. The
      text plays on the coupling of east-west (the master-teacher relation), for, as a compound,
      it also means "thing" in Chinese; moreover, the term "room to the east" (Dongjia 东家)
      now means landlord or employer, for the reason above, which is impossible to render
      (—Trans.).

20   See for reference a verse below about a tutor's being pushed around at a village private
      school, from which we can see the general living conditions of a tutor:
          "When the master vented, tears were immediately shed. The misery of his position is
      difficult to sum up in a word. Thinking of it how couldn't one cry? There was not just one
      day when the master couldn't do it. His remuneration only brought a miniscule amount,
      but his dealings were innumerable. When it rains, pack the mule, when the sky clears up,
      send it off. Reflecting on the details, it was worse than begging for food. The most measly
      business in the world today is incomparable to teaching. By tearing his throat, in a year of
      yelling his ultimate result was to become '*zhaodaosunli*' [just ordinary, like everybody];
      by exhorting force unceasingly from morning till night was to teach '*tiandixuanhuang*'
      [everything]. Who wants to offer tea, which family would offer food or one bowl of ginger
      sauce noodles, while hoping to temporarily fill his stomach; and when he was resting, the
      Zhangs would appear to invite him for a drink, or the Lis invite him to their house for a

their chests are few, a mere square inch of them, all the rest of them are only seeking a good tutoring position just to make a little more on tuition fees, to eat a little better, if the master's treat is generous, then so be it. I was not at all planning to spend my autumns and springs by peoples' households, ultimately it wasn't my far-reaching plan. Giving up my own field to plough other people's fields, having gone through all these perils I treated myself poorly, and my aspiration died down, the hollowest of the plans is the affair of teaching, for teaching is merely a temporary plan for eking out a simple living, when it becomes the ultimate life plan then it is just abnormal."[21]

"Treated poorly," "aspiration died down," "hollowest of the plans" can be said to be the true conditions of tutors' survival. Liu Dapeng could never escape poverty, but undertaken with his head high and full of disdain, not willing to give in to whining, just wrecking his mind's passion, that's all; and also filled with self-consolation, but not really moving forward, that's all. Even if this is the case, in the diaries we still find this remark:

> … Mid-way, I met one teacher, he was in commerce and still frustrated. We sat down for a friendly chat. He talked at length about teaching little boys, five to six of them, each contributing one thousand six hundred coins respectively. In one year that would amount to less than ten thousand, not enough even for simple living. How could one feed a family, truly desperate misery! After hearing that I also felt unhappy …
>
> … Fifteen years afterward I myself set up a school and started instructing students. I couldn't count the hardships I experienced …
>
> … Yan said: "If a family has three *shi* of grain [roughly 800 grams], there is no need to become a boys' teacher. It seems like he knows that teaching is not an easy job, if one scholar can find another job, one would not need to do this, not only because it wastes one's time, but also because it is no way to strengthen virtue."[22]

---

chat. He has two sweet cakes, weighing them [to see which one can] relieve his hunger. [The festival gifts, Bao Wen himself had never seen ones like those today]; [but] payments for his classes were nothing on top of absolutely nothing and he still had to check homework. Wearing an old [scholar's] hat, one was told that one was good at divination [was respected]; dressed in a beat up robe one was scolded for being poor and pedantic, as if he was an educator of barbarians."

21   Liu, *Diaries in Meditative Purity*, 57.
22   Liu, *Diaries in Meditative Purity*, 59.

Probably due to cherishing his "own virtue," Liu Dapeng was not always overly concerned about money, and considered, instead, how well he was treated by his landlord: "After breakfast, I came to the lecture hall from home, the landlord prepared food and wine for me, this virtue and ritual is [the] very [sign of] hospitality" (1893). "This dragon boat festival, all the villages and families celebrate it, the disciples in my lecture hall prepare wine and food for the sacrificial ceremony for old sages; it was also magnificent" (1894). "This rich man treats teachers many time in each year, and knowing the ritual of respecting teachers, this is the big benefit." "The landlord prepares all the food I need when I am in the lecture hall. My son Xuan also studies with me, and the fee for shared food is waived by the landlord too, the landlord treats me very well in this way. In the lecture hall, three meals are included, a boy serving in the lecture hall prepares the food for me. I always select the food I like—more vegetables and less meat. For me, it is already too luxurious, for others, they laugh at me for being too frugal" (1901). Between excessive luxury and frugalness, Liu Dapeng consoled himself, which is also reflective of his hypocritical and tragic life.

Liu Dapeng, who held to his will, was far less like Confucius. In terms of being poor with a positive attitude, there are some similarities with Yan Yuan![23] It is worth emphasizing that this positive attitude has become the basic content of the Chinese teacher's self-discipline.[24]

---

23   Yan Hui 顏回 (521–481 BCE), courtesy name Yuan 渊 or Ziyuan 子渊, was the most important disciple of Confucius. Yan Hui grew up in a poor family, but he had an immense love of learning. The Master esteemed Yan Hui very highly and praised him for his noble and humankind behavior. "He was flagging when I set forth anything to him," the Master said, and: "Yan Hui was such that for three months there would be nothing in his mind contrary to perfect virtue. With a single bamboo dish of rice, a single gourd dish of drink, and living in his mean narrow lane," Yan Hui was admirable for the Master. For Confucius, Yan Hui was a model of virtue and an equal to himself, progressing each day on the way of kindheartedness.

24   What is worth noticing is that by the time voluntary Chinese education arose and thereafter, the designer of China's modernization (or rather we should say the upper level school "vitalizer") demanded the image of the teacher be "Yan Yuan." The teacher of education "understood the greatness of his own responsibility and would often waver in belief due to depression in life. Because of this, those serving as the heads of primary school teachers would have to have a diligent and enduring spirit, work through complications without fear, harbor no resentment in the face of destitution, eat poorly, live uncomfortably, and even less so have peace of mind, while dedicating one's whole heart to the children, and undertaking one's duties with the spirit to survive only having 'one bamboo container of food, one ladle of drink, unbearable worries going down the decrepit alleyways, and upon returning having no way to alter one's own joy.'" (For reference, see *Voluntary Education*

"I'm serious about doing trifling things." In the time of Liu Dapeng's life, the road to becoming a Confucian official was much more crowded than before. The choice of entry exams for selected Confucian officials had become unattractive to many families, and the abandonment of Confucianism for the sake of doing business had gradually become a trend. Liu found that

---

Teacher Qualification Training and Refining [Zhonghua Shuju, 1939], Feb. Ed., p. 8. Cited from Xiong Xianjun's work: *One Thousand Autumns of Basic Enterprise: Research on China's Recent Voluntary Education*, ECNU Press, 1998, p. 182.) This "anxiety" and "worry" is what the commoner worries about but the *junzi* finds no shame in (those who are ashamed of bad clothing and bad food are unworthy of mention), the will of the teacher is set on seeking *Dao* and transmitting *Dao*, and the seeking of non-desire in life became a matter of integrity and even transformed into a sense of moral superiority, and, combined with the inherent cultural capital possessed by the teacher, it constitutes the symbolic capital held by scholars in authoritative society. Looking at it from the teacher's own perspective, this is both the self-expectation and also the self-relief, making him capable of keeping a "clean and high" distance from the commoner's life (although clean does not necessarily mean high, just as "harmoniously alone" does not necessarily mean "highbrow") to particularly establish a unique sense of superiority to maintain the dignity of studying and teaching. The teacher's sense of responsibility manifests as: "having high thoughts and an enduring will, if the high thoughts lower one portion, his sense of responsibility will lower one portion; if the enduring will is worn down one portion, his sense of responsibility will be worn down one portion" (See for reference Chen Baoquan: *Poetic Preservation of Diaries in Meditative Purity*) From the perspective of those running the school, endowing teachers who have achieved enlightenment (who have removed the veil of ignorance) and even liberation (no longer restricted to the cognitive level of the student, expanding to the entire life of the student; no longer restricted to the relatively self-enclosed school, and rather taking the school as castle, expanding to the deeper levels of the entire social life), and motivating teachers with rising aspirations. This endowment of meaning was never a spiritual discipline. The teacher is someone rather sensitive to signs and meaning. (The intellectual was someone who became habituated to using "abstract knowledge," namely those who easily enter deep reflection. Ye Qizheng once divided people into "prescient," "hind-sighted" and "ignorant," and although the teacher was not necessarily the "prescient," at the very least he should not have been "the ignorant.") The cultural habits that come with them give them the meaning of seeking to "establish a life" outside of home, and transcendent aspirations also make them not only live in a pressing-in uniformity of space-time. Meaning expands mental space outside of the teacher's material life and even above it; it also becomes a region of reliable, safe and extremely strong strength of resolve. This region resolves the direct conflict between the teacher's body and the institution, or rather, meaning allows the teacher to accept the institution in the mind, and even to begin participating in the establishment of the institution. Meaning accomplishes the motivation of the teacher's life and body through motivating the teacher's spirit—ceaselessly overcoming and ascetic. The making of such aspirations became the teacher's managerial practice across time (and even continues to this day); while it resolved the teacher's own vocational tensions caused by the choking cost of running an extensive education system in a poor country, in what sense did it construct the image of the Chinese teacher?

[T]he bad trend of late in my hometown is very popular, and people look down upon the study of Confucianism and regard business as more important. The talented children are all headed for business, and there are very few students; there are very few students studying here, most of whom give up studying and choose to do business instead.

The reason is that "the scholars suffer hunger and cold; if you are businessmen, your family will have wealth and flourish." And "recently the teachers are often despised, and even mistreated by the landlord, but they still would not quit their jobs. The landlord takes the mistreated behavior as what they deserve. The world is like this, and no one ever shows pity, who knows where this bad situation will end up?"

Liu has a painful feeling, stating
... this time, the school is decadent and the morale is weak. Therefore, even though the family has children, and paid for the teacher to teach them, it is only trifles, not to mention [the lack of] respect for teaching and teachers. For the teachers, because the landlord is rich, they ignore the disrespect and impolite behavior, and even flatter the landlord, the trend is like this, one can only sigh deeply.
LIU 1990, 147

In 1893, the teacher has no self-respect, how can others respect the teacher? (Liu 1990, 147). "The Dao of teaching is declining ever faster today." Because "everyone does not take studying seriously," and "students do not take the teacher seriously, and do not know the ritual of respect," meanwhile, "the teacher is not virtuous, and students do not know to change teachers." He continues, "the teachers themselves have the feeling of inferiority, often willingly following the will of [the landlord in the] lecture Hall, then on to earning money, and only enough to feed oneself for a year,"[25] suggesting that the decline of the world is worsening.

Although teaching is a trifle for the landlord, Liu Dapeng is still doing his utmost, for example, maintaining an aloofness (not flattering the landlord), even though he is in poverty—

After leaving the lecture hall, the landlord is inhospitable. When I come to the lecture hall, we seldom meet, the food prepared is far different than in earlier times, but I cannot turn a cold attitude to my students

---

25   Liu, *Diaries in Meditative Purity*, 140.

because of the cold attitude of the landlord, and with respect to studying and teaching, I can only try my best. Recently, there is a man who passed two selected exams and got the title of salaried student (*linsheng* 廩生); it seems like madness, but actually he is not crazy; he is happy when there is profit; if there is no profit, he gets angry. Regardless of whether one is his uncles or his brother, he treats them like strangers, there is no order of respect and humbleness in his mind, and he does identify the natural connection with relatives, he acts whatever he feels is right, and claims others' faults, never admitting his own problems, what a pity and shame. Last year, I was paid one hundred coins for teaching, this year, the landlord gave me one hundred and twenty without any reason whatsoever, so I only accept one hundred and turn twenty coins back, just afraid that the landlord uses profit to seduce me to give up my independent personality.[26]

Even if the emperor gives orders to stop the imperial examination, and the scholars are not in the mood to focus on studies and practice, but nor are students motivated to study, most of them are beginning to find other jobs, "The world has changed to this, and it's fearful. When I got up, I was hopeless, I saw that everything is empty, and there is nothing that can last forever. Only my gathered virtue can last with heaven and earth. But gathered virtue is not easy, unless one dedicates it to everyday practice."[27]

"Withdrawing and mediating as the roots of my joy." In 1891, Liu Dapeng wrote the following words when he was teaching in the house of banker Wu Youqing, located in Nan Xi village, Tai Gu county:[28]

Five Precepts: quit meddlesomeness, meddlesomeness leads to regret; quit talking too much, talking too much leads to troubles; quit acting too much, more action leads to being blamed [without any reason]; quit more desires, more desires disturb the heart; quit wasting too much, wasting too much will lead to suffering in poverty.

Seven Examinations: examine ones' own laziness, if one is lazy, then it is difficult to achieve anything; examine ones' arrogance, arrogance is annoying; examine oneself to see if one always thinks one is right, if so, it will lead to unreasonable behavior. Examine oneself to see if there is self-deception, deception disturbs the heart; examine ones' complacency, complacency is the company of bad luck; examine one's anger, anger will

---

26   Ibid., 88.
27   Liu, *Diaries in Meditative Purity*, 146.
28   Ibid., 1.

harm one's body; examine if you ignore yourself too much, ignorance will lead to regret.

Ten seekings: Seek the harmony of *yin* and *yang*; seek the generosity of human relationships; seek the teaching of customs; seek the joy of parents; seek the righteousness of the mind; seek the good starting point of character; seek the advancement of virtue; seek more good friends; seek the peace of a quiet house; seek a strong body.

Eight roots: humility is the root of the preservation of the body; peace and joy are the roots of doing things; the content is the root of cultivating one's heart; not desiring too much is the root of cultivating oneself; withdrawing and meditating are the roots of joy; patience is the root of advancing virtue; indifference to fame and wealth are the roots of cultivating health.

> LIU 1990, 1

3   The Dead End

If scientific research is abolished, my generation will lose the way. If I want to make a living, then I will have no way to work. What should we do?

When the imperial examination is stopped, many scholars will lose their jobs in the lecture hall, and there are no other jobs for them, what should they do?

There are many people like me who lost their jobs, if one has fields or other business, one can handle it without suffering poverty, what of scholars only rely on teaching without any other business? In these changing times, how can they find a job?[29]

In 1904, Liu saw from the "newspaper of Jin" that "the government wants to reduce teaching positions in various provinces and counties. The dismissal of teachers and all the incidents in the education department should be handled by the provincial departments of school." According to the old Qing dynasty system, *juren* 舉人 who pass the *datiao* 大挑 "big pick" exam, can become local teachers (although there may be a ten year or *longer* waiting period from the time of being selected to actually becoming a local teacher), but this is also one of the ways to enter the official system. Liu Dapeng had been waiting for a long time, and was only one step away from this. Now this path would be closed.

---

29   Ibid.

He immediately realized that "there is no way out for scholars." In the middle of February of 1905, Liu Dapeng knew that "the lecture hall of the world has been changed to a school; the school is the name shared by the foreign countries; all the rules of schools are in accordance with Japan" (Liu 1990, 139). In October, he was informed that the imperial examination had been abandoned. "My heart is dead, and everything in my sight is empty." The abolishment of the imperial examination was a major change to something that had existed for thousands of years. In traditional society, there was political Confucianism or there were families that ploughed the field while reading Confucian texts. From farming to political Confucianism, it was a far way to fall, but at least such an option existed; now there was no way to rise to the upper class, which meant that the entire society's upward mobility had to turn in another direction.

You cannot establish something without breaking something. The imperial examination was abolished, and establishing schools would become the most important thing. Zhang Zhidong said: "I think the reasons for good luck and bad luck from the ancient world till now, the flourishing and decline of talented people, is, on the surface and by appearance, politics, but actually, in reality, it is [the act of] study." Therefore, the world needs to run many schools, "the schools are not yet set up, people are not yet educated, but one seeks talents in a rush; it is like not planting any trees but hoping to have a good pillar, not having a big pool but hoping to have big fish."[30] It is significant to run a school, but the foundation of a school is neither located in the existing society, nor does it rely on what Liang Qichao called the scholars (like Liu Dapeng) who "do not totally understand the six arts, not to mention the four histories, do not know the existence of the five continents, and cannot distinguish the eight stars."[31] China's modernization is focused on flourishing schools; if they allow millions of students to be trained by these people who only read books but do not understand the books; it is "lifelong hovering over what is under one's legs without knowing that there is a bigger world." It is tantamount to "who wants to open up the wisdom of the people but fools them, and who wants to make the people strong but weakens them" (Chen 1983, 143). The establishment of a new school means repelling Liu Dapeng's lecture hall and reshaping the education system in China with new strengths and new ideas.

---

30   Zhang Zhitong, "Exhortation to Learning Edited," in Chen Xuexun, ed., *Selected Writings on China's Recent Education* (Beijing: People's Education Publishing House, 1983), 237.

31   Liang Qichao, "On Normal Education," in Chen Xuexun, ed., *Selected Writings on China's Recent Education* (Beijing: People's Education Publishing House, 1983), 142.

At this point, Liu Dapeng can only passively lose his lecture hall. When the imperial examination was abolished, Liu Dapeng repeatedly described in his diary,

> [O]ld friends who made a living by teaching, because of the new policy, lost their jobs; they sigh that they have no food. When I go out, my friends are all worried about the world, only the reformed people encourage us: changing the old system is like this, breaking the old and establishing the new, great chaos can lead to great order, then all under heaven can be ruled in order soon, "What are you worried about".
>
> LIU 1990, 149

But people like Liu Dapeng can't be reassured,

> This time, when I went out, I saw all the people suffering. The peasants said, "The year is not good for farming, and people will suffer hunger, but what can we do about it?"; the scholars said, "Students prefer to learn new studies and abandon Confucianism, and scholars are suffering because of it, but what can we do?" Workers said, "Now we have machines, and there is no need for handmade things, and there is no work, but what should we do?" Businessmen said, "The taxes are getting higher by the day, and there is very little profit, but what can we do?"
>
> LIU 1990, 155

By 1907, many villages had abolished the old lecture halls and set up new schools, had abandoned the study of Confucius and Mencius, and students had begun to learn science. The students in the provincial schools were mainly dressed in foreign styles. Upon seeing "traditionally dressed people," the students drove them away. The students in the new schools talked about the gains and losses of politics without any fear, and the state of rebellion had already come to light. Although people like Liu Dapeng saw and heard this with a chill, they lamented again, "The traditional teachers are suffering, but they don't know how to handle it." These "'poor' sad people who have bad luck" have no way to live a life. At this time, many said, "I was not born in the right time" (Liu 1990, 159).

Liu Dapeng experienced an important conflict in spirit, that is, the conflict between the new and the old, the East and the West. His attitude towards the studies promoted by foreigners also went through a process of development, from contempt to fear, and finally the decision to stick to his own knowledge, dejected and lonely.

In Liu's view, learning relied on ethics. The essence of ethics lies in righteousness, closeness, difference, order, and faith. These were the five ethics, and, "If one does not teach the five ethics, how can the training be called teaching?"[32] But, he continued, "Today, teachers teach students math, and take western knowledge as principle. How could this be the way to cultivate good people? The study of Western learning only focuses on utility, which is contrary to our own learning, and approaching the Western learning without knowing its faults, that's a pity."[33] The "utility" of western learning was completely opposed to the "righteousness" of Confucian teachings. It was popular to study Western subjects, yet people did not even know the most basic rituals. How was it possible to set up the *Dao* of teaching? What was point of running a school? Those who insisted on the path of Confucius and Mencius ere not tempted by Western learning, yet they were regarded as stubborn parties. When the imperial examination stopped, the scholars were pushed to engage in Western learning, but what was the use of Western learning?

China transformed into a modern country by virtue of outside powers, the sweeping changes in the late Qing Dynasty revolved around policies that had to be changed because Western countries had invaded China. It was easy to change at the concrete level, for instance by adopting machines and tools, but it was not easy to change people's minds at the level of principle. The new education system claimed "Freedom and equality, and ignored the closeness between father and son, and the importance of respect to teachers." The basic values which the scholar gentry insisted on were totally abandoned. "Everyone who enters the new school is engaged in the new habit," therefore "[f]or the father and the brothers, they know how ridiculous the new school is, do not allow the children to enter school, and [would rather] let them learn business" (Liu 1990, 162–163). The new schools were cut off from civil society on two levels. From the perspective of superficial utilitarianism, there was no longer an imperial examination, thus there was no possibility of becoming an official [by studying]. "Those who read books suffer from hunger and cold." Instead, if one does business, one can get more money and make one's family richer. The rapid decline in the status of scholars led to turmoil between the four different traditional levels of peoples (*shi nong gong shang* 士农工商). At the deeper level of principle, the occluded local society did not realize the significance of Western learning, so society lost the tradition of Confucius and Mencius and then lost the spiritual cohesion of integrating the hearts of human beings, and society suffered this heavy injury deeply. In this way, it was inevitable that

---

32   Liu, *Diaries in Meditative Purity*, 147.

33   Ibid., 144.

> ... in my hometown, the trend is bad, people dismiss studies and focus
> on business. The children of the talented are all going out to do business,
> and there are very few learners; there are very few who are insistent on
> learning Confucianism, most people are doing business. In general "eight
> or nine out of ten people are doing business, only one or two out of ten
> is studying."
>
> LIU 1990, 17

The people lost their inner interest in maintaining the lecture hall, and the
decline of the *Dao* of teaching occurred rapidly. "Students look down on their
teachers, and do not know the ritual of respect to teachers," ... "One does not
have the wisdom to change the teacher if the teacher is not virtuous enough," ...
"The teachers also look down on themselves, and [must] tolerate the landlord
who owns the lecture hall, earning only a little bit money to eke out a living.
The state of the world is declining."

In Liu Dapeng's view, schools were not only unprofitable, but even harmful. The harm was not only in the loss of the existing system of studying and
examination-taking, but also that the tradition of correlatively farming
and studying was broken—because there was no more 'studying.' Liu wrote,
"The intelligent children give up studying and choose to do business" (Liu
1990, 162–163), and "from then on, the population of scholars has been
reduced, day by day." Another blow was the erosion of the [literary] tradition
of Confucianism. "No one is focusing on the study of literature, I am afraid that
there will be no scholars left in ten years. How then is it possible to have good
literature? It is really hard to understand the will of heaven" (Liu 1990, 66).

As a *juren*, Liu Dapeng was fortunate enough to overcome the loss of traditional lecture halls relatively peacefully. By 1913, he was teaching at the Jinci
Mengyang (山西祠堂启蒙小学) Primary School, where mathematics, literature, gymnastics, etc., were taught. Liu taught Chinese and self-cultivation.
Every day, he offered the primary school students a basic education based
on the "four books and five classical texts" rather than text books. "Leisurely
teaching, there is no other thing to disturb my mind," he wrote. Although the
funding for the school was increasing, it was still insufficient, and also required
the support of students' parents. In spite of the effort, the school lost people's
support and Liu wrote, "People dislike the new school. The way the school
is set up now, it is doing whatever people dislike without doing anything people would like. Any desire to act contrary to this would create major unrest and
would necessarily fail." Having been a teacher at the primary school for half a
year, Liu did not receive the gift of pork that was standard for teachers and so
he resigned, stating the lack of ritual propriety (that would indicate respect) as
his reason, and subsequently he planned to do something else to make a living.

In 1914, Liu Dapeng's situation got even more difficult as he approached the end of his teaching career. He became even more introspective in his diary, convinced one should rely on the land or a consistent job to support one's family. He writes, "I have been teaching for 20 years, but because of the popularity of the new methods of learning, my consistent job is not reliable, and I am falling into a state of poverty. My only option is to find another job to keep myself living through the chaos." Eventually, he resigned his job as a teacher, "Due to poverty, I suffered in the countryside, without food or a job, I have no choice but this coal mine, and I often must go into the mountains. I live in a time of chaos, there is no use for my study. I rely on coal mining and stay there, this is what called awaiting my mandate." Liu Dapeng, at fifty years of age, was reduced to running a small coal mine to eke out a living.

The most formal activity recorded by Liu Dapeng in his later years was the "Letter from the County Office" received in 1938, inviting him to participate in the official ceremony held at the County Confucian Temple. The festival of Confucius' birthday is a great ritual for scholars.[34] Each county had a special temple for scholars where scholars would organize a clan meeting in honor of the ancient sages. Such ceremonies were organized by the county magistrate who is both the officer of policy and the officer of education. "Politics" was originally embedded in the "teaching," and the tradition of the rule of virtue in Chinese society was embodied everywhere. The 81-year-old Liu Dapeng rushed to the county early in the morning, he wished to "catch up," but he was old, weak, and slow, and when he finally walked into the Temple of Scholars, he later wrote, "the county magistrate, named Wu, and the village gentry have already finished the ceremony, and the other four streets have prepared and made the sacrifices" (Liu 190, 534). He slowly went with the crowd to pay his respects, although he did not bend his knees down, he had to bow three times; After registering with the county office, he happened to run into the distribution of sacrificial pork and mutton and so he received two or three pounds of meat which he took to his daughter's house in the city[35] (Liu 1990, 250).

Liu Dapeng concludes:

> When I was young, I had the aspiration of becoming a duke of a large estate. When I came of age, I studied military books, but when I reached middle age I was trapped in the imperial examination hall, continuously failing and stumbling, lamenting that my aspirations were greater than

---

34   Confucius became a cultural icon, the cohesive binding force maintaining the integral unity of political education in the so-called four people's society.

35   Liu, *Diaries in Meditative Purity*, 250, 534.

my meager talents, and could not bear to shoulder the great task. As I approached forty, although I had passed the examination, I ultimately had neither opportunities nor stable conditions, and could not help but to eke out a living by teaching. In the third year of the Guangxu era, the government was reformed and the *Dao* was abolished, until the third year of the Xuantong era, the revolutionary party has been harassing China, and the country has been broken. I have no place to teach and have been trapped in my hometown for several years. I am almost 60, there is no way to restore the Central Plains, and I really do not have talents to do other things, even though I am seven *chi* in height, that does not make up for the hardships in our time, and my life is empty, there is no end to my anxiety.[36]

References

Bourdieu, Pierre, Li Meng, Li Kang trans. 1998. *Shijian yu fansi: fansi shehuixue daoyin* 实践与反思：反思社会学导引 [Practice and Reflection: Introduction to Reflections on Sociology]. Beijing, Zhongyang Bianyi Publishing House.

Chen, Dongyuan. 1934. *Zhonguo jiaoyu shi* 中国教育史 [The History of Chinese Education]. Beijing: People's Education Publishing House.

Chen Xuexin. 1983. *Zhongguo jindai jiaoyu wenxuan* 中国近代教育文选 [Selection of Educational Literature of Modern China]. Beijing: People's Education Press.

Fei, Zhengqing, ed. 1993. *Jianqiao zhongguo wanqing shi* 剑桥中国晚清史 [Cambridge History of the Late Qing Dynasty of China] (Part I). Beijing: China Social Science Publishing House.

Gu Yanwu. 1983. *Gu tinglin shiwenji* 顾亭林诗文集 [Gu Tinglin's Collection of Poems and Essays]. Beijing: Zhonghua Book Company Limited. P.21.

He, Huaihong. 1998. *Xuanju shehui yu qi zhongjie—qinhan zhi wanqing lishi de yizhong shehuixue chanshi* 选举社会与其终结—秦汉至晚清的历史的一种社会学阐释 [Selective Society and its End: A Sociological explanation of the history from Qin and Han to the Late Qing]. Beijing: Sanlian Shudian.

Hu, Shi. 1997. *Sishi zizhuan* 四十自传 [Forty Autobiographical Notes] (Part I). Beijing: China Social Science Publishing House.

Kong, Feili. 1993. "The Decline of the Qing Empire and the Source of Rebellion." In *Jianqiao zhongugo wanqing shi* 剑桥中国晚清史 [The Cambridge History of Late Qing China] (Part I), edited by Fei Zhengqing. Beijing: China Social Science Publishing House.

---

36   Ibid., 198.

Liu, Dapeng. 1990. *Tuixiang zhai riji* 退想斋日记 [Diaries in Meditative Purity]. Taiyuan: Shanxi Peoples' Publishing house.

Mao, Lirui, and Shen Guanqun, eds. 1985a. *Zhongguo jiaoyu tongshi* 中国教育通史 [Comprehensive History of Chinese Education], Vol. 1. Jinan: Shandong Education Publishing House.

Mao, Lirui, and Shen Guanqun eds. 1985b. *Comprehensive History of Chinese Education* Vol. 2. Jinan: Shandong Education Publishing House.

Qu, Shipei, ed. 1995. *Jiang menglin jiaoyu lunzhu xuan* 蒋梦麟教育论著选 [Select Jiang Menglin Education Essays]. Beijing: People's Publishing House.

Sima, Qian (approximately 145 BC–approximately 86 BC). 1993. *Records of the Grand Historian [shiji* 史记]. *Qin Dynasty*. Hong Kong: New York: Research Centre for Translation, Chinese University of Hong Kong; Renditions—Columbia University Press.

Tang, Degang. 1993. *Hu Shi koushu zizhuan* 胡适口述自传 [Hu Shi's Oral Auto-biography]. Shanghai: ECNU Press.

Wang Junnian and Wu Jingzi. 1980. *Rulin waishi* 儒林外史 [The Scholars]. Shanghai: Shanghai Ancient Books Press.

Wu, Han and Fei Xiaotong et al. 1998. *Huangquan yu shenquan* 皇权与绅权 [Imperial Power and Gentry Power]. Tianjin: Tianjin People's Publishing House.

Wu, Jingzi. 1958. *Unofficial History of the Literati*. Beijing: People's Literature Publishing House.

Xi Zhou Sheng. 1981. *Xingshi yinyuanzhuan* 醒世姻缘传 [The Rousing Story of Fated Love]. Shanghai: Shanghai Ancient Books Publishing House. Chapter 33, p. 478.

Xiong, Xianjun. 1998. *Qian qiu ji ye—zhongguo jindai yiwu jiaoyu yanjiu* 千秋基业—中国近代义务教育研究 [One Thousand Autumns of the Basic Enterprise: Research on the Voluntary Education of Recent China]. Wu Han: ECNU Press.

Xunzi. 2014. *Xunzi: The Complete Text*, trans. Eric L. Hutton. New Jersey: Princeton University Press.

Yang, Nianqun, ed. 2001. *Kongjian, jiyi yu shehui zhuanxing* 空间、记忆与社会转型 [Space, Memory and Social Transition]. Shanghai: Shanghai People's Publishing House.

Ye, Qizheng. 1984. *Shehui, wenhua yu zhishifenzi* 社会、文化与知识分子 [Society, Culture and the Intellectuals]. Taipei: Taipei Dongda Book Company.

Ye, Qizheng. 1998. "*Guowai shehuixue* 国外社会学 [Who are 'the Intellectuals'?]." *Foreign Sociology* (No. 1).

Ying, Xing. 1996. *Shehui zhipei guanxi yu kechang changyu de bianqian—1895–1913 nian de Hunan shehui* 社会支配关系与科场场域的变迁—1895–1913 年的湖南社会 [Social Control Relationships and the Transformation of the Examination Site: Hunan Society from 1895–1913]. Peking University Sociology Department Master's Thesis, in *China Social Science Quarterly* (1997 Spring–Summer Volume), Altogether No. 18–19.

Zhang, Zhongli. 1991. *Zhongguo shenshi—guanyu qi zai 19 shiji Zhongguo shehui Zhong de zuoyong yu yanjiu* 中国绅士—关于其在 19 世纪中国社会中的作用与研究 [Chinese Gentry: Research on their Role in Chinese Society in the 19th Century]. Shanghai: Shanghai Social Science Publishing House.

Foreign Resources

Freire, Paulo. 1968. *Pedagogy of the Oppressed*. New York: The Seabury Press.

Giroux, Henry A. 1988. *Teachers as Intellectuals: Toward a Critical Pedagogy of Learning*. Westport, CT: Bergin & Garvey Publishers, Inc.

Young, Michael. 1971. *Knowledge and Control*. London: Collier Macmillan.

Young, Michael. 1999. *The Curriculum of the Future*. London: Institute of Education.

CHAPTER 2

Vocational Education and Career in Modern Shanghai: an Oral History-Based Study

Liu De'en
Translated by Tom Smith

Abstract

During the 1930s, the professional class in Shanghai, modern China's economic center, already included as many as one million people, a number second only to industrial workers. However, with regard to their lives and education, little research has been done, and only a limited amount of historical information has been gathered or put into order. In light of this, this paper, based on oral historical research supplemented with archival evidence, examines the relationship among the family backgrounds, professional careers, and education of Shanghai's technical, nursing, and business professionals during the Republic era. A distinctive feature of this class was that most of its members were born to middle-class families of moderate economic wealth. That is, there was some surplus beyond expenditures on basic necessities. All basically had cultural and professional experience beyond the elementary school level, and all had more or less established a cultural and professional spirit belonging to their own class and profession. However, they were also influenced to varying degrees by the social movements of their time. The vast majority of them had well-developed personal drive, but they were also limited by socioeconomic conditions. This essay proposes that the decisive factor in the social status of the professional class had nothing to do with their numbers but rather relied on their economic strength, level of organization, level of specialization, education level, cultural influence, and other factors.

© KONINKLIJKE BRILL NV, LEIDEN, 2019 | DOI:10.1163/9789004409606_003

1 Introduction: Direction of Research on Republic-Era Shanghai Professionals[1]

Shanghai has been the vanguard of China's modernization. Its central position in modern China's economy, culture, and other areas has been acknowledged by many scholars (Mo and Luo 1986; Zhang 1990, 19–27; Xin 1997; Jiang 2001, 73–83), and for all the changes of social structure and lifestyles manifested as a result of modernization it is likewise also considered an archetype of modernization (Li 2002, 4–6). Precisely because of this, increasing attention is being paid to the research of its various social groups and their social lives, as with, for example, Zhang Zhongli and Wang Xianming's studies of the modern gentry (Zhang 1991; 2001; Wang 1997), Li Yuliang and Sang Bing's studies of modern intellectuals (Li 1990; Sang 1995), Hao Yanping's study of the comprador class (Hao 1988), Zhu Ying and Tao Shuimu's studies of businessmen (Zhu 1996; Tao 2000), Zhang Kaiyuan, Mu Min, and Zhu Ying's study on official-business relations (Zhang 2000), and so on.

However, do the studies thus far sufficiently give the full picture of modern society? Research on individuals or small groups has, in general, been relatively detailed and thorough, but it has concentrated on people of eminent social status, such as important military and political figures, business leaders, or famous cultural figures. *Compendium of Historical Materials of the Republic of China* (*Zhonghua minguo shiziliao conggao* 中华民国史资料丛稿) is a large, widely influential collection, with 23 volumes of biographies published from 1973 to 2002, and 11 supplementary volumes on Republic-era figures—a total of 1,280 essays. The scale of the project is such that it undeniably covers a vast area. However, among the 1,280 biographical essays, more than half are devoted to military and political figures; next come specialists, who account for 23%, and then businessmen, who account for 17%. Non-professionals of various kinds account for 9.6% (see Table 1). *Biographies of Historical Figures in the Chinese Communist Party* (*Zhonggong dangshi renwu zhuan* 中共党史人物传), compiled by the Committee to Research Historical Figures in the Chinese Communist Party (Zhonggong dangshi renwu yanjiuhui 中共党史人物研究会) and edited by Hu Hua 胡华, Wang Qi 王淇, and Chen Zhiling 陈志凌, was published jointly by Shaanxi People's Publishing House (Shaanxi

---

1 This article was translated from its Chinese version, which was originally published in *China's Education: Research and Review*, 2005, volume 7, pp. 209–261.

renmin chubanshe 陝西人民出版) and Central Party Literature Press (Zhongyang wenxian chubanshe 中央文献出版社) from 1980 to 2002. Its 83 volumes include more than 1,200 biographical essays, and it is clearly slanted toward important military and political figures. Moreover, the compendium *Figures of the Republic Series* (Minguo renwu daxi 民国人物大系), published since 1996 by Unity Press (Tuanjie chubanshe 团结出版社), likewise consists mainly of important, preeminent figures.

Such is the tendency on the mainland, but even the 82 oral histories in 87 volumes published by the Institute of Modern History, Academia Sinica in Taiwan from 1982 to 2003 in its "Oral History Series"[2] (*Koushu lishi congshu* 口述歷史叢書) reflect the same tendency. With the exception of titles such as *Interview with Taiwanese Women of Two Eras* (Zouguo liangge shidai de Taiwan zhiye funü wenji lu 走過兩個時代的台灣職業婦女訪問紀錄), *Interviews with Kaohsiung Residents Pertaining to the February 28 Incident* (Gaoxiong she er'erba xiangguan renwu fangwen jilu 高雄市二二八相關人物訪問紀錄), *Interviews with Philippine Overseas Chinese* (Feilübin huaqiao fangwenlu 菲律賓華僑華人訪問紀錄), *Interviews with Naval Personnel* (Haijun renwu fangwen jilu 海軍人物訪問紀錄), *Oral Histories on Martial Law-era Political Cases in the Taipei Region* (Jieyan shiqi Taibei diqu zhengzhi anjian koushu lishi 戒嚴時期臺北地區政治案件口述歷史), *Interviews on the September 21 Earthquake* (Jiu er yi zhenzai koushu fangwen jilu 九二一震災口述訪問紀錄; this cannot really be considered historical in nature), and *Taiwanese in "Manchuria" During the Era of Japanese Rule* (Rizhi shiqi zai "Manzhou" de Taiwanren 日治時期在「滿洲」的台灣人), these are all basically the histories of "important" figures, of whom most are leading political persons, with famous business people and cultural figures next.

Research on society's great masses, meanwhile, has concentrated on the worker and peasant classes, especially the worker class, but the basic focus has been on revealing their difficult living situations and their actions in resistance and struggle. The six-volume *History of Chinese Workers' Movements* (Zhongguo gongren yundongshi 中国工人运动史) edited by Liu Mingkui 刘明逵 and Tang Yuliang 唐玉良 and published by Guangdong People's Publishing House (Guangdong renmin chubanshe 广东人民出版社) in 1998, as well as various other works purporting to be on labor movements, are classic examples. Most

---

2 Based on the content of the oral histories page on the Academia Sinica Institute of Modern History website: <http://mhorh.mh.sinica.edu.tw/books.php>.

studies of this kind exhibit two clear tendencies: (1) they are researched from a political or ideological perspective, so their conclusions are all more or less the same; and (2) because they focus on groups, they lack individuality and detail. Research on the history of peasants is relatively scattered, but it likewise has a tendency to overlook the details of individual peasant lives. There have been only a few exceptions, like Lin Yaohua's study on peasant families, Yang Maochun's study on farm communities, and Elizabeth J. Perry's study on strikes by Shanghai workers (Lin 1989; Yang 2001; Perry 2001).

TABLE 1   Statistics on biographies in *Compendium of Historical Materials of the Republic of China* (Zhonghua minguo shiziliao conggao)

Main categories	Subcategories	Number of biographies	Number of combined biographies	Subtotals
Important military and political figures	Qing court figures	26		26
	Anti-Qing revolutionaries	23		23
	Revolutionary party figures	92		92
	Important figures in provisional government	29		29
	Important figures in the Beijing government	202		202
	Important figures in the Nanjing government	175		175
	Important figures in other parties	37		37
	National traitors	39		39
	Important foreign military figures	24		24
	Subtotal	647	0	647/50.23%
Industrial and business world	Jiangsu-Zhejiang	88	4	92
	Beijing-Tianjin	39		39
	Guangdong	15	2	17
	Shandong	8		8
	Central China	13		13
	Southwestern China	20	1	21
	Northeastern China	19		19
	Northwestern China	11		11
	Subtotal	213	7	220/17.08%

TABLE 1   Statistics on biographies (*cont.*)

Main categories	Subcategories	Number of biographies	Number of combined biographies	Subtotals
Social groups	Women	18		18
	Minorities	37		37
	Overseas Chinese	33	1	34
	Religious figures	13		13
	Criminal societies	22		22
	Subtotal	123	1	124/9.43%
Specialists	Social sciences	65		65
	Law	13		13
	Education	34		34
	Literature and arts	84		84
	Science and technology	43		43
	Medicine and health	23		23
	Journalism and publishing	35		35
	Subtotal	297	8	297/23.06%
Total		1,280	8	1,288/100.00%

SOURCE: LIST OF "BIOGRAPHIES" IN THE APPENDIX, "BIOGRAPHIES OF REPUBLICAN CHINESE FIGURES (ZHONGHUA MINGUO RENWU ZHI 中华民国人物志)," 1987

In fact, between the social elites and the worker-peasant classes, there is another, middle class that has been overlooked. After the termination of the Shanghai International Settlement in 1943, this class grew steadily, and it grew even faster after the establishment of the People's Republic. It grew from 75,000 persons in 1895 to 960,000 persons in 1949. Ultimately it became the second-largest social class, behind only production workers (see Figure 1).

The members of this class accounted for as high a proportion of Shanghai's total population as 13.3%–17.7% (Zhonggong Shanghai shiwei dangshi ziliao zhengji weiyuanhui et al. 1999, 13–19; Hu 1987, 47). The proportion would be significantly greater if their dependents were added. For example, in 1946, the proportion of professionally employed residents as a share of the total population was as much as 34.8%[3] (Shanghai shi zhengfu tongjichu, 1947, 1946). In

3 Even though the largest group of employed persons in Shanghai were workers, their families were smaller in size than those of professionals. This may have been due to their

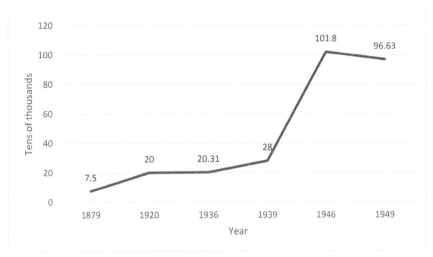

FIGURE 1   Growth of Shanghai professionals
SOURCES: ZHONGGONG SHANGHAI SHIWEI DANGSHI ZILIAO ZHENGJI
WEIYUANHUI ET AL. 1999, 13–19; ZHU, HU, AND XU 1984, CHAP. 24; ZHANG,
XIONG, AND SHEN 2002, 464; SHANGHAI NIANJIAN WEIYUANHUI 1937;
SHANGHAI SHI SHEHUI JU 1935; SHANGHAI SHI ZHENGFU TONGJICHU 1947

other words, one-third of the people belonged to this middle class. This suffices to show the scale of the professional class.

I have thus far seen only three scholarly books on this class. Ling-ling
Lien, making use of indirect historical materials, analyzed the scale, family backgrounds, education levels, methods and directions of employment,
and social organizations of groups of professional women in Shanghai during the 1912–1945 period (Lien 2001). Xiaoqun Xu used similar methods to do
an in-depth exploration of professional organizations in medicine, law, and
journalism as well as their power relationships with government during the
1912–1937 period (Xu 2000). The third book, a doctoral dissertation by Zhang
Liyan (2003), investigated the issue of the specialization of lawyers, from the
aspects of institutions and policies, professional organizations, the establishment of professional standards, and so on. Besides these, there have been a

---

impoverished lives, making it difficult to raise more children—and many workers were
single. Professionals, however, not only could raise more children but could also take care
of relatives and servants outside the immediate family. For instance, in 1941, the average
consumption unit for the households of Shanghai professionals was 5.52 persons, but for
workers it was only 4.33 persons. Of these, the number of children in professional households was approximately 3.45, but the number of children in workers' households was only
1.8. See Iwama 2003, 41–53, 123.

number of articles. For example, Wang Qisheng fully investigated the collective selection and appointment, backgrounds, qualifications, terms, salaries, and professional responsibilities of county magistrates in the Yangtze basin from 1927 to 1949 (Wang 1999, 98–116). Chen Mingyuan researched the economic conditions (incomes, lifestyles) of writers, professors, and other intelligentsia in Beijing and Shanghai (Chen 2000a, 16–22; 2000b, 27–32). Tian Zhengping and Xiao Lang investigated the group characteristics of modern Chinese educators (Tian 1999, 47–52). Liu Yunshan drew upon a wide range of materials to analyze the life history of a private school teacher living around the time when the old civil service testing system was abolished (Liu 2002, 143–174). The Japanese scholar Iwama Kazuhiro analyzed the living conditions of Shanghai professionals in the 1930s and 1940s, making use of surveys of such people's lives conducted by Gu Zhun, a local underground communist party member, and by the Industrial and Social Division of the Municipal Council, Shanghai International Settlement (Iwama 2003, 41–53, 123). These studies broke with the former model of abstract generalization on top of generalized explanations of the material and replaced it with revealing the individual characteristics of the different professional groups based on a comprehensive gathering of historical materials relating to particular groups. They all describe the ordinary conditions of those in the middle class but do not delve deeply into the details of their professional lives. At the same time, their conclusions are generalized mainly from government documents, the documents of professional groups, and published newspaper reports, but they still cannot express the various classes' diversity. In sum, the scale of these studies does not correspond with that of this professional class.

The next question is why there has not been more research on the middle class. There may be two reasons: (1) this class, lacking in importance or independence, belongs to another one; (2) current research models are inappropriate for researching this class, so that it is impossible to discover or interpret its characteristics.

Once we dig deeper into this class, we soon discover that the first "reason" above does not hold water. For example, scholars have discovered that this class not only differs from those above and below it but also that its existence is greatly significant, and one might even say that the process of modernization was the process of middle-class growth, and that one could hardly speak of modern society if not for the strength of the middle class (Mills 1987, Introduction; Ōkōchi Kazuo 1960, 18–21). There is, however, some basis for the second reason. On the one hand, members of the middle class do not play the roles of important military or political leaders, or of industrial leaders. Their actions do not directly influence the lives of ordinary city-dwellers of their time. Moreover, they are a relatively new group, so they are not so easily recalled, let alone recorded. On the other hand, they are not, as a rule, elite intellectuals. Few of them express their voices via the written word or the fruits of learning. They do not even cluster together to the same extent as workers or form ties to show their collective strength as a class. Their silent, scattered qualities have even been described as conservatism (Zhu, Hu, and Xu 1984, 24). Precisely for these reasons, historical materials for this class are much fewer than for the two classes above and below it.

For example, for members of the elite class in the military, political, commercial, and intellectual spheres, there are plenty of biographical works, and historical materials on them have been compiled and published in series. Most of the literary and historical materials published even by various local publishers relate to the elite class. Since the 1980s, there have been nearly 3,000 publications of literary and historical materials, and 110 volumes from the *Selected Shanghai Literary and Historical Materials* (*Shanghai wenshi ziliao xuanji* 上海文史资料选集) have also been published.[4]

As for the worker and peasant classes, there have been several specialized publications of literary and historical materials,[5] as well as series of selected histories of worker and peasant families, which are equivalent to literary and historical materials.[6] These historical materials were gathered and organized in accordance with the class struggle line, and some of it involves the lives and social movements of worker and peasant groups. The family history series also has touches of individualized color.

However, there have been no historical material series for the middle class and only a few publications under separate cover, which also follow the class struggle line. For example, there have been collections of historical materials on teachers' political movements (Shanghai shiwei dangshi ziliao zhengji weiyuanhui 1997), on movements among Shanghai postal workers (Shanghai gongren yundong shiliao weiyuanhui 1986), on workers' movements at Shanghai's Wing On Department Store (Zhonggong Shanghai hualian

---

4 This series, edited by Zhongguo renmin zhengzhi xieshang huiyi 中国人民政治协商会议 [Chinese People's Political Consultative Conference], Shanghai shi weiyuanhui 上海市委员会 [Shanghai Municipal Committee of the CPC], and Wenshi ziliao gongzuo weiyuanhui 文史资料工作委员会 [Committee of Cultural and Historical Data], is published by Shanghai renmin chubanshe.

5 For example, Liu 1985; 1993; Zhonghua quanguo zonggonghui Zhongguo gongren yundongshi yanjiushi 1980, 1981, 1982, 1983, 1984, 1985, 1986.

6 For example, Shanghai shi jianzhu gongcheng ju gonghui 1976; Shanghai shi qinggongye ju chang shi xiezuo zu 1975; Shanghai shi yijin gongye ju chang shi xiezuo zu 1975; Shanghai shi zonggonghui xuanjiao zu 1975.

shangxia weiyuanhui 1991), and so on. As for materials on individual persons in this class, there are only a few autobiographies or memoir collections, for example: the autobiography of Tang Diyin, the owner of a small stationery shop (Tang 1983), the autobiography of Ren Tongjun, a female teacher (Ren 1989), the biography of Zhang Binggui, a business professional (Dong 1986), the autobiographies of Zhang Youyu and Zhu Zheng, who were both reporters (Zhang 1982; Zhu 1999), the short memoir pieces of Shao Gongwen, an employee of Life Bookstore (Shenghuo shudian 生活书店) (Shao 1993), and so on.

To sum up, research on the middle class has been very inadequate, and what little researchable historical data exists is rather scattered. In this light, I feel that it is necessary to strengthen the research on the individual lives and group development of this class. Moreover, it is necessary to resort to methods besides documentary and historical data-based research and to uncover new historical material. My own choice is the oral history approach.

The oral history approach is quite well-developed in the West (Yang 1998, 2–6; 1998, 2–7), but it has also had some development in China. Before the 1970s, oral histories served mainly to provide a little supplemental evidence or further notational material for document-based history whose conclusions had already been set, e.g., in "on-site surveys" on the Taiping Heavenly Kingdom, Yihetuan Movement (Boxer Rebellion), the 1911 Revolution, the May 4th Movement, and recollections of the Communist Revolution, etc., where this tendency can be seen. Beginning in the 1980s, a few scholars greatly expanded the function of oral history. For example, Wang Qingxiang's career of oral history-based research on Pu Yi and his family have been a breakthrough, in terms of content and perspective, over document-based history. *Hu Shih's Oral Autobiography*, compiled by the Taiwanese scholar Tang Degang (Hu 1993), is not only content-rich but also very careful in its methodology; it makes the most of the advantages of oral history research. Besides function, the scale of oral history has also been expanded. For example, Zhang Xiao's oral history research on the Miao women of Jiangxi (Zhang 1997), Ling Tianhe's research on a farmer's life history (Ling 2003), Ding Yizhuang's and Li Xiaojiang's separate research on women's life histories (Ding 1999; Li 2003a, 2003d), and Liu Zhonglu's and Liu Xiaomeng's separate research on urban educated youths' life histories (Liu 1995; Liu 2003) turn the object of research away from famous people and leaders to ordinary people. However, I have not yet seen oral history research on the lives of professionals, apart from a few small biographies.

Seeing that research on the lives of professionals is rather thin and that the related historical materials are quite sparse, this study aims to use the oral history survey as the main research method for discovering historical truth and to make the data obtained from the oral history survey into descriptive history and to serve as a primary basis for judgment; essays, books, survey data, archival material and other contemporaneous documentary material will be supplementary, used for explaining the historical background, discerning truth from falsehood in the oral materials, and explaining the classic significance of oral historical materials.

My oral historical survey was conducted in two installments. The first surveyed 16 elderly persons, and after gaining a general understanding, I determined the focus for the second survey. The second survey filled in a few details, corrected some misunderstandings; it placed an emphasis on re-interviewing seven elderly persons of the most archetypical significance, and set aside two cases deemed not to have much bearing on the subject of this study. These elderly persons came from professions like engineering, business, medicine, education, public service, and so on, and in general they represented the basic situation for the professional class.

2   Destiny and Choice: Professional Class Backgrounds

The term "professional" (*zhiyuan* 职员) used here corresponds with the "middle class" as described above. The reason this term is used is purely customary, because "middle class" has not been used very often, either in the past or today in China.

Professionals are employed in a modern sector and have certain educational qualifications; they are salaried persons, not leaders, who assume a certain specialized professional capability. They are not limited only to white-collar workers (those who work with their brains) but also include technicians. Due to the limitations of research method and research conditions, the scope of the oral historical survey in this essay (which includes nurses, technicians, and business professionals) is only partial—it does not cover all professions. Other professionals would include teachers, public servants, various specialists, and so on, but others have already researched teachers and specialists. Although public servants were originally a part of my research, I was not able to include them here due to time- and research condition-related limitations.

Chinese terms equivalent to "professionals" include "the middle class (*zhongchan jieceng* 中产阶层)," "the bourgeoisie (*zhongchan jieji* 中产阶级)," related abbreviated terms (*zhongjian ceng* 中间层, *zhongchan ceng* 中产层), "white-collar (*bailing* 白领)," and so on, but in English usage these are all basically the "middle class." There are two connotative layers in the term: the first is "the old middle class," i.e., the managers of capitalist productive entities apart from the big capitalists themselves, including farm managers, factory superintendents, the owners of medium to small businesses, etc. The second layer of connotation is "the new middle class," made up of the increasingly large number of knowledge laborers who clustered in large business enterprises, government, and the public sector after the formation of monopolistic capitalism in the late nineteenth and early twentieth centuries, which was accompanied by the explosive growth in the scale of business enterprises (corporatization) and state organs. These laborers include the various levels of managers hired by businesses and governments, office workers, salaried engineering and technical staff, persons hired by various public sector entities in the areas of journalism, medicine, education, and transportation, and various free professionals such as lawyers, physicians, artists, clergy, and accountants. Of course, the owners of small and medium businesses were still middle class, but the agricultural middle-class as understood in the Western world shrank quite significantly (Mills 1987, chapt. 1–2; Ōkōchi Kazuo 1960, 18–21).

The modernization of Chinese business may have begun with the establishment of the Thirteen Factories, or Hongs, in Guangzhou (Canton) during the Qianlong and Jiaqing periods of the Qing dynasty. At that time, some Chinese merchants were able to deal directly with Western merchants, and even though they were under various restrictions imposed by the Qing government, they were all more or less influenced by the concepts and technologies used in Western businesses. Modern businesses established during the Westernization Movement in the mid-nineteenth century took the initiative to nurture a group of new-style Chinese professionals, even though most of them were concurrently serving as officials. The Treaty of Shimonoseki, signed after China's defeat in the First Sino-Japanese War (1894–1895), permitted foreigners to set up factories in China, which led to a large increase in the number of persons employed in foreign businesses. At the same time, it tacitly permitted a movement among Chinese-operated businesses to "save the country through business," and so the earliest Chinese business professionals emerged. However, the rapid development of Chinese businesses occurred after the founding of the Republic. Sun Yat-sen's ideas and policies on people's livelihood significantly stimulated an enthusiasm among Chinese for doing business. Chinese businesses also got a rare development opportunity as a result of World War I; they entered the so-called "Golden Age" of Chinese business development, when the speed of their development obviously accelerated. As a result, the number of new-style professionals rapidly grew, so that by the end of the 1930s they had emerged on the stage of history as a distinct class (Iwama 2003).

   Due to the constraints on employment conditions and employment scale, it was very difficult for children from workers' or farmers' families to enter the professional class. Mr. Fan, who attended a technical school and became a mechanic, introduced his own background this way:

> I was born in Changshu, Jiangsu (in the outskirts of Suzhou at those days) in 1914. After my father graduated from a normal school, he had always worked as a teacher and once was working in administration and served as the head of the Education Board. My mother was a housewife—didn't have a job. She died in her thirties, when I had just turned ten. I was the second child in my family—I had an older sister and a younger brother. My sister, after she graduated from normal school, worked her whole life as a teacher, first as a primary school teacher, later as the principal of her school, and finally as a middle school teacher. My younger brother had an art background, and he taught in Yangzhou Middle School ...

Mr. Shen originally graduated from China Vocational School and later became a civil engineer. As for his family background:

> I was born in 1920 in rural Pudong, Shanghai. Grandfather became an old-style Chinese medicine practitioner through apprenticeship, and he had a bit of fame in the area. After he died, his more than 3,000 books on traditional Chinese medicine were given to the College of Chinese Medicine. Father originally was a graduate of the Dept. of Shipping at Jiaotong University, but once, after he encountered a storm at sea, Grandfather wanted him to change jobs. So he sought out Huang Yanpei from our same village and taught at China Vocational School and later on became the instructional director. He taught there for more than 60 years. Father told us he could only support us through high school and couldn't afford to send us to university, and if we wanted to go to the university, the only way was to think of a way ourselves, work and then study. There were six of us, three boys and three girls. Four of us enrolled in China Vocational School. I studied civil engineering, two of my younger sisters studied business at China Vocational School, and one younger brother studied shipping, went on to study shipping in the university, and became a ship's captain. My older brother studied Chinese medicine from Grandfather and later changed to Western medicine. This could be reckoned a knowledgeable family—to the point that our nanny, from being influenced by my family, paid great attention to her

son's education, brought him to our house, let him learn by example, and form good study habits. Later on he was accepted at Tangshan Jiaotong University.

In 1934, when I graduated from elementary school, I was admitted into China Vocational School, which had a five-year civil engineering program. The reason I went there was mainly for economic considerations. On the one hand, my father was the instructional director, so I could study there tuition-free, and on the other hand, the expenses for studying at a vocational school were lower, and once you learned the skills of your field, you could find work.

The two individuals above had come from the homes of teachers, so their families had a stable income and could send their children to school. Even though some respondents came from rural villages, all met certain economic conditions. Mr. Shi, for example, who later became a mechanical engineer, came from a family that held certain assets and whose father and sister could also earn some income:

> In 1930, I was born in the Shanghai town of Chongming. At that time, our family was a big clan in decline. We had many houses, but they were all built during the Qianlong era. By my father's time, however, these old houses had mostly been sold off. Father's first wife and her children, a boy and a girl, and already died, so when he married my mother he was already rather old. My mother had four children—two boys and two girls—and I was number four. Father was an old intellectual and often did work for wealthy people, like calligraphy, bookkeeping, and so on. When I was little, we weren't at all wealthy and depended mostly on my two older sisters, who worked for a private business, to feed the family. Although I went to school in the town, from elementary to the first year of senior middle school, the tuition was waived because of Father's connections.

The family of another professional who had come from a rural village, Mr. Ye, owned several tens of *mu* of fields, but that could not guarantee he could enter middle school: he was able to study at China Vocational School only because of an uncle's financial assistance and a government scholarship:

> I was born in the countryside of Songjiang, Shanghai. When I was fifteen, my father died, leaving my mother, my younger sister, and me. Our family had ten *mu* of land but economically things were straitened. The cost of schooling was paid by my uncle's family. My sister studied at the normal school. In 1947, when I was in my second year of senior middle school

in Songjiang, I felt that it would be hard to find work without having mastered a skill, but there were no vocational schools in Songjiang, so I decided to go to China Vocational School in Shanghai. At the time there happened to be slots for public scholarships, where the government paid the tuition, so I applied for admission as a student on public scholarship to the Dept. of Mechanical Engineering at China Vocational School, and was accepted as a result.

Medical personnel, who were archetypes of Westernization, often came from families with better backgrounds. For example, Nurse Mao's family had two people earning salaries, and her older sister's income as a nurse was relatively high for the time:

I was born, raised, and educated in Nantong City. My father was a middle school teacher, and my mother was a housewife. After finishing junior middle school, I entered a nursing school for two reasons. One was that my family was not well-off, but the tuition for nursing schools was not high, and food and lodging were provided free. The second reason was that my older sister was a nurse, and when she had her nurse's uniform on I felt she looked quite dashing. She herself also felt good about it. So I entered the Nursing School attached to the foreign-run Nantong Christian Hospital (Nantungchow Christian Hospital).

Nurse Tao's family background was even better:

I was born in Shanghai in 1933, and my family's situation was rather good. Father had studied at a medical school but did not graduate—later on he became a teacher at St. Ignatius High School. Although Mother was a housewife, she was educated, a graduate of Qiming Girls' Middle School. But people in those days still didn't recognize the nursing profession (called "attendants" then) and thought it was a kind of low-grade occupation. Thus, after entering nursing school, it still wouldn't do to let other people know I was studying there, and others thought I was studying at some outstanding school!

Other nurses' families were bore similarities. Ms. Jiang's father worked in a bank, and Ms. Liang's could pay the tuition of three *dan* [150 kg] of rice. As for those working in business, the situation was more complex. It seems that the better their families' backgrounds were, the better their opportunities and job situations. Of the five persons who studied business, three had been professionals (a bank clerk, a business manager, and an employee of the water company), and two had come from rural villages—one was a part-time manager of a small business, and one was an extremely poor tenant farmer.

In general, although it was hard for sons to inherit their fathers' occupation, the tendency of professionals to come from the families of professionals is still evident. Material from Ling-Ling Lien (2001, 52) shows that among Shanghai's 30,519 elementary school students in 1930, 51.27% were from the families of professionals, and among the 815 middle school students at the time, 86.38% were from the families of professionals. This illustrates not only the economic ability of professionals to support their children's study but also the reproductive function of the professional class that was borne by professional families, i.e., the families of professionals created professionals.

3   Qualifications and Training: the Education of the Professional Class

A certain level of education is a requirement for entry into the professional class. From Tables 2 and 3, one can see that the degree of education among postal workers was lower than that among textile industry professionals. By paging through files from that era I also discovered that the educational levels among the vast majority of textile industry professionals did not measure up to those professionals employed by China Textile Industries Inc., and that within the same company, the educational level among the older professionals did not measure up to that of younger professionals. From this we can infer that the education levels of earlier professionals were lower than those of later professionals. As for business professionals, there were comparatively large gaps among different companies and individuals.

Many of the professional staff did not become professionals all at once. Many of them needed to receive three to four years of formal education, and more than a few had asked for a semester of study or other period of study.[7] The apprentice system in old-style shops more typically had a training period limited generally to three years, but some were longer. Moreover, the training systems in public agencies and new-style companies, on the other hand, more typically had a somewhat shorter training period, generally of one to two years.

That Mr. Fan could finish his studies smoothly and later become an inventor was, to a large extent, determined by his solid training in two engineering schools that combined theory with practice.

---

7   There was an apprentice system even for textile workers with simple skills, but the learning period may have been somewhat shorter.

TABLE 2   Educational levels of staff of China Textile Industries Inc. (mid-1940s)

Education levels		Formal education		Specialized training classes	
		Number of persons	%	Number of persons	%
Among them	Middle school education	17	37.78		
	– Middle school (senior	10	22.22	11	24.44
	middle or junior middle)	5	11.11		
	– Senior middle	2	4.44		
	– Vocational school				
Among them	Post-senior middle education	28	62.22		
	– University	12	26.67		
	– Junior college	15	33.33		
	– Study abroad	1	2.22		
Total		45	100.00		

SOURCE: ZHONGGUO FANGZHI JIANSHE GONGSI 1950

In 1931, I was admitted to the Textile Department, in the School of Advanced Industry at Zhejiang University, in the tuition-free Meiya special class, so I was able to continue my studies. Here, even though it was free and I was also getting a little living stipend, getting by was still difficult. So every Sunday morning I would go to wash steel plates, and for each plate I washed I could earn twenty cents. Before lunchtime I could wash several plates. In the afternoon, I'd go to the lab to watch how my teacher worked, and I'd try my own hand at something. The rules were that the students in the Meiya class could not return home during summer and winter breaks—they had to work in a factory, but there was some allowance. After graduating, I still had to work in a factory for three years.

During my time at Zhejiang University's School of Advanced Industry, I had practical training in a silk mill in Shanghai. The factory superintendent was very mean—he didn't let the interns freely take apart machinery. One day the factory revamped a machine, so I said to the foreman, "I'll help you take it apart and you watch me, okay?" He agreed, and gave pointers from the side—how I should arrange the parts, so I wouldn't forget. This way, with his guidance, I finished the dismantling and installation, and tested it successfully. After taking this machine apart, I understood how to dismantle other machines. Later on, one of the

TABLE 3   Statistics on educational level of Shanghai postal staff

Educational level	Post office workers	Post office assistants	Post office workers and assistants		Postal deliverers of various kinds	Total	
	Number of persons	Number of persons	Number of persons	%	Number of persons	Number of persons	%
Junior college or higher	138	8	146	10.40	–	146	4.58
Middle school or higher	676	422	1,098	78.21	286	1,384	43.37
Elementary school or higher	7	67	74	5.27	1,058	1,132	35.47
Special education	14	12	26	1.85	6	32	1.00
Private education	14	19	33	2.35	220	253	7.93
Not educated	–	–	–	–	63	63	1.97
Uncertain	10	17	27	1.92	154	181	5.67
Sum Number of Persons	859	545	1,404	100.00	1,787	3,191	
%	26.92	17.08	44.00		56.00		100.00

SOURCE: SHIYE BU ZHONGGUO LAODONG NIANJIAN BIANJI WEIYUANHUI 1934, VOL. 1, 323–330

factory's imported machines needed a major overhaul, the first. It was very complex, and there weren't any diagrams—no one dared to touch it, and they couldn't find anyone to do it. So I said to the manager, "Shall I try?" He didn't believe me and said, "If you destroy it, can you afford to pay for it?" I promised I wouldn't destroy it. "If it's ruined, then what'll you do?" "You can fire me." An old master next to us said, "He'll do, let him try taking it apart. He'll probably not ruin it—he's taken apart many machines, and his methods are good." As a result, the manager let me take it apart, and many people were watching me do it. In the end I took it apart, switched the worn part, put in a new one, and tested it successfully. The manager gave me a $15 reward for this.

After studying for four years, I worked in the Meiya factory, but in one and a half years I was admitted to the Dept. of Aviation Mechanics at

Hangzhou Aviation Finance and Economics School. The President of Meiya supported my continued study very much, so I only worked at Meiya for two years, and then went into the Hangzhou Aviation School, where I studied for another four years. Tuition at that school was entirely at public expense. Not only was tuition waived, but it provided a full living stipend and uniform. The school adopted German methods of teaching. In the first stage, students studied a little entry-level theory, coupled with practical training. I went to class in the morning and trained in the afternoon. In the second stage, we studied theory in greater depth.

There was an Indian teacher at the Aviation School, whose Chinese name was Wen Ge'er; he taught us heat treatment. At the time all the shock springs in aircraft landing gear were imported and extremely expensive. They had to be bought with their weight in silver. I felt that since China could already manufacture the shock springs for trains, it should be able to make them for airplanes, too, but the difficulty was mainly the inability to do the heat treatment. As a result, I started doing experiments and often took my bedding with me to the lab when I worked overtime there at night. After three months of repeated experimentation, I finally succeeded and made a spring that was identical to the ones imported from abroad.

After Mr. Wen expressed praise for my methods, he showed me his working notes, but let me read them for only one week. He had a worker's background and had a great wealth of technical experience. In the notes, he used many very easy methods to solve complex technical problems. I felt these were very precious, but I didn't have enough time to read them to the end. I could only take a full month's salary and ask someone to copy them all out. Inspired by Mr. Wen, afterward I would take notes on my work every day, and I persisted until after Liberation.

Being trained at China Vocational School was also endlessly beneficial for Mr. Shen.

When I first entered the school I got a deep sense of its special atmosphere: the campus was especially clean, and the studious atmosphere was very strong. Everywhere on campus, signs with slogans like "Two hands, endless capability," "Be dedicated and sociable," "Labor is divine," and "Use hands and brain together" were set out. China Vocational School advocated doing everything with your own two hands, and they had a semi-militarized student management. It practiced a unified system of work and rest, there were special residential supervisors responsible for supervision. Books and different clothes had to be set neatly in their places, and there were special rooms for boxes and so on. All of us men had our heads shaved, and all the women wore their hair behind the ears. Everyone put on their uniforms and school badges at the same time. The school president and teachers did the same. At around six in the morning (a little later in the winter, earlier in the summer), as soon as the whistle sounded, all the students had to jump out of bed, finish washing up, and have their bedding folded very neatly. We started with doing morning exercises, quickly finished eating breakfast, and then started class. The tests were very rigorous and there were rather a lot of them. Normally there were quizzes, midterms, and finals. If there was cheating, you'd get a zero and a warning, and a repeat offence would result in expulsion.

In the beginning I was a little unused to it, but quickly formed new life habits. Because the school president and teachers took the lead and did the morning exercises and ate breakfast together with the students, our self-awareness was soon elevated, so that we no longer needed the teachers to call our names in order for us to get up, do the morning exercises, and go to class. Studying for our classes then was very intense—we were deeply aware that knowledge was the most important thing—so we read and read, and read some more. We were quite self-aware when reading, and even during rest times we still kept reading. If the residence supervisors found out, they'd order us to go to sleep. Their supervision over us consisted mainly of urging us to go to sleep earlier.

From the junior first to junior third years what we learned, essentially, was the basics. The senior second year was mainly learning professional knowledge, the senior third was mainly internship. In those days there were few suitable ready-made teaching materials. Most of our materials had been translated from Japanese—Mechanical Drawing and Engineering for example. There were also English-language materials, for instance, in classes like Reinforced Concrete Structures, Road Design, and Engineering Design. At first we'd feel that learning was difficult, but after a year, through our teachers' gradually deepening instruction, we had grasped the rules and studying became easy. By the senior third year, we could read original, specialized English books on our own.

The vast majority of our teachers had returned from study abroad and were familiar with how things were done in practice. For instance, our President, the chairman of the engineering department, and the chairman of the civil engineering department had all come back from Japan. All the professional teachers had on-site work experience or had worked in the past or were teaching part-time while working. Our physics teacher was a university lecturer, and our professional drawing teacher was an engineer for the Shanghai Municipal Bureau of Public Roads. The teacher for Reinforced Concrete Structure was an old Jiaotong University graduate, an old engineer. The Engineering Design teacher had a professional certificate in engineering design, but he didn't have much practical job experience in engineering.

The school also put rigorous demands on the teachers. The President would often sit in on classes, and he'd raise opinions on the teacher's inadequacies. In 1936, there was a graduate from Shanghai Jiaotong University who was teaching Reinforced Concrete Structure, and he couldn't answer the students' questions. The students lost interest in his class, and the school thought him unqualified (mainly because his practical abilities were too weak), so he was let go.

The most distinctive feature of this school's education was its tight integration of theory and practice. "Use hands and brain together" was thoroughly and consistently applied. Full emphasis was placed here on basic skills training. For instance, in the Business Department, there was training on writing characters in the Song style, using an abacus, typing. Writing in the Song style ran from the first to the fifth years, and they were strict about using only the left hand with the abacus, and mastering it with accuracy. As another example, the basic training in the Engineering Department included Drawing, Measurement, and so on. Drawing continued from the first to the fifth year, and Measurement had to be practiced in various types of engineering projects. Field measurement and local measurement each took two months. Basic training in the Mechanical Department included welding, drafting, etc. The school reinforced the basic training through competitions and awards. Students in the Engineering Department had to go to work sites, and students in the Business Department had to go to banks for practical training. The school also set up a Chinese Store for the students' training.

The school also frequently invited well-known society figures to come and give lectures on campus—once every one or two months. For instance, Gen. Feng Yuxiang came once. After hearing a lecture, the students had to write an essay.

After graduates of our school's Mechanical Department went to work at the Central Machine Works, the evaluation they got was: no worse than university graduates. At the time, university graduates' ability to work with their hands was low. Society had a shortage of people with practical talents who could "use hands and brain together," so China Vocational School was highly evaluated. Students had no problem finding jobs. For example, according to regulations, interns from our school were one rank below interns from universities, so there were many work projects that we could not participate in—we could only assist. But after a while, our strengths were revealed: we could handle much of their work, but they [university students] could handle less than we could.

Nurses' education was perhaps even more rigorous, but the result of this rigorous education was a high level of professional quality, and hence a certain socioeconomic status. Nurse Mao describes her education as a nurse thusly:

As soon as we entered the school, we did six months in the hospital of basic nursing work like making beds, scrubbing, and so on. At the time there were no family members [allowed to visit], so all activities of daily life were assisted by first-year nursing students. After six months, the students could choose whether they wanted to continue in the Nursing Department, but the hospital also required them to pass an exam—if they didn't qualify, they were dismissed. It was only after this that one formally became a first-year student nurse and began taking courses in nursing. All of our classes were small—between ten and twenty students in all the basic courses. There were also many students who withdrew along the way, so that by the time my class graduated fewer than ten were left.

Ours was a four-year system—three years of study, one year of internship, but the practical training basically was scattered through the three-year course of study. Normally there was always practical training—every morning two hours in the ward and two hours of class, the same in the afternoon. Work and class were closely combined. For example, when we learned nursing for critically ill patients, we went immediately to practice it in the hospital. All of our teachers worked in hospitals, and there were graduates of Peking Union Medical College.

The teaching administration was very rigorous. The content of what was learned each year, qualifications, internship duties—everything was marked off very clearly, and you couldn't go beyond the bounds of your job. For instance, the main first-year duties were in activities of daily life—things like scrubbing, washing, food and drink. You couldn't perform higher-level nursing work like giving injections, issuing medicines, and so on, otherwise you'd be punished by not being allowed to wear your nurse's cap for a month. Also, informal teacher-student relations formed between students at different year-levels, with students from advanced year-levels teaching students from lower year-levels. If a student from a lower year level encountered a problem, she'd ask advice from a student in a higher year-level. I felt this system was quite good.

Before graduation, we had to sit for the nationwide exams of the Chinese Nursing Association. We were first tested on basic nursing skills. If you couldn't pass that, you couldn't go on and take the next exams—you'd be disqualified. If you were disqualified, you were held back a year and could not graduate. Only after graduation could you become a chief nurse.

Nurse Jiang's experience went even deeper:

Right after classes started, I felt so intimidated that I ran back home, because the work requirements there were rigorous, the responsibilities great. Later I was forced back to school again. But soon after returning there I took a liking to this work, and for the rest of my life I liked it.

In my first class in Nursing School, the school president said something that left a lasting impression on me—"The patient is the first"—meaning that the patient must be at the center. At first what we did was basic nursing—cleaning bedpans, scrubbing floors, giving seriously ill patients sponge-baths—all these things. I did the morning nursing in a third-class ward and had to give six patients their sponge-baths and none said they were uncomfortable, and the other nursing tasks were like this. If I didn't show up for three days, the patients would anxiously ask, "Why didn't you come? We all missed you a lot."

In the past they were very particular about the nurses' uniforms and put a lot of emphasis on the nurses' image. Hair had to be kept short, level with the ears, and if it grew longer they'd snip it off immediately. We wore skirts that covered the knees, a short-sleeved blouse, everything extremely neat and clean, and semi-high heel shoes that didn't make a sound as we walked. We couldn't go outdoors wearing our uniforms and had to put on a coat in order to prevent the spread of disease. We felt that the uniform and doing nursing work were very sacred. We weren't like doctors and nurses nowadays who wear their uniforms running around on the streets. They're afraid of the patients' germs spreading to themselves but not afraid of bringing germs from outside to the patients!

In those days the work of nursing was very regulated, with strict division of work among different grades; you couldn't go beyond your job responsibility, and the practical training was strict. The year I graduated, there was an appendicitis patient who couldn't get to sleep from post-operative pain. A classmate named Wang Huijuan gave him aspirin, but

forgot to tell the next shift about it. When the doctor came to the ward
and asked the patient how he had slept, he mentioned the aspirin, and
as a result that classmate was punished and expelled from school. We
classmates went on strike about this, and later three of us representatives
negotiated with the hospital—I was one of them. This way, she wasn't
expelled, and she was sent to Hangzhou—she wasn't held back. At the
time, the hospitals were afraid of us striking because nurses were scarce,
and they depended on the nursing students to do a lot of the work. If we
went on strike, the hospital's work was disrupted.

Possibly because working in business depended more on soft skills, the education and experiences of business professionals were somewhat more
complicated, and the pathways and methods of their study were multifarious.
Mr. Tu is a typical example.

After working in the book store for more than three years, the work
was simple and monotonous. The working hours there were long, and
I didn't have time in the evenings for study. I felt that I wouldn't have
any future going on here, so I left that job and became a low staffer in
China Investment Facilities Co. on Fuzhou Rd. There I could read books
and newspapers, and I could go to a tutorial school in my time off, so
I was learning more. Later on I was hired by Yifeng Bank, where I did
accounting. Although it was rather small and had only just more than
ten employees, it was a new kind of business for me. During this time, I
completed senior high courses at a tutorial school.

In 1946, I was accepted into the Dept. of Industry and Commerce at
China Tutorial School of Industry and Commerce. Here I went to class
from six to nine in the evening from Monday to Friday, and during the
daytime on Saturday and Sunday. There were more evening students
studying there after work than daytime students, and basically all of
my classmates got admitted there by studying on their own or going
to tutorial schools—working and studying at the same time. But the
achievements of the evening students were not at all inferior to those
of the day-students, and many later on became the backbone of various
fields, like university professors, engineers, senior government officials,
and so on.

Ms. He had more complex learning and work experiences even though conditions at home were good:

After graduating from senior middle school, I first went to a jointly run Sino-Russian pharmacy to work as a bookkeeper. This was a new-style enterprise, so that during my time off I could go to an accounting school to take accounting courses. Later on, I got some inside information that one of the big four department stores wanted to hire accountants, so I went to take their exam. The exam subjects included accounting, an oral test, and English composition. In the end I was fortunately accepted. The difficulty would have been much greater if it was an open recruitment exam. Our accounting department (the General Accounting Office) had several dozen accountants, taking half a floor, and the abacuses were always clicking. I worked hard there, but I also got a higher salary, and besides the basic salary there were dividends and bonuses.

Later on I realized that the best accounting school was Lixin Accounting School, so I applied for admission, and as a result I was accepted into the Accounting Tutorial School in the University Division. Every day after work I rushed to school and went to class from six to nine. I also went to classes during the day on Saturdays and Sundays. In those days Lixin Accounting Tutorial School had a Morning Class, Evening Class, Sunday Class, Correspondence Class, and so on, and the students in these classes were far more numerous than those in the day school. Around the country, there were more than 100,000 students. There were two levels, intermediate and advanced. In the two and a half years I studied here, I completed five courses. In 1945, I graduated and received the Advanced Accounting Diploma from the University Division.

Mr. Wu was a good student, and even though he did not work for very long in accounting, he retained deep memories of China Vocational School.

The teaching at China Vocational School was very distinctive—emphasizing the combination of theory and practice. A third to a half of the teachers had come from business and they required knowing how to use both the head and hands and doing solid, basic training. For example, the basic training in the business department included the abacus, Chinese and English typing, bookkeeping in accounting, bank accounting, industrial accounting, and cost accounting. Abacus training was three times per week, and one could use only the left hand in order to free the right hand to handle documents. High demands were put on speed and accuracy. The teaching materials used in industrial and cost accounting were the same as those used in the universities. Later on, when I worked for Wusong Gas Company, I learned from the accounting director—a graduate from National Southwestern Associated University—that the textbooks used in its industrial accounting courses and the ones I used were the same—all written by Lawrence. The technical level of all our graduates were higher than those of the existing workers at the time. Furthermore, the basic skill levels in the Dept. of Mechanics were so high that our graduates were exempted from the mechanical drawing exam when applying for admission to Jiaotong University.

In sum, all professionals had to receive a certain amount of specialized education and training, and this special training built not only professional skills but also a professional spirit; it built not only professional qualifications but also a professional culture. However, there were differences in the education for different lines of work. The technical sectors put greater emphasis on technical rationality, the nursing profession emphasized quality of service, and the education of business staff could be linked flexibly with the students' work environments.

4   Surviving and Searching: the Life of the Professional Class

Despite modern China's social turmoil, the life of the working class, generally speaking, is relatively stable, to the point that it neither struggles to survive as the worker and peasant class does, nor is it rich enough to interfere with others' lives as the managerial class does. Most of them do not have high positions. Their incomes are sufficient to support their families, but they also do not have much surplus.

Take Mr. Fan, for example. His expertise was taken seriously, and even during the War of Resistance Against Japan, his life was not greatly affected.

After graduating in 1938 from the Hangzhou Aviation Finance and Economics School, I worked first as a technician in an aircraft repair plant. Later, during the "War of Resistance," I taught in the College of Engineering at Tongji University for half a year as a mentor at the practice factory. With a teaching assistant's status, I guided students in their internships. Of the education there my memory is still fresh: in the first year, the students studied German; in the second, they began practical study, and then they more systematically studied the theories of their profession. The year of practical courses generally went like this: first the teacher would lecture and give demonstrations for about 15 to 20 minutes, and then the students would practice while the teacher made his rounds, giving advice. If the students encountered a problem or something they couldn't do, they could ask the teacher at any time. Our students did a lot of hands-on activities. When their year of practical study was finished, all of them could operate and repair machinery independently, and they could take apart all kinds of machines. For instance, after repairing an aircraft engine, they could reinstall and tune it, so that the airplane could fly successfully.

Half a year later, the school wanted to move from Kunming, Yunnan to Sichuan. By that time I was already married. My wife was a Meiya factory worker whom I got to know when working there. The university president, considering that I had a family, said, "You don't have to move. Right now the National Resources Commission wants the school to send people each year to go and work, and the Central Electric Works very much needs people like you who understand technology." So, through the school's introduction and passing the selection exam, I went to work for the Central Electric Works of the National Resources Commission. I started as a clerk, equivalent to a technician nowadays, and about six months later I was promoted to an assistant engineer.

After the victory in the War of Resistance Against Japan, I was about to be sent to Westinghouse Corp. in the United States to study elevator starter installation, but I didn't go. For three reasons: one was my father was sick and hoped I would go a little later, but I already had three kids and couldn't leave. Second was that China Iron Works had invited me several times to go to them; they treated me very well—40 *dan* (5400 *jin*) of rice per month—and promised to send me to the United States to study. Third, because I didn't like that area of specialty—I felt elevator starter installation was too narrow and not very useful.

It was through the introduction of Huang Yanpei's younger brother, Huang Boqiao, that I went to work for China Iron Works. Originally, he was a board member of China Iron Works, and during the "War of Resistance" he was the plant manager of Liuzhou Textile Machinery Factory. At the time I was working for Central Electric Works, I was seconded to him to help as an engineer and chief of works. In this way, I went to work for China Iron Works in Shanghai as chief engineer. They said after I worked for two years they could send me to visit the United States without having to stay there to study. As a result, I went to work for them.

Mr. Shen, as a vocational school graduate, likewise made full use of his own technical expertise and sensed its value.

> Because the "War of Resistance" was pressing close, the central government moved to the interior. When I graduated in 1939, I was 19, and places in the interior like Kunming were recruiting all kinds of graduating students. I and a dozen or so others were hired to repair the Xufu (Yibin)-Kunming railway. Transportation, food, and other expenses were paid by the government. There, the university graduates were "interns" for one year, while graduates of secondary vocational schools were "probationary staff" for two years. Our probationary staff could only record the engineers' or interns' measurements. Our work at that time was hard—we had to walk a lot of mountain roads to desolate places to do measurements. Although our wages were 60 yuan, not considered low, and one yuan could buy 60 eggs, there was nowhere to spend it, so we were always eating peanuts. It was also hard for letters to get through—they had to go through Hong Kong and Vietnam before they could finally reach Kunming.
>
> The people working there were all highly qualified. There were low-level engineers in their forties, senior engineers in their forties and fifties, there were graduates from Tsing Hua University and Beiyang University, and members of the first graduating class from Tangshan Jiaotong University. Originally, we graduates from China Vocational School wouldn't have been able to get in, but they got in only because of connections with the Transportation Minister. However, after we had worked for some time, the bosses saw that our accomplishments were remarkable, so they sent recruiters to China Vocational School in 1940, 1941, and 1942, getting anywhere from 15 to 30 people. They were working separately on the construction sites of the Southwest Railway and Highway. And so it was at this time, and this place, that we graduates of China Vocational School set up an alumni association.

Nurses' professional treatment may have been even better than that of engineers. Recalling those years, Ms. Mao said:

> When we graduated, jobs were easy to find—no one was unemployed. After graduating in 1942, I remained in the hospital working, and in the second year, there was a doctor in Shanghai's Renji Hospital who went to work at a private hospital in Nantong, and he said to me, "You nurses are quite good. If you're willing to work in Shanghai, I'll help introduce you."

As a result, I started working at Renji Hospital,[8] and worked there for 45 years.

We worked eight hours per day, starting each day at seven o'clock. There were no weekends. We had two half-days of rest each week and they weren't connected. In addition, we had to take turns on the night shift for one month continuously. When we had our half-day breaks, students would come and substitute for us. After starting work I did not do much basic nursing but had to undertake advanced nursing—like nursing for seriously ill patients, psychological nursing, and so on.

Nursing at that time was very meticulous. For instance, for a serious post-op patient, the nurse had to check his/her blood pressure, check urine and feces, see if there was any internal bleeding, inquire about eating and drinking, how he or she was feeling, and so on. For any patient, we nurses, together with the doctors, always did our utmost to save him. In addition to routine care, whenever we had the chance, we'd observe patients' condition and talk to them. Ward nurses naturally had to understand fully the condition of the patients under their care, and there were also nurses making rounds who would check on each patient once every two hours.

At that time, I paid great attention to psychological nursing. Besides asking about the patient's condition and medical history, I would also ask about the patient's family situation and economic situation, feelings and opinions on treatment and nurses, and many other areas. For example, there was a patient who wasn't eating, so I asked him why, but he was too embarrassed to say. The result was, after patiently talking with him, I learned that he was reluctant to eat because his family was poor. For patients who were especially poor, after we clearly understood their situation, we'd report it to the hospital's Social Services Department that would then talk with them in order to resolve their economic difficulty. As another example, if a patient needed surgery, the nurse would use comforting tones to explain why the surgery was needed, what exactly it was, what preparations were being made, what things would need attention, and so on, so that the patient's fears were eliminated, and he'd go into surgery with peace of mind. Then we'd accompany the patient when

---

8   Renji Hospital (formerly known in the West as "Lester Chinese Hospital") was founded in 1846 by William Lockhart of the London Missionary Society, with funding from the Hong Kong branch of the Chinese Medical Missionary Society; it was Shanghai's first teaching hospital, to which was attached Shanghai Renji Nursing School.

doing the anesthesia and going to the operating room. The anesthesiologists and surgeons also had to do similar thought-work.

I was always working wholeheartedly and often was so busy I'd forget to eat. I remember once when I was getting off work I met a patient at the door and thought I might have to send him in to the ward I was in charge of, but then I thought, "Who'll be on duty tonight?" It turned out it would be a lower-level nurse who might have difficulty competently handling the nursing for this patient. So I returned to the hospital and continued to work. I felt this was my responsibility. Schools did not consciously cultivate this sense of responsibility but instead naturally formed such habits through the work—and everybody was like that, so they didn't feel tired, or bitter, or that there was anything noble to this, but they felt this was as it ought to be. In those days, the doctors and nurses were all patient-centered in their work.

In those days, there was a very close relationship between doctors and nurses; one didn't sense any grade-level relationship. Doctors also respected nurses. Nurses knew the patients' conditions and treatments like the back of their own hands. The chief physicians, interns, chief nurses, and nurses all checked the wards together. Besides doing the nursing exams, nurses often had to help interns to perform medical examinations. And if a minor surgery was going to done the next day in the ward, the nurse on the night before would prepare all the necessary items like disinfectant, knives, brushes, gloves, gauze, and so on. During the surgery, the nurse would be assisting next to the doctor—not like the way it is now, with the doctor doing it himself.

The hospital's management was strict. When we went out for fun in the evenings, we couldn't be out past ten, and if you wanted to be out later, you'd have to ask for holiday leave, otherwise you'd be called in for a chat and be punished. The uniforms we wore had to be just right. The caps had specific marks, so that the nurses' grade or status could be told at a glance. We couldn't wear the uniforms outside but had to put on a coat, in order to prevent [the spread of] contagious diseases. Students could not fall in love, and to work you couldn't be married. The female doctors, too, could not marry—once they did, they could not work anymore.

However, our lives and treatment were better. The hospital's living services were comprehensive, including food and housing, there was lunch for the early shift and a midnight meal for the night shift. The food was good, too. Our wages were higher than for teachers. We also had custodians doing our laundry and cleaning our rooms. They'd wash our clothes once every other day, and they were folded very neatly. They worked ten hours per day, so on the eve of Liberation they went on strike, under the underground party's leadership, and demanded an eight-hour day, too.

Ms. Jiang was full of deep feelings toward her work. Despite being troubled by the war, her sense of responsibility and sense of values are palpable.

When graduating in 1942, more than twenty were left of the more than thirty of our classmates. After graduating, I stayed and worked in the hospital. I have never regretted working as a nurse, and even though there were some opportunities to leave my nursing position, there always has to be someone to do this job—not to mention that the position of nurses at the time wasn't low, and they earned higher wages than teachers. One month's wages could buy one *liang* [37.5 g] of gold. In addition, the hospital included room and board, conditions were good, and after work there were custodians to wash and scrub our clothes and shoes. Although doctors' wages were higher than ours, they also respected us very much. For example, Zhang Zhiyong, who is now a fellow of the Engineering College, was an intern in those days—he was my student. I taught him how to do intravenous injections and so on. He has always respected me, always called me "Teacher Jiang." There are numerous such examples! There was mutual respect between us doctors and nurses, and we coordinated our work together. We were happy working. At that time, no one looked down on us nurses—the patients' families, society all respected us.

I also valued my work very much. We always went to work willingly, with a lot of compassion and empathy for the patients. There was basically no concept of money. My whole life I never cared about the wages. Once I used two months' salary to by a pair of leather shoes on Nanjing Rd. I felt—I don't have to be so particular about clothes, but I definitely had to buy good shoes, because they were needed for work. Those shoes were really good value for the money, and though I wore them out they never got misshapen. We took the initiative in our work, and it was exactly like Chairman Mao said, nurses are "scouts" who have the most contact with patients. Besides our nursing operations, we were constantly checking the wards, observing patients' conditions, solving the patients' problems. General medical problems were all attended to by nurses.

In 1943, when the Japanese were controlling Shanghai, I was forced to go into the interior. At the time I had nothing at all, just my diploma from the Nursing School attached to Shanghai's first teaching hospital, so I went to the Renji Hospital in Hengyang, the best one there. We suffered a lot while there, but the ones who suffered even more were the seriously ill patients. We were very sympathetic to them and overcame all kinds of difficulties and did our best to work for them. Once, right when we were eating, suddenly there was a kaboom sound—a bomb fell, and we couldn't finish eating.

When I worked for the Christian hospital in Kunming [Church Missionary Society Hospital, Zhonghua shenggonghui Huidian yiyuan], many colleagues there were Christians, and many students were, too. I was already rather familiar with Christianity, and at this time I was further influenced by them and was baptized as a Christian.

However, things did not go so smoothly for everyone. Ms. Tao's professional life was full of twists and turns. She was originally a business student, but she was forced to drop out of school during her third year of junior middle school due to economic reasons, and then could not find any work in the business area. She had to run around looking for work as a substitute teacher.

In the fall of 1941, I could only help out with household tasks at home. These household tasks were originally all handled by my older sister. At this time she got married, so I needed to take her place. Then our family was worse off than it was before the war. A wall of the shop and our sign were destroyed by a Japanese bomb, a lot of the bricks, tiles, and lumber got carried off, and my family didn't have the money for repairs—we could only surround the shop with a bamboo screen and continue operating. At the time there were Japanese not far from our house, and my sister-in-law and I were afraid of them. As soon as there was any movement, my sister-in-law and I would hide.

Before long I learned that a cousin of my father's was running an elementary school, and I asked my father to ask whether I could teach at that school. As a result, the principal, my father's cousin, agreed to hire me, and this was the beginning of my teaching career. I was responsible for first and second grade arithmetic and senior high abacus, teaching more than twenty classes per week. Since I had never received training at a normal school, and it was my first time at the lectern, I felt it was very exhausting, and when I returned home I still had to help with the household duties. My sister-in-law took turns cooking dinner. I wasn't good at housework and could only learn by doing. I only asked of the principal not to make me teach during the last class hour. I went on this way for more than four years, until the victory in the "War of Resistance."

After the Japanese surrender, my third older brother was very glad and took me out to have fun in Shanghai. After he had graduated from Suming Vocational School, he went to work on the staff of one of Shanghai's four biggest department stores, Sun Sun Department Store. By that time he had already transferred to another privately operated commercial company, where he worked as the head of the Receiving Department.[9] I stayed in their company's women's dormitory for one night. This colleague of his, together with my brother, was voluntarily teaching children's evening classes in his spare time. My brother also gave me a few books by Soviet authors like Gorki to read. He often said to me, "Teaching is good— you can teach others the things you understand."

On December 3, 1945, I received a letter he had left for me, explaining that by the time I would receive it, he would already be in the liberated area. I felt very lost, and cried again. My second older sister had also gone to the liberated area. When she was little she had been sent to my father's cousin, and when she was in her second year of senior middle school, she went to Yan'an. My third older brother may have been influenced by her. During the period of Nationalist and Communist cooperation, he had also frequently sent letters, but couldn't speak of revolution—only of a few situations in life. I've kept his letters to this day. As early as the "War of Resistance," he had been seized by the Japanese for reading progressive books. Once when he was tortured, he had glue poured into him. He suffered a lot. I was constantly sending him clothes and food. Later on, really for some unknown reason, he was released again. After Liberation, because he was terribly ill (hysteria), he went back home to Shanghai to recuperate. If he wanted to see our eldest sister, he could only depend on my income of three *dou* of rice.

At the end of 1946, the mother of a second cousin of mine passed away, and I represented our family at the funeral. While there I learned that the elementary school no longer operated in the countryside but had moved to Shanghai. After returning, I asked my father to introduce me to this school that his cousin operated in Shanghai, to teach. At the time there happened to be a female teacher who had asked for maternity leave, so I could take over her teaching. Thus, in January 1947, I started my teaching life in Shanghai.

---

9   The boss of this company, and the boss's wife, were both university graduates with progressive ways of thinking.

This school was called Hongqiao Rd. Primary School (next to present-day Jiaotong University). The principal, just to make money, ran two evening classes for children, taught by me and another new teacher. We were only volunteer teachers—only the principal could benefit. I taught there for one year, then I went to teach at a primary school in Pudong.

I went to teach in Pudong because I wanted to get married to Mr. Shen, and their family in Pudong had links with the local education department. When I got married, I had only a little income, and my family couldn't raise the dowry. But my eldest brother and Mr. Shen's father were colleagues, and they agreed that the Shen family would prepare a few simple items of the trousseau. Thus I carried two pretty enamel-ware night pots[10] to the Shen home, which counted as getting married. This was in 1948. In Shanghai in those days there was much discussion of wedding arrangements, but our wedding was very simple. Such simple habits we have maintained throughout our lives. The clothes I'm wearing have more than ten years' history. The cotton shoes were made during the Cultural Revolution, and there are plenty of patches in the lining. The jacket was made when khaki cloth just came out. Mr. Shen's Zhongshan jacket was made when wool was first released. At the time, his salary was only ninety-plus yuan. I don't demand much in life. Our family has never done business and has never played the stock market.

Regardless of the ups and downs of her career path, Ms. Tao, through her own unremitting efforts plus her husband's social capital in China Vocational School, eventually developed into an excellent teacher and abacus expert. Moreover, her career pursuits went far beyond her material pursuits.

In fact, in normal circumstances, a professional's economic life is still decent: the income level is more than double that of workers, and the income of one professional can basically support one family (Perry 2001, 74). For example, in 1916, Shanghai's largest department store, Wing On Department Store, had 400 employees, of whom nearly fifty (12.5%) were high-level staff; most of them had come from Guangdong. The remaining 350 employees (87.5%) were ordinary staff members, mostly from Jiangsu and Zhejiang (Zhonggong Shanghai hualian shangxia weiyuanhui et al. 1991). Similarly, The Sun Company (Daxin gongsi 大新公司) had few high-level professional staff, only 11.5%, but ordinary staff members and trainees accounted for 88.5% (see Table 4).

---

10   The rule in Pudong at the time was that when the bride went to the mother-in-law's house to spend the night, she had to carry two night pots to make a pair—not just one.

TABLE 4   Numerical distribution and wage levels of the 584 employees of the Sun
            Company, 1938

Level	Number of persons		Wages			
	Number of persons	%	Highest	Average	Lowest	
Managers	7	1.20	600	329.43	200	High-level employees
Department / Section heads	60	10.27	165	75.23	40	High-level employees
Professionals / operational staff	403	69.01	38	14	5	Low-level employees
Trainees	114	19.52	4	2.71	2	Low-level employees

SOURCE: SHANGHAI SHI DIYI BAIHUO SHANGDIAN 1986

The labor structure comprised of factory technical staff was similar to that in commercial businesses. Even though the scope of the statistics may differ somewhat, the number of technical staff, i.e., the persons who had an actual grasp of the technology, judging from the employment structure in many factories, was generally less than 15%, and in some factories there were only single-digit percentages.

As for the social lives of professionals, Mr. Fang seems to be most typical. Originally he studied civil engineering at China Vocational School, but because of connections through his social life, the center of his life and subsequently the direction of his career changed.

> When I started at China Vocational School, my grades were good, and I received a scholarship. I served as class head, and then became chairman of the student assembly. In addition, I joined the work-study activities of the underground party so we could better obtain funding for tuition and living expenses. We often brought watermelons and other food from Caohejing to the south market for sale. Through these work-study activities, I was influenced by the Communist Party, the underground. Not only did those activities resolve the tuition funding problem but also cultivated in me the spirit of hard work and struggle, and I united with my classmates, which expanded the Communist Party's influence and elevated its prestige.

TABLE 5   Make-up of technical staff in Chinese factories in the 1920s

Name of factory	Occupation		No. of persons	%
Jiuda Salt Co.	Experienced workers		75	13.5
	Inexperienced workers		481	86.5
	Subtotal		556	100.0
Shanghai silk filatures	Experienced workers (male)			5.0
	Semi-experienced: reelers			60.0
	Inexperienced: women, children			35.0
	Subtotal			100.0
British American	Skilled workers (men)		350	14.9
Tobacco Co. (Tianjin)	Female workers, child laborers		2,000	85.1
	Subtotal		2,350	100.0
Danhua Tobacco Co.	Skilled workers (men)		200	10.0
(Danhua yanchang;	Nonskilled workers	Ordinary male workers	300	15.0
Tianjin, 1926)		Female workers, child laborers	1,500	75.0
		Subtotal	1,800	90.0
	Subtotal		2,000	100.0
Yuyuan Cotton	Skilled workers (men)		2,000	31.2
Factory (moved from	Nonskilled workers	Male workers	3,700	57.8
Shanghai to Tianjin		Female workers	600	9.4
in 1926)		Child laborers	100	1.6
		Subtotal	4,400	68.8
	Total		6,400	100.0
Zhongxing Coal	Mechanics		212	<5
Company (1924)	Electricians		234	Appx. 5
	Semi-skilled workers		913	Appx. 20
	Non-skilled workers		Thousands	>70
Danhua Firewood	Skilled male workers		200	10
Company (1926)	Non-skilled female workers, child laborers		1,800	90

SOURCE: LIU 1985, 225

In July 1945, I joined the Communist Party of China (CPC) as an underground party member. As my participation in political activities were rather numerous, my grades declined, so that I was just barely passing. In 1945, the New 4th Army entered Shanghai, and our underground party dispatched representatives to the assembly. As a result, two classmates were arrested by Kuomintang (KMT) forces. One of them reached the liberated zone in September 1945, and the other was killed in action during the attack on Jinan. After the War of Resistance victory, the political activities that China Vocational School was involved in intensified. I participated in all the big student movements, like the memorial service for those who died in the Kunming Tragedy, the "623 Movement" of 1946, and the "520 Movement" of 1947. In the 520 Movement, all the students—more than 900 of them—went on strike, and more than 300 joined the parade. Of the more than 20 students in my class, four or five joined the party. But rather few of our school's teachers did, even though the school's leadership was quite supportive of our progressive movements.

I remember one fall day in 1947 when a classmate and I rode a bicycle—he in front, me behind—to deliver the underground student magazine put out by the underground party. At the intersection where we turned from Xizang Rd. to Huaihai Rd., we were struck by an American ambulance turning right from west to east, and I lost consciousness right there. When I came to, I found a lot of people had gathered round to stare, but the police had not come yet. I became very anxious, because if a policeman discovered those magazines, it would be unthinkable. Fortunately, I found another insider classmate and immediately signaled to him to take the magazines away. Later I passed out again. When I woke the second time, I was already being taken to the Public Security Bureau on a three-wheeler. It was already evening by the time the Public Security Bureau let me go home. After applying plasters for three months, the wounds on my chest could finally be considered healed. But later on I had repeated spells of pleurisy and the like.

After graduating, I didn't go to work, but ran instead to the liberated area in northern Jiangsu, where I worked in the East China Party School (Huadong dangxiao 华东党校). Three months later, I participated in the work of the Jiang-Huai Work Team (Jiang-Huai gongzuotuan 江淮工作团), my classmate Wang Jishan and I were sent to work on the railroad at the Dongpu section. I lost contact with my family. They were very worried and went everywhere asking my whereabouts. In fact, they were already rather worried about me when I was at school—they were afraid

I'd be arrested for my political activities. Later on they received a letter from me in the liberated zone, telling them not to worry.

At the time of Liberation, I was the military representative of the Receiving Group, so at the Receiving Station I was in charge of railroad receiving. The engineer there, who was more than 50 years old, was quite obedient and handed over the railroad work to us. Then I was the political director there. Later on, I went to the Hefei section of the project as director, and then became the Confidential Secretary and Office Director in the Political Office of the Bengbu Branch Railroad Bureau.

Mr. Tu had a similar experience:

China Vocational School at the time had plenty of progressive teachers and students. Among the students, there were 118 Communist Party members, and there were a few teachers as well. There was one teacher among them who joined a movement and was beat to death by the KMT, and they stuffed the body into a hemp sack and threw it into the Huangpu River. Although I never joined the party, I was a radical and participated in several student movements. I graduated in 1948, when I was 23.

Modern Chinese society was in a period of turmoil. War, political and social movements came one after the other, so that all social strata were inevitably affected. However, Mr. Fang may have been one of the more radical persons. Students' level of participation in social movements seems to have been related to their occupational position and the level of their goals. For example, Ms. Tao was wholeheartedly devoted to her work and not too concerned about political activities. Several of the nurses basically never participated in political movements; only Ms. Jiang, as student representative, had negotiated with her school's authorities to prevent the expulsion of a classmate. Mr. Fan and Mr. Wu were also not enthusiastic about political movements, to the point of not knowing that there were still people organizing political movements.

Another important factor influencing professionals' careers was the employment issue. Even though many people only had a middle school education level, that did not at all mean that a middle school education level could make one a professional, because the employment situation in those days was rather challenging. One can discern this issue already from Ms. Tao's narrative above. In fact, the difficulty of finding employment was widespread. Statistics on students who graduated from middle school in Jiangsu Province from 1912 to 1921 show that the only students who had relatively stable outcomes (both

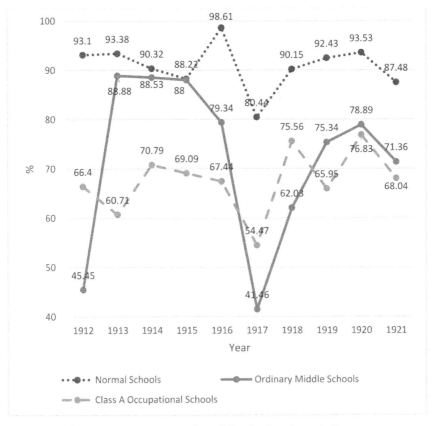

FIGURE 2   Changes in career outcomes for middle school graduates in Jiangsu, 1912–1921
SOURCE: SHENG 1930

in terms of further study and employment) were graduates of normal schools. The career outcomes for graduates of ordinary middle schools and occupational schools fluctuated widely, and during the worst times nearly 60% of the students had no job outcome (See Figure 2).

Furthermore, their career outcomes were rather uniform—the vast majority became teachers (see Table 6). This phenomenon of returning to one's school to teach after graduating from it was satirically referred to at the time as "reincarnation education." If this was true of Jiangsu (including Shanghai), a relatively developed region, one hardly need to mention what was occurring in other areas.

TABLE 6   29 top occupations of Jiangsu area middle school graduates, 1915–1921

Occupation type	No. of persons	%	Occupation type	No. of persons	%
1. Elementary school teacher	3,004	60.98	16. Farm technician	28	0.57
2. Elementary school principal	103	2.09	17. Self-employed sericulture	27	0.55
3. Bank employee	97	1.97	18. Normal school employee	24	0.49
4. Exchange employee	93	1.89	19. Normal adjunct elementary school teacher	22	0.45
5. Mill employee	78	1.58	20. Private school teacher	22	0.45
6. Teaching trainee, Type A	64	1.30	21. Teaching committee member	20	0.41
7. Middle school teacher	62	1.26	22. Lecturer / teacher in sericulture	20	0.41
8. Teaching trainee, Type B	61	1.24	23. Land Assessment Bureau employee	18	0.37
9. Postal employee	58	1.18	24. Aquaculture teacher	18	0.37
10. Self-employed agriculture	50	1.02	25. Specialized academy teacher	16	0.32
11. Self-employed commerce	43	0.87	26. Bookstore employee	16	0.32
12. Commercial company employee	39	0.79	27. Customs employee	12	0.24
13. Railroad employee	38	0.77	28. Foreign bank employee	12	0.24
14. Agricultural forestry zone employee	33	0.67	29. Teaching trainee, Type A normal school	10	0.20
15. Measurement, Water Conservancy Engineering Bureau	29	0.59			
Total employed	4,926	100.00	Subtotal of those employed in top 29 occupations	4,117	83.59
Total employed in teaching-related occupations	3,446	69.97	Total of those employed at elementary schools	3,129	63.52

SOURCE: SHENG 1930

In sum, the professional class was leading a moderately prosperous economic life, its politics tended toward the middle, and it was happy to lead a stable, moderate social life. However, the social turmoil of the time and the resulting employment problems were seriously threatening this class's lifestyle and ultimately constrained its growth.

5   Study and Change: the Development of the Professional Class

While the professional class maintains its survival, it also seeks room for development. On the individual level, this is a problem of learning and improvement; on the group level, it is a problem of improving the organization, adjusting policy, and perfecting the system.

In fact, each person I interviewed was seeking constant improvement. For instance, Mr. Fan was an excellent inventor and was receiving very favorable treatment, but he was not satisfied—he wanted to continue developing. However, Mr. Fan focused on the improvement of his technical level, not receiving a higher degree:

> Two years later, I felt that the manager of the China Iron Works lacked an open vision. He didn't attach importance to improving technology or to R&D. He was unwilling to improve the conditions for R&D—he was satisfied only with earning the money before his eyes. It was hard to have any development there, and I could only provide a little consultation—not any ideas. I remember once he wanted me to design a new diesel motor. I spent a whole month, anxiously doing research and design work, and for half a month I didn't sleep—I was relying on some imported medicine to keep my energy up, so I could go days and nights without feeling tired. Later I often had headaches—an aftereffect from it. In the end, the design wasn't successful, but the factory didn't attach any importance to it. Thus, even though they gave me a high salary, twice as much as at the Central Electric Works, and gave me 10 *liang* (375 g) of gold at Lunar New Year, I felt unhappy, and I put in my resignation. When I wrote the letter telling Huang Boqiao I wanted to resign, he was not willing to let me go and said he hoped I would improve the factory. But I still left.
>
> In the end Huang still recommended me to the president of Shanghai Textile Construction Co. (*Shanghai fangzhi jianshe gongsi* 上海紡織建設公司), Song Yongzhang 宋永章. He was a favorite of Song Ziwen 宋子文—a famous businessman. The president told me they wanted to run a new business—China Cotton Processing Works (Zhongguo

mianchen jiagong gongchang 中國棉產加工廠) and set up a company in Shanghai that had five factories under it—two in Shanghai, and one each in Zhejiang, Tianjin, and Beijing. I came here to serve as its chief engineer and vice president. These five factories opened at the same time in 1948, and they used new industrial techniques to process the raw cotton, so that the entire cotton boll could be processed and used: cotton floss spun into yarn, the short fibers outside the cottonseed were put to military use, cotton oil was used as an industrial preservative, and cotton residue for feed. My salary was high and my work pleasant.

Mr. Shen had already found a good job after graduation, but he resigned in order to get admitted to a university:

In 1940, I applied for the university entrance exam. First, because times were changing. The construction projects in the southeast were finished, so I didn't have any good work to do. Second, because I had been planning for a long time to continue doing more advanced study and learn more new things. When I graduated from vocational school, I was clamoring to study at a university, but my family's conditions would not allow it, and I could only give up. In addition, after working I felt the necessity of continuing my studies. So, though I also had the chance to go to other units to find work, I still applied for university.

All the well-known schools like Southwest United University, Zhejiang University, Fudan University, and Chongqing University had graduates from our China Vocational School. Most of them had worked for two or three years before being accepted. Tangshan Jiaotong University recruited China Vocational School graduates on the condition that their grades were 70 points or higher, and they had to have recommendations from three or four classmates, and then they would waive the admission exam. My admission exam score for Yenjing University was 96 points, only 1 point less than that of Mao Yisheng (first place).

Classmates who were accepted at Shanghai Jiaotong University likewise had excellent scores. When students from the Business Department went to the interior to work, even the university graduates could not surpass them. However, only a small number of China Vocational School graduates could go to the university, even though later on many of them took correspondence and evening courses.

It appears that continuing on to more advanced study was not an individual phenomenon. Even though the focus of Mr. Fang's work had shifted from technology to administration, he never stopped seeking to learn:

Compared with others of my generation, I'm still counted lucky. First, I hadn't expected that I'd be able to return to Shanghai. The upper ranks at the time were calling for the advancement of science, and many people went to the northwest, but I was able to return instead to Shanghai. Second, I had already been to many places—Yen'an, Xi'an, Yantai, Fuzhou, Qingdao, and so on—only Kunming, I never went to. I had friends everywhere in the country. This was not only pleasing but also increased my knowledge. So at heart I'm comparatively happy.

I feel that my good fortune may be ascribed to two things: one is the influence of Huang Yanpei's thought in education, and the second is the party education. But Huang Yanpei's thought and the thought of the CPC are consistent. Huang emphasizes that everything should be done to serve the unit, while the CPC emphasizes that everything should be done to serve the people. Of course, one's own efforts are also essential. I have always been, "Love whatever job you take up." For instance, if I hadn't taken the initiative to ask for things, I would never have been able to go to so many places and increase my experiences and abilities so much—and I would not have been able to go to graduate school at Renmin University of China.

Even people like Mr. Tu, the bookstore apprentice, let alone people like Ms. Tao who never gave up pursuing their careers, were able to upgrade their knowledge step by step. Mr. Tu was very proud of his experience studying at China Vocational School. This is not only because he completed his learning from the second year of lower middle school to the third year of senior middle school through self-study and tutoring, but more importantly because most of the students who graduated from that school became high-ranking business and industry executives—and also, because of that school's progressive tendencies, many of its alumni became leaders in various sectors.

None of the nurses I interviewed held a bachelor's degree. In fact, before Liberation, there already was a bachelor-level nursing program. It was only after nurses' education was unified on the eve of Liberation, that the nursing profession was designated as a high school / academy-level profession (Nie 1987, 195–204). Such restrictions on academic qualifications, coupled with the requirement of repetitive working methods, limited the development of nurses as individuals and as a group.

The issue of professional organizations and the setting of professional standards also had a comparatively large impact on professional group development. The relatively high rank of professional organizations and professional standards reflects a level of professional development. However, apart from a few of the professional organizations and professional standards where

TABLE 7   Types of tests and numbers of qualifying persons (1931–1947)

	Beginning time	Totals		Time period		
		No. of persons	%	1931–1937.7	1937.7–1945.9	1945.9–1947.6
Total		2,054,155	100	4,578 / 0.22%	620,239 / 30.19%	1,429,338 / 69.58%
Appointed staff exam	1931.7	139,309	6.78	3,714	43,122	92,473
Specialized professional and technical personnel exam	1942.2	21,007	1.02	0	6,694	14313
Exam for candidates for government positions	1941.6	1,890,875	92.05	0	568,780	1,322,095
Civil service exam	1931	2,677	0.13	864	1,356	457
Exam for agricultural, industrial, and mining technicians sent abroad	1944	287	0.01	0	287	0

SOURCE: LUO 1998, 4386

TABLE 8   Specialized occupational and technical personnel examination and number of passers (1942.2–1947.6)

Year	Total	High-level exam (37.45%)					
		Subtotal	Accountancy exam	Lawyers		Agricultural technicians	Technicia
				Verification	Exam		
Total	21,007	7,867	938	1,589	1	125	3
1942.2–12	618	618		618			
1943	1,268	1,102	117	256		15	
1944	2,334	1,292	222	171		35	3
1945	3,966	1,438	191	168		42	3
1946	4,441	1,438	183	193	1	18	
1947.1–6	8,380	1,978	225	183		15	

SOURCE: LUO 1998, 4394

standards are rather sophisticated, such as those for engineers, accountants, doctors, lawyers, and reporters, the level of sophistication for many other professions, such as for teachers, nurses, and technical workers (technicians) is still not high. This not only limits the individual development of those who work in these professions but also affects the social class and the contributions of these professional groups.

With respect to professional standards and examinations, the increasing numbers of and the standardization of qualifying examinations during the era of the Nanjing government, especially during the 1940s, had positive significance for the development of the professional class.

Of course, the function of such examinations and trainings were subject to some restrictions. First, this practice started relatively late—basically, it was something that occurred after the 1930s and was concentrated mainly in the 1940s, especially after the War of Resistance ended. Second, such tests were not universal, and only a few agencies and departments made use of this testing method. In the case of national examinations, the number of persons who took the specialized technical examinations accounted for only 1% of the total number of examinees, and among the persons taking those specialized technical examinations, those taking the Chinese medicine examination accounted for 52% (see Table 8). Third, the dissemination of information on examinations and training programs and the determination of results could more or less still be influenced by personal networks and human feelings. For example,

				Ordinary exam (10.57%)			Special exam (51.98%)		
trial technicians	Medicine			Medical personnel			Chinese medicine		
cation	Exam	Verification	Exam	Sub-total	Verification	Exam	Sub-total	Verification	Exam
	99	3,143	23	2,220	2,167	53	10,920	10,558	
		409	8	166	157	9			
		490	5	305	296	9	737	737	
		578	4	223	212	11	2,305	2,305	
	99	507	6	748	724	24	2,254	1,892	
		1,159		778	778		5,624		

the national examinations for appointed staff and candidates for public positions had a certain spurious quality—and the two accounted for 98.83%. The underdeveloped, imperfect examination system may also have been one of the important reasons why the Chinese professional workforce was weak and the middle class was undeveloped. However, no matter which kind of examinations they were, they were all institutionalized efforts to adapt to the development of the professional class.

6   Conclusion: Research Development

Earlier, it has been pointed out that there is plenty of room for further research on the life histories of modern professionals, both in terms of content and methodology. The research done in this paper is only a preliminary attempt. In view of this, I would like to explain here the specific characteristics of this study, its basic findings, the existing problems, and remaining issues.

Chinese professionals, as a class, had already formed around the end of the 1930s and had gained social recognition (Iwama 2003). During the Republic of China period, the professional class had already achieved considerable size. They all had primary school or higher education levels (those who had studied at private schools or only attended primary school were a minority), and economically they all had some surplus after expenditure for basic necessities, such as food, clothing, housing, and travel, which could be used for their own or their children's education. In these areas, they were clearly superior to the average peasant or worker. However, if compared with capitalists, the intellectual elites, and leading military and political figures, the status and power of the professional class was not so noticeable. So what exactly are the differences between the professional class and other classes? We shall further discuss their basic characteristics below.

Obviously, the determining factor of the social status of the professional class does not lie in the number of people in this class. Economic strength, organizational level, degree of specialization, education level, cultural influence, and other factors play a more important role.

6.1   *Economic Strength*
The economic foundation is the most important determining factor. As far as the professional class is concerned, such economic factors include at least the following:

Production capacity. The production functions of professionals are embodied primarily in several kinds of position—technical (such as medical and engineering technicians), service (such as public service staff and ordinary civil servants), managerial (such as senior managers), cultural (such as teachers and journalists). Of course, these positions are indispensable. Strikes by railroad workers, seafarers, postal employees, and shopkeepers all had serious impacts on society at the time. However, at that time, society depended on them to a degree that differed from developed countries. Because of low productivity levels, China's modern economy has been mainly capital- and labor-intensive, and the level of dependency on technology has been low. Consequently, it is impossible to attach importance to the development and promotion of technology—the demand for technical personnel was also very limited. Moreover, not only was the number of business enterprises relatively small, their scale was also rather small, so it was impossible to hire a large staff. At the same time, people's expectations and demands for life services such as medical care, transportation, communication, and dining were relatively low, so the development of modern public utilities and service industries was limited. These factors also further restricted people's educational and cultural needs and spending power. As a result, professionals lacked places to apply their abilities, and employment paths were limited.

Such social conditions constrained not only the size of the professional class but also the level of production (i.e., labor productivity) (Toda 1950). In other words, although the posts occupied by professionals were indispensable, and this irreplaceability was rather prominent in modern sectors, they were less obvious in traditional sectors, which made up the main body of the economy. For example, doctors of Chinese medicine could replace doctors of Western medicine, and family members could substitute for nurses. Family handicrafts could replace the products of industry, which meant that engineers and technicians could be eliminated. People could walk or ride in rickshaws without receiving any services from transportation sectors such as modern railways, highways, and aviation. Due to low demand for communication frequency and speed, the postal and telecommunications industries had difficulty developing, so they did not need large numbers of high-quality postal and telecommunications personnel. Since various sectors were underdeveloped, the work of government agencies was also much more leisurely than in developed countries, so the quantitative and qualitative demands on public servants were not very high. All of these phenomena indicate that although the professional class shouldered important productive functions, which had a certain irreplaceability, it was not very obvious, which limited the social status of this class.

Spending power. The economic returns of members of the professional class are related to their productivity. Their income levels are significantly higher than those of workers, and their expenditures other than for basic material

necessities account for a large proportion of their overall consumption structure, thus enabling them to spend on education, culture, social interactions,
and entertainment without having to struggle all day like workers just to keep
themselves warm and fed. According to a survey of female students' families
at that time, expenditure on education and culture accounted for only 43.11%
of their total expenditure and 55.09% if entertainment were added, but the
proportion of their spending for necessities (i.e., the Engel coefficient) was
approximately 20% (Pei 1925), so they were living at the middle level of urban
residents. In contrast, at that time, miscellaneous expenses for Chinese families, including education and cultural expenditures, accounted on average for
only 5.94% of total expenditures, while those for food, clothing, shelter, and
fuel accounted for as much as 94.30%. Although later on the incomes of city
residents rose and the consumption structure made some improvement, by
1936 expenditures on these four basic items still accounted for as much as 85%
(see Table 2).

This difference is of great significance, because consumption for cultural
and social interaction plays a critical role in the reproduction of the class. Most
expenses for the working class and peasants were for the barest life necessities,
so it could only maintain the reproduction of the working population at a low
level, but the professional class could spend more on their cultural and social
lives. This made it possible for them to constantly expand the forces of their
class (for instance, since their children were educated, they could be added to
the professional class). Hence the quality of personnel in this class could be
continuously improved.

As far as the professionals' own education was concerned, if there were
no family burdens, and especially if they were single, as with Ms. He, Mr. Tu,
Mr. Shen, Mr. Fang, and Mr. Wu, it was possible to rely on their own economic
ability to continue to study and improve themselves. However, most families
at the time had more children, and if several children were using up a professional family's educational and cultural budget, their situation was obviously
not so comfortable. Based on the materials I have seen, if most families of
professionals had two or more children—which is more than in workers'
families (Iwama 2003)—then most could only support their children through
middle school. Those who could go on to study in a university were very few—
generally, these were from well-situated families. This illustrates that there
was little hope of a person from a professional family background of becoming
a member of society's elite class.

In addition, even though individual spending by professionals was significantly greater than that of workers, their numbers were limited, so their
aggregate purchasing power was still less than that of the vast number of

workers. At that time, the consumer goods that had a decisive impact were rice, cloth, and other agricultural products—and during the period of inflation in the 1940s, rice even replaced the banknote and played a monetary function.

In short, the economic status of the professional class had a certain irre-placeability, but the overall amount of its purchasing was less than that of the huge working class. In particular, when compared with the elites, such as the capitalists, even though they were both minority classes, the economic power of the managerial class could often affect the country's financial situation, as well as the start-up and bankruptcy of business enterprises. In comparison with nearby Japan, the development of China's professional class appears to have lagged far behind. As early as Japan's Taishō period (1912–1926), Japan's professional class expanded rapidly. After the beginning of the Shōwa era (1926–1989), a middle-class society composed mainly of professionals had basically formed (Ōkōchi 1960). However, our country, even today, is still a soci-ety composed mainly of peasants.

6.2   *Level of Specialized Professional Organizations*
If the level of production and consumption determines the economic status of the professional class, then the organizational level of professional groups determines its political power. Although the political power of a class is to a certain degree affected by the size of that group, they are even more con-strained by their level of organization.

Dispersion and variability among modern professionals are far greater than among the working class (Zhu, Hu, and Xu 1984). Due to the rather small size of modern Chinese businesses and their low technology level, most of the pro-fessional class is dispersed in small- and medium-sized enterprises, and the number of professionals within the same enterprise is limited. This objectively determines the dispersion of professionals. At the same time, the business enterprises to which the professionals belong are also complex and varied, and their content and systems of operation are of all kinds. Not only are there new and old styles of operation, there are also differences due to industry, region, and even family background. This further increases the heterogeneity among professionals, which creates many organizational inconveniences.

The most typical organization for professionals in commercial businesses are guilds, and virtually every line of work has its own guild (Negishi Tadashi 1951 [1998]). However, most of them evolved from traditional guilds, often called "clubs," "fraternities," and so on, closely related to the chambers of commerce organized by capitalists but distinct from the unions organized by workers. Because they were led basically by business owners and senior staff, they advocated labor-capital cooperation and were skeptical of actions like strikes and revolutions. In a way contrary to the unions' acceptance of Communist Party leadership, guilds accepted more guidance from the Kuomintang (Ma 1966, 28–39). However, due to oppression by the imperialist forces, they often organized relatively benign strikes. In this regard, their interests were closer to that of the chambers of commerce. However, these organizations were not as well-known as the chambers of commerce (they were often under the latter's leadership), and socially they were less effective than unions.

Accounting associations, medical associations, nursing associations, engineering associations, education associations, journalism associations, and so on were higher-level professional organizations whose membership were always high-caliber, good-quality professionals. But they had a more academic quality and their social organizing function was weaker.

Not one of the twenty people I interviewed took the initiative to mention these organizations. When I mentioned them, they did not even quite understand what they were or even denied their existence. What they did take the initiative to mention were alumni associations like the Alumni Association of Lixin Accounting Tutorial School, the Alumni Association of China Vocational School, and so on. In other words, the cohesiveness of a well-known school seems to have outstripped that of the various professional associations.

However, the guilds organized for professionals were often split by the different lines of work, thus creating much inconvenience in the communication of information and exchange of personnel, which in turn limited the consensual actions taken among members. Hence, in this regard, they clearly differed from workers' unions. The professionals had difficulty showing the same organizational strength that the working class did.

During the historic period of class antagonism, the propensity of professional organizations to take the third road was considered by revolutionaries to be insufficiently progressive or revolutionary (Mao 1991, vol. 1; Zhu, Hu, and Xu 1984). At the same time, due to their innovative tendencies and dispersed quality, they could not be fully valued by conservatives. These factors put the professional class into a politically awkward position and were even attributed to the weakness and volatility of the petty bourgeoisie. In other words, the professional class lacked independent political ideas and positions, and it could not effectively organize itself to fight for its political rights and interests (Mills 1987).

6.3   *The Culture of the Professional Class*

A specialized professional life, a modestly prosperous level of material life, and a moderate political orientation created a distinctive professional class culture, and this culture continues to be nurtured and handed down through many means, such as through daily interactions, apprenticeship training, school education, and so on. This class culture can be summarized in at least the following respects.

Professionalism. The specialization and irreplaceability of professionals are such that they identify with their own professional roles and values. The professionalism of one profession is not entirely the same as another (for example, the pursuit of technical value by engineering technicians, the value placed on life by medical staff, the pursuit of wealth by business people, etc.), but they all can unify their personal values with the social functions of their line of work, and they expect thereby to gain respect as members of this class from external society.

This kind of professionalism is also related to our own business and industry traditions. We can all find these traditions from various texts such as the shop rules of old-fashioned industrial and commercial enterprises, Huizhou merchants' ballads, and so on (Wang 1999, 86–93).

Organizational consciousness. Due to the relatively small scale of Chinese business enterprises, professionals easily sensed the limits of their organizations. At the same time, apprenticeships of three or more years were not only commonly practiced in business—their traces could even be seen in the fields of culture, education, banking, and even the military and political sectors. This tradition, based on the teacher-disciple tradition, further strengthened a sense of belonging among members of the organization, so that there was a "home" feeling. This organizational consciousness was not only expressed in the relationship between business organizations and their staff but was also further extended to the relationship between the staff and the whole industry (Niida 1951).

This organizational consciousness among the professional class was often one of the reasons why they were criticized by activists as being "feudal" and "conservative" (Shi Bing 1985; Zhu, Hu, and Xu 1987), while at the same time they were able to accept the labor-capital cooperation advocated by the Kuomintang (Ma 1966, 28–39) as well as the leadership of the chambers of commerce. Of course, another influence on this organizational consciousness was the family- and relative-centered nature of businesses, so that there was a certain closed-door quality to their professional staff.

Pragmatic attitude. Due to their extreme poverty, it was hard for peasants and workers in old China to discover the value of their own labor or even hope for an unseen future (Chen Da 1980). This sort of class position easily generated in them a spirit of risk-taking adventure, so that they participated in strikes and revolutions (Perry 1993). However, the specialized nature of professionals and their more guaranteed income ensured that they could see the relationship between their own work and return, so that they were not very receptive to radicalism. At the same time, because their income was not so abundant, they had to be busy with their work, so that they were not as idealistic as middle school and university students and free intellectuals. In their beliefs, perhaps only gradual improvement and development were the most realistic.

However, in disaster-stricken modern China, both traditional culture and Western culture were being questioned. Only revolutionary culture was a good, progressive culture, so it came to be regarded as a commendatory term. The result is that both the managerial class (excluding the capitalists) and the toiling masses—the workers and peasants—developed a sincere respect for revolutionary culture. But there seemed to be some distance between the culture of the professional class and this near-mainstream revolutionary culture, so it occupied an isolated position. This may be one of the important reasons why the professional class could not be promoted.

6.4   *The Cableway Principle: Why the Professional Class Could Not Grow*

The professional class in our country formed relatively late, and after forming it still developed slowly, so that even today we are still a society whose population is mainly agrarian. The reason it is so hard to change this pyramidal social structure may be explained with a cable-car analogy.

We may liken the upward mobility and improvement of class status of society's members to the ascent of a mountain in order to see scenery. Many people (peasants, workers, housewives, etc.) want to go up the mountain, and they come from all over. But the mountain we face (a higher social class) is steep, and there is only one simple, crude cableway (employment departments and positions) by which one can go up. When everyone reaches the foot of the mountain, the vast majority cannot even get close to the cableway, so they have no choice but to stay there.

On account of this, the cableway managers (government and business managers) stipulate that people going up the mountain must buy tickets (diplomas), and even though many have already received theirs, too many people still cannot get tickets. Only some of the people have the opportunity to go up the mountain. The rest have to "graduate into unemployment." Tickets are devalued as a result, and people lose due trust of education. The devaluation of tickets in turn serves as an excuse for the guardians of the cableway (employee recruiters) to use social capital, resulting in the prevalence of apprenticeships, guarantors, and so on, which depend on social relations. In this way, the children and relatives of the higher classes get priority as they climb to higher strata, so that the higher the stratum, the more closed it is.

So, why does everyone want to go up this mountain? And why is there only one cableway? Generally speaking, it is because of China's internal and external problems. On the one hand, various powers robbed us of our wealth, so that we could not fully develop industries and expand employment opportunities, while long-term political upheaval and war squandered what little fortune was left. Meanwhile, due to backwardness in many areas, many mountain peaks (such as foreign trade, mining, heavy industry, communications, public utilities, etc.) had been occupied by foreigners, or were simply desolate mountains, or were inaccessible to Chinese.

6.5   The Relationship between Education and Professionals

All of the above are more or less related to the relationship between education and professional development. I do not wish to repeat this idea—I only want to use one set of data to offer a bit of supplementary explanation (see Table 9).

TABLE 9   Distribution of the occupations of 1930s Shanghai professionals and their children's educations (unit: %)

Occupational category	Employees in the international settlement (1935)		Occupation of students' fathers (1930)	
	Male	Female	Primary school student	Junior middle school student
Agriculture	0.18	0.06	17.81	5.40
Industry	31.40	11.33	24.56	2.09
Commerce, Finance	35.77	1.26	43.30	57.18
Communications, Transportation	2.56	0.02	2.40	3.07
Specialized	2.51	0.44	1.39	3.68
Public service	1.50	0.02	1.57	6.99
Military, police	0.08	0.00	1.15	0.98
Home economy	0.68	0.02		
School staff/teacher	8.08	4.30	2.61	15.46
Art	0.54	0.26		
Miscellaneous (inc. unemployed)	16.70	82.30	5.22	5.15
Total no. of persons	525,596	336,565	30,519	815
White-collar (%)	43.56	2.01	51.27	86.38

SOURCES: LIEN 1980, 107

Table 9 shows that the professions were virtually monopolized by men, and that the ratio of women entering the professional class was very small—only 2%. Most women were in occupations outside of the modern sectors or were housewives. The most reasonable explanation for this is that women at the time received less education and were denied access to the professional class. However, a secondary reason is that medicine, public services, military and police, churches, and even some schools refused to hire married women. This reflects the conservative nature of professional systems and practices.

As for the occupational distribution of the fathers of primary and middle school students, nearly half of the fathers of primary school students belonged to non-professional occupations, and more than 40% belonged to the worker and peasant classes. By contrast, 86.38% of the fathers of middle school students belonged to the professional class, and among them nearly 60% were in the commercial and financial sectors. This shows that despite the large number of workers and peasants, very few of their children could go to middle school; middle schools seem to have been designed mainly for the professional class. This suffices to illustrate the educational needs of the professional class as well as the power of its educational spending.

However, this adaptive relationship between the professional class and education was not at all well-developed. If we focus on historical development, how can we promote or further improve this relationship?

Professional qualifications: the institutionalization of the relationship between education and professionals.

Modern society is full of metabolic processes, and the growth of the professional class is no exception. The new-style professionals transitioned from the old-style clerks, handicraft workers, aides, private school teachers, and so on. Even though spontaneous transition can also bring changes in social structure, the Chinese, awakened from their deep slumber, can by no means tolerate this slow process and they attempt to speed it up through institutional and policy efforts. Occupational qualification systems are one of the most important areas of action.

The significance of professionalized testing. The purpose and content of the ancient civil service examinations emphasized general cultural accomplishment; the goal was to cultivate the ordinary scholar-official—to the point that accomplished administrative officials of the time had little operational capability and had to rely on instructors and other staff with practical skills (Liu 1998). This reflects the underdevelopment of social enterprises at the time: even incompetent officials could deal with them without causing any serious problems. However, since modern times, all kinds of occupations gradually developed, to the point that some political, economic, and social undertakings that touched on the foreign community must also link up with the way things are done in developed countries. As a result, problems existed with the old personnel standards and methods of selecting talent. This was the inherent reason for the reform of the academic system. Social qualifications from the past civil service examination rankings were converted into the records (diplomas) of the new academic system.

However, the fineness and the quickness of the differentiation between "occupation" and "profession" were such that the establishment of the academic system alone was unable to satisfy demand, so a more specific yet more flexible qualification system and examination method were needed. These various vocational examinations were already being conducted during the Nanjing government period (see Tables 7 and 8 for details). Among the exams initiated by the government, the exams for the hiring of public officials accounted for the absolute majority, followed by the examinations for specialists in engineering, medicine, and attorneys. Large numbers of people sat for the professional examinations in those days—often ten times and several dozens of times more than the actual hiring quota. On the one hand, this reflected society's approval of such exams and people's aspirations for modern employment sectors (mainly, professional positions), but on the other hand it also reflected the employment dilemma of the time: more and more people chasing fewer and fewer jobs. In addition, a variety of private sector examinations were flourishing. Most of these were in large, new-style business enterprises. Moreover, the accountants' qualifying examination was the most typical and had the broadest impact (Guo 1988).

Such professionalized examinations were, on the one hand, a recognition and encouragement of education, but it was impossible for people without the culture or education level to pass them, and on the other hand they were a recognition of the quality of the current professional class and of the regulation of this quality.

Relationship between vocational examinations and school education. Although the qualifying exams recognized the value of education in principle, they were not direct and simple endorsements of the results of school education (as are academic records). Both the public and private sector exams more or less inserted professional content, so that they had a certain degree of specialization. The demand for such specialization was often not easily attainable with schooling. In fact, this tacitly acknowledges the possibility and legitimacy of obtaining qualifications by other means. In other words, working on the job, short-term training, part-time classes, and other non-school means were means of obtaining the experience demanded by the examinations. Under such circumstances, various kinds of tutorial education and short-term training programs were developed during the Republic era (Guoji laodong gongju Zhongguo fenju 1949), and the number of students attending Lixin Accounting School far exceeded the number of students in Japanese schools (Pan 1996, 17:740–746).

It is evident that the relationship between professional examinations and school education is not direct, but cross-cutting and flexible. In other words, what the professional class needed was more than just schooling: it required both general education and specialized education, both formal schooling and more flexible forms of education like correspondence courses, part-time evening courses, and short-term training programs, as well as apprenticeships and even private schools. Each of these forms of education is adapted to different conditions and needs.

6.6   Structural Change: the Driver of the Interaction between Supply and Demand

We may suppose that if education were to adapt to the needs of professional staff in terms of system, content, and form of schooling, then would the professional class be able to develop rapidly? As described above, if society does not have enough of a pioneering spirit, if its economic structure has no major changes, and if the pathways to employment for professionals are still limited, then there is only a low level of adaptation between education and the professional class. The development of both education and professionals will be restricted, and so the significance of this adaptation will still be limited.

Most educators of that time advocated giving full play to education's leading edge and to giving priority to developing education and a store of talented persons. However, the "unemployment upon graduation" phenomenon forced some scholars to reflect on the problem, and they pointed out that education, besides its positive significance, also has a negative function. When resources are extremely scarce, education not only cannot promote social and economic development but instead generates competition between citizens and creates a large quantity of idle waste (Gu 1934). In view of this, many educators such as Tao Xingzhi 陶行知, Huang Yanpei 黃炎培, and Xu Teli 徐特立 turned their attention to political and social movements.

It can be said that in view of the need at the time for the development of the professional class, there was no peaceful, stable, and relaxed social and political environment that was conducive for their being able to retain their jobs, work with peace of mind, and respect the freedom and values of all, including their staff. In fact, it was impossible to expand the scale of the professional class, improve their skill levels, and ensure that the education relevant to them would generate greater demand and resources.

References

Chinese-Language Sources

Chen Da 陈达. 1980. *Woguo kangri zhanzheng shiqi shizhen gongren shenghuo* 《我国抗日战争时期市镇工人生活》 [Urban Workers' Lives During Our Country's War of Resistance Against Japan]. Beijing: Zhongguo laodong chubanshe.

Chen Mingyuan 陈明远. 2000a. "Ershi niandai zhishi jieceng jingji zhuangkuang—Beijing jiaoyujie he xuezhe qunti 20 年代知识阶层经济状况—北京教育界和学者群体 [Economic Condition of the Knowledge Class in the 1920s—Beijing Education and Scholar Groups]." *Shehui kexue luntan* (5): 16–22.

Chen Mingyuan. 2000b. "Ershi niandai zhishi jieceng jingji zhuangkuang 20 年代知识阶层经济状况—上海的作者群体 [Economic Condition of the Knowledge Class in the 1920s—Shanghai Writers' Groups]." *Shehui kexue luntan* (7): 27–32.

Ding Yizhuang 定宜庄. 1999. *Zuihou de jiyi—shiliu wei Qiren funü de koushu lishi* 《最后的记忆—十六位旗人妇女的口述历史》 [Last Memories: Oral Histories of Sixteen Manchu Women]. Beijing: Zhongguo guangbo dianshi chubanshe.

Dong Shanyuan 董善元. 1986. *Zhang Binggui jutai shengya wushinian* 《张秉贵柜台生涯五十年》 [Zhang Binggui's Fifty-year Career at the Counter]. Beijing: Gongren chubanshe.

Gu Mei 古楳. 1934. "Fazhan xiangcun jiaoyu de zhongxin wenti 发展乡村教育的中心问题 [Core Issues in Developing Rural Education]." In *Zhongguo jiaoyu zhi jingji guan* 《中国教育之经济观》 [Economic Perspectives on Chinese Education], 27–40. Edited by Gu Mei. Shanghai: Minzhi shuju.

Gu Mei. 1934. "Zhongguo jiaoyu yu shengchan wenti 中国教育與生产问题 [Chinese Education and the Issue of Education]." In *Zhongguo jiaoyu zhi jingji guan*. Edited by Gu Mei. Shanghai: Minzhi shuju.

Guo Daoyang 郭道扬. 1988. *Zhongguo kuaiji shi gao (xi ace)* 《中国会计史稿》 (下册) [History of Chinese Accounting, vol. 2]. Beijing: Zhongguo caizheng jingji chubanshe.

Guoji laodong gongju Zhongguo fenju 國際勞工局中國分局 [ILO China Branch]. 1949. *Shanghai jishu xunlian yu jishu jiaoyu* 《上海技术训练与技术教育》 [Skills Training and Technical Education in Shanghai]. Manuscript.

Hu Shi 胡适. 1993. *Hu Shi koushu zizhuan* 胡适口述自传 [Hu Shih's Oral Autobiography]. With translation and commentary by Tang Degang 唐德刚. Shanghai: Huadong shifan daxue chubanshe.

Iwama Kazuhiro 岩间一弘. 2003. "1940 nian qianhou Shanghai zhiyuan jieceng de shenghuo qingkuang 1940 年前后上海职员阶层的生活情况 [Living Conditions of Shanghai's Professional Class Around the Year 1940]." Trans. by Gan Huijie 甘慧杰. *Shilin* 史林 73(4): 41–53, 123.

Jiang Yihua 姜义华. 2001. "Shanghai: Jindai Zhongguo xin wenhua zhongxin diwei de xingcheng ji qi bianqian—jianlun bianyuan wenhua de jiju ji qi xiaoying 上海: 近代中国新文化中心地位的形成及其变迁—兼论边缘文化的积聚集其效应 [Shanghai: The Formation of Its Position as a Modern Chinese Cultural Center and Its Changes—With Discussion on the Fringe Culture Clustering Effect]." *Xueshu yuekan* 学术月刊 (11): 73–83.

Li Changli 李長莉. 2002. "Shanghai shehui shenghuo de dianxing yiyi 上海社会生活史的典型意义 [The Archetypal Significance of the History of Social Life in Shanghai]." *Shilin* 史林 (4): 4–6.

Li Xiaojiang 李小江, ed. 2003a. *Rang nüren ziji shuohua—duli de lichen* 《让女人自己说话—独立的历程》 [Letting Women Speak for Themselves—The Path of Independence]. Beijing: Sanlian shudian.

Li Xiaojiang, ed. 2003b. *Rang nüren ziji shuohua—minzu xushi* 《让女人自己说话—民族叙事》 [Letting Women Speak for Themselves—Peoples' Narratives]. Beijing: Sanlian shudian.

Li Xiaojiang, ed. 2003c. *Rang nüren ziji shuohua—qinli zhanzheng* 《让女人自己说话—亲历战争》 [Letting Women Speak for Themselves—Experiencing War]. Beijing: Sanlian shudian.

Li Xiaojiang, ed. 2003d. *Rang nüren ziji shuohua—wenhua xunzong* 《让女人自己说话—文化寻踪》 [Letting Women Speak for Themselves—Cultural Pursuits]. Beijing: Sanlian shudian.

Li Yuliang 李玉良. 1990. *Dongtang shidai de zhishifenzi* 《动荡时代的知识分子》 [Intellectuals in a Turbulent Age]. Hangzhou: Zhejiang renmin chubanshe.

Lin Yan 林焱 and Wu Lisheng 吴励生. 2001. "'Geming' shiqi de huayu lilun fenxi '革命' 时期的话语理论分析 [Analysis of Speech Theory in the 'Revolutionary' Era]." In *Lun caozuo yu bu ke caozuo: Wang Xiaobo xiaoshuo taolun bing zhi youren* [On Operability and Inoperability: Wang Xiaobo's Discussions on Novels and Addresses to Friends]. Ed. by Wu Lisheng 吴励生 and Ye Qin 叶勤. Fuzhou: Haixia wenyi chubanshe.

Lin Yaohua 林耀华. 1989. *Jinyi—Zhongguo jiazu zhidu de shehuixue yanjiu* 《金翼—中国家族制度的社会学研究》 [The Golden Wing: A Sociological Study of Chinese Familism]. Trans. by Zhuang Kongshao 庄孔韶 and Lin Yucheng 林余成. Hong Kong: Sanlian shudian.

Ling Tianhe 麦天和. 2003. *Ling yizhong lishi—Pan Yuanfa koushu shilu* 《另一种历史—潘元法口述实录》 [Another Kind of History: Pan Yuanfa's True Oral Account]. Taiyuan: Shanxi renmin chubanshe.

Liu Mingkui 刘明逵. 1985. *Zhongguo gongren jieji lishi zhuangkuang: 1840–1949* 《中国工人阶级历史状况：1840–1949》 [Historical Situation of the Chinese Working Class: 1840–1949]. 第 1 卷，第 1 册 Di 1 juan, di 1 ce [Part 1, Vol. 1]. Beijing: Zhonggong zhongyang dangxiao chubanshe.

Liu Mingkui. 1993. *Zhongguo gongren jieji lishi zhuangkuang: 1840–1949*《中国工人阶级历史状况：1840–1949》 [Historical Situation of the Chinese Working Class: 1840–1949]. Di 1 juan, di 2 ce 第 1 卷，第 2 册 [Part 1, Vol. 2]. Beijing: Beijing Zhonggong zhongyan dangxiao chubanshe.

Liu Xiaomeng 刘小萌. 2003. *Zhongguo zhiqing koushu shi*《中国知青口述史》 [Oral Histories of Chinese Young Intellectuals]. Beijing: Zhongguo shehui kexue chubanshe.

Liu Yunshan 刘云杉. 2002. "Diguo quanli shijian xia de jiaosheng shengming xingtai—yige sishu jiaoshi de shenghuo shi yanjiu 帝国权力实践下的教师生命形态——一个私塾教师的生活史研究 [A Teacher's Life under the Exercise of Imperial Power—Research on the Life History of a Private School Tutor]." *Zhongguo jiaoyu: yanjiu yu pinglun* 中国教育：研究與评论 3.2: 143–173.

Liu Zehua 刘泽华, ed. 1998. *Zhonghua wenhua tongzhi, di 4 dian, zhidu wenhua*《中华文化通志，第 4 典，制度文化》 [Compendia of Chinese Culture, 4th Series, Institutional Culture]. Shanghai: Shanghai renmiin chubanshe.

Liu Zhonglu 刘中陆, ed. 1995. *Qingchu fangchengshi—wushi ge nü zhiqing de zishu*《青春方程式—五十个女知青的自述》 [The Youth Equation: Self-Narratives of Fifty Young Intellectual Women]. Beijing: Beijing daxue chubanshe.

Luo Yuanjing 罗元铮. 1998. *Zhonghua minguo shilu: minguo yuan—sanshiba nian*《中华民国实录：民国元—三十八年》 [Records of the Republic of China: 1912–1949]. Changchun: Jilin renmin chubanshe.

Ma Chaojun 马超俊 et al. 1966. *Zhongguo laodong yundong shi*《中国劳工运动史》 [History of Chinese Labor Movements]. Beijing: Zhonghua dadian bianyinhui and Zhongguo yundong fuli chubanshe.

Mao Zedong 毛泽东. 1991. "Zhongguo shehui ge jieji de fenxi 中国社会各阶级的分析 [Analysis of the Various Classes of Chinese Society]." In *Mao Zedong xuanji*《毛泽东选集》 [Selected Works of Mao Zedong]. Vol. 1. Beijing: Renming chubanshe.

Mills, C. Wright 米尔斯. 1987. *Bailing—Meiguo de zhongchan jieji*《白領白领—美国的中产阶级》 [White Collar: The American Middle Classes]. Trans. by Yang Xiaodong 杨小东 et al. Hangzhou: Zhejiang renmin chubanshe.

Mo Fei 墨菲 and Luo Zi 罗兹. 1986. *Shanghai—Xiandai Zhongguo de yaoshi*《上海—现代中國的钥匙》 [Shanghai—Key to Modern China]. Shanghai: Shanghai renmin chubanshe.

Nie Yuchan 聂毓禅. 1987. "Xiehe yixue yuan hushi xuexiao de bianqian 协和医学院护士学校的变迁 [The Changes of the Nursing School at Xiehe College of Medicine]." In *Huashuo lao Xiehe*《话说老协和》 [Talking About Old Xiehe], 195–204. Ed. by Zhengxie Beijing shi weiyuanhui wenshi ziliao yanjiu weiyuanhui 政协北京市委员会文史资料研究委员会. Beijing: Zhongguo wenshi chubanshe.

Pan Xulun 潘序伦. 1996. "Lixin kuaiji xuexiao de chuangban he fazhan 立信会计学校的创办和发展 [The Founding and Development of Lixin Accounting School]."

In *Zhonghua wenshi ziliao wenku wenhua jiaoyu bian* 《中华文史资料文库·文化教育编》 [Chinese Cultural and Historical Materials Database: Cultural Education]. Beijing: Zhongguo wenshi chubanshe, 17: 740–746.

Pei Hua 裴华. 1925. "Nüxuesheng de jiating zhuangkuang 女学生的家庭状况 [Female Students' Family Situations]." *Funü jie* 妇女界 11.6.

Perry, Elizabeth J. (Pei Yili 裴宜理). 2001. *Shanghai bagong: Zhongguo gongren zhengzhi yanjiu* 《上海罢工：中国工人政治研究》 [Shanghai on Strike: The Politics of Chinese Labor]. Trans. by Liu Ping 刘平. Nanjing: Jiangsu renmin chubanshe.

Ren Tongjun 任桐君. 1989. *Yige nüjiaoshi de zishu* 《一个女教师的自述》 [Autobiography of a Female Teacher]. Beijing: Sanlian shudian.

Sang Bing 桑兵. 1995. *Qing mo xin zhishijie de shetuan yu huodong* 清末新知识界的社团与活动 [Associations and Activities in the New Intellectual World of the Late Qing]. Beijing: Shenghuo dushu xinzhi sanlian shudian.

Shanghai gongren yundong shiliao weiyuanhui 上海工人运动史料委员会. 1986. *Shanghai youzheng zhigong yundong shiliao (diyi ji): 1922 nian–1937 nian* 《上海邮政职工运动史料 (第一辑)：1922 年–1937 年》 [Historical Materials on Shanghai City Postal Workers' Movements (Vol. 1): 1922–1937]. Internal document.

Shanghai nianjian weiyuanhui 上海年鉴委员会 [Shanghai Yearbook Compilation Committee]. 1937. *Shanghai shi nianjian (minguo sanshiliu nian)* 《上海市年鉴》 (民国三十六年) [Shanghai Yearbook (1937)]. Shanghai: Zhonghua shuju.

Shanghai shi diyi baihuo shangdian 上海市第一百货商店 and Shanghai shi baihuoye Daxin gongsi dangshi ziliao zhengji zu 上海市百货业大新公司党史资料征集组. 1986. *Shanghai Daxin gongsi zhigong yundong shiliao: 1936–1949* 《上海大新公司职工运动史料：1936–1949》 [Historical Materials on Workers' Movements at The Sun Company, Shanghai: 1936–1949].

Shanghai shi jianzhu gongcheng ju gonghui 上海市建筑工程局工会. 1976. *Chuangchuang "yanglou" you xielie: Shanghai shi jianzhu gongrenjia shiliao* 《幢幢"洋楼"有血泪：上海市建筑工人家史选》 [The Ornate "Foreign Buildings" Have Blood and Tears: Historical Selections on Construction Workers and Families in Shanghai City]. Shanghai: Shanghai renmin chunbanshe.

Shanghai shi qinggongye changshi xiezuo zu 上海市轻工业局厂史写作组. 1975. *Changye jinglei: Shanghai qinggongye gongren jiefang qian douzheng shi pianduan* 《长夜惊雷：上海轻工业工人解放前斗争史片段》 [Long Nights, Startling Thunder: Historical Episodes of Shanghai Light Industry Workers' Struggles]. Shanghai: Shanghai renmin chubanshe.

Shanghai shi shehui ju 上海市社会局 [Shanghai Municipal Bureau of Social Affairs]. 1935. *Shanghai shi gongren renshu tongji* 《上海市工人人数统计》 [Statistics on Numbers of Workers in Shanghai City]. Internal document.

Shanghai shi yejin gongye ju chang shi xiezuo zu 上海市冶金工业局厂史写作组. 1975. *Luhuo xiongxiong: Shanghai yejin gongren douzhengshi pianduan* 《炉火熊熊：

上海冶金工人斗争史片段》[The Raging Fire: Historical Episodes of Shanghai Metalworkers' Struggles]. Shanghai: Shanghai renmin chubanshe.

Shanghai shi zhengfu tongji chu 上海市政府统计处 [Shanghai Municipal Statistics Office]. 1947. *Shanghai shi tongji zong baogao*《上海市统计总报告》[Summary Report of Shanghai City Statistics]. Internal document.

Shanghai shi zonggonghui xuanjiao zu 上海市总工会宣教组. 1975. *Tiechui zasui jiu shijie: Shanghai gongrenjia shi xuan* (3)《铁锤砸碎旧世界：上海工人家史选》[The Old World Shattered with a Hammer: Selected Historical Materials on Shanghai Workers and Families]. Shanghai: Shanghai renmin chubanshe.

Shanghai shiwei dang shiliao zhengji weiyuanhui 上海市委党史资料征集委员会. 1997. *Shanghai shi zhongxue jiaoshi yundong shiliao xuan: 1945–1949*《上海市中学教师运动史料选：1945–1949》[Selected Historical Materials on Middle School Teachers' Movements in Shanghai City: 1945–1949]. Shanghai: Shanghai jiaoyu chubanshe.

Shao Gongwen 邵公文. 1993. *Cong xuetu dao zongjingli—shudian shengya huiyi*《从学徒到总经理—书店生涯忆》[From Apprentice to President: Recollections of a Bookstore Career]. Beijing: Chaohua chubanshe.

Shao Zugong 邵祖恭. 1934. *Fan zhiye jiaoyu lun*《反职业教育论》[Against Professional Education]. Nanjing: Jinghua yinshuguan.

Sheng Langxi 盛朗西. 1930. "Shinian lai Jiangsu zhongdeng xuexiao biyesheng chulu tongji 十年来江苏中等学校毕业生出路统计 [Statistics on Career Outcomes of Middle School Graduates in Jiangsu for the Past Decade]." *Jiaoyu zazhi* 教育杂志 17.4 and 17.5.

Shi Bing 史兵. 1985. *Zhongguo gongren yundong shihua*《中国工人运动史话》[Historical Anecdotes on Chinese Worders' Movements]. Vol. 1. Beijing: Gongren chubanshe.

Shiye bu Zhongguo laodong nianjian bianji weiyuanhui 实业部中国劳动年鉴编纂委员会, ed. 1934. *Minguo ershier nian laodong nianjian*《民国二十二年中国劳动年鉴》[Labor Gazette 1933]. Shanghai: Shiye bu laogong si.

Tang Diyin 汤蒂因. 1983. *Jin bi yuan: yige nü gongshang yezhe de zishu*《金笔缘：一个女工商业者的自述》[An Affinity Between Gold and Brushes: Autobiography of a Female Industrialist]. Beijing: Sanlian shudian.

Tang Shaojie 唐少杰. 2001. "'Ren you bing, tian zhi fou?': Jidujiao fanzhao xia de Zhongguo geming lunli yanjin ji yuanliu wenti '人有病，天知否？'：基督教反照下的中国革命伦理演进及源流问题 ['Does Heaven Know if People Are Sick?' The Evolution of Chinese Revolutionary Ethics under the Reflection of Christianity, and the Issue of Sources]." *Kaifang shidai* 开放时代 (8): 34–40.

Tao Shuimu 陶水木. 2000. *Zhejiang shangbang yu Shanghai jindaihua yanjiu* 浙江商帮与上海经济近代化研究 [Zhejiang Merchant Organizations and Shanghai's Economic Modernization]. Shanghai: Shanghai sanlian shudian.

Tian Zhengping 田正平 and Xiao Lang 肖朗. 1999. "Zhongguo jindai jiaoyujia qunti tezheng zonglun" 中国近代教育家群体特征综论 [Summary of the Group Characteristics of Modern Chinese Educators]. *Jiaoyu yanjiu* 教育研究 (11): 47–52.

Wang Qisheng 王奇生. 1992. "Minguo shiqi xianzhang de qunti goucheng yu renshi shandi—yi 1927 nian zhi 1949 nian Changjiang liuyu shengfen wei zhongxin 民国时期县长的群体构成與人事嬗递—以 1927 年至 1949 年长江流域省份为中心 [Group Structure and Personnel Succession of County Magistrates in the Republic Era: With Focus on the Yangtze Basin Provinces from 1927 to 1949]." *Lishi yanjiu* 历史研究 (2): 98–116.

Wang Xianming 王先明. 1997. *Jindai shenshi: yige fengjian jieceng de lishi mingyun* 《近代绅士：一个封建阶层的历史命运》 [Modern Gentry: Historical Destiny of a Feudal Class]. Tianjin: Tianjin renmin chubanshe.

Wang Zhenzhong 王振忠. 1999. "Huizhou shangye wenhua de yige cemian—fanying minguo shiqi Shanghai Huizhou xuetu shenghuo de shi feng shuxin 徽州商业文化的一个侧面—反映民国时期上海徽州学徒生活的十封书信 [An Aspect of Huizhou Commercial Culture: Ten Letters Reflecting the Life of Huizhou Apprentices in Republic-era Shanghai]." *Fudan xuebao (shehui kexue ban)* 复旦学报 (社会科学版) (4): 86–93.

Xin Ping 忻平. 1997. *Cong Shanghai faxian lishe: xiandaihua jincheng zhong de Shanghairen ji qi shehui shenghuo (1927–1937)* 《从上海发现历史—现代化進程中的上海人及其社会生活》 [Discovering History from Shanghai: Shanghai Residents and Their Social Lives in the Process of Modernization]. Shanghai: Shanghai renmin chubanshe.

Yang Maochun 杨懋春. 2001. *Yige Zhongguo cunzhuang: Shandong Taitou* 《一个中国村庄：山东台头》 [A Chinese Village: Taitou, Shantung Province]. Trans. by Zhang Xiong 张雄, Shen Wei 沈炜, and Qin Meizhu 秦美珠. Nanjing: Jiangsu renmin chubanshe.

Yang Yanfu 杨雁斌. 1998. "Koushu shixue bainian toushi 口述史学百年透视 [Perspective on A Century of Oral History Studies]." *Guowai shehui kexue* 国外社会科学 (2): 2–6 and (3): 2–7.

Zhang Kaiyuan 章开沅, Ma Min 马敏, and Zhu Ying 朱英, ed. 2000. *Zhongguo jindaishi shang de guanshen shangxue* 《中国近代史上的官绅商学》 [Official-Gentry Business in Modern Chinese History]. Wuhan: Hubei renmin chubanshe.

Zhang Liyan 张丽艳. 2003. "Tongwang zhiyehua zhi lu—minguo shiqi Shanghai lüshi yanjiu 通往职业化之路—民国时期上海律师研究 [On the Road to Professionalism: Shanghai Lawyers in Republican Shanghai (1912–1937)]." PhD dissertation. Shanghai: Huadong shifan daxue.

Zhang Xiao 张晓. 1997. *Xijiang Miaozu funü koushu shi yanjiu* 《西江苗族妇女口述史研究》 [Study of Oral Histories of Miao Women of Xi River]. Guiyang: Guizhou renmin chubanshe.

Zhang Youyu 张友渔. 1982. *Baoren shengya sanshi nian*《报人生涯三十年 [Thirty Years of a Reporting Career]. Chongqing: Chongqing chubanshe.

Zhang Zhongli 张仲礼, ed. 1990. *Jindai Shanghai chengshi yanjiu*《近代上海城市研究 [A Study of Modern Shanghai City]. Shanghai: Shanghai renmin chubanshe.

Zhang Zhongli [Chung-li Chang]. 1991. *Zhongguo shenshi: guanyu qi zai 19 shiji Zhongguo shehui zhong zuoyong de yanjiu* 中国绅士: 关于其在 19 世纪中国社会中作用的研究 [The Chinese Gentry: Studies on Their Role in Nineteenth-century Chinese Society]. Trans. by Li Ronglü 李荣吕. Shanghai: Shanghai shehui kexue yuan chubanshe.

Zhang Zhongli [Chung-li Chang]. 2001. *Zhongguo shenshi: Zhongguo shenshi de shouru* 中国绅士：中国绅士的收入 [The Income of the Chinese Gentry]. Trans. by Fei Chengkang 费成康 and Wang Yintong 王寅通. Shanghai: Shanghai shehui kexue yuan chubanshe.

Zhang Zhongli 张仲礼, Xiong Yuezhi 熊月之, and Shen Zuwei 沈祖炜. 2002. *Changjiang yanjiang chengshi yu Zhongguo jindaihua*《长江沿江城市與中国近代化》[Cities Along the Yangtze and China's Modernization]. Shanghai: Shanghai renmin chubanshe.

Zhonggong Shanghai hualian shangxia weiyuanhui 中共上海华联商厦委员会. 1991. *Shanghai Yongan gongsi zhigong yundong shiliao 1918–1949*《上海永安公司职工运动史料：1918–1949》[Historical Materials on Workers' Movements Among Staff Workers at Shanghai's Wing On Company: 1918–1949]. Beijing: Zhonggong dangshi chubanshe.

Zhonggong Shanghai shiwei dangshi ziliao zhengji weiyuanhui 中共上海市委党史资料征集委员会, Zhonggong Shanghai shiwei dangshi yanjiushi 中共上海市委党史研究室, and Zhonggong Shanghai shi shangye gongzuo weiyuanhui 中共上海市商业工作委员会. 1999. *Shanghai dianyuan he zhiyuan yundongshi: 1919–1949*《上海店员和职员运动史：1919–1949》[History of Movements Among Shanghai Store Employees and Professionals: 1919–1949]. Shanghai: Shanghai shehui kexueyuan chubanshe.

Zhongguo fangzhi jianshe gongsi 中国纺织建设公司 [China Textile Industries, Inc.]. 1950. *Ben gongsi zhiyuan baozhengshu ji zhiyuan füli biao, 1946 nian 2 yue–1950 nian 9 yue*《本公司职员保证书及职员履历表，1946 年 2 月–1950 年 9 月》[This Company's Staff Certificates and Resumes, February 1946 to September 1950]. In the collection of Shanghai dang'an xinxiguan [Shanghai Municipal Archives].

Zhongguo shehui kexueyuan Jindaishi yanjiusuo Zhonghua minguo shi yanjiushi 中国社会科学院近代史研究所中华民国史研究室 [Department of Republican Chinese History, Institute of Modern History, Chinese Academy of Social Sciences]. 1987. *Zhonghua minguo shi ziliao conggao, renwu zhuanji*《中华民国史资料丛稿，人物传记》[Compendium of Historical Materials of the Republic of China, Biographies], vol. 22. Beijing: Zhonghua shuju.

Zhongguo shehui kexueyuan Jindaishi yanjiusuo Zhonghua minguo shi yanjiushi. 1988. *Zhonghua minguo shi ziliao conggao, renwu zhuanji* [Compendium of Historical Materials of the Republic of China, Biographies], vol. 23. Beijing: Zhonghua shuju.

"Zhonghua minguo renwu zhi 中华民国人物志 [Biographies of Republican Chinese Figures]." 1987. In Renwu zhuanji 人物传计 [Biographies], vol. 22. Edited by Zhongguo shehui kexue yuan Jindaishi yanjiusuo Zhonghua minguo shi yanjiushi 中国社会科学院近代史研究所中华民国史研究室, Compendium of Historical Materials of the Republic of China. Beijing: Zhonghua shuju.

Zhonghua quanguo zonggonghui Zhongguo gongren yundongshi yanjiushi 中华全国总工会中国工人运动史研究室 [History of Chinese Workers' Movements Office, All-China Federation of Trade Unions], ed. 1980. *Zhongguo gongyun shiliao, di 10–12 qi* 《中国工运史料，第 10–12 期》 [Historical Documents on Chinese Workers' Movements, Vols. 10–12]. Beijing: Gongren chubanshe.

Zhonghua quanguo zonggonghui Zhongguo gongren yundongshi yanjiushi, ed. 1981. *Zhongguo gongyun shiliao, di 15–16 qi.* [Historical Documents on Chinese Workers' Movements, Vols. 15–16]. Beijing: Gongren chubanshe.

Zhonghua quanguo zonggonghui Zhongguo gongren yundongshi yanjiushi, ed. 1982. *Zhongguo gongyun shiliao, di 17–18 qi.* [Historical Documents on Chinese Workers' Movements, Vols. 17–18]. Beijing: Gongren chubanshe.

Zhonghua quanguo zonggonghui Zhongguo gongren yundongshi yanjiushi, ed. 1983. *Zhongguo gongyun shiliao, di 22–24 qi.* [Historical Documents on Chinese Workers' Movements, Vols. 22–24]. Beijing: Gongren chubanshe.

Zhonghua quanguo zonggonghui Zhongguo gongren yundongshi yanjiushi, ed. 1984. *Zhongguo gongyun shiliao, di 1–8 qi huibian.* [Historical Documents on Chinese Workers' Movements, Vols. 1–8 General]. Beijing: Gongren chubanshe.

Zhonghua quanguo zonggonghui Zhongguo gongren yundongshi yanjiushi, ed. 1984. *Zhongguo gongyun shiliao, di 25 qi.* [Historical Documents on Chinese Workers' Movements, Vol. 25]. Beijing: Gongren chubanshe.

Zhonghua quanguo zonggonghui Zhongguo gongren yundongshi yanjiushi, ed. 1984. *Zhongguo gongyun shiliao, di 26 qi.* [Historical Documents on Chinese Workers' Movements, Vol. 26]. Beijing: Gongren chubanshe.

Zhonghua quanguo zonggonghui Zhongguo gongren yundongshi yanjiushi, ed. 1984. *Zhongguo gongyun shiliao, di 27 qi.* [Historical Documents on Chinese Workers' Movements, Vol. 27]. Beijing: Gongren chubanshe.

Zhonghua quanguo zonggonghui Zhongguo gongren yundongshi yanjiushi, ed. 1986. *Zhongguo gongyun shiliao, di 28–29 qi.* [Historical Documents on Chinese Workers' Movements, Vols. 28–29]. Beijing: Gongren chubanshe.

Zhu Bangxing 朱邦兴, Hu Linge 胡林阁, and Xu Sheng 徐声. 1984. *Shanghai chanye yu Shanghai zhigong* 《上海产业與上海职工》 [Shanghai Industry and Shanghai Staff Workers]. Shanghai: Shanghai renmin chubanshe.

Zhu Ying 朱英. 1996. *Shangye geming zhong de wenhua bianqian: jindai shangren yu "haipai" wenhua*《商业革命中的文化变迁:近代商人與 "海派" 文化》[Cultural Change in the Commercial Revolution: Modern Business People and the "Shanghai School" Culture]. Shanghai: Huazhong ligong daxue chubanshe.

Zhu Zheng 朱正. 1999. *Xiao shushing da shidai: Zhu Zheng koushu zizhuan*《小书生大时代:朱正口述自传》[A Young Student, a Great Era: The Orally Narrated Autobiography of Zhu Zheng]. Ed. by Zhu Xiao 朱晓. Beijing: Beijing daxue chubanshe.

Zou Yiren 邹依仁. 1980. *Jiu Shanghai renkou bianqian de yanjiu*《旧上海人口变迁的研究》[Study of Demographic Changes in Old Shanghai]. Shanghai: Shanghai renmin chubanshe.

Non-Chinese Language Sources

Lien, Ling-ling. 2001. "Searching for the 'New Womanhood': Career Women in Shanghai, 1912–1945." PhD diss., University of California, Irvine.

Negishi Tadashi. 1951. *Shanhai no girudo* 上海のギルド [Shanghai's Guilds]. Tokyo: Hyōronsha.

Negishi Tadashi 根岸佶. 1998. *Chūgoku no girudo* 中国のギルド [China's Guilds]. 1951; rpt. Tokyo: Ōzorosha.

Niida Noboru 仁井田陞. 1951. *Chūgoku no shakai to girudo* 中国の社会とギルド [Chinese Society and Guilds]. Tokyo: Iwanami shoten.

Ōkōchi Kazuo 大河内一男. 1960. *Nihon no chūsan kaikyū* 日本的中産階級 [Japan's Middle Class]. Tokyo: Bungeishunjū.

Perry, Elizabeth J. 1993. *Shanghai on Strike: The Politics of Chinese Labor*. Stanford: Stanford University Press.

Toda Yoshirō 戶田義郎. 1950. *Chūgoku kōgyō rōdō ron* 中國工業勞働論. Tokyo: Ganshōdō shoten.

Xu, Xiaoqun. 2000. *Chinese Professionals and the Republican State: The Rise of Professional Associations in Shanghai, 1912–1937*. Cambridge: Cambridge University Press.

CHAPTER 3

The Spirit of Modern China: Life Stories of Influential Educators

Ruth Hayhoe

Since[1] I began my studies of Comparative Education, more than twenty years ago, I have often been asked to explain what exactly this field of study is. Inevitably, the answer tends to get tied up in sociological terminology—the study of education across several societies or cultures, the understanding of education's relation to social change, the investigation of learning and schooling in different societal contexts, the solving of problems in education through comparative investigation and reflection ... While I have greatly enjoyed reading philosophy and history over my years in the field, I have always somehow felt Comparative Education was, first and foremost, a macro-sociology of education. As sociologists probe the patterns of interaction between the educational and social, or the political and cultural systems in one society, comparativists link two or several societies in a search for patterns of explanation.

As sociology has moved from uni-dimensional positivist assumptions about structure and interaction in describing and explaining societal systems to experimentation with ethnomethodology, critical theory and narrative, an increasingly rich array of methodologies has been available to the comparativist. Personally, I have been attracted in recent years to narrative approaches to the study of education, and have come to appreciate the efforts of sociologists to bring the lives of individuals back into the structures and interactions they have theorized about. Goodson and Walker (1991, 139) provide an overview of this development in sociology of education in England, in what they describe as a project "of reconceptualising educational research so as to assure that 'the teacher's voice' is heard, heard loudly and heard articulately." Clandinin and Connelly (2000) demonstrate through illustration and example what it means to think narratively and do narrative inquiry, exploring the conflicts that arise at the boundaries with formalistic theoretical inquiry on one side, and with

---

1   The Chinese version of this article was published in *China's Education: Research and Review*, 2001, volume 1, pp. 1–74. See also Ruth Hayhoe, *Portraits of Influential Chinese Educations* (CERC and Springer, 2006) for a later version of six of these portraits.

reductionist inquiry within the "grand narrative" of educational science at the other.

The rich potential of personal narrative for illuminating educational processes across cultures is evident in Mary Catherine Bateson's *Peripheral Visions*, where the author's personal experience of learning and teaching in Israel, Iran and the Philippines is drawn upon to illuminate basic learning processes in these distinctive cultures and societies, and their similarities and differences with learning within the American context. The artistry with which this volume ties together profound insights into human development through one life lived with intense awareness and meticulous attention to detail is a powerful lesson for comparative educators (Bateson 1994).

My own personal experience as a comparativist has been intensely focused on deepening layers of understanding of a society and educational complex very different from my own, that of mainland China. In studying Chinese education, both comparative education and history were essential elements from the beginning. One could not hope to understand contemporary patterns or structures of education and their wider societal or cultural links without reading a great deal of history and without coming to terms with the profound impacts made by a number of external educational and cultural influences over the 20th century. Major educational borrowings came from Japan, the United States, France, Germany and Britain, as well as from the Soviet Union. In addition, many fascinating minor sets of influences can be found from countries such as Denmark, Canada, Italy and New Zealand.

On one level, whole systems and sets of structures were introduced, beginning with the first modern educational system modeled after Japan in 1902–3 and culminating in the total restructuring of education in the Soviet image between 1952 and 1955. On another level, individual institutions were consciously shaped to emulate preferred models from specific countries, through particular sets of relationships, such as Cai Yuanpei's admiration of the University of Berlin, and Liang Shuming's interest in emulating the ideas of the progressive Danish educator, N.S.F. Grundtvig.

My research and writing has spanned the whole century, with a number of collaborative efforts that were seen as essential to take in the range of issues and levels calling out for consideration (Hayhoe 1984, 1992, Hayhoe and Bastid 1987, Peterson, Hayhoe and Lu 2001). However, I think what has fascinated me most has been the destiny of particular institutions, especially higher institutions, which combined values and patterns from other cultures with those of China's own rich history of educational development. I have regarded these institutions almost as personalities, and have enjoyed collecting many institutional histories that have been written in the period since 1978. This was a result of new freedoms from the constraints of a uniform system, which enabled them to re-establish identities that went back before the imposition of the Soviet model in 1952.

While it was important to identify and analyze broad patterns of educational and societal change over the century, it was valuable also to see how particular institutions conformed to these patterns or held out against them. It was helpful to draw on the sociological literature of education and social change, modernization, revolutionary transformation, imperialism and dependency, while also noting elements in the Chinese context that did not conform to these broad sets of theoretical explanation. In *China's Universities 1895–1995: A Century of Cultural Conflict* (Hayhoe 1996), I tried to link the momentous changes in China's higher education over the century with broader world trends, while at the same time developing an explanation that owed its main tenets to core values of Chinese philosophy and culture. Both the universal and the particular were integral to China's experience of change.

My own personal understanding developed through broad reading and observation, through intimate involvement with a certain number of institutions that I got to know well, and finally through long term and trusting relationships with some of the scholars whose lives had been dedicated to building up their own institutions and writing the literature which nourished the younger generation of teachers and scholars in education. Up till the present, I have written very little about these individuals, focusing rather upon the macro patterns of change in the major periods of the century and the differing experiences and destinies of important institutions which seemed to me to embody some of the core cultural conflicts that fascinated me: Peking University, Fudan University, Tongji University, Wuhan University, People's University, and many others.

In this paper, I wish to turn to six individuals, each associated with a university in a different part of the country, and each distinguished for their long-term service to their institution and to the field of education or higher education more generally. It might have seemed more logical to begin one's research with individuals, then move to institutions, and finally to broad patterns. However, there were good reasons to wait until relations of cooperation and mutual respect had been built up over nearly two decades before inviting some of the scholars I most respected to share their inner thoughts and views of a lifetime's experience through difficult and tumultuous times. In writing on "Biography and Society," Bertaux makes the point that "what is really at stake is the relationship between the sociologist and the people who make his work possible by accepting to be interviewed on their life experience" (1981, 9). I am deeply aware of the honor that has been accorded to me by the six scholars, giving their time and sharing their innermost thoughts.

In 1992, one of my doctoral students was able to carry out a survey of 1216 college students, under the auspices of a major project of cooperation between Canada and China in doctoral training. The survey took place in three locations, the major east coast city of Nanjing, former national capital during the Nationalist era; the central city of Xi'an, cultural center and capital during the Han and Tang dynasties; and the hinterland city of Lanzhou, in the province of Gansu. Survey questions focused on students' career goals and interests, and collated data about the educational level of both their parents and grandparents. One of the striking findings was the degree and rapidity of social change in terms of educational opportunity in all three cities, but most notably in the hinterland. About 52% of students in Nanjing had grandfathers who had been peasants, while the figure for Xi'an was 63% and for Lanzhou it was 64%. Of students' mothers, 33% in Nanjing, 45% in Xi'an and 53% in Lanzhou were peasants. Of their fathers, 20% in Nanjing, 25% in Xi'an and 38% in Lanzhou were peasants (Moody 1995).

To a large extent, those who built China's modern educational system and wrote the texts that explained it to the younger generation were individuals who had found a way from rural impoverishment and ignorance into the new opportunities provided by the modernizing educational system in the early 20th century. Most of the scholars whose stories will be told in this paper fit this picture, with three having fathers with very low levels of education and employment, and two having grandfathers who lived in rural poverty. Only one came from a family with several generations of a relatively privileged cultural background.

The choice of six life stories for this first effort to introduce biography into the study of Chinese education is obviously linked to my own personal network of connections in China. Each of the six are persons I have known for close to a decade, and with whom relations of mutual respect and cooperation have developed over time. There is thus the essential basis of trust necessary for the sharing of a life, and, equally, elements of my own life story emerged as our pathways crossed. Each has made distinguished contributions to educational thought and development in their own right, and each has been associated, for the most of their lifetime, with a major university in a different city and region of the country. While the focus is on their own lives, some attention will also be given to their affiliated universities and regions, thus bringing a comparative dimension in terms of institutions and regions.

One of the most difficult questions has been where to begin, and how to organize the life story material. My decision was to start with a brief picture of each scholar's present standing in each of the six institutions, so that the reader will get some sense of why it may be worthwhile to hear their life stories. From there the paper turns to childhood and the influence of family and schooling in the period before 1949. Then each scholar's career under socialism from 1949 to 1978 is described, along with their assessment of how education was influenced by the major movements that shaped China's development over this period. The final section deals with the perspectives they developed in the period after 1978, when Deng Xiaoping's reforms provided conditions for an opening up to "modernization, the world and the future." For each of them, this was a time when they were finally given space for rich professional contributions to China's development.

1   An Introduction to the Scholars, Their Institutions and Regions

1.1   *Li Bingde and Northwest Normal University*
Professor Li Bingde, the oldest of the six scholars, has been associated, since 1952, with Northwest Normal University in Lanzhou, Gansu, an important city in the Northwest region of China that encompasses three provinces and two autonomous regions. Northwest Normal University was founded in 1939, when Beijing Normal University escaped from the Japanese occupation of Beijing and moved to the Northwest for the whole period of the Sino-Japanese and Second World Wars. In 1952, under the Soviet style reorganization of the whole higher education system, it was made the major national level normal university for the whole Northwest region. In 1958, however, its name was changed to Gansu Normal College and it was placed under Gansu province. Later Shaanxi Normal University in Xi'an took up the role of the leading normal university under the national ministry of education for the Northwest region.

In spite of the ups and downs of the institution, Professor Li Bingde still holds the only center for doctoral training in education for the whole region; since the early 1980s he has guided the training of numerous master's and doctoral students in education. His doctoral graduates hold important positions in Beijing and Shanghai, as well as in the Northwest and Southwest of China. The first Tibetan to get a doctoral degree in education in China is among his graduates, and he has been responsible for numerous minority students at the master's level in education.

Li has authored a number of national level textbooks that have had a wide influence, including *Research Methodology in Educational Science* (1986) and

The Theory of Teaching and Learning (1991). In 1987, Shanghai Intellectual Press published an anthology on "Problems in the strategy of socialist economic and scientific development" which included an article by Li Bingde on educational strategies along with articles by the scientist Qian Weichang and the anthropologist Fei Xiaotong on other dimensions of China's development. Li thus stands alongside the most distinguished of an older generation of intellectuals. Li's family of four daughters and one son has been honored by the province as an "education family." Two daughters are university professors and have spent much of their careers teaching biology and chemistry in universities in Lanzhou. His son is a professor of engineering, formerly vice president of the Lanzhou Railway College, then vice commissioner for education in Gansu province, and most recently was elected vice governor of the province.

At eighty-eight years old, Professor Li is the most revered figure in education in the Northwest region. He continues to teach and guide the research work of graduate students, as well as taking a lively interest in educational developments in rural schools in the area. While Northwest Normal University is a provincial level institution, and thus not in the same league as such national level institutions as Lanzhou University, it plays a crucially important role in training teachers for the province and the region, and has a nationally funded center for the training of minority teachers for the Northwest region.[2]

One small vignette which may give readers a sense of the person can be sketched from a conversation he held with me in Toronto in October of 1992, when he had come to speak at a major conference we had organized on "Knowledge Across Cultures,"[3] and to confer over our joint program for training doctoral students in China and Canada that allowed twelve Canadian doctoral students to do research in six universities in China and twenty-two Chinese doctoral and postdoctoral students to do research in Canada. Four young faculty members from Northwest Normal participated in the program, and two continue to teach at the university, while the other two have moved to Beijing and Guangdong respectively. During the conference, Professor Li challenged me to plan for a new project of collaborative research to follow the completion of this project in 1995. When I replied that I hoped to take sabbatical leave and have some time for rest and personal research after the completion of this arduous six-year effort, he looked at me and said, "I have

---

2   During a visit to Lanzhou, I held two lengthy interviews with Professor Li Bingde, on May 8 and 12, 1998. Professor Li later read the manuscript, and made some factual corrections.

3   The conference papers, including a plenary address by Li Bingde, were published in both English and Chinese in *Knowledge Across Cultures: Universities East and West* [*Dongxifang daxue yu wenhua*] (Hayhoe et al. 1993).

never taken a sabbatical in the whole of my scholarly career!" Enough said. From that moment I began planning a second major project of collaboration that ran from 1996 to 2001!

1.2   *Zhu Jiusi and the Huazhong University of Science and Technology*

From the far Northwest, we move to Wuhan, the dominant city of the Central South region of China that encompasses six provinces and stretches from Henan province in the north, down to Guangdong province and Hainan island in the south. Wuhan is located at a strategic point between hinterland and coast on the Yangtze River, and through it runs the major railway line from Guangzhou, in the south, to Beijing and the Northeast. When the Central South region was created as a major administrative region in 1950, it was decided to locate a large number of national universities in this city, serving the whole nation and the region in the specialists they trained. The Huazhong Institute of Technology was newly created in 1953, at the time of the nationwide restructuring of higher education along Soviet lines, on the basis of engineering departments brought together from five older institutions in the region, including Wuhan University, Hunan University, Nanchang University in Jiangxi province, Guangxi University and South China engineering college in Guangzhou.

It was a fairly specialized institution, focusing on four areas of engineering which were important for socialist construction, including mechanical engineering, diesel and auto engineering, electrical engineering and power engineering. Although it was located in an important industrial center and placed under the administration of the Ministry of Higher Education, giving it a relatively high status within the overall higher education system, this alone could not account for its remarkable development into a leading university of science and technology, and also a leading comprehensive university, in the late seventies and early eighties. When the Ministry of Education decided to create a small number of schools of graduate study in 1982, four years after Deng Xiaoping launched the movement for modernization, opening up and reform in 1978, Huazhong University of Science and Technology (HUST) was one of only twenty-two universities nationwide deemed to have the academic standing and maturity to establish a school of graduate studies. In subsequent years, it was often placed in the top ten to fifteen universities in nationwide evaluative listings for its excellence in research.

One of the key reasons for this remarkable achievement lies with a visionary administrator and scholar who held important leadership positions at HUST from its founding in 1953, until his retirement in 1984, Professor Zhu Jiusi. First appointed vice chairman of its preparatory committee in 1952, he was made vice president in 1955, vice party secretary in 1956, party secretary in 1961, and party secretary and president from 1972 to 1984. Finding time for deep reflection on the past and future in a lacuna of time created by the Cultural Revolution, when most academic staff and students had been sent down for physical labor in the countryside, he developed a compelling vision for an institution that would give research equal importance with teaching, that would draw in the best talent that could be found throughout the nation, and that would become more and more comprehensive in its curricular offerings, bringing basic science, humanities and social sciences in to broaden its specialist orientation towards the applied sciences. As a result, this university gained tremendous respect nationally, and Zhu's policy advice and writings on higher education, including two edited books and many journal articles, had a definitive influence on national higher education policy in the reform period. In 1996, HUST's Higher Education Institute was given the right to establish a doctoral program in higher education administration.

In my own research on Chinese higher education and its burgeoning new developments in the early eighties, I quickly became aware of the important research being done by HUST's Institute of Higher Education Research, and the widespread influence of its scholarly journal on higher education. While I had heard Professor Zhu speak, in the autumn of 1988, at a meeting on higher education reform held at Nanjing University, my first opportunity for a personal meeting with him came in the spring of 1992, when I was engaged in a collaborative research project with members of HUST's Institute of Higher Education. I asked if he could give me his inside view of how HUST had achieved its standing as a nationally leading university, and what were the most important elements in the overall reform of higher education in China after 1978. Professor Zhu agreed to share his thoughts on this subject, and a time was set aside for our meeting. Once this was known to colleagues in the Institute of Higher Education, I was asked if I would mind of some of them also sat in on the interview, in order to hear his account.

The original plan had been for a meeting of about two hours, but this was extended into three meetings on subsequent days, lasting well over two hours each. In addition to myself, about 15 members of the Institute sat enthralled, listening intently as Professor Zhu shared the thinking that had inspired him to set HUST on a new direction in the early 1970s, and that had resulted in it becoming a beacon for fundamental reforms in higher education throughout China after 1978.[4] This was one of those moments when I suddenly got a deep

---

4   The content of this talk was later published under the title "Lishi de huigu" ("A retrospect of history") (Zhu 1992, 1–12).

insight into patterns of change that had interested me for a long time. The openness which Zhu Jiusi demonstrated over those hours, in sharing both his life experience and his deep thoughts and feelings, was a gift to be treasured, and an inspiration for this present project of linking up the life experience of China's influential educators, with the educational thought and practice of contemporary China.[5]

1.3   *Pan Maoyuan and Xiamen University*

From the city of Wuhan and the Central South, we move to the East China region, and the city of Xiamen in the south of Fujian province, opposite to the island of Taiwan. This region is made up of the prosperous east coast provinces of Shandong, Jiangsu, Zhejiang and Fujian, as well as the poorer inland provinces of Anhui and Jiangxi, and has been in the forefront of change during the period since 1978. Xiamen was designated one of four special economic zones in 1984, and given certain advantages in terms of foreign investment and development along with fourteen other coastal cities. The intellectual and economic center of the region is Shanghai, where a large number of major national universities are found, and the cities of Nanjing, Jinan, and Hangzhou are also important centers for higher education. The geographical location of Xiamen, in the southernmost part of the region and a twenty-two-hour train ride from Shanghai, has made it somewhat isolated in spite of its prosperity.

Xiamen University was founded in 1921 as a private university, funded by a Fujian native who had become a successful businessman in Southeast Asia and who wanted to help his own community—Mr. Chen Jiageng. It has a spectacular location, along the seafront, facing Taiwan, and its historical buildings reflect the generosity of the donor. In 1937, it became a national university supported by the Nationalist government, and soon thereafter had to move to Zhangting in Fujian province to escape the Japanese invasion. In 1946 it moved back to Xiamen. The fact that it was selected as one of two universities to become national comprehensive universities in the south eastern part of China under the Soviet model in 1952 indicates the high intellectual standing it had achieved over the years (the other being Zhongshan University in Guangzhou). In spite of his adherence to radicalism and revolutionary transformation, Mao Zedong invited Mr. Chen Jiageng back in the 1950s, in order to gain further support for the university and for a number of secondary schools in the region.

---

5   Details of Professor Zhu's childhood and growing up in the period before 1949 were shared in an interview held on November 18, 1999. Professor Zhu subsequently reviewed this manuscript, and made some factual corrections to the text in September of 2000.

Pan Maoyuan, the third of the scholars profiled in this essay, has been associated with Xiamen University throughout his career.[6] A graduate of its education faculty in 1945, and a lecturer there at the time of the revolution of 1949, he was asked by the president to stay on at a time when the whole education faculty was moved to Fujian Normal University. He was charged with the task of preparing education courses for science students in some specialties, so that they could become future teachers. He was also invited to preside over a total rethinking and re-development of the higher curriculum.

Beginning in 1956, Pan put forward the view that higher education required a set of theories distinctive from primary and secondary education, the field in which he had had his professional development. He got the idea of establishing China's first institute for higher education research. He now presides over this institute, which has master's and doctoral students from many different regions of China, and has produced an extensive scholarly literature that leads the field in China. Altogether he has graduated sixteen doctoral students and about eighty master's students, almost all of whom are working in various parts of China.

When I visited the university in December of 1997, in order to give some lectures and to carry out an extensive interview with Professor Pan, I was fortunate to be invited to the "salon" he holds every Saturday evening, in his house high up on a hill within the Xiamen University campus. His large and spartan study, on the second floor of the house, was lined with bookcases, and furnished with a sofa and extra chairs brought in for the occasion. About twelve graduate students from different regions of China, including Xiangtan University in a rural part of Hunan, Yantai Normal College in Shandong, and Hebei University two hours south of Beijing, had gathered for an exciting evening of debate and discussion. The focus on this particular evening was on an article written by one of the graduate students that critically attacked a sociological perspective on education put forth by a leading scholar in Nanjing because its premises totally excluded the functions of higher education as a field. This student was preparing a response to the published comments made by the Nanjing scholar on the critique. Hours passed in passionate and lively arguments put forward by various students, with an occasional interjection by Professor Pan, bringing everyone back to the core issue that had started the evening's event.

---

6   Most of the information here was collected in two lengthy interviews with Professor Pan Maoyuan, in Xiamen, December 6 and 8, 1997. Professor Pan later read the manuscript and made corrections to it.

1.4   *Xie Xide and Fudan University*

From Xiamen, we move to Shanghai and Fudan University, one of China's most prestigious comprehensive universities and the leading institution of the East China region. Founded in 1905 by a patriotic Chinese scholar in protest over French domination in the Catholic University, Zhendan or L'Aurore, Fudan developed as a private university up to 1941, when it was made a national university by the Nationalist government. Its leadership of the May 4th Movement in the Shanghai educational community gave it a high profile for patriotism and political activism and its teaching programs tended to be highly relevant to Shanghai's commercial and business needs during the 1920s and 1930s. It was less well known for high standards of scholarship in the pre-1949 period, but was designated a leading national comprehensive university by the new Communist government in 1950. Some of the best departments of basic sciences and humanities from other universities in the region, such as that of the famous Zhejiang University in Hangzhou, and also those of former missionary universities, such as St. Johns and Hu Jiang, were moved there.

In 1978, a distinguished physicist at Fudan University, Xie Xide, was appointed vice president with a particular responsibility for the university's burgeoning international relationships. From 1980 to 1982, I had the privilege of serving as a foreign expert under her leadership, a period which I treasure as a turning point in my own intellectual life. In 1983, she was made the first woman president of a major comprehensive university in China, a position she held until 1988. During those years Fudan broadened its programs far beyond the patterns left from the Soviet period, including the development of a school of management, a school of life sciences and a school of economics. Xie Xide emerged as a leading spokesperson for the intellectual community, both within China through her service on the Party Central Committee and internationally through her leadership of a number of major World Bank projects responsible for upgrading Chinese higher education in collaboration with major institutions in the West.

In 1992, we invited her to give a keynote address at an international conference on "Knowledge Across Cultures: Universities East and West" at the Ontario Institute for Studies in Education in Toronto, and she graciously agreed to come and speak on historical developments in Chinese higher education at our opening session. Two or three months before the conference, after all detailed arrangements had been made, she discovered that a once in five-year Party Congress would be held in Beijing close to the same date, and hesitated over whether she would be able to come after all. As it turned out, her status with colleagues in the Party was such that she was able to miss several important preparatory sessions in order to keep her promise to give our keynote lecture, and then fly from Toronto to Beijing just in time to play her role in the Congress itself. Two years later, in June of 1994, she came to Canada once again, this time to receive an honorary doctorate from McMaster University in Hamilton, where her outstanding achievements as a leading scientific figure were recognized.[7] The Chinese intellectual community and many international friends and colleagues felt a deep sense of loss when Xie Xide passed away from breast cancer in February of 2000, a disease she had fought bravely since its first onslaught in the dark days of the Cultural Revolution.

1.5   Wang Yongquan and Peking University

Our fourth institution, Peking University, reigns over the rest of Chinese higher education from its beautiful campus in the Northwest suburb of the capital Beijing, with its Nameless Lake and the classical Chinese architecture erected by culturally sensitive American missionaries in the 1920s and 1930s for Yanjing University. Founded in 1898 as the Imperial University, Peking University succeeded in combining some of the best features of German and French traditions with Chinese progressive scholarship under its distinguished chancellor, Cai Yuanpei, between 1917 and 1923. The May 4th Movement of 1919, which electrified and forever transformed cultural, educational and intellectual life in China, started there. No other institution has had its destiny intertwined with that of the country to such a degree.

Under the Soviet influences of the early fifties, Peking University was made the sole and supreme comprehensive university in the capital, and in many ways reflected Cai's German-influenced vision for the university as a center of pure arts and sciences. Its faculty of education was moved to the Beijing Normal University, while engineering, medicine and agriculture were also moved to other institutions.

In the mid-1980s, Professor Wang Yongquan, the Provost of Beida, as the university is also known, and the fourth scholar who will be profiled in this paper, established an Institute for Higher Education Research which became the second center for doctoral and master's degree study in higher education after that of Xiamen University. Its affiliation with China's leading institution has meant the capacity to attract some of the brightest and best students from the whole nation to study in this Institute and enabled it to play a leading

---

7   Interviews were held with Professor Xie Xide on October 16 and 17, 1998, in Shanghai, and an earlier draft of this paper was sent to her in September of 1999 for her review. It is not known whether or not she found the opportunity to read the draft before her untimely death of cancer in March of 2000. However, the author has read a biography (Wang 1993) she approved, and found corroboration for most of the details she shared in the two interviews there. The biography was also helpful for minor corrections to this text.

role in higher education research. A physicist and radio engineer by training, Professor Wang's whole professional life has been intertwined with the life of this leading university.[8]

In May of 1998, Peking University celebrated its 100th anniversary, with a series of commemorative events that brought back 60,000 graduates, and attracted presidents of more than 100 universities from all over the world. The foremost ceremony was held in the Great Hall of the People, where 10,000 people gathered in the presence of President Jiang Zemin, Premier Zhu Rongji, and all of the nation's top leaders, who showed their respect in this way for this premier intellectual institution and its role in the strategy of "Education and Science to revitalize the nation." A university presidents' seminar was organized by members of the Higher Education Research Institute, and overall responsibility for all of the commemorative events lay with the executive vice president, Min Weifang, a former Director of the Research Institute and a former graduate student of Wang Yongquan. In the informal seminar for visitors from Hong Kong held at the Institute on May 4th, Professor Wang presided as a serene director emeritus, confident that this research institute was now well established and able to carry forward the Beida spirit of scholarship in its work on higher education.

1.6   *Lu Jie and Nanjing Normal University*

Professor Lu Jie, the youngest of the six scholars profiled in this paper, was born in 1930, one year after Wang Yongquan. Her whole career has passed at Nanjing Normal University in Nanjing, a provincial level university for teacher education that is one of the few to have a national reputation for excellence in education and other fields in basic arts and sciences. One of the reasons for this is its strong historical foundation. As the premier educational institution in Jiangsu province, a province renowned from the early part of the 20th century for the progressive thinkers in education which it spawned and its many experiments in progressive education, it drew together some of the best scholars in China. The first president after 1949 was Chen Heqin, China's most renowned scholar in early childhood education. Chen had studied with John Dewey at Columbia University and returned to China in the 1920s. In the early 1980s, Lu Jie was the first female professor to be formally recognized as qualified to recruit and supervise doctoral students in education (*bodao*).

---

8   An interview was held with Professor Wang Yongquan on May 3, 1998.

She has a pre-eminent professional standing in the field and has brought much honor to Nanjing Normal University.[9]

The university is located on the campus of the former American missionary institution, Jinling Women's College, and its graceful Chinese style buildings, yellow in color, grouped around a lovely quiet central yard, remind one of the heritage of China's own scholarly and artistic sensitivities. In 1996, Lu Jie convened an international conference on Chinese culture and education, attracting scholars of Chinese background from around the world, and focusing on the special contribution Chinese thought and culture can make to contemporary education. The papers from this conference have recently been published, and provide a rich repository of ideas that have relevance beyond the borders of "Greater China" (Lu 1999). In a sense they reveal a China that has finally "come of age" after more than a century of trauma, and is able to make its own unique contributions to the international world of education.

Lu Jie herself has been a leader in the field of moral education, and has made substantial contributions to thought and theory around rural educational development, an aspect of education that has tended to be neglected yet is crucially important, given that eighty percent of the children of China's schools live in rural areas. A sociologist by training, she has devoted her whole life to both the theory and practice of education, and to the development of Nanjing Normal University.

This first section of this paper has provided a brief introduction to each of the scholars, their institution and their region. In every case their individual destiny was closely linked to that of their institution, a pattern that is common in China over the latter half of the twentieth century. In the next section I turn to their early lives, hoping to illuminate the early experiences in the family, in school, and in a turbulent and changing social context that shaped their educational ideas, and contributed to their development into educators of influence. How did they integrate early learning experiences, in regions and circumstances that differed greatly for each of them, in such a way as to be able to make a difference in the institutions they led, and in the teaching, research and writing they undertook?

---

9 Two interviews were held with Professor Lu Jie on October 14 and 15, 1998. She was subsequently given a copy of the first draft of this paper, and made some minor factual corrections.

2   Early Lives: Family and Schooling

The oldest of the six scholars, Li Bingde, was born in 1912, the year after the
1911 Revolution, while the second, Zhu Jiusi, was born four years later in 1916.
The third, Pan Maoyuan, was born in 1920, the year after the May Fourth
Movement of 1919, and the fourth, Xie Xide was born one year later in 1921. The
fifth, Wang Yongquan, was born in 1929, the year after the Nationalist government was established in Nanjing and the sixth, Lu Jie, was born one year later
in 1930.

Each of these three periods represented an important turning point for education in China's modern history. In the years after the 1911 Revolution, efforts
were made to establish republican forms of education, and move away from
the Japanese influences that had dominated the period from 1900 to 1911. The
early twenties, after the May 4th movement, saw strong interest in progressive
ideas in education, and considerable American influence, with the visit of John
Dewey and other American educators, and the return of many young Chinese
scholars who had studied in the United States. However, political disunity and
economic problems stood in the way of effective educational development.
The period after 1928 saw a renewal of effort to develop a national system of
education, with considerable influence from Europe and the League of Nations
Institute of Intellectual Cooperation, but this was disrupted by Japanese hostil-
ity beginning in the early 1930s.

In the accounts of the early life and education of each of the six scholars
that follow, we will see how they were affected by the educational conditions
and spirit of the time, and the ways in which family and school influences
shaped their early years.

2.1   *Li Bingde: Growing Up in Henan, 1912–1949*

Li Bingde was the eldest of four in a very poor family in the city of Luoyang,
Henan province. His father had no land, no established profession and no
house, but managed to eke out a living with part time jobs doing accounts
on the abacus. He had studied for a few years in a traditional *sishu*, or private
school, and loved to read so much that when he had to go out to work at an
early age, he put all his books together in one place, and cried because he could
not continue to study. He was therefore greatly concerned that his children
should have an education. Li's mother came from a peasant family and was
illiterate, but a very good person, kind and warm.

Li started primary school in 1919, the year of the May 4th movement. He
went to a traditional private school, a *sishu*, which cost three dollars at the
end of a year. Before long this private school became a government primary

school, and from there he went on to a government lower secondary school in Luoyang. Henan was a part of the country that was greatly disturbed by fighting among warlords during the 1920s, and Li remembers poor teaching constantly interrupted by outbreaks of fighting among warlords. When school could not open, Li studied at home with his father, reading the Four Books of the Confucian canon, as well as the Book of Odes and the Book of History. His father was often out of work so was able to make up for what the school could not offer, at home.

After three years of lower secondary school, Li was eager to go on to upper secondary, but there were no schools at that level in Luoyang. In neighboring Kaifeng, however, there was an excellent upper secondary school attached to Henan University, and he was able to gain entry to that school through passing examinations against stiff competition. The fees were twelve dollars a year and there were also costs of food and lodging, 59 Chinese yuan for a term, as well as travel, with the train ride from Luoyang costing over 3 yuan each way. In addition to worrying about his own expenses, Li had three younger brothers, all as eager to study as himself, and he felt responsible to take care of them.

This problem was quickly solved when he found a job teaching English in a private secondary school for 12 yuan a month, as well as doing individual tutoring. With these earnings, he was able to cover his own expenses and help his brothers study. In upper secondary school he chose to study humanities, purely by chance, as he did not understand the difference between humanities (*wen*) and science (*li*), when he was asked which entry examination he preferred to take. He was warned on entry to the school that if he failed two subjects or more, he would be kicked out, so he studied extremely hard. His English teacher, an American-born Chinese who could speak a little Ningpo dialect, but did not speak Mandarin and thus did all of his teaching in English, inspired him to work very hard in that subject. He also did extremely well in math, and passed all subjects. On entering university, after two years in upper secondary, he decided to choose English as his major field, and education as his minor field. He felt that he could study literature and history on his own. After one year in university, he decided to change to education as his major field and take English as a minor field. He felt very strongly the need to have a profession, as well as an area of specialist knowledge; also he felt that he would never be as good at English as native speakers.

In the years at Henan University, both in the upper secondary preparatory school and at the tertiary level, he was inspired by some excellent teachers. Generally, American returned Chinese scholars dominated. He had vivid memories of Tai Shuangchiu, who had returned with a PhD from Columbia University and had worked under John Dewey. Not long after returning, Tai had changed from Western clothes to traditional Chinese clothes, emulating his friend Tao Xingzhi, and in his impassioned lectures on educational reform to save the country he made use of newspaper articles and contemporary events for illustration. Often the tears flowed down, as he lectured on "a way out for China through education." These passionate lectures were decisive for Li Bingde, in shaping his decision to make education his lifelong pursuit.

On graduation from Henan University in 1934, Li had such good marks that he applied to the provincial education bureau for a job as principal of a provincial secondary school. He soon discovered that such positions only went to those with high-level connections. Instead he took up a position as a rural primary school principal in a lower primary school three miles from Kaifeng, that was part of an experimental district managed by one of his professors, Li Lianfang, who was following the ideas of the Belgian educator, Decroly. He thought it would be a very simple job, but he found it to be extremely demanding, preparing the teachers and materials for an experimental approach that was to have primary school children master Chinese reading and mathematics in two and a half years, rather than the normal four years. This was the beginning of a life-long interest in educational experimentation for Li, and the results achieved in this experimental school attracted considerable interest from scholars such as Jiang Wenyu, Meng Xiancheng and Huang Yanpei, who visited. Huang wrote an influential article in *Dongfang Zazhi* describing the experiment.

After two years working in this rural experimental school, Li saw an advertisement in the intellectual newspaper, *Dagong Bao*, which caught his eye. The Rockefeller foundation was offering five scholarship places for graduate study at Yanjing University in Beijing. There were also parallel programs in medicine at Union (Xiehe) Medical College, in economics at Nankai University and in agriculture at Jinling University in Nanjing. It was a five-year program in all, with two years of study for a master's degree, followed by a year in the United States, then two years to work in the famous Ding Xian experimental site run by James Yan Yangchu.

Li was thrilled to have a scholarship of 600 dollars, plus 300 dollars in travel money, which enabled him to live well and support his younger brothers. He completed all his course work in 1936 and 1937, then used the travel money to visit as many experimental educational sites as possible. He started with Liang Shuming's rural education site in Zouping County, Shandong, then went to Ding Xian in Hebei and Tao Xingzhi's Xiao Zhuang School in Nanjing. From there he continued south to Guangzhou, Guangxi and finally Hong Kong. At this point the Japanese invasion disturbed all of his plans—it was impossible to return to Beijing.

In observing and reflecting on these different cases of rural experimental work in education, Li felt that Liang Shuming's efforts were entirely based on traditional Chinese ideas, Yan Yangchu's were drawn from his work in France and from Western thinking, while Tao Xingzhi was most successful in integrating Western and Chinese ideas. Li felt that all three were linking their educational work with broader political change, and there was genuine educational value in what they were doing, in contrast to the empty talk of many of the American returned Chinese scholars teaching at Henan University.

After a summer of travel, Li returned to Henan and found a job in the provincial teacher training school, from 1937 to 1941, training primary school teachers. When that institution had to close due to the Sino-Japanese War, he took up a position as inspector for the provincial education bureau in Hubei for 8 months, and then was appointed associate professor at Henan University. Although this meant a significant drop in salary from 380 to 260 Chinese yuan a month, he took it with alacrity, as he had always wanted to teach in the university. From 1941 to 1945, Henan University operated in a remote rural village in Song county, two days' travel through difficult countryside from Luoyang, and Li took his whole family there with him. His fourth child and only son was born in a tiny hamlet during a difficult journey, as the university had to move even farther inland to escape Japanese incursions.

As soon as the war was over, the university moved back to its campus in Kaifeng, and Li's eye was once more caught by a new opportunity. The Nationalist ministry of education in Nanjing was offering 100 full scholarship places for study abroad, and another 1,000 places for self-funded study abroad. He was successful in getting a full scholarship to go to Switzerland, while two of the three brothers he had helped through school secured places to USA, under other scholarships. All three were to return and make distinguished contributions to education, medicine and science in China.

In Switzerland, Li went first to the University of Lausanne, where he attended a range of lectures, and once a week was able to hear a major lecture by Jean Piaget, who came over from Geneva once a week to teach. During his year in Lausanne he lived with a local family, and took the opportunity of visiting local schools. In 1948 he went to the University of Paris for 4 months, and then returned to the University of Geneva, where Piaget was dean of the Institute Jean Jacques Rousseau. The major attraction for him was vice dean Dottren, who was a specialist in educational experimentation, the field of his greatest interest. Yet he felt the opportunity to attend lectures by Piaget over a two-year period introduced another dimension to his understanding of educational psychology, which had been dominated by American scholarship such as the ideas of Thorndike and Gates up to this time.

Before returning to China in 1949, he went Paris once again, then visited England, the Netherlands, Belgium and Italy, pursuing his interest in learning patterns and educational experimentation. He arrived back in China just days after the formal establishment of the People's Republic, in early October of 1949.

2.2   *Zhu Jiusi: Growing Up in Jiangsu and Joining the Revolution 1916–1949*

Zhu Jiusi was born in 1916, five years after the 1911 revolution, in the city of Yangzhou in southern Jiangsu province, a city with strong cultural traditions in a province known for its leadership in progressive education. Because of its location at the point where the imperial canal crossed the Yangzi River, it had been relatively well developed economically since the Tang dynasty. Zhu's father was a small businessman who had started out as an apprentice in a shop and who was later able to open his own small shop selling clothing. His mother could recognize some Chinese characters and was familiar with traditional stories, but was unable to read Chinese texts for comprehension. He was the youngest of a family of four, with an older sister and two older brothers, one of whom died at the age of 18. His father and surviving brother had the greatest influence on his early educational experiences.

As was common at the time, he had his early education in a traditional private school or *sishu*, where he memorized the Four Books of the Confucian canon, but never had any discussion or explanation of their content. The effect of memorization was to store this ancient wisdom in his mind for future reference and reflection. Later he felt the influences of Confucian thought in his development were considerable, due to this early experience of studying the classics. By contrast he had little exposure to Buddhism beyond finding Buddhist temples a pleasant location for play as a child, and even less to Daoism. Even in his phase of traditional education, neither Buddhist nor Daoist texts had played a role.

When he reached the age of ten, in 1926, Zhu's father decided to put him into a modern primary school. Every summer one of his cousins, the son of his mother's sister, used to return to Yangzhou and visit the family. This young man was studying at the famous Qinghua preparatory school, getting ready to go for higher studies in the United States, where he went in 1927. It was he who persuaded the elder Zhu to send his youngest son to a modern primary school. At the same time, father decided to give his son a new name, drawn from the Analects (*Lunyu*), the first of the Four Books in the Confucian canon. *Si jiu* means simply to think about (*si*) nine things (*jiu*), and these nine things, enumerated in the Analects, include listening carefully, observing carefully and seven other recommendations for good conduct which Zhu can no longer remember. Somehow this new name signaled a new beginning in his life. Because he had already learned some English, and mathematics, in the last year in the *sishu*, he was able to enter the first year of upper primary school, and graduate within two years, not needing to attend the four years of lower primary schooling.

On graduation from primary school in 1928, Zhu entered Yangzhou Secondary School, one of only three secondary schools in Yangzhou at the time. It was his own choice to study there, and he remarked how his family gave him complete freedom in the choice of which school he would attend, and which subjects he would study, much greater freedom than he feels most young people experience today in China, where parental choice plays a very strong role in young people's education. His six years at Yangzhou Secondary School turned out to be extremely important, laying a foundation in knowledge and academic orientation which had a profound influence on his thinking later, as a university leader and administrator.

The principal of Yangzhou Secondary School at the time had a master's degree from the Massachusetts Institute of Technology (MIT), and was a member of the Nationalist Party, a connection that enabled him to get high-level government support for the school. At the same time he never attempted to influence his students politically, but focused on academic excellence. He recruited teachers from all over the province, in order to get the very best, and put a strong emphasis on the effective learning of English by all students. For this purpose he regularly had an English newspaper, published in Shanghai, the *Dalu bao*, posted on the bulletin board where all students could read it. The leading English teacher was a graduate of Yanjing University in Beijing, an American missionary university known for its high standards in English. Equal emphasis was put on humanities and science in the school, and a special building was built to house science laboratories that made possible a strong emphasis on experimentation in the learning of science. The school also had an excellent library. Every year more than 100 students graduated, and most furthered their studies in the best universities in China. Yangzhou Secondary School had a nationwide reputation for excellence and was often regarded as the southern counterpart of the famous Nankai Secondary School in Tianjin. Nevertheless, because the school was funded by the provincial government, fees were low and Zhu's family was able to support him throughout the six years.

When he graduated from secondary school, however, his father felt it was impossible to provide the support that would be needed for him to undertake university studies. Rather, he contacted a relative who was head of the chemistry department at Zhejiang University (Zheda) in nearby Hangzhou, and arranged a clerical position for him at Zheda, where he could earn 20 yuan a month, and gain some experience of life in a university environment. The year was 1935, and the psychologist Guo Renyuan was president at the time. However, Guo had been so harsh and unreasonable in suppressing student activism that Chiang Kai-shek felt it best to replace him and appointed Zhu Kezheng to the presidency of Zheda later that year. Zhu Kezheng was an excellent choice, a distinguished scientist who had been recruited to the Academica Sinica by Cai Yuanpei some years earlier, he proved a dedicated university leader, insisting on greater financial support from the government and autonomy over all academic appointments as conditions of his acceptance of the presidency. In the years of the Sino-Japanese War, Zheda had to move to four different locations, but Zhu Kezheng had a powerful vision that enabled it to develop a remarkable degree of academic excellence under the most turbulent of wartime conditions.

Zhu felt his year working in a modest position at Zheda gave him much food for thought. He was extremely grateful to his remaining older brother for persuading his father, one year later in 1936, to support him in undertaking university studies. His father suggested that he go to the National Central University in Nanjing, just six hours away by boat on the imperial canal and the Yangzi River, but Zhu was determined to make a different choice, as he did not want to live in the national capital under the regime of Chiang Kai-shek. Once again, he was extremely grateful to his family for allowing him to make his own personal choice of Wuhan University, also an excellent national university, and enroll in its program in philosophy and education, with a minor in English.

Altogether, Zhu was to spend three terms as a student of Wuhan University. During the first year, he had five courses in education and philosophy, covering philosophical concepts, moral reasoning, educational psychology and educational principles. Only one of these courses, philosophical concepts, was intellectually challenging, and he still remembers the teacher, Fan Shoukang, using dialectical materialism in an effective way. The others were dull and poorly taught, simply a regurgitation of ideas from English language textbooks imported from abroad. By contrast, the teachers and courses taught in the foreign languages department were of higher quality, and this influenced Zhu to change to English as his major in the second year. He still remembers several excellent courses taken that year, including one in phonetics taught by Li Rumian, the content of which remains helpful to him now, sixty years later!

Overshadowing the experiences of his first year at university was a deep sense of national destiny that Zhu felt had occupied his mind ever since the

September 18th incident of 1931, when Japan began its incursions into Chinese territory. In his view, young people in China today are not able to grasp the influence that this incident, and the subsequent escalation of Japanese aggression, had on youth of his time. In his upper secondary years, he had done a lot of reading of literature and social theory that affected his thinking about university study, and his decision to avoid Nanjing at all costs. He became more and more aware of the activism of progressive students while working at Zhejiang University and was frustrated that he could not participate, since he did not enjoy the status of a student. Finally, as a student at Wuhan University, he was able to take positive action.

This is how it came about. In a basic course in Chinese literature taught by a very conservative lecturer during his first year, he had been criticized for progressive ideas expressed in an essay he submitted. The lecturer denigrated what he had written as a kind of "proletarian eight-legged essay" (*puluo bagu*). Deeply discouraged by these comments, Zhu showed the returned essay to a fellow classmate, who immediately introduced him to a group of about 40 progressive students who met secretly to discuss national affairs and what they could do to save their country. While this underground group had no formal connection to the Communist Party at the time, it did have links to progressive student groups throughout the country. One year later, in October of 1937, Zhu decided to join the Communist Party. The most important reason for his decision was the impact of the Japanese invasion on his thoughts and feelings. He felt only the Communist Party could give hope for China's future.

In November of 1937, Zhu received the last letter his brother was able to send him, a letter that enclosed 70 yuan from the family, and let him know that the Japanese had already entered Shanghai, and were expected in Nanjing and Yangzhou before long. There was a strong sense of impending disaster in the letter, yet his brother urged him to continue his studies, and follow the university inland when it was forced to move. From the moment he received this letter, Zhu was no longer able to concentrate on his studies. He made up his mind to apply to go to Yan'an, along with the other two students who had joined the Party, a decision he was required to keep secret, and could not communicate to his family. While he guessed his father and brother would not approve of his decision, he nevertheless felt a sense of their support and understanding.

In reflecting on the subsequent years, from 1937 to 1949, Zhu feels he was extremely fortunate to survive the difficult conditions of the Anti-Japanese and the Civil Wars. He always keeps in mind the many close friends and comrades who lost their lives over those years. He reached Yan'an in December of 1937 and spent a year there, first as a student of the Anti-Japanese Resistance University (*Kangri junzheng daxue*), known as Kangda, for six months, graduating in June of 1938, then as teacher of political education at Kangda for three months, and subsequently as counselor (*zhidao yuan*) in another section of the university. In December 1938, the decision was made that Kangda should establish two branch campuses in other bases behind enemy lines. The first was set up in the southeast of Shanxi province, and the other in Jin Cha Ji, a mountainous area of Hebei province, northeast of the City of Taiyuan and northwest of Shi Jia Zhuang. Zhu remembers the moment when Luo Ruqing, vice president of Kangda, read out the list of names of who would go to which place, and he was assigned to Jin Cha Ji. One went where one was told, with no discussion.

From 1939 to 1945, Zhu lived in this remote region in the mountains. For the first three years, he continued to teach in Kangda, giving courses on the history of the Chinese revolution and the history of social development to large groups of students, who sat on the ground in the village square—there was no building large enough for classes. Nor were there any books available for study purposes—all teaching materials had to be prepared from memory and experience. In 1942, Zhu was given a new assignment as a head of publicity in an area near the famous Ding County, where Yan Yangzhu had done so much literacy work, and thus where the cultural level of the peasants was quite high. In that year, he also finally felt able to write to his brother and ask for news of his family. He told them he was now a rural primary school teacher in Hebei, and he received word back that both parents had died that year.

In January of 1946, after the defeat of Japan, Zhu was appointed deputy editor of the daily *Qunzhong ribao*, and moved to Rehe. He had been invited to take up this role by Li Rui, editor in chief of the newspaper, who got permission from his superior in the army for his release. The following year, Li Rui sent him to Harbin to buy some materials for publishing, and there he met his future wife who followed him back to Rehe in the spring of 1947. They were married in January of 1948.

The People's Liberation Army reached Beijing in February of 1949, and Zhu had been appointed editor-in-chief of the Tianjin Daily (*Tianjin ribao*) under the direction of the Tianjin city Party committee from January to May of 1949. Subsequently he was sent to Changsha, first as vice editor-in-chief, and subsequently as editor-in-chief of the Hunan Daily newspaper, working under the provincial party committee from August of 1949 till December of 1952. During these years in journalism his role was mainly to ensure the dissemination of accurate information and political directives from the party, and there were relatively few opportunities to write analytic pieces himself. Nevertheless, he felt these years greatly broadened his perspective, causing him to reflect deeply on political, economic, cultural, military and agricultural concerns ranging from local to national and international arenas. From December of 1952 till

May of 1953, he was appointed the first vice head of the Hunan Education Department.

In May of 1953, he was informed of the decision that he should be transferred to Wuhan, where the newly established administration of the Central South region wished him to take up a leadership role in establishing the Huazhong Institute of Technology, along with Zha Qian, the first president. The Head of the Publicity Department for the region was familiar with his work and felt he would be suitable for this role. Again, there was no discussion of this new appointment and it was a matter of Party discipline for him to accept. But it was an opportunity he greatly welcomed.

So we leave Zhu Jiusi at this point, the only one of our six scholars who had lived and worked in Yan'an and other liberated areas before 1949, having a strong academic foundation, rich revolutionary experience and a significant career in higher education, journalism and publicity work. All of these varied experiences were to contribute to his efforts to build a university of distinction that would have a nation-wide influence, in the years from 1953 to 1984.

2.3   Pan Maoyuan: Growing Up in Southeast China 1920–1949

Pan Maoyuan was born in Shantou, a city on the northeast coast of Guangdong province, near Fujian, in 1920. His family was extremely poor, having neither land nor profession, similar to the family of Li Bingde. Only three of the ten children born to his parents survived to grow up, and the family at first could not afford to send him to school. He was taught to read by an older brother and his father, then, at age eight he was put into the third grade of a local primary school. The main content of the curriculum was traditional classical texts, beginning with the *Three Character Classic* (*Sanzi jing*). On finishing primary school, there was no possibility of further education and he was kept at home to help his father grind rice and make rice flour and cakes.

Fortunately, one of his teachers had noted his flair for writing and intervened at this juncture to help him get into lower secondary study in a Confucian school in Shantou, with an exemption from normal fees. He remembers that his teacher in this school had a *juren* qualification from the traditional civil service examination system. After completing lower secondary school at age fifteen, he was asked to teach in a primary school for some months, and this experience gave him a sense of how significant a teacher's work could be, also of how much he would have to learn if he wished to pursue teaching as a profession. He decided to enter an upper secondary school for training primary school teachers, Haibin Normal Secondary School in Shantou. He managed to pay the fees and support himself through teaching evening classes. On graduation he started teaching in a rural primary school. From 1937 to 1939, he threw himself into primary school teaching with great enthusiasm, but also found himself increasingly drawn to the Anti-Japanese War effort. He helped with organization and propaganda work and had connections with the underground work of the Communist party.

By 1940, he was drawn to further educational study, and decided to take the entry examinations for Xiamen University. It took him over a week of difficult travel through mountains to reach the university's new location, inland in Fujian near Jiangxi, where he took the examinations but failed to gain entry. Instead, he found his way into a provincial government program for primary school teachers of Chinese, and followed further studies there for a year. His background had been Chinese literature, and he had published numerous stories and articles. However, he knew the study of education was his greatest interest. A year later he applied again to Xiamen University and this time was accepted into its department of education.

In spite of the difficulties of the war years, he found the years of study from 1941 to 1945 to be wonderfully stimulating. Most of the professors were American returned Chinese scholars, and the chair of the department, Li Peiyou, had translated a number of Dewey's works into Chinese. Professor Chen Jingpan was on the faculty, a scholar who was later to spend many years at Beijing Normal University. In order to support himself while studying, Pan taught part-time, first in a primary school, later in a secondary school. During his fourth year of study at university, he was head of the teaching affairs section in the county middle school. He thus had constant opportunities to put everything he was learning into practice.

Pan felt that Dewey's educational ideas were very progressive and these years of study prepared him extremely well for his career in education. After he graduated in 1945, he taught briefly in county schools in Jiangxi. Xiamen University had meanwhile moved back to Xiamen and in 1946 he was invited by the president and the head of the education department to become principal of its attached primary school, while also working as a teaching assistant in the university's college of education. He found Tao Xingzhi's books most helpful in running the school and also made use of them in his teaching at the university. In this he concurred with Li Bingde, who felt Tao's ideas and writings best fitted China's education needs. Neither Pan nor Li ever met Tao in person.

We will leave Pan Maoyuan at this point, twenty-nine years old, a budding scholar of education, primary school principal and activist, ready for a whole new phase of his career at the time of the successful Communist Revolution of 1949.

2.4   *Xie Xide: Growing Up in Privileged Educational Circles 1920–1947*

Xie Xide was born just one year later than Pan Maoyuan, and they were des-tined to be students together at Xiamen University during the Japanese occupation of China. From every other perspective, however, her early years passed in a totally different environment than the impoverished and difficult situation in which Pan grew up. Her father had studied in the United States for many years, and held a master's degree from Columbia University and a PhD from the University of Chicago in Physics. She was born in 1921, and spent the first four years of her life at her mother's side in Xiamen, where her mother was a student of Xiamen University. Her mother died in 1925, and two years later her father returned from the United States and took her to Beijing, where he took up a teaching position at Yanjing University (the same institution where Li Bingde spent a year in graduate studies in 1936–37). Her father remarried, this time to a Yanjing graduate, and had three sons, her half-brothers growing up within the same family with whom she was very close.

It was a life of remarkable privilege, given the difficult times China was going through; a sheltered life in which she had the best possible educational opportunities. She attended the attached primary school of Yanjing University, and had many of her lessons taught in English, and gained, as well, a good foundation in Chinese. On completion of primary school, she was enrolled in the famous Bridgeman Academy, an exclusive private school for girls run by Christian missionaries, one of the oldest and best known of its kind. Both the teaching of English, and of science and mathematics, were at a very high standard.

In addition to these excellent school experiences, she received constant sup-port and encouragement from her father and stepmother. Her father was very traditional in his family values, in spite of the many years in the United States, and very much wanted his children to conform to his own patterns and bring honor to the family through their studies. He was thus very pleased when she chose to study physics, and prepared her from an early age to pursue advanced studies abroad. He also upheld her as an example to three younger brothers, all of whom pursued careers in various fields of engineering. While he was open-minded as a scholar and professor of physics, in many ways he retained the role of a Confucian father. He took an interest only in his children's studies, not wishing them to "waste time" on extra-curricular activities, and was deter-mined that they should stay away from student activism or any direct political involvement in the nation's affairs. While Xie Xide pleased him with her aca-demic choices, and successes, as she grew up, her life decisions diverged from the patterns he had laid down. One of the reasons for her independence of spirit may have lain in her educational experiences, and she felt her secondary education in a series of excellent girls' schools was particularly important.

When the Japanese invaded Beijing in 1937, Xie Xide was sixteen years old and only part way through her secondary education in the Bridgeman Academy. Along with her family, she had to escape Beijing, and she followed her father first to Wuhan, then to Changsha. For six months, she studied at St. Hilda's, a missionary school for girls in Wuchang, then subsequently completed her secondary education in the Fuxing Secondary School, a school for girls attached to the Yale in China missionary college in Changsha. She thus experienced three different missionary schools for girls, and she felt this gave her tremendous confidence in her own ability to make independent decisions and choices, also to prepare for a professional career as a woman. For her, the most crucial phase was upper secondary education, a period when girls tend to be overshadowed by the sudden rapid development of boys as they seek to overtake the girls in their classes in co-educational schools. In a girls' school, this is the period when a strong sense of self-confidence and preparedness for leadership is developed, she explained.

In 1938, when she graduated from secondary school at the age of 17, her father moved to Xiamen, and took up a teaching position at Xiamen University. She followed the family there, and for four years she had to rest at home, in order to recover from a severe attack of tuberculosis in the hip-joint, something that was to leave her slightly handicapped throughout her life. During this period of convalescence, the Japanese invasion reached southeast China, and Xiamen University had to move inland to Zhangting, a small town near the border of Jiangxi province, which was a secondary base for the Chinese Communist Party, their major base being in nearby Ruijin. It was a remote mountainous area, difficult to reach for the invading Japanese troops.

In 1942, Xie was able to begin her university studies in physics within the department of math and physics. There were only about six students majoring in physics, and they all shared one textbook borrowed from their professor. Conditions were extremely difficult but they did have electricity in the classrooms up to a certain hour in the evening, after which they studied by kerosene lamps. Pan Maoyuan was studying one year ahead of her, in the department of education, and she knew him and his wife well.

Generally the students at Xiamen University in those years were of very high standard, being students who fled there from excellent universities in Zhejiang, Jiangsu and Hubei when these areas fell under Japanese control. There was a very active student movement, with many students supporting the underground activities of the Communist Party. She was fully aware of this, but strongly influenced by her father's desire that she keep out of politics. She also refused to join any of the activities organized by the Nationalist Party's Youth organization on campus, the San Ching Tuan.

In 1946, Xie graduated from Xiamen University, while it was still in Zhangting, but was preparing to move back to Xiamen, where a new class of students was being recruited. With the help of her father's connections in the academic community she was able to obtain a position as teaching assistant in physics and math at Hu Jiang University in Shanghai, a missionary university affiliated with American Baptists, and there she prepared for the period of study abroad that had been a part of her career plans from an early age. She was successful in gaining a scholarship at Smith College, where she spent two years doing her master's degree, and from there she went to Massachusetts Institute of Technology, where she was able to complete her PhD in physics in a brief two and a half years, with a focus on semiconductors. On completion of the degree she stayed for another six months in order to do collaborative research with a group working in the area of solid-state physics.

As Xie moved through this important phase of her development as a scientist, differences of view with her father became more and more acute. He moved to the Philippines in 1946, where he taught at the Oriental University in Manila and later moved to Taiwan when he was unable to gain satisfactory residential status in the Philippines. From her high school days, she had a boyfriend who was also an excellent science student, and who went on to study at Yanjing University in Beijing and then followed it to Chengdu where it was combined with West China Union University during the Sino-Japanese War, graduating there in 1943. He got to know Dr. Joseph Needham, and had an opportunity to work with him in a collaborative scientific research center Needham had established, then gained a Sino-British scholarship to study chemistry at Cambridge University in 1946. Her father claimed to believe that marriage should be a matter of free choice, but in the case of his own children, it was a different matter. He did not approve of her boyfriend, and was only persuaded to give his permission to their engagement in 1946, when he learned of the scholarship to Cambridge and association with Dr. Joseph Needham!

A second and much greater conflict arose with her father over her decision to return to China, after completing the PhD at MIT. He wrote her many letters, begging her to stay in the United States, but she and her fiancé were determined to return to China. They had been corresponding between the two "Cambridges" for some years, and it was difficult for her to leave the United States for China in the Cold War atmosphere that existed. She was, however, able to get permission to visit England, with the help of Dr. Needham, and she and her fiancé were married in an Anglican church near Cambridge, whose vicar was known as a "red priest" for his socialist sympathies. Within a few months, the two returned to China on the Guangzhou Hao, arriving in Shanghai in 1952.

The decision to return to China, in spite of all the uncertainties and difficulties of the period, was never a matter of struggle or self-questioning, but somehow a natural choice. Both she and her husband wished to contribute the scientific expertise they had gained in the world's most prestigious universities to the development of their own country. It was only later, in 1956, that each separately made application to join the Chinese Communist Party, and discovered they had been accepted on the same day. The decision was linked to patriotism and a deep-rooted sense of Chinese identity.

Xie's father was never able to come to terms with her decision to develop her professional career in China, and refused to acknowledge any of the letters or parcels that she sent to him after returning to China. He died in Taiwan in 1986, having sent no communication to his only daughter over the 34 years that passed since 1952. However, it was a great comfort to her, when a friend brought some of his personal possessions to her after his death, to find that all of the photos she had sent, since the time of her marriage in 1952, had been kept by him over the years. He was a determined, even stubborn person, a Christian, but most of all a scholar. That was her characterization of him, as she reflected back over the years from the autumn of 1998. When she visited Taiwan for the first time in 1997, she felt some comfort in connecting to the region where her father had spent the last twenty years of his life, and where her grandfather had first taken him at a young age, in the late 19th century.

So we leave Xie Xide at this point, a highly qualified and dedicated young physicist, settling in Shanghai with her husband in 1952, both determined to use their knowledge and skill for the betterment of their country, and full of hope for a satisfying professional future. Her background and life story had been very different from that of Li Bingde, Zhu Jiusi and Pan Maoyuan, but her ambitions and commitments converged very closely to theirs, as they prepared for long years of service respectively at Northwest Normal University, Huazhong Institute of Technology, Xiamen University and Fudan University.

2.5   *Wang Yongquan: Growing Up in Beijing and the Hinterland 1929–1949*

Wang Yongquan, the fifth scholar in our narrative, was born in 1929, to a father who had grown up in an impoverished rural family, similar to that of Li and Pan, in rural Hubei. His father's brothers were all peasants but they had saved up to send him to a good secondary school near Wuhan in Hubei province, and from there he had been successful in entering Peking University. In about 1917, his father went to France, with the famous Work Study Movement [*Qingong jianxue*] of young people from working class families who supported their studies through labor in French factories. He studied philosophy and logic at the University of Lyons, and returned to China in 1925. Before leaving for France, he had married an illiterate young peasant woman, in a marriage arranged by the family, and had one daughter. On return, he and his wife lived in Shanghai until eight months after Wang Yongquan was born in 1929, then moved to Peking, where he taught at National Beiping University and the Université Franco-chinoise.

Wang has happy memories of his first seven years, living in an old-style courtyard house, with a mother who may have been illiterate but who was schooled enough in the Confucian virtues of politeness, sincerity and honesty to bring up her two children well and maintain a happy and harmonious marriage. His father was a strict Confucian, in spite of the many years studying Western philosophy. He emphasized the Confucian virtues of clear social hierarchy, filial piety, loyalty to ruler and country, sincerity with friends; he advocated strict demands upon oneself and a spirit of broadmindedness and forgiveness towards others. He saw Buddhism and Taoism as somewhat passive and negative, while Confucianism, in his view, showed the way to social harmony and well-being.

In 1937, when Wang was just eight years old, this peaceful family life was disrupted by the Japanese invasion and the Marco Polo bridge incident in Beijing. At this very time, Li Bingde had been cut off from his Rockefeller scholarship at Yanjing University, Zhu Jiusi had made his momentous decision to leave university and go to Yan'an, Pan Maoyuan had just started teaching in a rural primary school in Fujian, and Xie Xide was in her last year of secondary school. For eight-year-old Wang it meant the end of formal schooling for several years. His father hurried away from Beijing in order to avoid being pressed into service in a Japanese-controlled higher institution and the parting instruction to the children's mother was that the children were not to go to schools that were in Japanese hands.

For several years, Wang studied under his older sister at home, while waiting for the chance to rejoin his father. Father went from Wuhan to Guilin, to Kunming, where Wang and his sister and their mother joined him. He studied for one year in the secondary school attached to the Sino-French University, which had moved to Kunming along with Peking University, Qinghua and Nankai, the three that formed Southwest Associated University. In 1940, his father moved to Chongqing to teach at Sichuan University, and he studied at its attached secondary school. In both of these schools the teachers were associate professors in the university who gave some of their time to teaching in the secondary school. His memory was of excellent teaching, particularly in English, Chinese and mathematics. Some of his mathematics and science texts were in English, and he remembers one English teacher who had perfect mastery of the language and who introduced a whole culture, along with the language. He particularly remembers that teacher introducing Beethoven's Moonlight Sonata, and singing while teaching.

However, the school of life was in the end even more important, he felt. His mother took ill in Chongqing, and he stayed at home to do the shopping, cooking, washing and all household chores while his father crossed the river every day to go to his work at the university. His mother died in 1941, when he was only twelve years old. In retrospect that year was one of the most important in his education, as he had to be totally independent, and he gained the sense that there was nothing he could not do, given the way he had managed in these very difficult circumstances.

The following year Wang's father moved to Northwest United University in Shaanxi province near Hanzhong. Southwest United in Kunming had a philosophy department dominated by the returned group, and he was more comfortable with those influenced by European philosophy who had congregated at Northwest United University. In 1943 he married a professor of mathematics from Sichuan University, and Wang found her to be a wonderful stepmother. Wang particularly loved Chinese language and literature, and wanted to study in a classical academy or *shuyuan* after completing secondary education. However, his stepmother insisted that he learn something practical that would enable him to earn a livelihood, and keep his interest in Chinese literature as a hobby, something to be taken up in his spare time. As a result he took the examinations for Qinghua University in Beijing, and was accepted into the physics department in 1946, graduating in 1950. He lived on the Qinghua campus, and by this time his parents had also returned to live in Beijing and his father was teaching at Beida.

Wang had been educated to obey and be loyal to his family in the true Confucian spirit. He feels he had never been a rebel in any sense of the word. His family influence was more important than schooling in his overall development, and he kept a diary that was read by his parents, from time to time. Out of respect to his father, he did not join the Communist Party during his student years on the Qinghua campus, but studied hard and only attended some of the major demonstrations. He has particularly vivid memories of the debates that went on in December of 1948, just two months before Beijing was liberated by the Communist Party, over whether the Soviet Union was an imperialist or a socialist country. The conclusion of Qinghua students, at that crucial time, was that it was imperialist, but the question remained an open one and it was quite acceptable for some to maintain the other position. This student debate had been organized by the underground Communist Party group at Qinghua, and the difference between this even-handed approach in 1948, and the later insistence that everyone adopt the "correct" line was a striking one, in Wang's view.

When the People's Liberation Army liberated Beijing in February of 1949, Wang was in his last year at Qinghua University, about to graduate in physics. His father and stepmother had also returned to Beijing to teach in universities there. He was about to transfer the absolute loyalty to family that he had learned from his father, and that he saw as part of the Confucian value system, to the Communist Party that was now taking charge of China's future.

2.6   Lu Jie: Growing Up in Shanghai, 1930–1949

Lu Jie was born in Shanghai in 1930 to a family that was seen as privileged at the time, but that had overcome many odds to reach that position. Her grandfather grew up in rural Sichuan province, in the county town of Langzhong, twelve hours drive and many more hours by foot from the capital of Chengdu. A small businessman working under difficult circumstances, he had only one son, Lu Jie's father, who was left an orphan at an early age. Lu's father was able to study in Christian mission schools, and was such a good student that the missionaries wanted to train him for church leadership. He preferred medicine, but finally settled for education as his chosen field. During the First World War, along with other impoverished students from rural Sichuan he was able to go to France under the work-study movement which Wang Yongquan's father also joined. Working as a translator, he was able to save money for his further education. He returned to China right after the war, and with further help from the church, as well as his own savings, he was able to go to Columbia University for an MA program under John Dewey in education and psychology. During his years at Columbia he became good friends with both Chen Heqin and Tao Xingzhi.

Returning to China in 1922, he taught briefly at Zhejiang University in Hangzhou, and then settled at the private Da Xia University in Shanghai, where he was to spend his whole career, up to 1949. The beautiful campus of this university, in a western suburb of Shanghai, was given to the newly established East China Normal University in the early 1950s. It has since become one of China's leading institutions in education. Her father built his own house very near the campus in 1923, taking out a loan from the bank to pay the mortgage. The room in this large house that she remembers with great poignancy was the library, full of the many books that were his greatest delight.

Lu Jie's mother was also a very important influence in her life, and she came from a background quite different from that of her husband. Hers was a well-established Shanghai family that owned land and was very prosperous. She was educated at St. Mary's School, a girls' school associated with the prestigious St. John's University. Her parents planned to choose a husband for her, but she refused, remaining single until her late twenties, and pursuing a career as a private teacher. When she elected to marry a person from outside Shanghai (*waidi ren*), who had neither money nor land, the family was strongly opposed. They finally gave in, due to her new husband's professional standing as a university professor. Lu Jie felt that her mother's independence of mind and choice, which was quite unusual for a woman of her time, was an important element in her own development.

Family education was extremely important, and Lu Jie remembers her parents as being strict and putting great emphasis on the education of their three children—an eldest daughter, born in 1923, a son, Lu Ping, born in 1927, and Lu Jie, born in 1930. Their parents made it clear that they had the highest expectations of their education and they should study hard and improve themselves. While they held to traditional Confucian values in terms of respect for elders and family discipline, they were unusual in giving the three children absolute freedom over their career decisions, and other life choices. Her father's theories of education were strongly influenced by John Dewey, and this, together with her mother's independence of spirit, resulted in a remarkably liberal household for the times.

Lu Jie's early years were very happy ones, growing up in her father's large house and going to a progressive kindergarten on the university campus. She remembers starting to write characters with her mother's help at age 3, learning more during her year at kindergarten, then being sent to primary school at age five, along with other children of professors at the University, in one of the progressive schools founded by the Shanghai Municipal Council. Chen Heqin was principal of this school.

The Japanese invasion of Shanghai in 1937, when Lu Jie was just seven years old, shattered this idyllic childhood world. Her father's home was destroyed by the Japanese and the whole family had to take refuge in a tiny apartment within the international concession. Her father's beloved books were scattered in the homes of various friends and relatives, and never again was he able to have the luxury of his own personal study and library. Lu Jie noted how her brother, Lu Ping, who became famous as the Director of the Hong Kong Macao Office during the years leading up to Hong Kong's reunification with China in 1997, never accumulated a personal collection of books. This was because of the trauma associated with his father's loss in these early years.

During the Japanese occupation of Shanghai, her father elected to stay in Shanghai, while the university relocated to Guiyang, and to take responsibility for a school affiliated with Da Xia University that continued to function in

Shanghai. He was trusted with this task, she felt, because of the fact that he had been known as strongly committed to his profession, and totally non-political. It was a very difficult task, and she remembers vividly the day in which her father received a threatening letter from the Japanese authorities, demanding that he join other "Hanjian" (traitors to the Han) in cooperating with Wang Jingwei, the Japanese puppet governor. He immediately fled to Guiyang, waiting until he was sure their attention had been deflected from the Da Xia school, then returned to Shanghai.

The family remained in Shanghai throughout the war years, and Lu Jie was sent to a girls' Catholic school associated with L'Aurore (*Zhendan*), a French catholic university. The strict discipline of the nuns presented quite a contrast to her primary education in the progressive school run by Chen Heqin, but her parents felt this would be beneficial to her. The principal of the school, Yu Chingtang, was a famous educator, and there were numerous other Chinese teachers as well as the European nuns. Overall, she felt the influence of the church was a very positive one, with the sisters showing real care for the students, having tremendous patience and never getting angry.

During these years in secondary school, she saw the brutality of the Japanese and the various incidents of national protest, although she was too young to participate. She remembers seeing Japanese soldiers on horseback, attacking civilians in the streets. She also remembers how the school itself became a kind of internment camp for nuns from all different parts of the city after the Japanese attack on Pearl Harbor and the American entry into the war. At one point, the Japanese insisted that their language should be taught to students, and they sent a man to give them Japanese lessons. Within one week, he gave up because the students hated the lessons and refused to learn.

These years were very important for her in developing a strong sense of "*minzu*" or national identity. When the war was over, she remembers the celebration and relief, and joined with others in celebrating Chiang Kai-shek as a hero. However, it soon became evident that there was very little real change, and China remained weak and vulnerable. Supposedly one of the five powers that had won the war, along with Britain, France, the USA and the Soviet Union, it actually faced worsening conditions of poverty and economic collapse. She remembers how much she hated seeing the American soldiers in Shanghai after the war, and how bitter were the feelings aroused by the infamous case of a Chinese student being raped by an American soldier.

In 1947, two years after the end of the war, Lu Jie completed secondary school. There had never been any question in her mind that she would pursue higher education, but where would she go for her studies? Her brother had chosen agriculture at St. John's University and her sister had studied chemistry at Da Xia University, both in Shanghai. She decided that she would like to leave Shanghai and be more independent of the family, so chose Jinling Women's College in Nanjing, where she started studies in chemistry in 1947. Her father was happy with the decision, and greatly respected the then president, Wu Yifang, a female scholar with a PhD in biology from the USA. After a short period of study in chemistry, she found the subject bitter and dry (*kuzao*) and decided to go into the sociology department in her second year, choosing its program in child welfare as her focus. With all the suffering of the war, she felt drawn to work with children, and hoped some day she might be able to run an orphanage.

When she wrote to her father to let him know her decision to change her field of study from chemistry to education, he was delighted. He wrote her a four-page letter explaining how happy he was to have one of his children freely choose to enter the same field he had chosen. It was important to him that his children have complete freedom of choice, but his lengthy exposition of the meaning and value of education in this letter showed how much the decision meant to him. After two years of study at Jinling Women's college, Lu Jie took ill with tuberculosis and had to rest for two years, returning in 1952 to what had become the education department of Nanjing Normal University, and graduating in 1953.

The years of the Sino-Japanese War, the Second World War and the Civil War were extremely difficult ones for the family. Her father worried constantly about the dangers faced by his children who were becoming more and more politically involved. He also agonized over his own future, finally deciding to move to Hong Kong in 1949.

Lu Jie felt there were three great influences that shaped her life: family, school and the political situation China faced throughout her teenage years. Due to this third factor she believed that both she and her brother, Lu Ping, reached political maturity very early, and felt a deep sense of the need to sacrifice themselves for the country (*ziwo xisheng*). Her father did his very best to persuade them both to take the opportunities available for study abroad. He actually secured a scholarship for her brother at Stanford University, and asked her to fill in forms to apply for study in the United States. However, both resolutely refused these opportunities. Many, particularly friends and schoolmates who did go abroad, and lived very different lives, have asked her whether she now regrets this decision. Her reply is that it was a very rational decision, given the situation of the times, not an emotional one, and that she has reaffirmed the choice as one based on sound reasoning throughout her life, in spite of the many unanticipated difficulties that came after 1949.

Her parents' latter years were not easy, given the life choices made by their children. While living in Hong Kong and briefly in Taiwan during the early fifties, they missed their children so much as to decide to return to China in 1958, only to find their oldest daughter had already died. With the coming of the Cultural Revolution, their son was sent to the countryside in Henan and they followed, living in terrible circumstances. Lu's father died in 1977, and her mother in 1978, having spent her final years with her daughter in Nanjing. In the forty years since they had lost their home in Shanghai, they had never been able to recapture the life of professional commitment and family solidarity that had been their dream in the early twenties.

Lu Jie herself graduated from Nanjing Normal University at the age of 23 in 1953, and was asked by the university to join the staff as a political instructor. Having joined the Communist underground in the late forties, she was one of the few with the necessary combination of political and academic qualifications for the task. Her husband was also a committed Communist Party member, and held a leadership position in the university as head of the Department of Political Science. Both of them believed that China was now at last on the right track, free of war, independent, led by a political party committed to economic development and social justice. In their modest roles within a newly established provincial university, they could finally contribute in ways that would make a difference to their beloved China.

3   Careers under Socialism, 1949–1978

At this point we reach a new phase of each life story, and go forward to see how each of these six educators experienced and understood the first three decades under Communist rule. Li Bingde was thirty-seven years old, with a solid track record as associate professor of education at Henan University, a graduate qualification in education from Yanjing University and two years of research and study in Europe behind him. Zhu Jiusi was thirty-three years old, with solid academic credentials from an excellent secondary school and undergraduate studies at Wuhan University, and even more important, with thirteen years of experience as a revolutionary intellectual in higher education leadership, teaching and journalism. Pan Maoyuan was twenty-nine years old, held a degree in education from Xiamen University and had had considerable experience in both primary and secondary school teaching. At the time of the Liberation, he was principal of Xiamen University's attached primary school and an assistant lecturer in the college of education. Xie Xide was twenty-eight years old, working on her doctorate at MIT, and already determined to return to China on its completion. Wang Yongquan was twenty years old, about to graduate in physics from one of China's most famous universities, Qinghua, and was looking forward to his first job. Lu Jie was nineteen years old, suffering an interruption in her undergraduate studies, due to tuberculosis, but determined to continue her studies as soon as possible, and contribute her youth and energy to the new China.

All six of them had been deeply influenced by traditional Chinese thought and philosophy, mainly the Confucian canon, both through their families and through some aspects of their early schooling. They had also been exposed to American educational ideas, particularly Deweyan pragmatism, as interpreted by American-returned Chinese teachers, and to a lesser extent to European influences. Li Bingde and Xie Xide were the only two who experienced an extended period abroad as part of their intellectual and professional formation. Zhu Jiusi was the only one who had had a deep exposure to Marxism-Leninism and Mao Zedong thought, in both its theoretical and practical aspects.

For all six scholars, the victory of the Chinese Communist Party in 1949, and the decision of China's new leaders to lean towards the Soviet Union, and adopt its model of socialist construction, was a crucial turning point in their lives. The major part of their professional careers was to pass under a new order, and it was this that framed the development of their educational ideas. In this next section we will listen to their accounts of the first three decades of Communist rule.

3.1   *Li Bingde: Pioneer of the Northwest*

Li Bingde never considered any alternative but to return to China from Europe in 1949, to be reunited with the wife and five children he had left behind, and to contribute to building a new China under socialism. Fourteen other Chinese scholars on government fellowships in France, Sweden, Denmark and other parts of Europe returned, while many others chose to wait and to see what would happen.

As soon as he returned, only a month or two after the formal inauguration of the new regime, he sought guidance from the new ministry of education in Beijing, and was placed at Huabei University, one of the institutions set up by the Communist Party during the revolutionary struggle. It was renamed People's University in 1950, and was to play a very important role as the arbiter and guide of socialist orthodoxy for the new regime. All those who had studied humanities or social sciences abroad were expected to undertake this study, while those who had studied science or medicine, such as his two brothers returning from the USA, were not given the same requirement.

The study of Marxism-Leninism was entirely new for Li, but he was happy to take it up, and confident that China would now be peaceful, with the end of both the civil war and the Anti-Japanese War. There was a large group of others with him, some very young, others much older, including old professors such as Tai Shuangchiu who had taught him at Henan University and high-level officials of the Nationalist regime. In June of 1950, nine months after his return, the work of job assignment began, and it was done in a sudden and somewhat arbitrary way. He was staying in the Northwest corner of Beijing, not far from the Summer Palace, and had gone into the city one day to meet the provost of Fu Jen University, who wanted to discuss the possibility of him becoming a professor there. On return to his residence the next day, he was informed by the Ministry of Education that his future position had been decided and he should get his luggage ready for departure after lunch. A group of eleven scholars, all returned from Europe or USA, were hosted for lunch by the Ministry of Education and then told their fate after lunch: eight who had returned from USA were sent to the Northeast region, while three who had returned from USA, France and Switzerland, one in fine arts and two in education, were to go to the Northwest. They would first travel to Xi'an, where the Northwest regional education bureau was, and then would be assigned to a higher institution. The other scholar of education, Zhu Bo, had come originally from the southwestern province of Yunnan. The authorities in Xi'an decided to keep Zhu in Xi'an, at the newly established Shaanxi Normal University, and to send Li to Lanzhou, to Northwest Normal University, as they believed that since he came from Henan he would find it easier to adapt to the far Northwest. The scholar of fine arts was sent to Lanzhou University.

He arrived at Lanzhou for the first time in June of 1950, and his wife and five children joined him towards the end of 1950, after she had spent a period of study at Huabei University. He was appointed full professor and provost immediately. In 1957, he was accused of being a rightist and removed from all positions of responsibility. His salary was reduced by two levels, from 283 yuan to 208 yuan, but he was still allowed to teach and keep his professorial title. In 1959, the rightist appellation was removed.

In 1966, during the Cultural Revolution, he was again attacked and this time his punishment was to be sent to teach in the university's attached primary school. For him, no assignment could have been more welcome and he put tremendous energy and interest into the preparation of teaching materials for Chinese and mathematics. This experience was somehow a return to his early years of experimentation in the classroom.

He remembers the 1950s as a period when Soviet ideas reigned supreme and all that he had learned previously, especially that associated with USA, was criticized. It was a kind of total about-face in education, with one set of ideas, particularly the theories of the Russian educator, Kairov, dominating all discourse. For him, it was a striking contrast to the Nationalist period, when there had been lively debates among different groups in education, and many competing viewpoints had been tolerated. No Soviet experts were posted to Northwest Normal University, but several did visit, in the company of an official from the Ministry of Education. They inspected all that was going on, and gave their views on what was correct or incorrect in what they observed.

The rejection of the Soviet model in 1958 and the early sixties was equally abrupt and left Li feeling a sense of crisis, as one more set of foreign ideas was withdrawn before it could take root in Chinese soil. In his view there had been no resolution between two extreme positions—one of affirming Chinese thought and culture as the basis (*ti*) and external inputs as mere techniques (*yong*) that could serve it, and the other of seeing external theories—first capitalism, then socialism—as the only means of saving China. The deep problem which he felt awaited resolution after 1978, with the end of the Cultural Revolution and the beginning of the Deng Xiaoping era, was how to integrate Western and Chinese ideas and build a deep-level educational structure suited to a modern China.

In 1979, Li Bingde was accepted into the Communist Party, and from 1980 to 1983, he was president of Northwest Normal University. During those years he made great efforts to strengthen its professional and academic profile and help it to establish mutually beneficial relations with universities in the USA and Europe. However, it was in the years after his retirement from the presidency at age seventy-one that his most important contributions were made—in a series of scholarly works and textbooks which led the field of pedagogy and educational research, and in the master's and doctoral students he trained for the region and the whole country.

3.2   *Zhu Jiusi and the Development of Higher Education under Socialism*

For Zhu Jiusi, the success of the Communist revolution in 1949 represented the culmination of intense collective efforts by members of the Chinese Communist party and the People's Liberation Army to create conditions for a new China, free from the corruption of the Nationalist period and the humiliation of Japanese and Western incursions. Tears still come to his eyes, fifty years later, as he remembers many close friends and comrades who gave their lives for the success of the revolution, and wonders why it was that his life was spared and he had so many years to serve his country. In dialectical materialist terms, he regards this as a matter of random chance (*ouran*) rather than something predetermined by historical process (*biran*).

When he was informed by his superiors of the decision for him to leave his position in the Department of Education of Hunan province, move to Wuhan and take up leadership responsibility for a newly established institute of technology, he welcomed the opportunity. He moved to Wuhan in June of 1953, in order to take part in planning for the new institute, which was officially opened in October of that year. By 1955, Zhu was vice president of the institute, and in 1956 he was made vice party secretary. In 1961 he became party secretary, and from 1972 to 1984 he served as party secretary and president. He was thus in a position to have a defining influence on the development of this institution, and on higher education in China more generally.

Generally, Zhu felt the adoption of the Soviet model in the restructuring of 1952–3 was a positive move, as it made possible a concerted effort to train higher-level specialists to serve all different sectors of the newly established socialist economy. Excellent private universities of the pre-1949 period, including most of the Christian missionary institutions, were recognized by being integrated into restructured institutions, which held an important role in the new system, while poorer ones did not deserve to survive in any case. However, some elements of the Soviet model were applied in too doctrinaire and rigid a way, Zhu felt, when he reflected on the situation during the later years of the Cultural Revolution decade. This had resulted in the weakening of some of the great public universities of the Nationalist period, including Peking University, Qinghua University, and Wuhan and Zhejiang universities, among others. Both Qinghua and Zhejiang universities were designated polytechnic universities, with all of their distinguished scholars and departments in the basic sciences and humanities moved to other institutions, stripping them of a very significant part of their earlier heritage. Peking University and Wuhan University were designated comprehensive universities under the Soviet model, but this excluded professional fields such as education, medicine, agriculture and engineering, which were moved to other institutions. In retrospect, Zhu felt this created more loss than gain, and we can see from his efforts to develop the Huazhong Institute of Technology how these concerns affected his thinking from a fairly early period.

The first years of development involved establishing a new campus on a pleasant site in a fairly distant suburb of Wuchang, one of the three sister cities, along with Hankou and Hanyang that make up Wuhan. It was a challenging task to create a new identity, with teachers and students being transferred there from five other institutions in different cities and regions. By 1956, the new institution was well established, and had already begun to dream of reaching international standards in certain fields over the subsequent decade. With the Great Leap Forward's emphasis on rapid industrialization, there was considerable expansion of programs, from four departments with eight pro-grams to eight departments with 37 programs. While Zhu himself felt there were serious mistakes in the exaggerated efforts to move ahead quickly over this time, he also felt important lessons were learned.

For him, it provided the first opportunity to introduce two concepts that later became core to his higher education thinking. One was the integra-tion of research into the work of the university, contrasting with the Soviet model which made universities centers mainly for teaching, and consigned most research to the institutes of an academy of science. The second was an emphasis on integrating applied and basic sciences in the work of the univer-sity. Many of the new programs introduced in 1958 at the Huazhong Institute of Technology were in basic fields such as mathematics, physics and chemis-try, all of which were seen as a vital foundation for the specialist engineering programs. Zhu greatly regretted the fact that these new programs were closed down again in 1961, at a time of retrenchment, when the Sixty Articles for Higher Education determined an academically conservative approach to higher education development.

Overall, Zhu felt that the period from 1958–1960 represented a kind of "breaking the mold" (*tupuo*) of the Soviet model that had been copied with far too little reflection and adaptation to the Chinese context. He noted Mao's speech of 1956 on the "Ten Great Relationships," where the last of the relation-ships was that between China and foreign countries. Here Mao expressed his wish for mutually beneficial relations with all other peoples and countries in order to learn from their strengths, but stressed the importance of making crit-ical analysis of what was learned, avoiding mechanical or holistic borrowing, and rejecting shortcomings and mistakes. Mao had added that this approach should also be adopted in relations with the Soviet Union and other social-ist countries, and criticized the mechanical way in which Soviet patterns had been copied in the early fifties.[10] Zhu noted how these points had been added to Mao's speech when it was published in 1978, and that they were an impor-tant reference point in terms of the problems left by the Soviet model.

However, Zhu's most profound thinking on the form of higher education that would be most suited to socialist China took place during the disruption of the Cultural Revolution. In November of 1969, all of the university staff had been forced to move down to the countryside as part of the Cultural Revolution movement to learn from the peasants. In the atmosphere of the time, they feared there was no future for universities in China, but Mao's 1968 statement that "universities would still be needed, especially colleges of science and

---

10   Zhu Jiusi, "Lishi de huigu," *Gaodeng jiaoyu yanjiu*, No. 4 (1992): p. 4.

engineering ..." gave them some hope. Zhu himself moved back to the campus in 1970, one year before the other staff, and during that year he had time for a great deal of thinking. The campus was largely deserted, except for a factory that had moved in and taken over several buildings, and a few research workers under his supervision. All of his books had been moved during the critical attacks launched against him by Red Guards, so once again, as in his teaching years in the liberated areas, he had to depend on experience and memory. He was encouraged by the fact that the Army leader heading the Mao Zedong thought propaganda group responsible for the campus, Liu Kunshan, had a respect for knowledge and would support new ideas for the development of the college.

Two important aspects of his experience in pre-1949 China were germane to the initiatives he took to transform the college and prepare it to become a leading university in the period before Deng Xiaoping declared China's opening up to modernization, the world, and the future. The most important was his memory of six years at Yangzhou Secondary School, as described earlier. The second was his appreciation of several of the great university presidents of the Nationalist era, including Cai Yuanpei at Beida, Zhu Kezheng at Zheda and Zhang Bailing, president of Nankai University and one of the leaders of the Southwest United University (Lianda) in Kunming during the anti-Japanese War.

His reflections on the academic excellence of his secondary school made him aware that people were the most important asset of any academic institution. He remembered how Yangzhou's principal had searched the whole province to bring the best teachers to his school. In this spirit, and with the political standing and support he had at Huazhong University of Science and Technology, he was able to attract about 600 academics from all parts of China to HUST over the years from 1974 to 1983, during a time when many other universities were still paralyzed by the difficult conditions in the aftermath of the Cultural Revolution. In addition to bringing in new people, Zhu also instituted a program to provide all existing academic staff, especially those recruited during the years of academic disruption, with special classes in English and mathematics. This was to strengthen their ability to draw on international sources of information, and to do quantitatively based research. In this too he was inspired by the importance that had been given to English in his secondary school. A further aspect of his effort to develop people was the early restoration of the system of academic titles, and promotion opportunities that would encourage excellence.

He also remembered the excellent laboratories, in their own specialist building, and the remarkable library the principal at Yangzhou Secondary School had developed. This inspired early efforts to build up laboratories, acquire vital equipment and develop library resources at HUST, at a time when such resources were very difficult to get and required intense effort on the part of the college's leadership.

From his memory of the famous presidents of the Nationalist period, he reflected on the importance of research being an integral part of the life of a university, closely linked to teaching, and possibly even leading the teaching program. In order to create conditions for this, he took several steps. In 1971, the first national education meeting after the Cultural Revolution was held in Beijing. It was called by the Education and Science Group established by the State Council, and he was one of 10 people from Hubei province who were sent to participate. During the three months he stayed in Beijing for the meeting, he took the opportunity to make linkages with various national ministries, including the Ministry of Mechanical Industry (*jixie bu*), and the Ministry of Electronics Industry (*Dianzi gongye bu*). He found there was a real need for research and also for new programs in related areas. As a result, he obtained funding commitments from these ministries for research they needed, and established 10 new programs in areas such as lasers and electronics. He was delighted to find, on his return to Wuhan, that Liu Kunshan, the Army leader in charge of the campus, was fully supportive of these initiatives.

Another important step he took at this early period to establish strong research support was the creation of two journals of research information. One reported on international developments in science and technology, the *Guowai keji dongtai*, making the latest information available in Chinese. The other was a journal of translations, the *Keji yibao*, which selected important works in foreign languages relating to science and technology for translation. Both involved intensive effort by a group of senior staff who often had to travel to major libraries to search out the information.

These efforts to recruit excellent staff and support the continuous development of existing academic staff, and to secure research funding and disseminate research information from international sources put Zhu's institution far ahead of many others over this period. When Deng Xiaoping came to power in 1977 and started the movement of reform and opening up, a space was finally created for Zhu's vision to have a national impact. The one element of that vision which he had been able to do little about before 1978 had been his hope for a much more comprehensive approach to knowledge in the university. This was inspired by both his secondary experience and the memories he had of institutions such as Zhejiang University and Wuhan University before Liberation. It was to be confirmed by the impressions of a visit to USA and Japan in 1979. In this early period all he could do was note the potential of many of the new academic staff he had attracted, and create fundamental conditions for developments that would only become possible in the 1980s.

Zhu's powerful vision for a reformed university and his capacity to lay the foundations for the fulfillment of that vision in a difficult period after the Cultural Revolution may have been linked to the unique combination of political, academic and cultural experiences of his earlier life. As a student, he had made a clear choice, at great personal cost, to join the Party and serve the revolution. This gave him a respected standing in socialist China, and the confidence to think and act clearly and decisively when many others associated with higher education were paralyzed by the political movements of the time. As a revolutionary who had taught for many years in one of the Party's major institutions of higher education, he knew both the possibilities and the limitations of the "Yan'an model" upheld during the Cultural Revolution. He was able to draw upon his earlier experience with mainstream academic institutions of the Nationalist era to envision a form of Chinese university that could combine the best features of both. While Communist thought and dialectical materialist philosophy was the predominant factor in his thinking, he had an open mind to all forms of academic knowledge, and his moral integrity and deep commitment to his country had roots also in his early exposure to Confucian teachings.

3.3   *Pan Maoyuan and the Development of a New Field of Research in Education*

For Pan Maoyuan, the Communist revolution represented a new beginning that opened up a clear direction for his life as an educator. He was invited to remain as a member of staff responsible for teaching affairs at Xiamen University, and in 1951, a year after Li Bingde had moved to Lanzhou, he was sent to People's University to study education. In the group studying education were a small number of graduate students of education, like himself, and a much larger group of cadres or officials, who had sub-degree qualifications and were being prepared as educational administrators for the new regime. In his class of graduate students were several scholars who were later to become famous at Beijing Normal University, including Huang Ji in educational philosophy, Wang Cesan and Wang Tianyi in education and Zhang Zhiguang in psychology.

After six months at People's University, the reorganization of colleges and departments was completed and the education program was moved from People's to Beijing Normal University, where he was to spend the second half of his study period. He can still remember the names of the four Russian scholars who taught Marxism-Leninism, political economy and educational theory, but all of the Russian language he learned has since been forgotten.

He was impressed by the thoroughness and attention to academic quality that characterized the Soviet approach to education. He felt American educational ideas had been lively and flexible, but were somehow a poor fit after Liberation, when the system itself was rigid and controlled. By contrast, Soviet patterns were regular and orderly, and served to set high standards for China's higher education, especially in fields such as engineering and natural sciences which were crucial to socialist construction. During the first five-year plan, Pan felt that the Soviet model served China extremely well, forming experts that were greatly needed, and raising educational and professional standards dramatically. Later they may have become somewhat rigid and inflexible, in his view, hardening into forms that did not adapt to changing needs.

After one year in Beijing, Pan was called back to Xiamen University by President Wang Yanan, who asked him to help in writing the new teaching plans in all subjects for the university. His official position was section chief (*kezhang*) with the teaching affairs office (*jiaowuchu*). This gave him familiarity with the exacting demands and standards of the Soviet curricula, which were the model for curricular reform in all subjects.

In 1954, the education faculty of Xiamen University faced the reorganization of colleges and departments (*yuanxi tiaozheng*), which had started in Beijing in 1952, and fanned out to each of the six major regions. The Soviet model had dictated that comprehensive universities should have only arts and sciences, no faculty of education, nor other professional areas such as medicine, engineering and agriculture. Thus it was decided that Xiamen University's whole faculty of education should move to Fuzhou, and become a key component of Fujian Normal College, a provincial level institution. Pan wanted very much to go with the education faculty, and to concentrate on the history of education, but the President of Xiamen University was reluctant to let him go. He knew that graduates in subjects such as biology, physics, mathematics and history might well be assigned as secondary school teachers on graduation and would need courses in educational theory, teaching methodology and education practicums. Therefore he asked Pan to stay and teach these courses.

With his dual responsibilities, teaching courses in education and developing new teaching plans for all of the tertiary courses in the sciences and humanities at Xiamen University, Pan was in an ideal position to reflect on the whole field of higher education over the 1950s. He felt that the Soviet model suited China very well, having resonance with China's tradition of a centralized and systematic approach to knowledge, with emphasis placed on foundational understanding. While there were no Soviet experts at Xiamen University in the 1950s, partly because of its distance from the main centers of Beijing and Northeast China, there were a small number of Russian language teachers.

In 1956, at the age of 36, Pan came to a realization that was to shape his whole subsequent career. Most of what he had studied in the field of pedagogy and teaching methodology was relevant only to primary and secondary schooling, and there was a need for a whole different approach to educational thought and theory within higher education. He wrote an article concerning the necessity of studying educational theory and teaching methods in higher education institutions and published it in Xiamen University's Scholarly Forum (*Xueshu Luntan*) (Pan 1957). Subsequently he edited a book under the same title, with contributions from several colleagues working with him, and it was distributed to all comprehensive and normal universities, then formally published much later (Pan 1984). This constituted the first book on theories of higher education in modern China.

In 1956, at the 8th Congress of the Communist Party, the role of intellectuals in China's socialist development was affirmed, and the situation appeared healthy from Pan's perspective. Soon thereafter, however, Mao launched the Great Leap Forward, and in his position as provost he oversaw the educational revolution of 1958. While he agreed with the need for greater Chinese orientation in the content and approach to teaching, no one at the time knew what this really meant. The result was a highly politicized movement, in his view, in which students were involved in writing teaching outlines and doing research far beyond their capability, and labor was emphasized for its own sake, not as a way of revitalizing educational theory.

At this time there was some modification of the patterns of 1952, which had disadvantaged the southern part of the East China region, especially in terms of engineering. Part of the engineering faculty of Xiamen University had been moved to Nanjing in 1952 to help in the establishment of Nanjing Engineering College, now Dongwu University, and another part of the faculty had been integrated into Beijing Aeronautical University. This left Fujian province with no significant program in engineering. In 1958, the province decided to establish Fuzhou University, and some of their former staff were called back from Nanjing and other places to help. In the first few years Xiamen University helped by teaching the basic sciences courses. Lu Jiaxi, later famous as the president of the Chinese Academy of Sciences, had been vice provost and assistant to the president at Xiamen University in the fifties, and was sent to be vice president of Fuzhou University when it was established in 1958.

While there were some positive elements in the re-balancing of higher education that took place in 1958, overall Pan felt it started China on the wrong track, and culminated in the even more disastrous Cultural Revolution of 1966. In 1964, Pan was invited to Beijing to do research on educational theory at the Central Institute for Educational Research. He was a member of a small group that included Liu Funian of East China Normal University, Li Fang of Shenyang Normal College and several others. Their task was to write articles critical of the Soviet Union and its educational influence, however within a year the group was dissolved and he stayed on in Beijing to observe the outbreak of the Cultural Revolution as an outsider. The rebel group at Xiamen University (*Xiada Zaofanpai*) eventually called him back from Beijing but they were so busy with other matters, and many of them had gone out to "make revolutionary connections" (*chuanlian*) that he was largely left alone on return. He participated in labor, wrote daily reports to the revolutionary leading group to express his commitment (*jiaodai*), and was happy to be reunited with his family.

It was a period in which he felt deeply upset. All the achievements of the fifties were now condemned as Soviet revisionism, and there was a kind of lacuna, with nothing to fill it. Similarly, aspects of traditional Chinese thought and education, which had nurtured him in his early years of schooling, were criticized. For him it was a total reversal that seemed to make nonsense of all the efforts of the past.

Only after the death of Mao in 1976, and the establishment of a whole new direction for the country by Deng Xiaoping in 1978, was he able to pursue the dream of establishing a whole new area of research and study. In 1978 Xiamen University approved the first Higher Education Research Unit to be established in China, and in 1984, his book *The Study of Higher Education* was jointly published by Peoples Education Press and Fujian Education Press. While Zhu Jiusi might be seen as the leading figure in terms of policy and related action, for the revitalization of higher education after 1978, Pan Maoyuan was, without doubt, the leading theorizer and researcher into higher education.

3.4   *Xie Xide: the Ups and Downs of a Scientific Career under Socialism*

Xie Xide and her husband chose Shanghai as the place to develop their careers in science because it was a major intellectual center, a place where they could focus on their professional interests. Xie Xide had worked there for a year in 1946, before going to USA, and her husband was drawn to the Institute of Biochemistry and Physiology of the Chinese Academy of Sciences, which was the ideal location for his work in biochemistry. They took residence on Yueyang Road, a pleasant southwestern suburb of Shanghai, near to the Institute and not far from the famous Jiaotong University, one of Chinese oldest modern universities, going back to 1896.

Although this was now socialist China, where Mao had declared that "women held up half the sky," Xie Xide's job assignment was arranged to fit around her husband's appointment to the Institute. The Institute approached Jiaotong University on her behalf, and arranged for her to work under a professor of physics there. Before she could begin, however, this professor and most members of the department of physics were moved to Fudan University in a Northeast suburb of Shanghai under the reorganization of faculties and departments which brought Chinese higher education in line with the Soviet model. Jiaotong was now to focus on engineering and applied science, while Fudan was made the major comprehensive university of the region, with departments in basic sciences and humanities. It was a suitable intellectual environment for a young physicist, but she was reminded by the vice president and Provost, Su Buqing, a distinguished mathematician who had come to Fudan from Zhejiang University, that she still had a lot to learn, in spite of the PhD from MIT. She was offered the humble position of lecturer, since she had had little teaching or research experience.

Her memories of the Russian scientists she worked under during the period of Soviet influence, up to 1958, were mixed. It was a time when all Chinese university teachers were admonished to learn from Soviet science and scholarship, but she knew from her experience at MIT that the Russians lagged behind the Americans in many areas, certainly in her own field of semiconductors. She felt uneasy with some of the new Chinese textbooks that made claims for the superiority of Soviet science, and found the Soviet experts who had been sent to China to help were largely scientists of a second level, not the best in their fields. Most troubling of all, she was aware that some of their scientific findings had been distorted by the ideologically biased ideas and claims of Lysenko, Stalin and others. None of these reservations could be openly discussed in the political atmosphere of the time.

In 1956 she was asked to go to Beijing for two years to work with a small team of Chinese scientists in solid-state physics, developing the first textbook in Chinese for the newly developing area of semiconductor physics. She was made vice head of the group, working with the famous British returned Chinese physicist, Huang Kun. The preparation of this text and related teaching material was part of a national twelve-year plan for the development of science and technology. For Xie Xide, this contribution demanded a major personal sacrifice, as her only child, a son, was five months old at the time she left Shanghai, and had to be left in her husband's care over the two-year period. The team did the work at Peking University, which had moved to the former campus of the American missionary university, Yanjing University, in 1952. This was the campus where her father had taught physics for so many years, and where she had spent much of her childhood and early youth. This return, fifteen years later, must have been an interesting time for memory and reflection.

During these two years, she also threw herself into studies of Russian and was able to assist in the translation of two books in atomic physics from Russian to Chinese after her return to Fudan. Overall, her impression of the Soviet scientists she got to know at Peking University was that some were good, others were mediocre and yet others were quite chauvinistic. One of the Soviet professors of physics teaching at Beida was a woman, and Xie found her a very pleasant personality, not chauvinistic, but not of the highest caliber either. In her work on semiconductor physics, she was clearly aware that American research in this field was far ahead of Soviet, though it was politically necessary to give credit to Soviet achievements as far as possible.

When the Anti-Rightist Movement was launched in 1957, she was called upon to criticize others in the university community who were not seen to be supporting Mao's political directions. She felt extremely sorry to see many older professors suffer in this movement, although she herself was not severely affected. In 1958, Mao launched the Great Leap Forward, and she could see from the very beginning that there was no economic base to support the huge expansion in higher education that was attempted. One positive development that came out of this movement in Shanghai, however, was the creation of the Shanghai University of Science and Technology, closely affiliated with Institutes of the Chinese Academy of Sciences in Shanghai for the purpose of training their own scientists. Overall, most of what was said about involving students and younger faculty in research within the university community was little more than rhetoric, in her view. Most of the research funding still went to the Institutes of the Academy or the research institutes affiliated with major industrial ministries.

The fifties were not an easy period, with her mixed feelings over the all-out emulation of Soviet science between 1952 and 1958, followed by the sudden decision to move away from the Soviet patterns in 1958, just after she had completed two years of study at Peking University under Soviet experts. By contrast, the first half of the 1960s were very happy and productive years for her. She felt this was the time in which she was able to make great progress in the teaching of physics, and in 1962 she was promoted to full professor, at the age of 41, just 10 years after taking up a lectureship, and six years after being appointed assistant professor in 1956. In 1961 she made her first visit to the Soviet Union, and in 1965, she went to England to participate in an international physics meeting. These were the years in which higher education developed along more of an academic than politicized trajectory, under the Sixty Articles promulgated by the Ministry of Higher Education in 1960. It was also a time when Zhou Enlai made great efforts to re-establish diplomatic and educational relations with European countries after the disasters of the Great Leap Forward.

Xie's return from England in 1965 marked the end of this period and the opening of the Cultural Revolution, a movement in which Fudan University played a leading role. It was taken as a kind of intellectual base for the radicals around Mao's wife, Jiang Qing, many of whom were Shanghainese. Xie Xide did not wish to say much about those difficult years. She spent a great deal of time down in the countryside doing labor, with no books, no possibility of research and no teaching. The three classes recruited by Fudan in 1966, 1967 and 1968, often called the "*lao san jie*"—three old classes—were a total loss in terms of any serious scientific study, and no further students were recruited until 1971, the year before Nixon visited China. This was also a time when she had to face a major personal battle with breast cancer, which was first diagnosed in 1966, just as the Cultural Revolution was beginning. Her deep personal sense of commitment to the nation and its scientific development gave her courage to struggle hard against the disease, in spite of poor medical facilities and extremely difficult personal circumstances during the ten years of revolutionary turmoil.

When Deng Xiaoping came to power in 1978, she was 57 years old, one of the best qualified of her generation, and finally able to make the contribution to Chinese scientific and intellectual development that she had hoped to make many years earlier. In 1978, she was appointed vice president, and from 1983 to 1988 she served as president of Fudan University, one of China's best known and most influential comprehensive universities.

3.5   *Wang Yongquan and the Evolution of Peking University*

For Wang Yongquan, 20 years old at the time of the Communist Liberation, the transition was a natural and comfortable one. On graduation from Qinghua University in 1950, he was assigned a job as assistant teacher at Peking University in the Physics department. Within a short period of time he joined the Communist Youth League and then the Communist Party, and all that he had learned about loyalty and conformity to family values and traditional virtues from his parents was now transferred to the Communist Party. He describes himself as having a kind of absolutism in his thinking that encouraged unquestioning obedience and respect.

In 1958, the Physics department at Peking University was divided into four new departments, bringing in radio electronics, nuclear physics, and technical physics, in addition to the basic physics department. At age 28 he became chair of the department of radio electronics, reflecting his training in electronic engineering at Qinghua. As well as being department chair he was also Party Secretary for the department, and he made high demands on academic staff and students both in terms of professional knowledge, and moral-political behavior. In retrospect, he felt his emphasis was on preserving unity, and ensuring conformity to Party standards; there was little room for individualism, which was seen as unhealthy at that time.

Wang felt very fortunate to have been at Beida rather than at Qinghua in 1956 and 1957, when intellectuals were encouraged to speak out critically in the Hundred Flowers Movement and this was soon followed by the Anti-Rightist Movement. Ma Yinchu, Beida's famous president, was attacked and discredited at this time, but he had been more of a figurehead than an active leader on campus. The Party Secretary for the university, Jiang Longji, was the moving spirit and he had done everything possible to protect the academic staff. He persuaded them not to go out and demonstrate publicly, with the result that far fewer Beida professors were condemned as rightists than Qinghua professors, where the academic staff had been more active. In fact several of his fellow students from Qinghua who had stayed on to teach, were labeled rightists in 1957. As a result of this movement he began to have critical thoughts for the first time, and to realize that directions given from above were not necessarily correct. Meanwhile the Party Secretary whom he admired so much, Mr. Jiang Longji, was transferred to Lanzhou University as president.

On the legacy of the Soviet influence, he felt that most intellectuals had a deep distrust of the Soviet Union in the early fifties. They remembered how the Soviet army had entered the Northeast after the defeat of Japan in 1945, and taken away a lot of valuable equipment. They also remembered student protests at the rape of Chinese women by Soviet soldiers in the Northeast. In a lively student debate at Qinghua in 1948 over whether the Soviet Union should be seen as socialist or imperialist, the side judging it to be imperialist had won.

In spite of these negative feelings, Wang felt that, in the end, the academic staff at Beida got on well with the Russian professors who were sent as experts. They quickly gained respect—the teaching material they introduced was systematic, their presentation style was clear and the content was in-depth. He had expected to be sent to the Soviet Union for further study, and had an excellent Russian teacher at Beida in preparation for this. In the end, however, he was not sent, and he gradually forgot much of what he had learned.

When the Soviet model was repudiated, first in 1958, and then more vehemently in the Cultural Revolution of 1966–67, Wang felt deeply disturbed. In spite of the rhetoric about educational revolution, he felt a sense of nihilism. There was really nothing to replace the patterns that were being repudiated, no educational principles on which to build. As department head from 1958 to 1976, through both revolutionary periods, he discovered how impossible it was to solve educational problems, without clearly established educational principles. From 1966 to 1969, he was locked up on the Beida campus by revolutionary rebels from among the students. During that time he read a great deal of Marxist-Leninist literature, but he also read a lot of John Dewey's work, and had time for reflection on the process of education. In 1969 he was sent to Hanzhong, in southern Shanxi province, where the radio electronics department had an affiliated campus.

In 1978, he was appointed head of a newly established center for audio-visual education, and the interest in education which had grown through the turbulent experiences of cultural revolution now blossomed under new conditions. In 1982, he was appointed vice provost for the university and provost from 1984 to 1986. In this role he was involved in the total reconstruction of the university curriculum and the teaching process. In 1988, four years after Xiamen University, Peking University established a Research Institute of Higher Education, with Wang as its first Head. From this position he has been able to educate a large cohort of master's and doctoral students in the field of higher education, as well as fostering related research. China's premier university is thus able to exert significant influence in the field of education in spite of the fact that its college of education had been moved to Beijing Normal University in the reorganization of 1952.

3.6   Lu Jie and Moral-Political Education

Although she has never held positions of leadership such as president, vice president or provost, as have most of the other scholars profiled in this article, Lu Jie has a tremendous sense of pride in and loyalty to Nanjing Normal University. She feels it is like her own family, an institution she has given her whole life to building. She sees her work as having been not for the salary or the status, but for the sake of the health and wellbeing of her university. The sense of urgency and concern in this commitment has never lessened over the years. If anything it has grown stronger, as unanticipated disasters such as the Cultural Revolution disrupted higher education development.

In the early fifties, after the reorganization of faculties and departments (*yuanxi tiaozheng*), Nanjing Normal had every reason to be the one of the best of its kind. The normal college of National Central University, China's premier institution under the Nationalist regime, was given to Nanjing Normal, and the great progressive educator, Tao Xingzhi had been its first dean. Chen Heqin came from Zhongyang University to Nanjing Normal with the reorganization of 1952 and functioned as its president up to 1958. As a non-party member, it finally became difficult for him to exercise leadership, and he was moved to another role in 1958. Several other distinguished professors of education joined Nanjing Normal from Zhongyang University, while the Department of

Education of Jinling University, and the Department of Child Welfare of Jinling Women's University, were also placed in Nanjing Normal.

In terms of human resources, Nanjing Normal was far superior to the newly established East China Normal University in Shanghai, which had absorbed the education departments of private universities such as Da Xia, Guang Hua and Fudan, none of them having the prestige or leadership role of the Nanjing institutions in education. Subsequently, however, East China Normal University was given stronger support, as a national normal university directly under the Ministry of Education, and its location in Shanghai also gave it certain advantages. Furthermore, institutions of engineering and science tended to gain far stronger support in the early fifties under the Soviet model. Lu Jie noted with regret how the best libraries, equipment and even vehicles were given to the engineering universities in the reorganization of 1952, with inferior book collections, third rate equipment and the most derelict vehicles being given to the normal institutions.

There were many occasions when she regretted her decision to choose education as a field of study, sensing that fields such as basic sciences or engineering were much more welcomed in the early 1950s. She wished at times she had chosen engineering, like Wang Yongquan, or had stayed with her original choice of chemistry, which would have made a much more obvious and practical contribution to China's development. By contrast, education was closely linked to politics and it was often difficult to express honest views. There were times when she felt a deep sense of loss (*shiluo gan*), such as during the campaign to criticize Tao Xingzhi in 1957, when she saw the effects this had on Chen Heqin who had to step down from his role as president of Nanjing Normal at that time. Both had been close friends of her father at Columbia.

Generally, however, she felt the Soviet model was beneficial in its influences on Chinese higher education in the 1950s. Many subjects and specialties were developed that were important in China's economic development—especially in the field of engineering—and the growth from three to eight universities in Nanjing over a short period opened up opportunity to many more students and prepared much needed talent. She had the opportunity to study political theory at Fudan University for one and a half years, after her graduation in 1953, and during that time she learned some Russian and studied under Russian experts. On looking back at that period, she has tremendous respect for the Marxist classics that she read, and feels in many ways that China has not yet risen above the standard of knowledge and understanding represented in those works.

On the other hand, however, she found the teaching methods to be rather dogmatic, and the approach of the experts responsible for the course to be directive and unbending. Outlines had to be memorized, there was no provision made for discussion of varying interpretations of the texts, and only one explanation was countenanced. It seemed as if these experts were simply repeating what others had said, rather than providing a helpful or liberating educational experience. Generally, the greatest problem with the Soviet patterns, she felt on retrospect, was that they were a closed system, unable to reform themselves over time, and not open to divergent views. One can only guess the influence of her early years in progressive educational settings on these judgments! She felt students tended to embrace the Soviet patterns with great enthusiasm, seeing them as a kind of "ideal kingdom" (*lixiang wangguo*) which would carry China forward very rapidly, while professors hesitated, since many of them had studied in Europe or North America, and found them too constraining.

Whatever their limitations, Soviet influences were profound, transforming the structure and pattern of education thoroughly from the inside out. The influence of I.A. Kairov, Minister of Education in the USSR during the fifties and editor of a textbook which was widely used in Chinese translation, was particularly important in the early fifties. After 1958, it had less influence when the Soviet model fell under criticism. She moved to the education department of Nanjing Normal only in 1960, after the high tide of interest in Kairov had subsided. However, she recognized that his approach was widely accepted because it was seen as both academic and systematic, in contrast to the many eclectic theories of education that had been introduced from the West.

The Great Leap Forward of 1958 was a reaction to the intensity of Soviet influence, in her view. Mao had ideas of his own, and did not want to be simply a follower. His idea of "walking on two legs" and utilizing both formal and informal approaches to education was unique to China and suited to the practical needs of the time. In education, two new textbooks were developed which became as widely influential as the work of Kairov, one edited by Liu Funian of East China Normal University and one developed by a group of scholars at Nanjing Normal University. Meanwhile Zhou Yang was responsible for the development of new teaching material in the humanities. Lu Jie admitted that none of these new texts were of the highest academic quality, yet they were significant as an assertion of a Chinese approach to the various subject areas. Overall, serious problems of quality and sustainability arose from the over-rapid development, at this time, of many new higher institutions in the non-formal sector, called red-expert colleges. Also there was clearly a stronger role for the Party in higher education, and much greater political content than had been the case under the Soviet model.

With the early sixties and the publication of the Sixty Articles guiding higher education onto a more academic track, Lu Jie felt pleased to be able to take up teaching in the field of education, and delighted with the quality of the four classes of students recruited between 1961 and 1964. Her feelings were similar to those of Xie Xide, who found these the best years for higher education in the whole period between 1950 and 1978.

The outbreak of the Cultural Revolution in 1966 was deeply disturbing to Lu Jie, as a loyal Party member and political educator. She simply could not accept the reality that the revolution could take this kind of irrational direction. At first, she described her response to the early rebel attacks and accusations as "*mamu*," somehow numb with incomprehension. She recognized that there were real problems with the leadership, especially certain cadres at the basic level who abused their power, which was one of the purported reasons for the movement. However, it turned out to be those leaders with the greatest integrity who became subject to attack, and were brought down. Her own husband, who was head of the political science department at Nanjing Normal, was labeled as part of a "black line" (*heixian*) and attacked in numerous big character posters (*dazibao*). She herself was an ordinary lecturer in the education department at this time, so was not a target of attack, but she found herself subject to criticism because of her husband.

From the beginning, she simply refused to go along with the rebel group, and their criticisms, even though this stance was to cause her much suffering. She felt her ability to stand firm was linked to the Western style education she had had. She insisted on thinking independently and had a rebel streak of her own. She had always been critical of leaders whose style and approach she considered unhealthy, and she feels she may have offended some, who took this opportunity for revenge.

She was among the first group of 108 to be sent to a remote village in Jiangsu for physical labor. She did not mind the labor at all, and was glad to clean any number of toilets, but it upset her deeply to see old professors of her father's generation subject to terrible indignities and forced to endure hard labor under bitter winter conditions. Since she spoke out when others did not, she was forced to go on innumerable parades. She absolutely refused to admit she was at fault in any way. She was considered extremely stubborn (*wangu*) by the rebel "authorities." Seven long years passed in the village, and she was unable to do any teaching or educational work.

What distressed her most of all was a particular meeting with all members of the university present, when she was accused of being part of an "international spy network," because her father had spent some time in Hong Kong and Taiwan. Another incident she remembers vividly was the demand of red guards, who were rampaging through her home, that she hand over all personal letters—she absolutely refused, as privacy was one of the basic principles in her family and professional life. As a result, she was again severely criticized in a public meeting. Many protected themselves in these circumstances by criticizing others, but this was something she refused to do. The rebel authorities tried to make her criticize her husband openly, but again she firmly refused.

What enabled her to remain strong through this period of terror? It was probably the same quiet rationalism that had lain behind the firm decision she and her brother made to devote their lives to China in the late forties. She could see that the Party itself was deeply divided, with urban intellectuals like herself who had joined the underground in the 1940s, being attacked by those with rural backgrounds who were grouped around Mao Zedong. It was a bitter pill to be labeled a "traitor" (*pantu*), after all the sacrifices made for Party and country, but it was a pill which even China's president, Liu Shaoqi, had to swallow. She recalled one moment of comfort in these difficult years. An old cadre, whom she greatly respected, made the following brief and cryptic comment to her one day: "only you yourself have the clearest understanding of your own personal affairs" (*ziji de shiqing, ziji zui qingchu*).

When the Cultural Revolution came to an end with the arrest of the Gang of Four in 1976, Lu Jie was 46 years old. After dealing with the death of her parents in 1977 and 1978, she threw herself into the task of rebuilding Nanjing Normal University into a strong center of education to carry forward the rich progressive traditions of the region that had nurtured her over many years. In 1978, she was made head of the department of education, and some years later became head of the institute for educational research. In the years between 1978 and the mid-1980s, 30–40 students were recruited each year into the department of education, and when they began to graduate in 1982, she selected the best each year to stay on as young lecturers, and rebuild the field. Among them were two who spent time doing research in Canada under the joint project with OISE/UT—Wu Kangning, and Tan Dingliang, both now well-known younger scholars in their fields. In fact it was Wu Kangning whose article on sociology of education inspired the fierce debate among graduate students at Pan Maoyuan's Saturday night salon in Xiamen, mentioned earlier!

Lu Jie's greatest sadness over the 1980s lay in the fact that a large number of the young lecturers whom she had selected, nurtured, and sent for study abroad, never returned to build up their university and country. She noted that it still gave her great pain to speak of this point, even though ten years had passed by 1998. The gap between the choice she had made in the late forties, when China was torn by war, and the choice made by many in this new generation was difficult for her to fully comprehend.

Her main focus in the twenty years since Deng Xiaoping declared China's new orientation towards modernization, the world and the future has been on two challenges: building up people, and rebuilding theory. She sees it as a huge challenge to develop a genuine theoretical understanding of the links between education, labor and rural life. Every year she takes students to visit rural schools and asks them to link what they are learning to the realities of these schools. She has also focused on problems of moral education, and the rebuilding of a framework for moral development in education after the devastation of the Cultural Revolution and the denigration of so-called class struggle into a series of vendettas in which vengeance over personal grievances was dignified as revolutionary ardor.

As one of a very small number of senior scholars qualified to supervise doctoral students in education she has guided a new generation of scholars at her own institution and elsewhere where she has served as external examiner. She has also published a number of influential volumes in the areas of moral education, rural education and the sociology of education.

4   Perspectives on the Period since 1978

There are certain commonalities in the narratives of these six scholars. Each was able to make a substantial and ongoing contribution to education, in spite of the difficult turns of their own lives, both before and after 1949. Each was affiliated with one institution for the most of their professional lives, in some cases having crucial leadership roles. Each also nurtured a large number of graduate students who now hold influential positions and will shape China's future. In family history and life opportunities there are clear differences among them, but these do not seem to be of fundamental import. Each had a somewhat different view of the Soviet contribution to China's educational development, ranging from relatively positive, to greater reservation. All concurred in expressing grave concern over the educational outcomes of Mao's revolutionary projects, especially the Cultural Revolution. For all of them, Deng Xiaoping's accession to power in 1978, and the modernization and open door policy he initiated, represented an important new beginning. In many ways the most productive years of their careers took place in the twenty years from 1978 to 1998. This was a time when it was finally possible to blend elements of their own cultural tradition and experience of socialism with ideas introduced from abroad, and build something that had authenticity and gave hope for the future.

4.1   *Li Bingde: Harmony as the Watchword*
For Li, Confucian morality, taught in his father's home, remains important for China, and its special feature lies in the fact that it rejects nothing, but absorbs

all things into itself. Chinese intellectuals are also greatly interested in and influenced by Buddhism and Daoism, something that is evident in their writings, in the concern for nurturing the spirit and engaging in quiet reflection. Yet Confucianism remains central, and at its heart is the practice of self-examination—three times a day, questioning one's inner integrity and the direction of one's life. In addition, Li loves to dip into the Daoist classics by Laozi and Zhuangzi, and appreciates what Buddhism has brought to China.

China's traditional strength in moral education must remain the core of the concept of "quality education" (*suzhi jiaoyu*) but at the same time it must adapt to modern socialist society, according to Li. He sees this notion of "quality education" (*suzhi jiaoyu*) as something very deep, something linked to China's national character (*guoqing*), a concept that cannot easily be translated into English. Looking back on China's modern century, Li believes that one of the greatest problems was the fact of overdependence on ideas introduced from outside.

Before 1949, Western ideas dominated the curriculum of colleges of education, and they remained largely on the surface; they did not penetrate deeply, nor have any lasting effect through educational experimentation. After 1949, Soviet or Russian ideas were introduced and emulated, but they likewise failed to take root, and the Great Leap Forward and Cultural Revolution left China in chaos. There was always a lack of balance, a tendency to lean too far towards external solutions (*pianmian*) and, as a result, an inability to absorb what was introduced from outside.

Li chose to spend considerable time speaking about the achievements and ideas of Deng Xiaoping in the period after 1978, as he felt this was a turning point for education. Deng could see that Mao's policies had not worked, and he could see the danger of Hua Guofeng's promise to continue upholding all of Mao's theories and ideas. Deng had lived in France for some years and seen a great deal of how capitalist countries developed, as well as the experience of the Soviet Union. This was in contrast with Mao and many of the other old cadres, who knew how to fight and suffer, but had no idea how to run a country. Most important of all, Deng was able to learn from bitter experience—he knew China needed a new way forward after Mao's mistakes. He set a context, after nearly three decades, whereby Marxism and socialism could finally be seen as a way of liberating the mind and seeking practical solutions to real problems (*shishi qiushi*).

In 1978, Deng urged Chinese people to look toward modernization, the world and the future. Instead of empty rhetoric, for the first time the criteria of what constituted socialism were opened up for discussion and debate, and the emphasis moved from ideology to the importance of productive development and a visible improvement in people's lives.

Deng gave special emphasis to education, Li believes, because of its importance for the economy. From Li's perspective, however, what matters most is the development of human talent, the development of China's people to their fullest potential, and for this there needs to be a full integration of Western and Chinese culture. For forty years, the theme of education to save the country was dismissed as a futile hope of the pre-revolutionary period, but now finally it has been recognized as crucial if issues of energy, environment, population, political culture, ethnic conflict and regional distribution of economic good are to be addressed. The spirit of Li's teacher, Dewey's disciple, Dr. Tai Shuangqiu and his lectures on education as a way forward for the country, now find a new resonance, in Li's view.

4.2   *Zhu Jiusi: Saving Education*

In the most recent talk held with Zhu Jiusi in November of 1999, he quoted from the famous progressive writer Lu Xun's story, *Diary of a Madman*, saying the phrase that ends this remarkable story, "Save the Children" (*Jiujiu haizi*) should now be replaced with "Save Education" (*jiujiu jiaoyu*). Zhu's greatest concern on the eve of the new century was that the tide of market reform and commercialization was sweeping through China's universities, creating a fever for immediate commercial advantage that threatened to undermine all of the achievements of the eighties and early 1990s. In his three-day marathon interview of 1992, Zhu had ended with the comment that he hoped to see maximum freedom of speech and action in China's revitalized universities, and there were only two principles which he considered non-negotiable: public ownership as the main principle of socialism, and the leadership of the Chinese Communist Party over all other political parties in China. By the late 1990s, he could see the necessity of encouraging various forms of private higher education to meet growing social demand, but still saw the major public institutions as the cornerstone of China's higher education.

Zhu had played a crucial role in the rebuilding of higher education in China under Deng Xiaoping. In August of 1977, fifteen university professors and fifteen scholars from the Chinese Academy of Sciences met with Deng Xiaoping in order to discuss the true situation of science and education in China, in advance of the March 1978 national science meeting and the April 1978 national education meetings which set the agenda for the reform period. Probably the most important point for higher education coming out of these deliberations was the commitment to universities becoming centers of not only teaching, but both research and teaching. Zhu personally presented a paper at the national science meeting, entitled "Scientific research should be in the forefront of teaching and learning" (*Kexue yanjiu yao zou zai jiaoxue de qianmian*), which detailed some exemplary experiences of scientific research. At this meeting only two universities were given special commendation for their research work, and one was the Huazhong University of Science and Technology.

In 1979, Zhu was part of a study tour to USA, Canada and Japan, supported by UNESCO, along with four other senior university leaders. The tour lasted two and a half months, with the largest period spent in the United States, and for Zhu it confirmed many of the convictions he had already acted upon, including the important role of research in the university. A key point for him was the observation of a world trend towards more comprehensive forms of knowledge in the university, with institutions such as MIT, Texas A & M University and the Tokyo University of Technology having moved, historically, from a specialist focus on applied sciences to comprehensive curricular coverage in their programs. This showed the limitation of the narrowly specialized patterns imposed by the Soviet model in 1952. Finally Zhu found himself in a position to do something about this for his own institution.

In 1980, he managed to persuade the ministry of education to approve a range of new programs and departments in areas such as Chinese language and literature, journalism, higher education and the laws and philosophy of science at the Huazhong Institute of Technology, putting the college on the road to becoming a fully comprehensive university. In 1982, it was given approval to establish one of the first twenty-two graduate schools throughout China, a striking recognition of the achievements in research since the early seventies and the quality of its academic staff. In 1987, it was retitled the Huazhong University of Science and Technology. Other elements in Zhu's leadership that had contributed to this remarkable achievement were the development of an excellent library holding many international titles, and the systematic acquisition of significant equipment for scientific research.

Since his retirement from the presidency in 1984, at the age of 68, Zhu Jiusi has continued a very active career in teaching, research and higher education policy, functioning as a treasured advisor to the university's Institute for Higher Education Research, and an active contributor to national debates on higher education policy. In the autumn of 1999, he was engaged in teaching a series of four courses to a new group of 19 doctoral students in higher education administration recently admitted to the Institute. The courses covered Soviet influences on Chinese higher education, Chinese intellectuals before and during the Cultural Revolution, higher education problems, and prospects for the present and future of higher education.

The richness and continuity of his life as a political activist, journalist, university leader, administrator, scholar and independent thinker can be seen in the close links between each phase of his career and the ways in which valuable experience and penetrating observation were turned into new ideas that were able to inspire and empower others. He was always open to external influences, but the key source of the ideas he used to shape China's university development came from within China. At the core of everything he did was a concern for the quality of people teaching and researching within the university and how this could be constantly enhanced, a concern rooted in Confucian philosophy as well as in the literature of socialism and progressive thought.

4.3   *Pan Maoyuan: the Integration of Several Heritages*

In reflecting on a whole lifetime in education, Pan felt that he had benefitted greatly from all three of the ideologies most criticized during the Cultural Revolution: Chinese feudalism, American capitalism and Soviet revisionism (*feng, zi, xiu*). From his early studies of Chinese classical literature, he had gained a basic moral orientation and a strong sense of Confucianism as a philosophical tradition that could adapt to every age. From all that he had learned about American pragmatism in education, he gained many useful ideas for school improvement, for more lively teaching methods, and for curricular reform. From his extensive experience with Soviet patterns in the 1950s, he had come to appreciate the value of well-structured teaching materials, unified standards across the country, and thoroughness in teaching preparation and presentation. In the end, he felt Soviet teaching materials and approaches were more suited to China's traditions of centralization in education, and the realities of China's development needs, than American patterns. This was so even though their weakness had been a tendency to become somewhat hard and inflexible.

For Pan, the period since 1978 has been the most productive in his life, and he takes great pride in the leading position of his center for higher education research, the first of only four throughout China that are able to confer doctoral degrees. The greatest challenge in contemporary higher education, he believes, is the need to emphasize students' ability and bring about reforms in teaching that give greater support to the full development of students' talent. This highlights the need for an excellent teaching force in higher education. A great deal has been done in graduate education over the recent fifteen years to provide for new blood in the teaching force.

Pan feels the focus of reform should be on teaching quality and support for the further development of university teachers, not only on changing the management structure and bringing about a redistribution of power, issues that are closely linked to overall reforms in the political system. He believes that Chinese higher education will follow world trends more and more closely in the future. There will be an emphasis on breadth of knowledge and adaptability, and also on the overall intellectual and moral quality of graduates. He sees private higher education as important for broadening access to higher education, and he feels that the concept of lifelong education will become more and more important in China. People will recognize the need to constantly upgrade their own knowledge in order to keep abreast of the rapid changes in society.

4.4   Xie Xide: a Vision for Science and Internationalism

Throughout her lifetime, Xie Xide had experienced intense periods of exposure to very different ideological and cultural influences, and somehow managed to create her own balance and a deep tolerance of spirit, which enabled her to adopt the best from each period, and turn it to the service of what was her major life-long commitment—China's development into a modern scientific nation.

As a child and young person, she was exposed to the liberalism and humanitarianism of an American missionary campus and American missionary schools for girls. The importance she attached to this single-sex education has already been noted above. Overall, she felt that American missionary universities made a very positive contribution to China's development, although the scope of their influence was limited to relatively elite circles. She noted that many graduates of such well-known missionary universities as St. Johns and Hu Jiang in Shanghai, Yanjing in Beijing and Jinling in Nanjing, became senior cadres in China's Ministry of Foreign Affairs after 1949. She noted that the Nationalist leader, H.H. Kung, had refused to give the name of Yanjing to the American missionary university established in Taiwan after 1949, as he felt Yanjing University had educated too much talent for the Communist regime! It was called Donghai instead.

On Leighton Stuart, the famous president of Yanjing University who later became the American ambassador to China during the Anti-Japanese war and Civil war period, it is her unequivocal judgment that he made a great contribution to China, and that there is a need for his role as ambassador to be re-assessed. She noted how Huang Hua, one of the most famous of the Yanjing graduates who served in China's foreign ministry, invited him to Beijing at the end of the war, before he returned to USA. She felt history might have developed differently if the American government had let him go. Stuart had asked to have his ashes buried on the Yanjing campus, and almost all the approvals had been given for this to happen during the 1980s. Unfortunately, the June 4th incident intervened, further delaying this final reconciliation.

Xie Xide's lengthy exposure to American missionary education was one element in her American heritage, the other being her years spent at Smith College and MIT. At Smith she appreciated the personal closeness with her teachers and mentors which the small size of the college allowed, while at MIT she was greatly impressed by the ways in which research and teaching were interconnected—a model she fought for throughout her career in Chinese higher education.

The second important influence in her life came with her decision to join the Chinese Communist Party and give wholehearted support to its leadership in the face of very strong opposition from her father, resulting in an estrangement that was to last until his death in 1986. This was not a blind or uncritical commitment, but a careful judgment arising from her determination to devote her professional life to China's development. The price was high, including the difficult experiences of the Great Leap Forward and the decade spent in a professional desert during the Cultural Revolution. It was a dedication she shared with a beloved husband, and the devotion of this scientific couple to one another was an inspiration to many.

The third influence, that of the Soviet Union, was one she accepted as part of her dedication to China's development, seeking to learn what she could from visiting Soviet scientists in the 1950s and adapting what was useful to the Chinese context. At the same time she remained critically aware of some of the shortcomings that others would only recognize much later.

Her vision for the future of Chinese education is that a small number of universities should attain full international status and standing and be able to give as much to the world community of science and scholarship as they may gain in their international interactions. For this to happen she feels there needs to be even greater national support for university based research, and a full integration of research and teaching in the best universities. Generally she feels Chinese higher education should be broadened, with each institution achieving a breadth of curricular range and moving beyond the narrow specialties that characterized Soviet patterns.

As a physicist rather than a specialist in education, she had little to say about Confucianism or Chinese cultural patterns, but her gentle pragmatism, tolerance, and ability to balance the several sets of influences that shaped her professional development, might be seen as indicative of the best of Confucian humanism. In many ways she had succeeded in moving far beyond the world of her father, with his unresolved inner tensions between Confucian traditionalism and Western science.

4.5   *Wang Yongquan: the Beida Spirit*

Wang Yongquan feels that his half-century spent at Peking University, China's most famous center of higher learning, has given him a unique perspective and set of experiences. What he values most about the Beida spirit is its openness, and the way in which lively debates over all kinds of topics have been able to go on. Beida has always been hard for the political leadership to manage and control. Avant-garde in embracing new ideas, its influences tend to cascade out into the wider society. At various crisis points the top leadership has tried to bring Beida to heel and make sure its members supported the dominant line, but this was never fully possible. Beida teachers and students always had an elusive quality in terms of their intellectual life. They were less unified and so less productive than Qinghua, in the direct sense of research and teaching for nation building, but by the same token they were, in some important way, a conscience to the nation.

Wang's own scholarship in higher education bears some of the marks of the Beida spirit. What he values most is the opportunity to think about new problems, and to raise new issues that relate to them, rather than focusing on the past and publishing traditional works of scholarship. Asked to write a book on the principles and philosophy of higher education, he is still hesitating to lift pen, as he knows many of his viewpoints and perspectives are likely to offend others. He recently aired views on the issue of quality (*suzhi*) in education, and found that they were not acceptable to the prevailing orthodoxy.

As he looks to the future, Wang feels that the quality of teachers is the most important issue for education, not only from the intellectual perspective, but also their affective ability and capacity to understand and connect to young people. A second concern is for an adequate emphasis on humanities as well as sciences and technology, when pressures for rapid modernization seem to give greater importance to the latter.

4.6   *Lu Jie: Developing a Chinese Theory of Pedagogy and Educational Development*

With the richness of China's cultural traditions and the wealth of experience of her huge rural population, Lu Jie is convinced that Chinese educators do not need to rely on concepts and frames of reference from the West, whether American, European or Soviet, but should be able to develop explanatory theories of their own.

Like Li Bingde, she feels that Confucianism forms a strong basis for Chinese education, and she finds herself constantly drawing upon the rich classical literature to which she was exposed in her school days. In human relations,

Confucianism emphasizes reliability and integrity. While filial piety is an important tenet that seems to draw attention to parents and the older members of society, actually children and youth are the center of Chinese family patterns. Parents will make any sacrifice for the next generation, and she herself still counsels young people having difficulty in their marriages not to seek divorce, for the sake of their children's wellbeing.

The most valuable aspect of Western educational influences in China has been the encouragement of the individual, in her view, and the nourishing of a sense of independence. She attributes her own rebellious spirit to her experience of progressive education. However, she feels this is not foreign to Chinese traditions in education. In recent years she has made the notion of "subjective consciousness" (*zhuti*) a centerpoint in a developing theory of pedagogy. Young people are not to be simply molded from without through educational experiences, but engaged in a process whereby their individual consciousness is enriched through interaction with external inputs and the ability to judge and discriminate is nurtured. What has been most detrimental in China's recent educational history has been the tendency to copy slavishly (*zhaoban*) one model or another, rather than building their own educational theories in interaction with a range of external ideas.

For the future, Lu Jie feels that China must develop its own framework, based in education, to encompass a globalization process in which human destinies and human benefits are closely linked around the world. China can no longer blame capitalism for crises that it is as closely linked to as all other countries, no matter what their political orientation. The environmental crisis and problems of economic instability, such as the Asian crisis that broke out in the autumn of 1997 are as much China's concern as that of any other country. It must carry its share of responsibility and contribute in positive ways. For the past century, nationalism has been China's most important preoccupation but now it is being drawn out of its nationalist identity into the kind of global integration that is part of globalization. The challenges of multi-media in teaching and instant global communication through the internet need to be taken up and used in a positive way by China to effect an integration into the global community that is genuinely interactive, rather than a passive accommodation to external trends.

5   Conclusion

What kind of conclusion might one hope to draw from these life stories, and how far can they give us deeper insights into Chinese education in the twentieth century? In his book on *Time, Narrative and History*, philosopher David Carr explores the way in which narrative activity constitutes a part of action in people's lives, opening up both past and future. "To be an agent or subject of experience is to make the constant attempt to surmount time in exactly the way the story-teller does. It is the attempt to dominate the flow of events by gathering them together in the forward-backward grasp of the narrative act" (Carr 1986, 61–62).

This is true for the group, as well as the individual, and Carr concludes his study with the assertion that "action, life and historical existence are themselves structured narratively, independently of their presentation in literary form, and ... this structure is practical before it is aesthetic or cognitive" (ibid., 184). Carr uses the concept of narrative to describe "our way of experiencing, of acting, and of living both as individuals and as communities." He sees it as "our way of being in and dealing with time."

In this paper, I have presented the life stories of six educators, their own personal narratives of family and early schooling, and also each phase of careers that stretched over periods of dramatic change in modern China's development, as seen through their own retrospective eyes. Each stepped onto the stage of history at a different period, two shortly after the 1911 Revolution, two in the years just after the May 4th Movement of 1919, and two in the years just after the establishment of the Nationalist regime in Nanjing in 1928. This difference in age affected the layering of their exposure to traditional Chinese, Western and Soviet influences in education. Likewise their geographical locations gave them somewhat different vantage points.

While their views on the respective value of Soviet, American and European ideas vary, all affirmed the importance of the foundation in Confucian values, nurtured through the family and early schooling. In looking to the next stage of China's development, they all emphasized the quality of human persons, both teachers and students, and found their hope for China's future lies more in the educative development of individuals than in broader structural change.

For those of us who see the study of Chinese education as more than an objective, detached process of analysis, we have much to learn from these insights of insiders into the past, present and future of China's education. We are invited to look backward and forward within their individual and group narrative, to understand the foundations in Chinese traditional thought that have given continuity and strength to lives lived through momentous and often disturbing forces of change. We are also invited to join hands with them in working toward a kind of educational synthesis that will weave the best ideas from world experience into China's own tapestry of thought and culture in a firm and abiding way.

References

Bateson, Mary Catherine. 1994. *Peripheral Visions: Learning Along the Way*. New York: Harper Collins Publishers.

Bertaux, Daniel. 1981. *Biography and Society: The Life History Approach in the Social Sciences*. London: Sage.

Carr, David. 1986. *Time, Narrative, and History*. Bloomington, Indiana: Indiana University Press.

Clandinin, Jean and F. Michael Connelly. 2000. *Narrative Inquiry: Experience and Story in Qualitative Research*. San Francisco: Jossey-Bass Publishers.

Goodson, Ivor and Rob Walter. 1991. *Biography, Identity and Schooling: Episodes in Educational Research*. London, New York, Philadelphia: The Falmer Press.

Hayhoe, Ruth. 1996. *China's Universities 1895–1995: A Century of Cultural Conflict*. New York: Garland Press.

Hayhoe, Ruth, ed. 1984. *Contemporary Chinese Education*. London: Croom Helm.

Hayhoe, Ruth, ed. 1992. *Education and Modernization: The Chinese Experience*. Oxford: Pergamon Press.

Hayhoe, Ruth and Marianne Bastid, eds. 1987. *China's Education and the Industrialized World: Studies in Cultural Transfer*. New York: M.E. Sharpe.

Hayhoe, Ruth, et al. 1993. *Knowledge Across Cultures: Universities East and West*. Wuhan: Hubei Education Press, and Toronto: OISE Press.

Li Bingde. 1986. *Jiaoyu kexue yanjiu fangfa* [Research Methodology in Educational Science]. Beijing: People's Education Press.

Li Bingde. 1991. *Jiaoxuelun* [The Theory of Teaching and Learning]. Beijing: People's Education Press.

Li Bingde. 1993. "A Brief Overview of Sino-Western Exchanges Past and Present." In *Knowledge Across Cultures: Universities East and West*. Edited by R. Hayhoe et al. Wuhan: Hubei Education Press, and Toronto: OISE Press.

Lu Jie, ed. 1999. *Huaren jiaoyu: minzu wenhua chuantong de quanqiu zhanwang* [Education of Chinese: The Global Prospect of National Cultural Tradition]. Nanjing: Nanjing Normal University Press.

Moody, Franklin. 1995. "Factors Affecting the Aspirations and Expectations of University Students in China." PhD diss., University of Toronto.

Pan Maoyua. 1957. "Gaodeng Zhuanye jiaoyu wenti zai jiaoyuxuezhong de zhongyaoxing [The importance of higher education problem in the study of education]." *Xuexhu Luntan* 1(3): 35–39.

Pan Maoyuan. 1984. *Gaodeng jiaoyu xue* [The Study of Higher Education]. Beijing: People's Education Press and Fujian Education Press.

Peterson, Glen, Ruth Hayhoe and Lu Yongling. 2001. *Education, Culture and Identity in Twentieth Century China*. Ann Arbor: University of Michigan Press.

Wang Zengpan. 1993. *Xie Xide* in *Fujianji kexuejia chuanji congshu* [A series of biographies of scientists from Fujian]. Fuzhou: Fujian kexue jishu chubanshe.

Zhu Jiusi. 1992. "Lishi de huigu [A retrospect of history]." In *Gaodeng jiaoyu yanjiu* [Journal of Higher Education] 4: 1–12.

CHAPTER 4

China Central Newsreel and Documentary (CCND) and the Narrative of Educational Film in Modern China

Mao Yijing
Translated by Chad Meyers

Abstract

This paper looks back on the history of educational documentaries released by China Central Newsreel & Documentary (CCND) between 1949 and 1976, and accesses the film archives of CCND to compile first-hand literature on educational film. Moreover, this paper corrects and rediscovers already existing literature, restoring and supplementing research on this period of educational history out of the scattered and fragmented historical materials of educational documentary films. From the perspective of narrative, this paper replays frame-by-frame the fragments of the educational stories that took place after the founding of the PRC, especially in the early period, in the attempt to penetrate through these historical images and recordings of educational scenes to reveal the educational significance implied within them.

Keywords

CCND – educational documentary – narrative

In[1] recent years, the perspectives and methods of researching Chinese education have only increased in richness and plurality, but research on education films is still rarely seen in the academic world. Film is an important medium following closely after text, and represents a cultural turn (Zhou Xian 2008, 245).[2] Turning from dependence on personal experience to dependence

---

1   This article was translated from its Chinese version, which was originally published in *China's Education: Research and Review*, 2014, volume 16, pp. 249–319.
2   In the original text, Zhou says: "Balázs in that year argued that the more important basis for the presentation of visual culture was film. If there were actually a transition from culture

on film, the latter has come to inform people's judgments with increasingly important support. Mare Ferro points out in *Cinema and History* (1993) that the newest trend is to use film as a recording instrument, utilizing it to write the history of our age. A classic example is the rebirth of narrative history in the 1970s as represented by Ray Huang's *1857: A Year of No Significance.*[3] But the narrative style of film documentary is simply the typical manifestation of squaring with "microscopic history." Documentaries are generally representations of another space-time made for the sake of different spectators; they are utilizations of film and recorded sound to describe (construct) history now (Weitz 2000). This way of writing history is an interpretation made with poetic means on the basis of limited historical recordings, whose strength is in making our knowledge of history turn from a chronological recording to the sensations and openness unique to the language of film, which ultimately reaches the truth of history through poetic means.

In fact, the early recordings used in education stopped merely at the functional aspects of objective recording like the educational topics in *Education of Blind Children, Education by Charity* and the early *News Brief,* all of which count as typical samples. Such films that stop at the level of recording—although similar to the chronicles and collections of news articles in history books—are not however works of cinematic historiography.[4] From the perspective of cinematic historiography, there are many films, especially the investigative reporting of documentary films, that use the memories and oral accounts of those involved to testify for history (Ferro 2008, 151–190). Although such historical data is not recorded in the fashion of written documents, it does still possess elements of the nature of written documents. At the same time, it insists that history expressed through optical images and visualized discourse, as well as our thoughts about them, are supplements to "historiography."

In this sense, the broadcasting function of documentary films is adequately explained. Educational films truthfully record the original condition and way of being of some things actually existing in the objective world by means of

---

revolving around language to culture revolving around pictures, would there not also be some transformations worth noticing in such an important form of visual art as film?"

3   In this work, the written form of history employs the methods of compressing space-time and the skills of scene setting often used in film and television, placing the focus of the narrative on a specific minor character or small stretch of time, which, in the process of narration, brings the atmosphere of the times into focus and draws a conclusion about the overall trend of history at the time. Because what it mainly explores is a singular event, it is therefore called "microscopic history."

4   Documentary film was officially established as an art form when Grierson brought up the idea of "the creative treatment of actuality." Similarly, cinematic historiography was also established as historiography.

media, and depict people's understanding of education and the influence that education brings to people's lives through the natural appearance of objective things in cinematographic works. From the researcher's perspective, the expressive means of education that are presented through film are the reflection of an educational activity. When we shift the focus to such basic facts of educational culture and educational life as student-teacher and student-student dialogues, the life of education is naturally drawn into open historical structures, each more wide-ranging and vivid than the next, and scenes of education circulating by way of empirical fact quietly start to rise to the surface, while furthermore composing richer and more colorful pictures of education, such that, meanwhile, research on educational narrative becomes an important form of theory (Ding 2008, 1). The living narratives in education put into focus the inner world and experiences of individuals and groups; they describe people's experiences and actions through the telling of educational stories, and thereby penetrate beyond these means to understand the rich significance of experience in everyday educational life. Meanwhile, film as a form of discourse simultaneously gains public recognition in everyday life.

Putting this aside, due to the popularity of Anderson's theory (Anderson 1991), many related explorations have emerged in the academic world in recent years. In the field of broadcasting alone there has been an upsurge in research on the construction and recognition of national culture. Several different angles of observation of national culture have emerged to take on this topic of "CCND" in text including the "political," "academic," "artistic," "cinematographic," and "mass cultural" perspectives. But the absence of the educational perspective is also an uncontested fact. Observing this stage of history from the educational angle, the "voice" of the documentary film composed out of the producer's story, the spectator's story and the story of the film itself is not merely broadcasting, but is much rather a reflection and recording of fact. The discourse of film expresses education, and conversely, education is also presented through the discursive means of film. The details that are reflected in these different perspectives in fact show the core values, orientations and problems in education.

1   **Educational Film in the *News Brief***

1.1   *The Historical Archives of "CCND"*
The predecessor of CCND (hereafter abbreviated "News Brief" *xin ying* 新影) was the Yan'an Film Group founded in 1938, which mainly shot films on the

war of resistance against Japan and news clips about the front lines and side-lines of that war. This period of film was constrained by conditions preventing larger scale filming activities. Limited film materials include *Yan'an Celebrates the Victory and Memorial Gatherings of the Hundred Regiments Offensive* (1941), *International Youth Day*, and *Chairman Mao's Speech at the Yan'an Arts Seminar* (1942), all of which basically reflect important social events and political life during the Yan'an period (Shan 2005, 81–83).

Following the victory of the war of resistance and the beginning of the war of liberation, the members of the group split up into separate factions heading to the liberated territory of Dongbei, and partook in the establish-ment and production work of Dongbei Film Studio. The Dongbei Film Studio (hereafter abbreviated as "Eastern Film") was established on the basis of taking over the film association ran by the Japanese (The Manchukuo Film Association). The news documentaries that "Eastern Film" produced also went under the name of *Democratic Dongbei* (17 Reels, Total 106 Editions),[5] and generally could be divided into two main parts: "the front lines" part, like Reel No. 3, *Surrounding Jiangnan, The Frontlines of Eastern Manchuria*, and *Reclaiming the Town of Shuanghe*, shot to record the state of the war of liberation in the Dongbei and Huabei territories; "the rear" part like Reel No. 7, *Class Education* and *Eastern Films Nursery*, a set of films documenting the story involving the army and the masses, all of which basically reflect the climate of the liberated territory of Dongbei.

In the autumn of 1948, "Eastern Film" received instructions from the cen-tral government: "No more than a year of war would basically topple the Kuomintang, you must not miss the opportunity to dispatch film crews to all of the front lines, race to film as many documentaries as possible, and put the films in production in nearby Huabei to speed things up" (Cheng 1983, 30). Thereupon, "Eastern Film" sent out the first group of four film crews, and in 1949 sent out six film crews to follow the army south. News cameramen and the core tasks of film production mainly shifted to the Beiping Film Studio founded in April 1949.[6] This newly founded film studio rapidly invested in the work of

---

5   From the beginning of 1947 to July 1949, "Eastern Films" altogether dispatched 32 film crews to scour the frontline and rear, shooting a total of 300,000 feet of film comprised of news material about the Dongbei war of liberation and the Dongbei liberated territory under the title "Fighting for Democratic Dongbei." The material was later edited into 17 reels for the journalistic film *Democratic Dongbei*, 13 reels of which were news documentary films.

6   The Beiping Film Studio was founded on April 20th, 1949, and composed of the members of three departments: one was the "Eastern Films" Documentary Department and the film crews dispatched by "Eastern Films"; the second was the founder of Shijiazhuang Film Studio; the

film-making, and quickly completed five short documentaries and one long documentary entitled *Brief Report* Nos. 1–4, merely in the time span between the founding of the studio on April 20, 1949 and December 1 of the same year. Meanwhile, "Eastern Film" sent members of all other areas to merge with the regional film studio and the film studio of the previous Kuomintang government, and founded some film groups like Shijiazhuang Film Studio and the Huabei Film Crew (also called "The Grand Vehicle Film Studio"), while shooting news documentaries on the war of liberation during the same time period.

After 1949, the literature and art world proposed both launching a great convention of literary and artistic workers from around the country and founding a new organization of the literary and artistic world at the tea talks of the Beiping literature and arts workers on March 22. In April of the same year, Beiping established the Central Film Management Bureau. In August, Yuan Muzhi hosted and convened a meeting uniting news film workers. At the meeting, the CCP Propaganda Department issued *On the Resolution to Strengthen the Film Enterprise*, on the basis of which news film crews throughout the country were greatly adjusted and consolidated, whereby Dongbei Film Studio founded the general news filming headquarters, and divided it into the administrative regions of Dongbei, Huabei, Xibei, Zhongnan, Huadong, and Xinan territories. In summary, what took shape was the north to south configuration of "one corporation with three studios" (The China Film Release and Exhibition Corporation with Dongbei Film Studio, Beiping Film Studio, and Shanghai Film Studio).

At the beginning of the founding of the PRC, the main production companies of news documentaries were: the Beijing Film Studio,[7] the Shanghai Film

---

third was the personnel who took over the third studio of the original China Film Studio (Shanghai Film Lab).

7   Beijing was called Beiping as early as September 12th, 1368, and would only later change its name to Beijing in 1427 as the capital of the Ming dynasty, so Beiping is earlier than Beijing by nearly 60 years. During the first republic it would again change the city name to Beiping on June 20 of 1928. The Japanese puppet government would again change the name from Beiping to Beijing on October 12, 1937, but it did not actually gain wide recognition in the Chinese government and broader masses, so the name Beiping was still in use at this stage. After Japan surrendered in 1945, it was again changed to Beiping, and remained so until after the capital of China was officially fixed at Beiping on September 27 of 1949, at which time it was change from Beiping to Beijing. During this span of time from June the 20th of 1928 to September the 26 of 1949, it could basically be called Beiping. Beijing Film Studio of the early liberation period was precisely the Beiping Film Studio of the Republic period. This article alternates the names Beijing and Beiping according to these nodes and demarcations of time.

Studio, the Dongbei Film Studio, and the August 1st Film Studio[8] (Shanghai Film Studio and Dongbei Film studio would gradually transfer the task of shooting news documentaries to the Beijing Film Studio). As both the companies made adjustments and production grounds shifted, Beijing would become the "central shooting ground" of news documentary film production. Founded in 1953, CCND (News Film) was the specialized and indeed sole company engaged in news documentary filmmaking after yet another central reorganization. Qiao Tongqing (2005, 9) points out:

> The news documentaries that the CCND studio piled up like mountains were the image of the republic, "the people's will," and were the most important source of images revealing such issues as the formation of classes in China during the 20th century, the birth of the nation and the people's liberation. But worth noticing is these images and scripts articulated a unique grand narrative—the model of the nation's ideological narrative.

For the Chinese people of the 1950s and 60s, the *News Brief* was the "news network" everyone watched—at theatres or in open-air public squares.[9] It was not just politics, it was culture and even entertainment, a window opened up for the Chinese people, and for a time, it was even the only window open (CCND 2009, 1). There is even a saying that Chinese film during this time was the *News Brief*.

The numerous *News Briefs*[10] started publication in 1949 so as to memorialize the new China. Each brief came out once a week, each about 10 minutes long,

---

8   The August 1st Film Studio was founded in 1952. Before 1956, it was called the Chinese People's Liberation Army Film Studio. Initially, when the studio was constructed, it mainly produced news documentary films, and the studio's address was set in Beijing.

9   Circulating in the 1960s was a rhyming jingle: "China Film is all news and briefs (*xin wen jian bao*), North Korean Film is all cries and laughs (*ku ku xiao xiao*), Vietnamese Film is all planes and bombs (*fei ji da pao*), and Armenian Film is neither heads nor tails (*mo ming qi miao*)." Another version is: "North Korean Film is all laughter and crying, Romanian Film is all embraces and hugging, Vietnamese Film is all planes and bombing, and Chinese Film is all news briefs and reporting." Such an image vividly shows the monopolistic position, quality and characteristic of the *News Brief* in China at the time.

10 *News Brief* is a film type among news documentaries. The length of every issue was only about 10 minutes, the content touched on pressing political news along with economic, cultural, military and social life and the progressive figures on all battle lines. Every issue had five or so minor themes, but in them there had to be two or three major domestic news topics like the headlines at the front of a newspaper. Short and efficient, quick

mainly using film to document and disseminate news with content including every sphere of social life. From 1950 to 1952 it was called *The New China Brief*, and from 1953 to 1954 *News Brief*, but later it was also named differently depending on the theme, from *News Weekly, Rural News, Rural Brief, Young Pioneers* and *Sports Brief* to *Science News, Liberation Army Brief, Today's China, The People's World, International News Brief* and *International News*, etc. In 1978 the name was changed to *The New Look of the Fatherland* up until the end of 1993. In that year, the editor of CCND, Wang Wei, recalled:

> By the time I came to the CCND organization, the name had already changed to *News Weekly* with an issue coming out every week. By the year of 1955, the CCND studio decided to film mainly short features, listing miscellaneous features as the chief task of film production; they then changed *The News Weekly* to *News Brief* with an issue coming out every 5 days, which increased the production quantity. After several years, the time it took to issue a *"Brief"* was changed to one every week without any changes to the basic form.
>
> During that time, I was mainly editing *"Briefs."* The *Brief* group at that time was like a mobile military camp, often with news film editors editing documentaries, documentary film editors editing miscellaneous magazine features, and also editors who newly joined the studio along with other editors from sister studios studying the art coming and going all the time. By now, I already cannot remember clearly ultimately how many people joined the *Brief* work. Later the studio split into the documentary room and the news room, at which point the respective members settled down, relatively speaking.
>
> WANG WEI, 2009

Considering the changes in the name of the *News Brief*, it was basically like the specialized columns of the news produced in today's TV stations, but it was much more synthetic, basically encapsulating every sphere of society. At the beginning of the founding of the CCND in 1953, the leaders of the Publicity Department (CCPPD) and the Ministry of Culture (MOC) indicated: "In the task of strengthening the production of news documentary film, educational film and short story film to satisfy the pressing needs of the broader masses of laborers, farmers and soldiers, the plan is to found specialized organs and editing departments for educational film and news documentary film." (Cheng

---

and timely, it reported the newest information (relatively speaking) on all aspects of the fatherland through cinematic images. In the historical conditions of the times, it became an indispensable film type in the cultural life of the broader masses.

1989, 30) The Government Administration Council's 131st meeting on the 4th of April 1952 discussed the MOC's proposal *1952 Plan for Film Production Work*, and approved the *Plan's* proposed request to set up specialized organs for news documentary film. Through the analysis of the series of meetings and documents around the founding of the CCND studio, the guiding principle of handling the studio, which could basically be generalized as the CCND, was to set up a "Figurative Party Brief."[11] Its core purpose was that of dissemination and education: disseminate the plan and guiding principle of the CCP and its government, educate the broader masses on how to implement the plan and guiding principle of the party and government, and struggle hard to realize communist ideals.

Film during this stage could basically be summarized into three types: film following the army (the Yan'an film group), film productions by the studio for central news documentaries (previously the Beiping Film Studio), and *News Brief*. The number of films included under the *News Brief* type was particularly massive with the themes, style and form diversifying as well. With respect to exploring artistic aspects of news documentaries, this part of filming was strongly representative of the times with extremely special and classical samples. Basically every big social event was reflected and manifested in the film materials: from recovering national territory to resisting the US, from restoring the national economy to reforming all of the issues left over from the old China, from establishing the people's communes to catching up with the great leaps in progressive movements in Britain and the US, from opposing the right wing tendencies to following the cultural revolution ... in this respect we may assume that the CCND was the biggest organ of documentary film production in China at the time that took on the key creative tasks of the Chinese people's cultural life. Before the TV entered the Chinese household, it was an extremely widespread and effective channel of mass dissemination.[12] CCND's work took

---

11   *Strengthening the Determination of Film Production Work* issued in the 01-12-1954 *People's Daily*, published the editorial: "News documentary is 'figurative political commentary, it is the brother of the newspaper, it should quickly report to people on all the events and phenomena actually occurring, and show the leading figures in all movements and struggles.'"

12   The CCND Studio was also called the CCND Film Group. With the China Central News Documentary Film Studio and Beijing Science Education Film Studio as its core, it was approved by the State Administration of Radio and Television, and in 2010 they collectively set up the national film group. Its predecessors were the Yan'an Film Group founded in 1938 and Beijing Film Studio created during the initial founding of new China in 1949. On July 7, 1953 it was officially founded as the China Central News Documentary Film Group. Extant film materials consist of 42,000 reels, combining 7,000 hours, with a small amount still classified and not open to the public. Among them, the CCND is China's only professional organization producing news documentary films; it is the state's precious historical document archive. The Beijing Science Education Film Studio is currently

on the function of filming and documenting Chinese national history, it was the cinematic expression of the political narrative.

Among all the types of *News Brief* film we can now see, they generally come in two forms: the first type is original films, the central news documentary studio collectively published them as film materials in recent years; the second type is the new documentary films re-cut and re-edited out of original materials in recent years and especially after 2008, which were used mainly to remember and represent the historical situation of those early years.

1.2   *The Cinematic Presentation of Educational Discourse*

Although we could say that the educational scene is disproportionately less than others in the *News Brief* film pool, the educational scene under the persisting lens of history is exceptionally interesting. The original film materials of the *News Brief* became material evidence expressing a sense of history which was disassembled into shot after shot and inserted one after another into segment after segment of new footage. Through recombination, such materials are reconstructed once again by the editors who place them in new discursive bodies of interpretation.

Let us take the long documentary film shot in 1950 by CCND entitled *Liberated China* (editors: Xu Xiaobing, Su Heqing, in color, 1950)[13]—the lens scanned every corner of society at the time like old China, the concessions, old Shanghai, foreign militaries, Sino-Russian relations, land reform, each and every industry, universities, higher education, Tsing Hua University, Children, *The White Haired Girl*, and theatre. Through these films, every aspect of society

---

China's largest studio producing science education video programs. The News Film Materials Department was established in 1953 and mainly takes on the gathering, sorting, preserving and utilization of the film materials of all time periods. Presently, as the sole business that possesses large quantities of historical film materials, it provides foreign and domestic TV stations and film producers with many materials. At the same time, the CCND archive also provides quick computer queries, film projection and videotape selec tions of film materials, as well as videotape conversions and CD writing, film to video conversions and high definition television materials.

13   The film was coproduced by Soviet and Chinese film workers, and it was the first color documentary film that more or less comprehensively reflected China's geography, history and culture as well as the recent Chinese struggle for liberty, pursuit of liberation, struggle for revolution and ultimate victory. It concentrated on describing the history of China's birth after the founding of the CCP and the CCP leading the Chinese people in the struggle against feudal forces and imperialism. The film won first prize in the outstanding full-length film category from the Ministry of Culture from 1949–1955, and in 1951 it won the first Stalin Prize in the Soviet Union.

in the early years of Chinese liberation was touched upon, through these life-like films it seems we can foresee China greeting a new age, an era following the thematic words of "carrying the revolution to the end." At the same time, these documentaries also became the materials about those years most frequently used in today's much more numerous historical documentaries. The documentary *Chronicle of New China's Education* and CCTV's documentaries under the column of *Witness* mostly select what amounts to original film materials from the CCND film pool for the purposes of recreating them. With respect to creating, today's historical documentaries basically all use this method to express history, the only difference being the degree of involvement of the editor during the processing and shooting. For instance, 1949 in the documentary *Memory of the Year of Chou* for the *Film Annals* of *Witness*, three original film materials from those years were used, *The Liberation of the Chinese People* (1949), *Memories of a Prostitute's Turn Around* (1949) (Zhang 2009, 230), *Beijing Students After Liberation* (1949). While using these three films, the new film uses the original sounds and original materials for the sake of seeking the feeling of returning to those historical scenes. The director pre-inserts commentary and then chronologically inserts historical events. If shots that do not suitably express the commentary are not found, pictures or still shots are used to fill in the gaps. The director processes a set of footage in this way:

> [commentary] On the first of January 1949, there was not one bit of New Year feeling to be seen in the city of Beiping and the city gate only opened briefly in the morning and at night. Beiping at this time had already been entirely encircled by the PLA for 10 days.
> [footage] The shot shows a painting of the PLA entering the city in the 1949 documentary film *The Liberation of the Chinese People*, car after car entering the city from outside, detachments aligned in columns carrying guns on shoulders walking down the winding village roads.

At this time the commentary says:

> [commentary] The French filmmaker Henri Cartier-Bresson passed his own New Year in Beiping. At the end of the previous year, he carried an old Leica camera with him here. He shot films for the American magazine *Life*. When *Life* published the picture, it added a note stating that the arrow of war was on the string and about to be released, that they let the famous French filmmaker Cartier-Bresson fly from Myanmar to Peking and finally take a look at the city, which the world knows as

affluent in terms of way of life. On the verge of deep winter, Cartier-Bresson captured a warm record of this city.[14]

[footage] The scene uses subtitles, white block letters in three columns evenly aligned as the foreground of the picture. For the sake of plentiful layers, the subtitles and background were processed half-transparently, and folded into the center of the picture with the picture of Beiping shot by Cartier-Bresson, faintly shining through from the background. The film explained it as a warm memory of the city frozen in the lens, which is also the decisive moment.[15] This shot is continuously held until the male voice commentary finishes reading the words. Afterward the shot switches to the next scene.

In this cinematic dialogue, the director uses citations from historical figures' diaries to prove and recall history through old pictures and letters. Not only does the scene contain segments of cinematic materials from that time, but also recombines these segments and flashes back between different shots to fill in the historical and educational scenes. The whole film does without the method of performing historical re-enactments, and instead uses the common expressive means of written documents, and attempts to restore true history by means of supplementing where historical materials are lacking. Due to the shortage of film materials of the time, motion picture cameras were not present at many scenes, so stills filled in the rest (the filming method of sweeping across old photos with a moving camera attempted to make the photos have the optical illusion of a moving lens, and by transitioning between different photos, the fading in and fading out effect increases the sense of movement and framing).

Editing techniques similar to those in the film above were commonly used methods in documentaries representing educational scenes. For instance, the documentary *Childcare Workers—The Trickle of the Spring* (2006) from *We are the Glorious 8 Great Members* is the classical example of film using original

---

14   Henri Cartier-Bresson (1908–2004), French, world-famous photographer of humanity, was the one who created and practiced the theory of the decisive moment and has been praised as "the father of modern photojournalism."

15   *The Decisive Moment* (New York: Simon and Schuster, 1952) was Bresson's first famous photobook, and it later became the synonym of Bresson's photographic method. In the book he defines photography in the following way, "To me, photography is the simultaneous recognition, in a fraction of a second, of the significance of an event as well as of a precise organization of forms with give that event its proper expression." In 1948, Cartier-Bresson accepted the invitation to do an edition of *Life* magazine, and in early 1949 he shot a set of news photographs, some of which were published in 1949 in *Life* magazine and some of which were chosen for inclusion in his famous work *The Decisive Moment*.

materials and contemporary interviews to trace back history. In the film, the director used original materials in the following way:

[commentary] In this way, Zhen Yuzhen remained in the New China Social Childcare Institute for over 20 years. The New China Social Childcare Institute established kindergartens at Yan'an in 1948, at which time the liberated zones consecutively established many such childcare institutes, Eastern Film's Childcare Institute was one of them.

[Original Film and Commentary] "Eastern Film established a small childcare institute under the current conditions, internally divided it into two departments, the nursery and the kindergarten—for the sake of allowing mothers who had work experience to participate in work as far as possible, it was also for the sake of our next generation, cultivating their wisdom in collective life under organized scientific management, raising good habits and safeguarding their healthy growth—this organization was very good in many respects. Although it was still very basic and still had weaknesses, it wouldn't hurt to introduce it here as a reference for childcare work at other organizations and factories in the hope that this type of organization could be popularized."

[commentary] This is a documentary film shot at the Eastern Film Production Studio in 1948, at which time, it had just been democratically liberated, and the entire country was about to be liberated, one region after the next. Directing added shades of accurate perception to the documentation of life in the liberated zone's kindergarten at the film studio, and was somewhat focused on popularizing the experience to other areas that were not yet liberated.

[footage] Simultaneous with the speaking commentary above, what the lens showed were segments from the documentary *Eastern Film's Childcare Institute*. Since the original film had been shown during commentary, the lens did not shoot the scene of Eastern Film's Childcare Institute. The mode of presentation was black underlined rolling subtitles displaying the commentary. Because of this, in order to make the picture in the lens more beautiful in *Childcare Workers—The Trickle of the Spring*, and also in order to help the viewer return to the historical scene with the film images, the director in one respect retained the original (female) voice of the original commentary and in another respect alternated the pictures with original scenes of children putting on clothes and folding blankets, mothers taking children to the institute and childcare workers feeding children. When the voice of the commentary in the original footage drops but the picture still has not completely returned to present reality, a new male voice continues the commentary:

[commentary] During the shooting of this film, Wang Yurun was the one responsible for the childcare center. After the founding of the new China, Wang Yurun went to the Beijing Central News Documentary Film Studio, at which time, people of all stripes and practices invested in the passion of establishing the new state and the problem of nursing children had to be raised higher on the agenda. CCND was no exception and Wang Yurun participated in establishing the CCND studio's kindergarten.

[footage] Cuts to interview, the interview target is Wang Yurun (the member responsible for the original Eastern Film Childcare Center); the interview location appears to be a library in a house. Wang Yurun says with a full head of white hair in the present day:

[interview] Wang Yurun: "Very many young workers have a meager income, and if you say tell them to work as a nurse they can't do it. What would we do if our young workers give birth at that time? Actually our first guiding principle is to (resolve) the workers' difficulties. Second is to raise the virtue, wisdom, health and all-around development of the children. This guiding principle looks just like this. Actually it is to serve the children and the workers and resolve productivity problems."

[commentary] Since the first purpose of the kindergarten is simply to take good care of the children, there were not too many concerns that arose when handling the selection of kindergarten employees. Wang Yurun selected several female workers from the studio in line with his own understanding of kindergarten work.

[footage] The scene again returns to a documentary segment (Eastern Film's Childcare Institute). In the childcare institute, the children are putting on a performing and painting pictures, while the doctor examines their health and the nanny tells them stories.

[interview] Wang Yurun: "First is we don't want any trachoma. At that time we were still very simple, if we needed a nurse, having an healthy appearance is most important. At that time we wanted uprightness, and if there are any specific flaws too outstanding, we don't want them."

"For example if you say, who goes to work caring for the children? There is that elderly wife over there, who can resolve the problem of looking after them. If there is a child staying at home, he or she can't stay alone, and the kindergarten on the street solves this problem. Solves the problem, but it is still falling behind in other respects, isn't it? With respect to food and education it has to catch up. But it solves this, that is, as long as it supports the children."

Perhaps because an interview with only one manager of the childcare institute wasn't enough to explain or convey clearly the situation in those years, the director immediately attaches and sets up another interview target.

[commentary] Zhen Yuzhen is a teacher at the New China Social Childcare Institute. Over 20 years ago, a child sprang a fever and changed her whole life's direction. At that time, she hadn't been working at the kindergarten for even a month's time.

[footage] Interviewing Zhen Yuzhen (teacher at the New China Social Childcare Institute), a woman about 50 years of age, the interview takes place in the present day in the kindergarten, in the background is a pretty and clean kindergarten classroom.

[interview] Zhen Yuzhen: "At that time, I felt this small child sprang a fever, and afterward I carried him over; he was very uncomfortable, lying there on my shoulder. At this point, the head teacher came in asking me how he was. I said he had come down with a high fever. He asked, 'Were you observing? He sprang a high fever, what caused it?' This veteran teacher woke me up with one sentence. I said he has a bump, aside from that just a high fever. This veteran teacher came right out with it, 'mumps.'"

[commentary] Zhen Yuzhen caught the mumps. She never would have thought such gers lurked in work caring for children at kindergarten.

[interview] Zhen Yuzhen: "Later I stayed at home and rested for a while. I then came back (to the kindergarten). Before leaving the house that day, I thought about it, and decided 'today is the last day.' Then I spoke with the leader and I quit, saying, 'I won't do it anymore.' Because at that time I had not signed a contract with him, I simply came to class carrying this mood. It was just when I stepped into the classroom, when all the kids encircled me in a great commotion, saying, 'Teacher why didn't you come?' I said I been sick. 'Aww, teacher, I missed you, have you just come back?' As a result of saying that, my immediate reaction was to truly forget about that whole affair of quitting."

[commentary] In that way, Zhen Yuzhen stayed at the New China Social Childcare Institute for over 20 years.

[footage] A plain shot of the bronze placard of the New China Social Childcare Institute on a red brick wall, on it is a column of red official script "New China Social Childcare Institute," under it is posted the date of the founding of the institute: 03-16-1948.

This is one of the most frequently seen way of processing film—by fusing together original materials with interviews. The film not only talks about the working and living situation around the childcare institute at that time, through interviews, but also involves cuts of cinematic materials shot in those years in the process of talking (the entire film largely uses footage shot in 1948 of *Eastern Film's Childcare Institute*). The purpose of doing it this way is for the sake of drawing the spectator much closer to the historical scene. In order to avoid the monotony of narrating events, the film also brings up another similar kindergarten: the New China Social Childcare Institute. But since there is no historical footage of that kindergarten, the only thing the director could do is fill it in with a plain shot of present times with added explanation. Considering the aspect of cinematic expression, although there is a shortage of historical footage, which is regrettable, it does not seem to stand out so obviously in terms of how it reads and is presented.

From this we can see that although the lack of new or additional material in terms of cinematic images doesn't return viewers to the historical scene in the true sense of the term, it in fact plays the role of correcting history through the very process of the film tracing back the event. That aside, in documentaries that represent historical scenes, stories that lack historical images are ordinarily supplemented by using still images, and sometimes the theme is expressed by means of inserting still images with moving images.

Through the lens we not only get a look at the clothing and daily life of children in the early years of liberation along with the care they received at the kindergarten, but also peer into the attitude and demands that society and the government had toward childcare. Although the experience of the children speaking is entirely lacking and there is no feedback of parental opinions or thoughts and feelings of the childcare institute staff throughout the whole film, through the lens we can still get a feel for the importance of childcare work. In the end the children have a place to go and the benefit of this place is, "I was honored and happy to be a child of the new China in this era."[16]

Use of the lens in a way similar to this type of documentary is also reflected in the documentary film *New Child* (directed by: Gong Lian, filmed by: Wang Shaoming, in black and white, 1950), *Summer Camp* (directed by: Tan Zhen, filmed by: Tian Li, in color, 1955), *Happy Child* (1953), *Small Training Group* (directed by Duan Hong, filmed by Zhou Kai, in black and white 1955),[17] *In the Childhood Palace* (directed by Jiang Yi, filmed by Zhen Guangze, in black and

---

16   Cited from the commentary in the documentary *New Child*.

17   Outline of the film: Classmates of Beijing's No. 4 Middle School organized a small training group to do physical training, including long distance running, horizontal bar, high jump, grenade throw, rope climbing, double bars. During spring break, each small group held heavy load marching competitions, the classmates had to prepare beforehand, and when the competition began, everyone fought courageously to get ahead. The scattered

white, 1956),[18] *Two Summer Camps* (directed by Liu Caiyao, filmed by Wang Zhixiong, in black and white, 1957), *Child Party* (directed by Wang Chen, filmed by Zhen Guangze, in color, 1957).

In these films children not only learn in class but also visit farms to study.

1.3   Educational Film and the Barriers of Life

Ordinarily, phenomena occurring and observed in educational situations all have their intrinsic, understandable and constitutive meaning. The ordinary person's activities, speech, thoughts and emotions make up a scroll painting of complex interactions, and the narration of the lens provides a practical possibility for explaining such things. Formatted figures, thoughts, voices and experiences converge together to make up an educational event awaiting our observation.

In the early years of liberation, urban and rural peoples remolded themselves through wave after wave of reform. For children of the 1950s, beginning in 1956, "little buddies, the little trumpet has started to broadcast," *The Little Trumpet* (1962) broadcast became the unchanging concern in their memory of their childhood years. Another apparent change was:

> Before the Chinese New Year, the State Council passed bills about popularizing Mandarin Chinese and the simplification of Chinese characters. During the Spring Festival [Chinese New Year] of this year, peoples north and south of the Yangtze started trying to use Mandarin Chinese to extend New Year's greetings and to use simplified characters to write Spring Festival couplets.
>
> ZHANG 2008, 214

Whether it was way of life or habits of education, as long as they could reflect the great project of socialism and keep up with the powerful trend of the times, everyone wasted no energy in changing, especially the innocent children.

What type of child is a child of new China? The state provided a standard of reference. *Gao Yubao* (1953)[19] became the time's storytelling model as well

---

     classmates reached the finish line where the title read: "Prepared to Work and Defend the Nation."
18   What this film documents is all the activities joined in by children at the Shanghai Youth Summer Palace. The Youth Summer Camp nourished children's broad interests and different hobbies. There was a gym club, group singing club, dance club, embroidery club, model boat club, ship building club and an electrical engineering club, etc.
19   In the 1950s, the illiterate soldier Gao Yubao wrote the novel *Gao Yubao*, which became a classic of worker and peasant creation. The publication of the novel led to an upsurge

as the representative of heroic historical figures in documentary film. Through the expression of such images, heroic figures are proceduralized, with flashing eyes, a fighting spirit, humble clothing and hatred of all things evil. Under this influence, the thoughts of the children underwent a thorough inside-and-out change under the overall reforms of the whole social environment. The documentary film *Advancing in Step* tells the story of the young student Bin Baozhu joining the Young Pioneers.

> [footage] In the classroom, a group of students wearing red neckties sit in a circle facing one another, everyone is joining in together to give suggestions to classmate Bin Baozhu.
>
> [commentary] Now all of his classmates were members of the Young Pioneers. In the past Bin Baozhu had a flaw, he was bad at listening in class and often disrupted the class. After the Young Pioneers opened a class group discussing advancing in step, everyone came to help Bin Baozhu. First they changed their own stand-offish attitude towards him, and frequently asked him to do homework together.
>
> Bin Baozhu wasn't bad at Physical Education, and everyone chose him to be the gym team leader. Bin Baozhu corrected his own flaw, and was admitted into the Young Pioneers, and their class became the red neckerchief class.

Although this part of the footage is pretty short and there were only a few words from people on the side, such that merely relying on these elements made it difficult to restore the look of education during the whole decade, no matter how, it was still able to capture the change in people's mentality and everyday life behind these few situational changes from brief identical footage (Gao 1991). Especially changes in education were huge.

---

in learning culture and soldier writing among members of the army. After the novel was published, it led to even more commotion, according to statistics, *Gao Yubao* was published in 7 different national languages. Han Wen's publication of *Gao Yubao* reached 45,000,000 booklets, and was revised into 24 kinds of illustrated storybooks, as well as 12 different kinds of artistic song forms and works in traditional opera. It circulated in mass as storybooks suitable for children to read. As a popular art form for the broader mass of people to enjoy, the illustrated storybook could produce the propaganda effect that theoretical articles and long treatises could not, and thus its development was also encouraged and supported by the government. In 1954, illustrated storybooks reached over 900 kinds, and 350,000,000 booklets, which added over 200 kinds and 150,000,000 booklets in comparison to the year of 1952. It reflects the fact that the new illustrated storybook of actual life began to be published in great quantity.

The early years of the founding of the new China witnessed the establishment of many new organizations and many new policy proclamations; this was an entirely new era of education. Everyone was very busy. Most of these policies were captured in film in the process of their formulation and implementation, and were documented in *News Brief*. Parts of the original material in the first collection of the documentary film *Chronicle of New China's Education* (2008)[20] came from *Democratic Dongbei Ed. No. 13: Brief No. 13* (directed by Xu Xiaobing, in black and white, 1949),[21] and *The New Political Consultative Committee Preparatory Meeting is Established* (directed by Gao Weijin, filmed by Su Heqing, in black and white 1949).[22] The opening scene is a shot of an important education policy being formulated.

---

20   *Chronicle of New China's Education* altogether comprised of 60 parts, beginning with true small stories in the context of 60 big events and important policy decisions in the history of education in the republic, it reflects the development of Chinese education and the practical history of the revolution. Each part is about 30 minutes, and in 2010 it aired on CCTV and the China Education TV channel, but at present it is not officially circulating.

21   The documentary film: *Democratic Dongbei No. 13: Brief No. 13*, produced by CCND studio in 1949, 1 reel. This film has five themes: 1. *Welcoming the Equality of Democratic Figures*, at the Beiping Front Gate Train Station, Lin Biao, Ye Jianying, Liu Yalou wait to greet at the train station. The historical figures appearing in the film are Zhu Xuefan, Shen Diaoru, Lin Boqu, Guo Moruo, Peng Zhen, Li Jishen, Ma Xulun, Li Dequan, Dong Biwu, etc.; 2. *The National Student Representatives Union Held in Beiping*, with representatives of all fields attending. The CCCPC representative Ye Jianying, the PLA representative Luo Ronghuang, the CCP Beiping Municipal Committee representative Zhao Yiwei, the KMT ruled region student representatives and liberated zone student representatives, and also the Chinese Youth Alliance Union representatives Feng Wenbin and Guo Moruo respectively spoke at the meeting; 3. *Dongbei Worker Politics University*, worker students study, hold meetings and discussions at the school; during extra-curricular time they play ball; the graduation ceremony and sending off of students to the south; 4. *Revolutionary Air Force Arrives in Jinan*, leading the revolt were the machinists. Together they fly from Shanghai to Jinan; 5. *Greeting the Nanjing Train*, the Nanjing train was sent to the Nanjing railway office after fellow workers at the Huanggutun train factory in Shenyang fixed it. They see off the Nanjing train heading for Nanjing.

22   The documentary film: *The New Political Consultative Committee Preparatory Meeting is Established*, produced by the CCND Film Studio in 1949, 2 reels. Outline of the film: On the 15th of June in 1949 The New Political Consultative Committee Preparatory Meeting was established in Beijing. The New Political Consultative Committee advocated establishing a democratic alliance government. Joining this preparatory meeting was the CCP, the KMT committee, CDNCA, and non-party affiliated democratic officials, the CAPC, the Peasant Workers Democratic Party, the China Zhi Gong Party, the PLA, the Workers' Union, the Youth Union, the Women's Union, the Students' Union, the industrial sector, cultural sector, democratic professors, Shanghai People's Alliance, minority peoples, 23 stations and 134 representatives of Chinese emigres abroad. The representative of each sector made a speech, and finally decided that the truly democratically united New Political Consultative Committee Meeting was about to start, and China's history was about to enter a new age.

[footage] The first national education work meeting (Dec. 23–31, 1949), with over 200 participants. In the frame you can see the representatives standing single file and entering the meeting hall, outside of which hangs the horizontal banner "National Worker and Farmer Education Meeting" written in traditional script; hanging on the corridor posts are slogans. The meeting hall is huge, and everyone is listening to the report of Ministry of Education minister Ma Xulun. He says: "Workers and farmers of the new China are pressingly in need of culture, and can only thoroughly turn themselves around and more effectively engage in productive work with culture (CCND 2009)." (This segment of Ma Xulun's speech was later cut out and left blank) At this time, the meeting hall exploded in a roar of applause with every representative's face covered in a smile.

[commentary] On the 20th of September 1950, over 500 representatives coming from education systems across the country and in every area converge in Beijing to join in a meeting with special significance—the National Worker and Famer Education Meeting. This was the first time in history that China raised worker and farmer education to the top of the state agenda. The meeting centered on discussing problems such as industrial and agricultural enterprises along with accelerated programs in education, industry and farming, and cadres of cultural extracurricular schools. At this meeting the first minister of the Ministry of Education, Ma Xulun, made the report.

Such documentaries offer footage of the speeches of representatives at the meetings, though they rarely use sound from the same time period, and even cut out the applause during later periods of editing. The audio in the film is extremely simple, usually only retaining the accompanying dubbed voice of men and women without playing any background music at all. We see from other important documentaries of meetings like *The Founding of the Preparatory Meeting for the New Political Consultative Conference* that only chairman Mao's speeches were partially retained in terms of contemporaneous sound, the rest being dubbed later on.

This was also the habitual practice of the *News Brief* in the early years of liberation, just like in the document records of the CCND studio documentary archive, which generally only had the names of the director and cameraman, and seemed not to have a sound recorder at all. Clearly, the most important work focused on at the time was the documentary function of filming along with the task of retaining the frame, while the person's voice was negligible.

Aside from the processing of the human voice, the environment was also an important element in the frame that could not be overlooked. In the new environment of the early years of liberation, getting rid of ornamentation and establishing simple and healthy cognitive and aesthetic ideas was the new lifestyle young students actively sought.

The documentary film *Student Life During Summer Break* (directed by: Wang Xingming, filmed by: Zhang Zhaobin, in black and white 1950), filmed young students and young children in Beijing starting out summer break under the direction of the Beijing Youth Summer Break Life Committee. It shows us the active and healthy student life championed by the government and society. In the frame viewers see them swimming in Kunming Lake, boating in the North Sea or collectively travelling to camping activities. In the Haibin summer camp held at Qinhuangdao, classmates participated in such activities as radio, chemistry, arts, music, theatre and physical education under the guice of teachers, and some classmates went to factories to learn from masters. The film ends saying: "Only youth living in the time of Mao Zedong can live such a pleasant life."

That pleasant life was expressed in such details as changes in clothing and dress. After the founding of the new China urban life underwent revolutions by itself, the most marked of which happened in front of the camera lens: pretty Western outfits were no longer commonly seen, and people's garments were simplified. Female clothing was stylistically simplified, and whereas before no female workers wore the blue cloth cheongsam, now simple blue unlined Chinese gowns were seen everywhere and the youth loved wearing Lenin style outfits; men chose a crop cut and women either cut their hair short or combed it into small braids, while female students rarely styled their hair in perms anymore. The blue streetcars that had previously parked in front of cinemas, theaters and hotel gates disappeared, and students rode their bikes to and from class.... In sum, being inspired by the lifestyle and habits of the PLA in the evolving times made everyone unintentionally change the way of life together. In the intellectual stratum, the traces of the old education system were undoubtedly retained the most. The state's attitude toward intellectuals and their knowledge and the transformation of education was the root of the changes in people's thought in the early years of the founding of the new China. Intellectuals in the camera frame, whether holding meetings or working, always wore a simple Chinese tunic suit or dual use overcoat. Trousers were loose fitting and wide legged, and gender differences between men and women were not marked.

Teachers and students walked to school as of old, but the school atmosphere was no longer the same as before. In the frame, the viewer can clearly get a feel for this naturally exhibited lively and bustling scene. Such a mood expressed in the documentary film reflecting school life entitled *Beijing Students After*

Liberation (directed by Gao Han, filmed by Tao Xueqian, in black and white, 1949) goes like this: in front of the camera lens, the director tells people the overall situation of Beijing students after the founding of the new China through describing the classes attended by university students, their labor on the southward march, participation in the municipal government, urban worker meetings, and work at factories and farms in Beijing. Through the camera lens you can see the life of students during time outside of school as well as during school activities themselves. Through the asides viewers discover that students were more concerned with how to throw off the constraints of the old era, and how to usher in the new era (Zhang 2007). Reflected in the documentary film *Happy Children* (directed by Liu Wenmiao, filmed by Nie Jing, in black and white, 1953), the happiness of the children was revealed in the following context: Liaotung province (which, under the direct assistance of the Soviet Red Army, was liberated rather early and its industrial and agricultural production recovered development rather quickly) created the conditions of a happy life and learning for children.

> [footage] Children from the countryside, in nurseries and kindergartens, joined hands with Soviet children on the June 1st Children's Day with group after group of outstanding children joining the Young Pioneers. They wore uniform outfits, the little girls either had cropped bangs or two small braids, while some children tied lightly colored butterfly knots onto the small braids; the boys cropped their hair short and smiles uniformly covered their small round faces.
>
> [commentary] Little kids reaching school age walked to school. They try hard to learn and exercise their bodies.
>
> During summer break, the children's summer camp was filled with laughter and singing. Children lined up in orderly ranks, hand in hand, dancing and singing, sometimes earnestly listening to the teacher with eyes concentrated on the platform in the classroom and sometimes engaging in recreational activities on the playground.

A documentary similar to this described the recreational activities of youth was entitled *Beijing Youth Summer Camp* (directed by anonymous, filmed by Tao Xueqian, in black and white, 1949). The frame expresses the scene of the summer camp held during the summer break for young students in Beijing (similar to today's summer camps). Shots were mostly panoramas with every frame capturing a group of students and set after set of footage collectively composing the all-around look of the camp filled with diverse activities. For instance the film shows the Beijing Library lending reference books to students, classmates apprenticing in building model airplanes and students riding bikes to the countryside to travel and explore. The sports meet after the graduation ceremony had roughly 3 minutes of footage shooting each track and field competition, gymnastic performances and tug of war matches. The final shot scans over students joining the pledge ceremony of "New Democratic Youth Group" members. In some footage, students appeared with smiling faces of elation and enthusiasm.

In the documentary film *Happy Children*, the kids in front of the camera appear in group form with group after group of children doing similar activities in the frame; basically the figure of small groups of children is in every shot. It is very difficult to record the full coherence of someone's activity and even harder to record an individual's psychological activity through the camera lens, because what the camera shows is always a group. We can easily observe the representative traces of the living environment, clothing and activity of children through such footage.

From the analysis of film materials, such films during the early years of liberation almost always show a picture of the Yangge dance. Students and even young teachers group together into Yangge teams. The people in the camera lens hold such instruments as fans, handkerchiefs, and colored silk, lightly stepping to the gong and drum rhythm, "dancing at heart is singing, and song in the end is dance." Concretely what is sung is not too clear (the contemporaneous film audio is cut out by means of later dubbing). But through the lens you can see that the scene is bustling and boisterous. People also change into different group formations, the bending hip movements are humorously interesting and simply adorable, leading groups of surrounding spectators to dance and sing along. The newspaper at the time said this was a silhouette of students' extra-curricular life, so it was possible see that every environment in this new age fully metamorphosed into something new, and everyone's passions and expectations were high by correspondence. In the end, the decade entered into a new phase, and the Yangge dance precisely reflects and expresses this swelling emotional state.

By the late 1950s, and especially after 1958, there emerged a scene unseen and unprecedented in Chinese history, namely wave after wave of movements beginning to show up on camera. A documentary shot in 1958 entitled *The People's Commune is Good* (directed by Xiao Xiangyang, filmed by Han Haoran, in color, 1958) truly reflects people's mentality at the time:

[commentary] Xushui satellite district's hogs—every one of them had to reach the weight mark of 5,000 *jin*,[23] and currently, the problem waving in front of every commune member's face is no longer anything of the type revolving around labor power, but rather how to launch a high productivity satellite in each production line.[24] This is a satellite cabbage patch, where every head of cabbage must collectively grow to 250 kg, which is not fiction, but rather must be secured through using these concrete measures. This stalk of corn bore 33 tassels, which is not only miraculous but the fruit of labor as well. Reporters from many countries have all come to see it and take a picture of it. The commune members are not satisfied with this momentary achievement, and on the walls here you can see such a mural everywhere, people in one respect use it to express their own ideals and beliefs in life and in another respect also use their own two hands to realize such ideals (Zhang 2009).

[footage] The film largely uses the montage method and angles the camera looking up to magnify the state of production in the people's commune. For instance, a commune member holds a massive cabbage, which takes up the whole frame. Another member holds an ear of corn filled with tassels brimming out the top swaying in the wind. Such free imaginings can be seen everywhere through the film.

What are the lens's free imaginings? They are the unrestrained imagination. We can see from some memoirs of scholars in the art world that creating is for the sake of expressing the soaring efforts and lofty ideals of the masses who must walk a path uniting the romanticism of revolution and the realism of revolution. What the documentary film *The Steelworks of Young Pioneers* (directed by Chen Jian, filmed by Zhang Jie, in black and white, 1958) presents us with is the romanticism of revolution:

---

23   The obviously hyperbolic over-inflation of figures here was part of common practice during and after the great leap forward to over-emphasize the impressiveness of the product being produced in a particular zone or area and thereby forge an immediate link in the popular imagination between a particular policy or state project and its "unbelievably" grand achievements. A number of such hyperbolic exaggerations will be seen in the following text (—Translator).

24   The word "satellite" in English doesn't adequately capture the meaning of the original Chinese term *weixing* 卫星, which although is the term for actual satellites that orbit the earth, literally breaks down to "protective star" or "security star" in Chinese, and so came to refer to "the outstanding production lines and high productivity towns or cities" the CCP was trying to "launch" everywhere to protect "the Chinese planet's" food supply.

[footage] After Students of the 2nd Western District No. 3 Elementary School of Luo Yang Municipality of Henan Province get out of class, they gather scrap metal and bring it to the Young Pioneer Steelwork Factory to make steel. They join in the work with great enthusiasm. The students split up into different groups and engage in production like steel workers.

[commentary] The students build furnaces with their own hands and learn to make steel. They work every day for six hours and study for four hours. The students do experiments at the steel factory and operate in front of the steel furnaces and hold production meetings.

[footage] Late at night, the furnace fire reflects red into the night sky, and reddens the steel forged by the students as well. The children joyfully sing and dance.

A similar scene can be seen in the documentary *Students Forge Steel* (directed by Wang Wei, filmed by Zhuang Wei, in black and white, 1958), the documentary *Little Ones Can Do Big Things* (directed by Xiao Shuqin, filmed by Chen Jinti, in color, 1960). *Little Ones Can Do Big Things* tells the story of the Jingshi Street Elementary School of Luoyang Municipality of Henan Province holding the "June 1st" Association of Factories. We can see through the film that students are both workers of the factory and the masters of the factory. In this school-run factory, there is a radio workshop, pharmaceutical workshop and paint workshop. Specialized teachers and technical workers act as the workshop assistants, who take on the responsibility of guiding the students to learn about the production.

In high school, humanities and sciences bury them in hard work. The documentary *Flying Beyond the Clouds* (directed by Wang Wei, Filmed by Zhuang Wei, in black and white, 1958) describes students of the Beijing Aeronautics Institute, and the story of them designing and making airplanes. In the film, students and teachers work hard, the masters of the factory also come to support, tensely rushing to assemble the whole plane, install the tailfins and wings, landing gear and engine. "Speed" becomes the most forward looking and lively verb for this time period. In another documentary describing the aeronautics institute *Work-Study Program* (directed by Xiao Xiangyang, filmed by Han Defu, in black and white, 1958):

[footage] Classmates go to the subsidiary factory of the school to participate in productive labor. In the factory they make a small imitation Czech MN80 multi-use lathe, they make an electricity meter and assemble a radio.

The camera turns to the workshop, and classmates split up into two classes, one day class and one night class, busily and ceaselessly, they work; they are producing a sowing machine. At the same time, another group of classmates go to the No. 13 Lingshui warehouse work grounds to labor.

Also in this year, through the "Great Leap Forward" across the nation, the government made a target for education work: "In about 15 years [the aim is to] make higher education universal" (film *My University* 2010) over 200 public high schools newly added across the country, and two high schools were founded on average every 3 days. By 1960, the number of high schools across the country had increased from 229 in 1957 to 1,289 in 1960. In 1959, to celebrate the 10th anniversary of the founding of the People's Republic of China, the Minister of the Ministry of Education Yang Xiufeng issued the article in the *People's Daily* entitled *The Great Revolution and Grand Development of Our Education Enterprise* (Yang 1959). The article asserted that the massive development in the Chinese education enterprise over the previous ten years was the result of ten years of education reforms and especially the education revolution and Great Leap Forward of 1958.

The expression of such cinematic images of the "Great Leap Forward" derived into a model for later documentary productions (including film). For instance, ordinarily magnifying such grain crops as corn, rice and cotton such that satellites, rockets or even trains cannot pull a corn cob nor can a person carry a tassel of rice. Likewise, a fish is made to look bigger than a boat and a person needs to climb a ladder to pick cotton or a piece of fruit that is bigger than a human. By applying the means of perspective and montage through the lens, what most films present is positive triumph.

Behind the prosperity and joy in the camera lens, on one hand is the social environment or the needs of the political terrain at the time, and on the other hand is artistic creation seeking exaggeration, which could only count as entertainment (an artistic sense of freshness).

After the festival celebrating the founding of the PRC in 1959, the Ministry of Culture ultimately decided to make a total of 18 films dedicated to the 10 year anniversary,[25] all basically reflecting the wheels of a decade's progress under

---

25   The film includes: Shanghai Film Studio's *Lin Zexu, Nie Er, Spring Fills the World, All Purple and All Red is Always Spring, Old Soldiers New Mission, Lotus Lantern*; Beijing Film Studio's *The Song of Youth, Firestorm, The Lin Family Store, Spring and Autumn on the Water*; Changchun Film Studio's *Five Petal Golden Flower, The Young People in Our Village, Sisters on the Water, The Face Opens through a Smile*; August 1st Film Studio's *Seahawk, Waters and Mountains*, and *The Hui People Detachment, The Sea in Battle*.

the mighty stream of history. These films dedicated to marking the anniversary became a peak of cinematic creation in the new China, and in its cinematic history: this year was called "the unforgettable 1959" (the Ministry of Culture held week long exhibition activities showing the new National Day Anniversary films across all the big cities, where the number of viewers reached 120 million). There were also scholars who called this the cinematic style of realism. By comparison, in the documentaries of 1957–1959, the cinematic images witnessing scenes of education were so surreal and inconceivable.[26]

Holistically considered, education type documentary films did not completely film everyday life. Neglecting the parts that exaggerate, other parts seem retain some content about everyday life in those years, with footage partially expressing the details of everyday life interspersed with all types of themes. For instance, the powerful architecture of the Tsinghua Library, the still and respectful atmosphere, and levels of mystery in the documentary *The Engineers of the Future* (directed by Chen Chunlie, filmed by Gao Zhenzong, in black and white) make people fully concentrate and find resonance in themselves through what the lens shows. From the perspective of architectural culture, you see another still view of educational life.

We can see from the Sino-Soviet co-produced documentary film *Great Friendship* (directed by Wang Yonghong, filmed by Wang Decheng, in black and white, 1954) that Chinese courses were set up in some Soviet schools. Similarly on Chinese campuses, middle elementary school foreign language courses were set up, and nearly all of which were Russian. We see the Liaoning Province Education Hall holding a test in the school in the documentary film *Black Mountain Northern Pass Elementary School Education Reform* (directed by He Zhongxin, filmed by Li Zexiang, in color, 1960) that compares a second grade experimental class with another 4th grade elementary school's class with respect to writing, character recognition and reading comprehension, and the 2nd grade experimental class students were superior to the other in each respect. The documentary film *The University Under the Qilian Mountains* (directed by He Zhongxin and filmed by Fei Long, in black and white 1960) allows us to see the situation of the agricultural university (during the Great Leap Forward) in 1958 from Lanzhou to Wuwei Huangyang Township under the Qilian Mountains. Classmates of all majors walked from classrooms to the open countryside; the classroom was no longer the only place where classes were held, and labor became an important class. The students in the film were

---

26   Premier Zhou Enlai at the State Ministry of Culture in Beijing held a long meeting of all film studios from the 1st to the 7th of November 1958, pointing out: "What we want is documentary art films, and not artistic documentary films."

shown in over 30 education-related scenes, studying while apprenticing and co-producing a series of specialized research. The documentary film *Cultural Revolution* (directed by Deng Baochen, filmed by Zhang Yitong, in black and white, 1958) offers an even more expansive view of China, from East to West, showing the revolutionary reforms in education.[27] The camera shows night-classes in all the regions with workers and peasants picking up lanterns after work and heading to night school. There are shots of their work breaks, where viewers are shown the commune members reaching down to grab books, newspapers and musical instruments. During work breaks, the commune members read books and newspapers, play the tambura, and sing and dance.

Looking more closely, it does not appear to be a cinematic image typical of that decade, the educational life as filmed was so tranquil. In a decade of such clamor, the lens pays respect to the calm everyday life of education through a few details. Education in the 1960s truly could be said to present two completely different extremes through the camera.

2   The Stylistic Characteristics of CCND Teaching Materials

2.1   *Early CCND's Selection of Education Themes*
The main feature of the *News Brief* in the 50s and 60s was to bring the cinematic monopoly under the state ideology into the foreground. Many news documentary themes were "figurative political theory" fully complementary with the social theory of the party newspaper at the time. According to Gao Weijin's statistics, from 1949 to 1966, China annually produced 250 collections of news film and documentaries. Complete documentary films include: long documentary films, 239 on 1,506 reels, short documentary films, 2,007 on 3,632 reels, news periodicals on 3,528 reels (Xiao 2005; Gao 2003).

The specific distribution for each year was: 11 in 1947, 21 in 1948, 29 in 1949, 57 in 1950, 39 in 1951, 30 in 1952, 53 in 1953, 62 in 1954, 86 in 1955, 104 in 1956, 71 in 1957, 119 in 1958, 87 in 1959, 93 in 1960, 61 in 1961, 36 in 1962, 47 in 1963, 47 in 1964 and 82 in 1965.[28]

In addition, starting in the spring of 1958, each province and autonomous region across the country (excluding Tibet) took the great leap forward to establish film studios, at the beginning of which conditions were such that

---

27   From the 1st to the 11th of June 1960, a meeting of representatives of progressive units and progressive workers in socialist projects in education, culture, sanitation, physical education and journalism from across the country was held in Beijing. It called on all cultural cultivation workers to push the cultural revolution to new heights.

28   I have based this on the statistics of the film catalogue publicly released at present on the CCND Film Studio official website, <http://www.endfilm.com>, 2012-01-20.

only news and documentary films could be shot. In 1958 alone the entire country had 31 film studios producing news documentaries, so that in 1958 and 1959 the total quantity produced was nearly equal to the sum of all that produced in the previous 8 years. From 1967 to 1976, CCND and August First Film Studio coproduced 509 long and short documentary films and 2,037 news periodicals. These figures do not even include all the film materials that never became films (Shan 2005, 117–225).

Summarizing educational types of *News Briefs* there are mainly:[29]

Year	Film name	Reels
	Beijing Youth Summer Camp	1
1949	*Dongbei Military and Political Academy*	3
	Beijing Students After Liberation	1
	World Youth Visiting China	5
1950	*Student Life During Summer Break*	2
	New Children	2
	Tractor School	1
	Women and Infant Hygiene	2
	World Youth Alliance Representatives Come to China	1
	Professor Hua Luogeng	1
	Welcoming Dr. Li Siguang	1
	Renmin University School Commencement Ceremony	1
1951	*Dongbei Work Academy*	1
	Central Committee Theater Academy Cheng Cuixi ce Research Group	1
1951	*Dong Bei and Xibei Youth Travel Groups Visit Beijing*	2
1953	*Happy Children*	6
1954	*Engineers of the Future*	2
1955	*Dedicating the Spring Youth to the Fatherland*	3
1955	*Advancing in Step*	2
1956	*Summer Camp*	1
	Asian Students Medical Treatment Academy	2
	The Petals of Youth	2
1956	*In the Youth Palace*	2
1957	*Our Holiday—June 1st Children's Day*	1
	Children's Party	2

---

29 The statistical data on the films in the table is from the CCND Film Group website's materials search. The film materials without the number of listed reels is from (Shan 2005).

(*cont.*)

Year	Film name	Reels
	We are the CCP Youth Group Members	1
1957	*About to Blossom*	3
	Successors of the New Countryside	2
	Two Summer Camps	2
	Dr. Ha Da in Beijing	1
	Professor Ma Yuehan	
	Winner of the Science Scholarship	
1958	*Students Make Steel*	2
	Work-Study Program	2
	Descents of Dogged Perseverance	1
	The Young Trailblazers Greening the Changjiang River	1
	The World's Children Singing	4
	Youth in the Battle	1
	Young Pioneer Steelworks	1
1959	*The Glory of Youth*	1
	Long Live the Youth	8
	The University Under the Qilian Mountains	1
1960	*The National Conference of the Heroes of Cultural Education*	2
	Black Mountain Northern Pass Elementary School Education Reform	3
	Asian-African Student Medical Treatment Academy	2
1961	*Celebration of the 50 Year Anniversary of Tsinghua University*	
1963	*The Young People in the Production Team*	1
	The Name Change of Yuwen University	1
1964	*Emulate, Learn, Catch up, and Help Struggle to Swim*	2
	Diary of the Young Contestant	1
	Rising Day by Day	2
	The Acoustics Laboratory of Modernization	
1965	*Cultivating Newcomers: Working One's Way Through Education*	1
	Jiangxi Communist Labor University	2

If we engage in "viewing" from the perspective of history, these film materials make up a cinematic China of the 1950s (Liu Jie 2007, 2), and bring about a rhetorical and linguistic form unique to Chinese documentary film. What most of the films of this period bring into focus is the scene of comprehensively unfolding the construction of the new China. For instance the films shot to commemorate the 10 year anniversary, *The 10th Spring* (1959) and *The National Conference of the Heroes of Cultural Education* (1960), show the bright light of the new China, where the camera lens captures those deeply moving pure smiles. The films seem to brim with a mood of gleeful talk and swelling satisfaction everywhere, yet the proportion of cinematic images of the state of life in the CCND archive is minuscule, and the film materials lack profound descriptions of everyday life in China. In the limited source of films the topics of Chinese education touched upon is basically wholly connected to politics.

Viewing these cinematic images one can only peer into the scene of education during that period from one angle, and taking them as significant historical documents outweighs all other considerations because, they are far from anywhere near genuine scenes of education and observations of the normal state of life in education.

In addition, there are story plots in the documentary films, most of which were predetermined beforehand, which is different from representing real scenes, and instead makes the films of a performative nature. For instance, *Advancing in Step* (directed by Wang Chen, filmed by Zhen Guangze, in black and white 1955) shows a young student, who having fallen behind, progresses and eventually joins the Young Pioneers with the help of the collective group. This actually happened, and the environment and historical figures are real, it is only that a Young Pioneer who was a good performer played the student in the film because the real student who fell behind was unwilling to be filmed (Shan 2011).

By the beginning of the Great Leap Forward in 1958, documentary film started to become absent. The serious natural and human disasters were nearly absent from documentation. Every venue was flooded with scenes of the surge in steel smelting and news of launching satellites, one *News Brief* in 1958 reports:

> Tianbei commune of Xingzi Township in Lian County, Guangdong Province created a huge agricultural satellite of over 60,000 *jin* of middle season rice per *mu*, Huancheng County of Guangxi Province also launched a 130,000 *jin* satellite. This moment has made those of the wait-and-see attitude exclaim: people are so bold, the earth produces so much, and the farmers of today have outpaced the immortals
>
> ZHANG 2009, 269

At this time the number of cinematic art films grew to over 100, while documentary films reflecting the Great Leap Forward approached 50. In just 1958 alone, there were 7 documentary films touching on the topic of education.

Behind this growing number of uniformly cut films, the famines, difficulties, tears and anger brought about by disasters were all but covered up and concealed from view entirely. School life also turned into *Work and Study Program* (1958), *Students Making Steel* (1958), *Young Pioneer Steelworks* (1958) and motivational films tightly tied to the state of production.

Directors shot films with the principle of maintaining an upward looking perspective, involving exaggerating, deforming and magnifying original images to emphasize a mighty scene of plentitude. Free imaginings about education were seen everywhere in films. Under the command of this powerful state narrative, the voice of the base weakened considerably, and although "the people" were present in the scenes of education, "the people" were in fact absent.

2.2   *CCND Documentary Films after the 1960s*[30]

By the 1960s several massive historical events became the focus of documentary film: the documentary film of the first Chinese athletes to climb Mount Everest, *Conquering the World's Highest Peak* (directed by Wu Jun, filmed by Wang Ximao, Mou Sen, Qu Yinhua, Shi Jing, Wang Fuzhou, Liu Qiming, in color, 1960), and that of the first successful nuclear test *The First Atomic Bomb Explosion was a Success* (1964). The instants and details of momentous historical moments that these films document have themselves become documentary film materials used today to reflect that segment of history.

Educational content is almost entirely lacking from such films. Partial footage like the extremely tragic scenes of Tsinghua University students smashing and toppling the Tsinghua Garden Plaque, burning books, calligraphy, paintings and temple statues, and group denunciations have been found scattered through some documentary films focusing on other historical themes. Although these frames, used to document events reveal shocking scenes, it must be pointed out that "the reconstructing and remaking of cinematic images" (disassembling and reassembling) can also be used to interpret and warp history.

In fact, in the *News Briefs* of the 1960s many news events and historical figures underwent a process of imaging and idolizing, and the discourse presented requires authenticating truth from fiction. Due to the background of the time of the creation of these filmed pieces, it is unavoidable that there

---

30   The cinematic expression of history is basically divided into two levels: one is historical documentaries, whose sole mission is to truly restore history; two is historical films and TV series that mainly demonstrate history, the common region of the two is the historical writing style of their narratives.

is suspicion about the re-making and beautifying of history. In utilizing these materials, we must exercise maximum caution and it seems we cannot replicate the past model and, even less, go along with it perfunctorily.

Cheng Huangmei points out that the central thought of documentary film creation is underscoring the "problem of truthfulness" in documentary film. He states: "News documentaries must describe actually existing things and describe events that actually occur, one cannot fabricate facts, otherwise one would make news documentaries lose all political prestige" (2005, 115–225). Looking at it today, this idea is powerful and sobering. If this reminder had been the long term guiding thought of CCND and had it been implemented up to today, China's cinematic history would necessarily have been rewritten. However, the facts sadly suggest otherwise. In the films of the 1960s it is hard to see film with a truthful and sober form of discourse.

For political reasons, not all film materials from the interval between 1966 and 1976, the period of the Cultural Revolution, can be released to the public at present. Yet merely from the limited footage available, the history concerning the Cultural Revolution is in fact documented richly in film. Basically, all film after 1966 in China is documentation of revolutionary movement. Every activity of Mao Zedong meeting with Red Guards was documented on film shot mainly by CCND and August 1st Studio.[31] The films CCND shot include: *Mao Zedong Meets Red Guards and Revolutionary Teachers and Students, Chairman Mao together with the Million Strong Army of the Cultural Revolution, Chairman Mao's Third Meeting with the Young Generals of the One Million Strong Revolution, Chairman Mao is the Red Sun in Our Hearts— Celebrating 17 Years of State Building, Chairman Mao's 5th and 6th Inspection of the Great Cultural Revolution Army, Chairman Mao Forever Connected to Our Hearts—Chairman Mao's 7th Inspection of the Great Cultural Revolution Army, Glorious Model of the Great Beginning—Chairman Mao's 8th Inspection of the Great Cultural Revolution Army*, etc. (Shan 2005, 235).

There are only two main roles in these films: The leaders and the masses. The leaders, aside from Mao Zedong, also include Lin Biao and Jiang Qing who don't leave his side and the members of the China Central Cultural Revolution Minor Organizations. Among the masses most of them are students, and in most of these films one rarely sees any special shots aimed at any one person,

31   From the 19th to the 26th of August 1966, Mao Zedong met with Red Guards and university and middle school teachers and students 8 times at Tian'anmen Square; the total number of people reached over 11,000,000. Such cinematic images were produced into film materials, but at present these parts have not been released.

the majority of the shots are of big public squares. Paying their respect to the leaders, students appear in the majority of frames as far as the eye can see like a green sea. In the footage it is impossible to make out their ages and genders, you can only see their energy and enthusiasm, and because they are overly similar looking it is impossible to distinguish individual differences.

For instance in the documentary *Chairman Mao is the Red Sun in Our Hearts—Celebrating 17 Years of State Building* (directed by anonymous, filmed by anonymous, in color), we find (CCND 1967):

> [footage] In the early morning of the 1st of October, masses in the millions congregate at Tian'anmen Gate. In the frame, marching and gathering teams wind back tens of *li*, human shadows thickly dot the scene and seem to all want to crowd into the frame. Chairman Mao comes to the Tian'anmen Gate Tower and waves to the masses. The masses passionately cheer him. 1.5 million of them flood through Tian'anmen Square, welcoming his inspection. Premier Zhou Enlai, Li Fuchun, Liu Baicheng, Xu Xiangqian, Nie Rongzhen, Ye Jianying, etc., are all at Tian'anmen Gate observing the ceremony. After the marching ranks walk by, the masses crowd toward Tian'anmen Gate. Chairman Mao walks down to Tian'anmen Gate and walks into the crowd. The night of the holiday, fireworks light the night sky red. Chairman Mao again comes into the crowd, and sitting on the ground, begins speaking affectionately with the crowd around him. The crowd, cheery and upbeat, set off fireworks in a spectrum of different colors.

The CCND documentary archive's footage of this film is described in the following way (film summary commentary from the documentary archive):

> [footage] Repetitively re-viewing the [original] film footage, there is a sea of people in front of Tian'anmen Square, between each shot there are great similarities, shots of the ranks inveterately use full-length shots. In a frame there are countless regularly arranged squares [of groups of people], and the camera lens continues to follow the low movement of the groups. In the shot, every square, because of uniform outfits, is a single block of color as far as the eye can see. Some ranks are holding up the red flag, which appear extraordinarily eye catching in the square blocks. The ranks slowly march forward, and upon reaching the front of Tian'anmen Tower, you see the groups break into cheers, with colorful ribbons and balloons flying up all over the sky.

Actually, the state at this time already had fallen into unprecedented turmoil, and the filming work of news documentary was in a state of turmoil as well (currently such footage still has not been publicly released, with much material missing and unavailable to corroborate history). The majority of the members of the CCND had all joined the Cultural Revolution, and only a small portion of the members shot some films reflecting scenes of the revolution under the leadership of the Military Propaganda Arm and the later Worker Propaganda Team (aside from the films mentioned above which reflect Mao Zedong meeting the Red Army, there is also *Fanning the Surge in Revolutionary Critique, The Red Sun Shining on the Beijing Opera Stage*, and *The Red Sun Shining on the Ballet Stage*, etc.), and continued to produce assorted news clips in *News Brief*. During the Cultural Revolution, although *News Brief* did not stop publication, the number of issued briefs dramatically decreased. Taking 1967 for example, only 10 issues were released that year (while normally at least 52 issues would be released annually, with, on average, one each week, and sometimes extra), and moreover, the time of release was not fixed (sometimes one issue would be edited in a night, and sometimes only one issue would be edited in over a month).

The main content of such films included big-character posters, debates, grand critiques, revolutionary tours, smashing the "four olds," long marches, Red Guard movements, critiquing leaders, etc. These come in black and white and color, with the lens basically adopting whole-scene compositions, showing big public spaces and usually using full-length shots. You can see that the cameraman's skills are consummate, shooting in such an environment of unstable turmoil, the camera is basically stably shooting and the frame composition is intact. Educational documentaries at this time were nearly wiped out completely, and the only few mentioned in the document summaries of a few scholars are no longer extant, like *After Class* and *One Day in Kindergarten*. In addition, there are also a few documentaries reflecting "education reform" like the film attacking "the trend of the right wing reversing cases" produced by CCND at Tsinghua and Beijing University (the film name is uncertain).

At present the materials available for research mainly depend on CCND's already published works and footage that may be aired after having received a permit, with some film materials circulating partially in underground channels. Because of this, the materials analyzed later on in this text are also drawn from these partial contents. It is imaginable that once the ban is lifted and these materials are collated, they will amount to a set of important historical materials in witness of Chinese education.

For the main content touching on education from 1966–1979 *News Briefs* see the table below (Shan 2005):

Year	Film name	Reels
	The People's Army in the Snowfields	1
1966	Learning From Chairman Mao's Good Warrior Liu Yingjun	2
1970	Model of the Revolutionary Youth Jin Xunhua	1
1973	Flower Petals Open in the Sun	3
	The May 7th Cadre School is Filled with Life	2
1974	The Vast World Nurturing New People	1
	Children's Day	1
1976	Young Sprouts	2
1977	Dazhai Small Martial Arts Team 1977	3
	New Sprouts	2
	Spring Buds	4
1978	Strong Growth—The Young People of the 7 li Camp	2
	Loving Science from a Young Age	1
	Young University Students	1
	Attending University at Ningbo	Unspecified
	The Mathematician Chen Jingrun	Unspecified
	Professor Chen Xingshen Comes to China to Give Lectures	Unspecified
	The Brush of Innocence	2
1979	For the Kids	5
	Professor Li Zhengdao Comes to China to Give Lectures	Unspecified

The footage from this period of documentaries appropriately expresses the political environment and atmosphere at the time. In the camera frame, the most frequently observed action is the saying of goodbyes at the train station.

[footage] In front of a train about to depart, every window is crowded with the silhouette of young children uniting and going down to the countryside. They lean out of the train windows waving goodbye to teachers and parents on the platform. Many are holding "The Little Red Book" in their hands. The train slowly takes off and everyone's hands wave continuously, many waving "the Little Red Book" in both hands. The

people on the platform throng together all elated in mood, the feeling of departure hurts and at the same time is also interspersed with passion and excitement.

At this time, the camera cuts to a close-up of a flag on which is written the following place names: Zhao Shan—Jing Gang Shan—Rui Jin—Zun Yi—Yan'an—Beijing, in the center of the flag is written in large Song dynasty font "Forever Following Chairman Mao." At the very bottom, a column of small characters reads: Henan Tongxu—Jin Song Long March. This is where this train is about to go. At this moment the frame is not accompanied by contemporaneous speech, the music accompanying the film is an impassioned revolutionary tune. The march melody incites the frame with an unspeakable emotion of worry and excitement.

[commentary] from Beijing to such revolutionary holy land as Yan'an to Zhao Shan to Jing Gang Shan, the students unite in great scope and carry on for over 2 years. (CCTV 2005)

Turbulent times and turbulent life. Swept along by the revolution, every single person whether the lowest plebes or the highest nobility like Chairman Mao were sincerely swept along in the vast ocean, insignificant, fragile and breakable, often swept away in total silence to who knows where. The cinematic images in the CCND and from the Cultural Revolution itself are more like documents of the survival conditions of a generation of youth and intellectuals. Looking at these film materials is like looking at every stage of Chinese history, facing the unavoidable heaviness in it will become history along with everything else.

Turning this page of the Cultural Revolution, CCND's creations entered a stage of greater documentation. Laying out the facts and talking about the truth, the camera lens in the *News Brief* is always proving the achievements attained in Chinese education. Every important historical moment and news event is extracted in 10 minutes using the news brief form. Like the documentary *Little Trumpet* (1962–50) (Dept. of Film Materials 2009, 99) which begins with lively language:

[footage] Now let all of us viewers go to the China National Radio station together to visit the little trumpet! This is the young announcer Yuan Jie. This is teacher Sun Jingxiu. This is "the Kitty Cat" performed by the Big Street Kindergarten child Shi Fuma. "Da-di-da, da-di-da, da-di-da—da—di—, kids, the little trumpet show is now broadcasting!"

[commentary] The content broadcast by the little trumpet show[32] is mainly children arts programs like the telling of stories, children's songs, children's radio plays, etc., it once continuously broadcast long feature stories like *Journey to the West, The Story of the Veteran Revolutionary when just a Child, The Story of Gao Yubao*, and *The Rubik's Cube Building*. Some works of famous children's literature authors like Zheng Yuanjie were once broadcast on this program. Some commentators point out that the radio story of the little trumpet was unique in linguistic style with meticulousness, considerateness, kindness and grace, it was filled with feelings of love and care for the children.

The style of these CCND documentaries shot in 1962 is the main style of the *News Brief* produced later on. The films began to consciously take up concern for some individuals in films like *Attending University at Ningbo* (1978), *The Veteran Teacher Wang Senran* (1981), *The Bridge Specialist Mao Yisheng* (1982) and *Female Ph.D. Wei Yu*.... When the films were shot, the perspective chosen was still upwardly focused, with the cameraman generally standing below the subject in a posture with the gaze looking up. From the documentary subject to the shooting angle, the documentary is basically treated as a political, propaganda or educational instrument (Guo and Chen 2009). The filmed subject is always higher up, an idol to be revered; filming a historical figure is almost like praising a deity. This idealized creation immediately resulted in the perspective presentation of that period of documentary film. With the narration regarding the individual entirely different from the documentary creations after the 1990s, the descriptive form is unique to that point in time. Considering the early style of *News Brief* as a whole, it is simple and general, while later it absorbed the methods of production used by feature movies and television documentaries with its touch stretching out to the individual and the record of actual events. Consider the incomplete statistics on these films (Shan 2005):

---

32   "The Little Trumpet" [*xiao laba* 小喇叭] is a famous children's program on CNR, it started airing on the 4th of September 1956 and continues to air today, it has accompanied the growth of the three recent most generations of Chinese people, and it is the only children's radio program with a set segment of time and is even the only one in all of China. Thus, it is a children's program with the broadest coverage and biggest influence in mainland China.

Year	Film name	Reels
	Messenger of the Youth	2
1980	*Shining Young Spring*	2
	Children's Voices Loud and Clear	2
	Politeness Class	1
	Make Kids Smarter	2
1981	*Studying Abroad in China*	2
	Kids' Day	2
	The Veteran Teacher Wang Senran	2
	The Budding of Theatre	2
	Nobility in Diligence	1
	Science and Technology Reserves	2
1982	*Senior Middle School Vocational Class*	1
	The Great People's Educationalist Tao Xingzhi	1
1982	*Professor Ma Bi Returns*	2
1983	*They are also Gardeners*	2
	Red Cross Youth	1
	Bridge Professional Mao Yisheng	Unspecified
	Female Ph.D. Wang Yu	1
	Home Kindergarten	1
1983	*Female Engineers*	2
1984	*The Native Home of Confucius*	2
	A Generation of New People—Communist Youth Group's 11 Great Sidelights	2
	The Strength of Young Sprouts	2
	The Cradle of Future Navigators	2
1984	*University Students*	4
1985	*Huangpu School friend Xi Zhongfeng—Commemorating Huangpu Military Academy's 60th Anniversary*	2
	Candle Light	2
	Prodigy	8
1985	*Brotherly Affection—Chinese and North Korean Youth Get-Together*	3
	Heart of Green Grass	11

(*cont.*)

Year	Film name	Reels
	Our Alma Mater Hangzhou University	3
1986	*The Strong in Life*	2
	The Deep Ocean—Record of Chinese Youth Visiting Japan	6
	The New School Model	2
	University of Science and Technology of China	2
	One Day in Kindergarten	3
	Young People in the Field	2
1987	*Qinqiao Summer Camp*	1
	Engraved in Fertile Soil	2
	Lijiang River Lute Child	2
	The Rhythm of Youth	1
	On University Campus	Unspecified
	Music Kindergarten	2
1988	*Vocal Music Professor Huang Youkui*	2
	From Child Star to Film Star	2
	Youth and Seeking	2
	Sketch of Beijing University	3
	China Series: Beijing University's Barren Farmland	2
1991	*Running a School in a Mountain Village*	2
1992	*To Life—Visiting the Lu Xun Arts Academy*	2
	Striking the Minds of Children	1
1993	*Mountain Nook Elementary School*	2
	The Villages of Confucius and Mencius	2
1993	*Cradle of Talent*	2
	Studying Abroad in the United States	2

As the state focused on film document materials, the Central China Film Studio's many years of dust covered documents were recompiled and edited into films. After the year 2000, these original materials were consecutively compiled and edited into series after series. Scanning, re-organizing and re-interpreting these historical materials became a chief task of current documentary creation.

For instance the original film commentary of *News Brief* (CCND 1962):

[commentary] Beijing Foreign Language Books is a bookstore providing foreign book materials for the capital's foreign readers, supplying

40 kinds of foreign language books. The over 25,000 books here include many world famous ones. In the phonograph department attached to the book store there are over 3,000 foreign records for people to buy.

The commentary from *News Brief—China: the People* 1961–1979 (CCND 2009):

[commentary] China is a state with a long enduring civilization of 5,000 years, and roaming the long aisle of history one can only get a taste of the broad depth of Chinese civilization through reading the ocean of its books. China has always focused on the compilation of history, from which emerged massive works like Sima Qian's *Historical Records*. In ancient times, the literate were originally just a minority of people. As a tool for disseminating knowledge—books passed through the first phases of Bone Oracle Script, Bamboo and Wooden Slips, Silk Manuscripts and then the later paper books, all of which only circulated among the minority of literate people and rulers and never came into contact with the broader working masses of people. Because of this, the emergence of the book store in the recent sense of the term, along with the popularization of culture, the spreading of knowledge and communication with foreign countries all played huge motivating roles. Today, our commonly seen book stores include Xinhua Book Store and the Foreign Language Book Store.

  Due to suffering the invasion of the strong Western powers, increasingly numbers of scholars in China in the recent era have taken a broad view of the world. The Westernization Movement of the Qing Dynasty age and the emergence of "Western Science Coming to China" have made Chinese people recognize their own inadequacies, from which sprang the hot trend of "Studying the West and Sinosizing it." Thus, leaving China to study abroad has gradually become a thing, and increasingly, many foreign language books have also entered China in accompaniment. Intellectuals are already unsatisfied with the translated works, and have begun to try to read the original foreign language texts themselves, because of which foreign language books have played important roles in China's modernization and opening up to the West.

Film source materials in the new films only play the role of restoring historical scenes, and the directors' intentions were to place the introduction of Chinese culture at the center of films, which differed widely from the introductory quality of film news. In viewing these types of films, this research was much more focused on the documentary value of education. For instance, "The Firsts" focusing on the field of education, *The First National Conference on Worker and*

Famer Education, The First Generation of Foreign Students in the New China, The First Comprehensive University: China's Renmin University, The First National Set of Unified Teaching Materials, The First New Institute Specifically Cultivating Public Servants: The Executive Academy of China, and *The First Teachers Day,* etc.

The documentary film *The First Comprehensive University: China's Renmin University,* source material *News Brief* (1950–45) (Central China News Documentary Film Studio 2009, 42–43) offers the following:

> [footage] Source materials: 1950 Opening Ceremony of China's Renmin University.
>
> [commentary] 10-3-1950, the first comprehensive university after the founding of the new China—the first school orientation ceremony of Renmin University held in Beijing.
>
> [footage] Source material: school gate of Renmin University
>
> [commentary] Among China's many higher education institutions, Renmin University's powerful humanities subjects draw attention. Undergoing 60 years of recent development, Renmin University as of now already has over 20,000 students at the school, nearly 1,700 teachers, currently 22 institutes, 12 inter-departmental research organizations, as well as the Physical Education Department, Institute of Continuing Education, Training Institute, International Institute, (Suzhou Research Institute) and Shenzhen Research Institute, etc., which all have formed their own subjects, levels, school-running scenarios and systems of cultivating all types of higher talent. As a nationally important university, the brilliance of today's Renmin University is enough to make people feel proud, and even more so makes teachers proud; this is the glorious revolutionary history of Renmin University.
>
> [interview] Wang Zongxian (the first student of Renmin University's Law Department): "I still remember Renmin University's first school orientation ceremony as if it happened yesterday, because we students woke up on time, and ate together. After eating we hustled to put on our uniforms, put them on nice and neat, including the female classmates. They were all those grey Lenin style uniforms, we wore belts, and also grey caps. Many of us were willing to wear those caps just like the People's Liberation Army!"

The documentary film *The First National Set of Unified Teaching Materials,* source material *News Brief* (1950–unspecified) (Central China News Documentary Film Studio 2008, 44–45) includes the following:

[footage] The 1950s consolidated teaching materials of the People's Education Publishing House.

[commentary] In the fall of 1951, the first national set of unified teaching materials were officially published across the country. After the founding of the new China, education around the country was brought under one effective unified management, and at the beginning of the 1950s, the first national set of unified teaching materials was used in schools.

New teaching materials, new people, new things; the teachers lectured with great vigor and the students listened with great interest. However in 1949, at the beginning of the founding of the new China, many schools were still using old teaching materials that had only undergone rough revision.

In China's old teaching materials, there were many problems, even in the science course materials, not only was the content insufficiently scientific, but it was also interspersed with many unhealthy things; even gambling was used as a subject of mathematics. In actuality, early in 1948, when Dongbei province had just been liberated, the government of the Dongbei Liberated Region had already started to solve this problem. The method chosen was to translate and draw lessons from Soviet teaching materials while autonomously editing them.

In September of 1949, at the dawn of the new China, at the first CPPCC, the education problems of the new China drew widespread attention. At the meeting, everyone voted for the political consultative leadership that brought up many problems concerning education. Everyone believed that the education of new China would be democratic, mass-oriented, and scientific.

In September of 1950, in order to unify the national middle elementary school teaching materials, the central committee decided to found the People's Education Publishing House, and rapidly enlisted a group of people from all areas of the nation to start immediately editing work on teaching materials. Within less than half a year, new teaching materials for all 12 grades were edited, which is truly miraculous!

[interview] Lei Shuren (executive chairman of the research council for the middle school physics and mathematics majors): "Those of us editing teaching materials understand a bit about the business, but we do not understand Russian, while the comrades who translate understand Russian but don't understand the business, the result is that I basically don't understand the things that are translated. I do not know what it says, so I can only start to learn by looking at the alphabet and learn

Russian by myself. Very quickly, in basically 3 to 5 months, let's say, I'm capable of translating the things in my trade."

[commentary] New teaching materials are edited partially based on old teaching materials, materials from the Dongbei Liberated Zone and Soviet teaching materials. In this set of teaching materials, new thoughts become the core of education, and course content is also more scientific and practical. The first nationally unified teaching materials of the new China have already become history, but they are still the first step on new China's journey in the enterprise of education.

From the documentary film *The First Generation of Foreign Students in the New China*, source material *News Brief* (1951–unspecified) (China Central News Documentary Film Studio 2009, 34–35):

[footage] A group photo of 20 Chinese foreign exchange students in the Soviet Union, source material: *Chairman Mao Greets Chinese Students Studying Abroad in the Soviet Union.*

[commentary] After the founding of the new China, we were faced with a poor and backward situation, yet the party and state leaders deeply felt the importance of human talent for nation building. In the 1950s and 60s, we sent over 10,000 exchange students to the Soviet Union and Eastern Block socialist states that shared diplomatic relations with China at the time. This is new China's first generation of foreign exchange students.

Actually, before selecting the team of foreign exchange students to go study abroad, the China Central Committee had to consider the needs of nation building, and so first sent a small group of exchange students to the Soviet Union. As early as 1948, when Dongbei province had just been liberated, the Party Central Committee considered the problems of building upon the founding of the new China, and sent the first exchange students to the Soviet Union, including Li Peng and Zou Jiahua.

Carrying wonderful aspirations and the mission given to them by the times, the first generation of exchange students overcame the linguistic and other obstacles with astonishing will-power and relentless spirit, investing their own youth into the struggle to learn for the fatherland.

[interview] Wang Yongzhi (Academician of the Engineering Academy of China): "Our notebooks in class are retrieved by the class monitor at the end of class and put in a classified department, if you want to look at your own notes again, you have to go borrow them, and basically cannot just take them out of the classroom; our graduation dissertations likewise were left there and could not be carried away. After returning home, the first thing the foreign exchange students did was recall those courses on rocket design."

Aside from detailing "the firsts" in education, these films are also partially "original" sources in deeply and widely influential education films up till today, for instance, *The Character Simplification Project, The Chinese Pinyin Project, The Great Canon Revised in the Period of Prosperity: The Great Chinese Encyclopedia, Birth Document of Hope Engineering*, etc. Such materials are undoubtedly most precious with respect to research on the history of education. In the historical moments of education that they document from the cinematic perspective, the meaning of the documents is even more apparent.

The documentary film *The Character Simplification Project*, source material *News Brief* (1951–unspecified) (China Central News Documentary Film Studio 2009, 46–47) reveals:

[footage] Source material: all the literacy classes and illiteracy elimination classes unfolding in every region across the country.

[commentary] In January of 1956, *The Character Simplification Project* was publicly released. After the founding of new China, nation building urgently needed vast numbers of workers with knowledge and culture. But at the time the number of illiterate people was staggering, and hence required massive forces to unfold illiteracy elimination activities.

Illiteracy, first of all, requires solving the problem of "knowing characters." Chinese characters are complicated, which actually brings great obstacles to people's learning and living: the number of characters is vast, the strokes are manifold, character recognition and writing are all quite difficult. Facing this new terrain, the work of character simplification is immanently pressing upon us.

Beginning in 1952, The China Writing Reform Committee began research by compiling the most popular characters needing simplification for the masses. In 1955, The Writing Reform Committee publicly released *The Character Simplification Plan (Draft)*; in 1956, the State Council approved *The Character Simplification Project*. After the stipulated simplified characters were publicly released, it greatly excited the passions of the masses to learn characters and cultural knowledge. Premier Zhou Enlai said at the PCC in 1958, "In the last two years since the public release of the project, simplified characters have already become universally adopted in newspapers, publications, textbooks and books in general, they have been warmly received by the broader masses, and specifically have done a great thing for children and adults beginning to study characters. As all the enterprises of the fatherland continuously develop, society using characters must also make a step forward in normalization."

The Character Simplification Project pushed four batches of simplified characters, compiled many opinions about them, and everyone believed in the need for a summary of the character simplification project. In 1964, the whole table of simplified characters that was published included 2,236 characters. This batch of simplified characters, regardless of whether one considers the situation at the time or in the later practical effect, was most successful.

In 1986, the National Written Language Work Committee published *The Table of Simplified Characters*, which made individual adjustments to the table of 1964. Because of this, the form and structure of simplified characters basically stabilized. Republishing the table of simplified characters made society's use of characters capable of following an order and gave it a basis to reduce confusion, and this helped the normalization and standardization of modern Chinese characters.

The new table was a new summary, providing a set of revisions of the past norms and also resolving some systematic problems, so it was also a development. Simplified characters inherit the advantages of traditional Chinese culture and also adapt to the needs of modern society.

[interview], Shen Jian (originally, deputy senior editor of the editing department of *China Social Science*): After Hu Qiaomu researched several revision plans at our "writing reform committee," he also thought about it after returning to the car. After getting home he called and said, let us also try something else, another method of reform. Sometime around midnight he called back again, saying to revise this and that, there was no day or night he did not think about it. He still needed the national people's representative congress to pass it.

The documentary film *The Chinese Pinyin Project*, source material *News Brief* (1951–unspecified) (China Central News Documentary Film Studio 2009, 46–47) contains the following:

[footage] Source material: the scene of the 1955 national writing reform committee.

[commentary] On the 11th of February 1958, *The Chinese Pinyin Project* was officially announced.

The founding of new China has given the broader working masses and young children the opportunity to go to class to learn the language and culture of China, and the first content learned is Pinyin and Chinese characters.

Actually, there had already been a method of adding pronunciation to Chinese characters in the early years of the Chinese Republic. The plan announced in 1918 was called the national phonetic alphabet, and was later changed to being called phonetic signs. It was only the slight simplification of ancient Chinese characters, slightly revised for usage. But the old phonetic signs were not too scientific and were of no help to the new culture of new China and to cultural communication with foreign countries. So researching a scientifically workable Pinyin system became the chief task of those working on the language.

In order to map out the Chinese pinyin system, the China Writing Reform Committee founded a professional committee, called the Chinese Pinyin System Committee. At the time, the main energy of the Writing Reform Committee was directed toward researching national forms of phonetic systems since Chairman Mao had indicated in 1951 that the main intention was that characters must be reformed, the alphabet should be national in form, and it must be produced on the current foundation of characters. So, according to Chairman Mao's indication at the time, the chief task of the Writing Reform Committee was to explore the national style of the alphabetic form.

The national form of our alphabet, although natively Chinese, was still inferior to the scientific and universally applicable Latin letters. So which kind of alphabetic form was best to adopt in the end?

In January of 1956, the China Central Committee held a conference on the issue of intellectuals. At the conference, the president of the Writing Reform Committee, Wu Yuzhang, made a speech about problems related to writing reform, Chairman Mao lauded Wu Yuzhang's opinion, believing Latin letters would be more suitable.

Previously, in 1955 during the opening of the national Writing Reform Conference, several systems were proposed. In February of the second year, the China Writing Reform Committee published the draft of the Chinese Pinyin system.

The fifth meeting of the First National People's Representative Congress began in Beijing on the 1st of February, 1958.

Wu Yuzhang joined the meeting bringing the Chinese Pinyin system drafted by specialists over 3 years of hard work, and gave the report entitled *The Current Writing Reform and Chinese Pinyin System*. Ten days later, on the 11th of February, the congress approved the Chinese Pinyin system.

The drafting of the Chinese Pinyin system fit the needs of new China's elementary school language education, and was of great help to the teaching of teachers and the learning of students. At the same time Pinyin was also capable of helping the broader middle elementary school students speak Mandarin.

This system was not the invented product of one person, but was that of collective wisdom, and at the time everyone was well satisfied with the system. After more than 50 years of practical usage, it still satisfies people today.

In 1982, the Chinese Pinyin system became the global international standard for writing the phonemes unique to China.

[interview] Zhou Youguang (original State Language Committee Researcher): "Premier Zhou Enlai took this affair very seriously at the time. He said it was not enough for the State Council to pass it, it also had to be passed by the national people's representative congress."

Though it was the biggest producer of documentary films in the system, CCND gradually went into a period of decline at the beginning of the 1990s after the peak period of creation in the early 1980s as a result of the ever developing terrain of television documentaries; the number of films continuously decreased. In addition, institutionally restrained, the creative style of CCND still basically followed the old narrative style of news-exhibiting cinema of the 80s and 90s, and so it was difficult for the editors to break through this in creation and practice. At the turn of the century, CCND basically gave way to television on the stage of documentary creation. This was effective until 2010, when China Central News Documentary Film Studio and Beijing Science Education Film Studio reorganized; but by this time, its function had already transformed, and CCND became the main archive responsible for compiling, sorting, preserving and utilizing the film materials of all periods. Its task was to provide the organizations producing documentary films with quick response to computer inquiries, film projection, and video selection, and service the copying of all footage via videos, CD writing, film-to-magnetic transfer, and high-definition television. The transformation of CCND was not only due to the vastly lower costs of videotape vis-à-vis film, but more fundamentally, because technology became more popular, and common people could use their own video cameras and create, at which point documentary film ceased to be the privilege of some group of people far above the rest.

2.3   *Comparing Foreign Media with the Creations of* CCND

China Film Publishing House published *The Portrayal of China and India on the American Screen, 1896–1955,* by Dorothy B. Jones in 1963. The film analyzed and examined the last 60 years of America's description of China and the transformation process of Chinese people on the silver screen. According to this book's statistics: ever since WWII, feature films about Asian countries appearing on the silver screen were mostly about China, and from June of 1947 to the end of 1954, during this period, all of the different films describing China amount to over 40 (Lu Xun 1930).[33] However, the Westerners who genuinely entered the world of Chinese film can be counted on one's fingers.

Joris Ivens was the forerunner among them. Early in 1938, he turned his gaze toward the war ravaged soil of China, with the camera lens focused on the raging fire and billowing smoke of the northern war of resistance against Japan. With the assistance of the "Contemporary Historical Film Company" and Chinese émigrés abroad, he personally went to the front lines to shoot the recovery of Tai'erzhuang; At Hankou, Ivens first met with Zhou Enlai and shot footage of the 8th Route Army holding an important military affairs meeting; stopping in Xi'an, he shot footage of the people of Xi'an protesting against the Japanese. These shots became landmark frames of the 1930s Chinese war of resistance against Japan.[34]

Under the influence of the Cold War, after the founding of the new China, Western directors filming in China were strictly checked by government organs, and came mostly from red areas: Ivens from the Netherlands and Michelangelo Antonioni[35] from Italy were both left wing Communist Party members.[36]

---

33   Early in January of 1930, Lu Xun translated the Japanese film theory researcher Iwasaki Akira's *Film and Capitalism,* and wrote a "translator's postscript" about China's current conditions. In the postscript, he wrote: "Euro-American imperialists use guns, making China [full of] strife with war and turmoil, and also use old films, making Chinese people astonished and confused. After reforms, they again moved inward to expand their confusing culture. I think such books as *Film and Capitalism* are most indispensable!" Looking at it, it seems the political understanding of Hollywood films drew the intellectual world's attention early on.

34   Later Ivens would edit the film he shot in China into the documentary *The 400 Million,* which was shown worldwide and led to great commotion. From the film name you can roughly see how Ivens understood and expressed China.

35   Michelangelo Antonioni, 1912–2007, an Italian modernist film director, was one of the most influential directors in terms of film aesthetics.

36   Left wing and right wing, in terms of traditional politics, refers to two kinds of ideologies in a society's internal politics, especially in democratic societies. In modern Western states, politics is generally divided into the left wing and right wing, namely conservatism (right wing) and socialism (left wing). In America, liberalism in the broad sense refers to left wing politics, but in Europe, liberalism refers to right wing politics in the broader

In the 1950s the Soviet Union entered into close diplomatic relations with China, leading Chinese documentary film to be deeply influenced by the Soviet Union. At the end of September, 25 Soviet documentary film workers came to China and in the span of 8 months, two film crews shot large quantities of material that would be edited into two big documentaries respectively, *Liberated China* (directed by: Xu Xiaobing, Su Heqing, filmed by Nikolai Blozhkov, in color, 1950)[37] and *The Victory of the Chinese People* (directed by: Leonid Varlamov, Wu Benli, Zhou Feng, filmed by: Vorontsov, Hao Yusheng, Li Bingzhong, Xu Lai, Li Hua, Ye Hui, in color and black and white, 1951).[38] After these two films were shown they generated widespread international influence and won the first "State Stalin Prize" and the first prize in the outstanding "full-length film" category from the China Ministry of Culture. *Liberated China* was the earliest color documentary shot by foreigners in China as well (He 2009).[39]

---

sense. As for what truly is left wing and what is right wing, has, up until today, still is not clearly defined. This paper refers to the left wing in accordance with the nomenclature of the "left wing playwright alliance" organized by the unified battle line of progressive playwrights led by the CCP, thus it refers to the revolutionary, progressive Western socialist organization.

37   Wang Meng: "I recall the documentary films co-produced with the Soviet Union in 1949 to 1950, entitled, *The Victory of the Chinese People* and *Liberated China* respectively, the latter film commentary writers were Liu Baiyu on the Chinese side and Simenov on the Soviet side." *Discussing 60 Years of Revolutionary Music with Wang Meng*, Feng Huang Blog, Wang Meng, 2009, <http://www.chinawriter.com.cn>, 2009-08-26, 08:50, *People's Daily*.

38   The director Shen Rong recalled: "In 1958, China and the Soviet Union co-filmed a documentary film, the Soviet director with whom I shot when filming the Volga was the director of *The Victory of the Chinese People*, Varlamov" (Rong 2005).

39   According to records, the moving story of this film was that Stalin had proposed the filming of a movie about the Chinese people winning victory, and after the China Central Party and Chairman Mao agreed, the China Central Film Department formally invited a Soviet film crew to help film new China's founding documentary in early September of 1949. Later, it was disclosed why the resulting documentary film was only several minutes long. Originally, the Soviet videographer was busy shooting the founding ceremony until 1 o'clock in the morning. Finally, he fell asleep early on the 2nd of October, but in the lower lobby sitting room a cigarette butt started a fire that burned up the film in the neighboring workroom, and at 5 o'clock when the fire alarm was rung, the firemen rushed onto the scene only to find the foreign videographers anxiously yelling—and the original several hours long film that had recorded the founding ceremony only ended up being several seconds long. Later, the vestiges that remained of this color footage after the fire were added to reshot footage and edited into the big color documentary films *Liberated China* and *The Victory of the Chinese People*. The former focused on the economic nation building in the rear, while the latter focused on the front lines liberating the entirety of China. According to the research of *The History of the Development of Documentary Film in China*, the Soviet videographer started the history of "reshooting" and "performing" documentary film in China. According to the shooting program Varlamov set up, he reshot the

In 1955, the French documentary director Chris Marker came to China to shoot *Sunday in Peking* (*Dimanche à Pékin*), 1956 (Marker 1956). Contemporaneous with him was the female director enjoying the French honor of being "the mother of the new wave" Agnes Varda (originally Arlette Varda). In 1958, Ivens shot the documentary *Early Spring* south of the Yangzi River (directed by Ivens, filmed by Shi Yimin, in color, 1958), it reflected the rural scene of people actively investing themselves in the building of socialism. In the 1960s extremely few foreigners came to China to film (Shan 2002), one of them being the British Television Journalist Felix Green, who shot *China!* and also the documentary *Tibet—the Roof of the World* (Green 1963), along with the Japanese film director Tokieda Toshie and Eizō Koten's shooting of *The State Before the Dawn* (1968) (Shan 2005, 224). The newest documentary film to be discovered is an amateur film shot by a French doctor entitled *China*, (1966). As a representative visiting China,[40] he had, by his side, a Super 8 film camera to shoot the film. After many years, the film producer said:

In May of 1966, my grandfather, accompanied by my grandmother, and several other French radiologist colleagues were invited to China to join a conference about the specific subject of cancer. At the time my grandfather possessed a Super 8 model film camera and would capture the living

---

four big war campaigns at Liaoning, Pingjin, Huai Hai and the Yangtze river crossing. The Chinese co-editor, Wu Benli, already shot the black and white film *1 Million Bold Troops Cross to the River's South* before this, then followed the Soviet professional to reshoot a 5 color segment, "Crossing the River." The Soviet professional also meticulously designed the famous long shot of planting the red flag at the Nanjing Presidential Palace. Later, he reshot the Liaoning campaign and even loaded and transported the original troops on a train. This film was later reworked in Moscow, and in mid-July of 1950 it was completed as a documentary film totaling over 8,000 inches long. According to records, the investigation was presided over by the Film Bureau Chief Yuan Muzhi. The projection room wasn't very big, but all the members of the Central Politics Bureau at Zhong Nanhai came. Wu Benli and the Soviet director Varlamov anxiously waited on the side. After the showing, Chairman Mao said loudly, "Very good, it passes!" Everyone cheered together, clapping. Liu Shaoqi, Premier Zhou Enlai, General Zhu, etc., and also Yang Shangkun all came over to shake hands with the directors Wu Benli and Varlamov, expressing their congratulations. Not long afterward, *The Victory of the Chinese People* was shown in the depths of winter in Beijing. At the celebration after the screening, Varlamov cheered in Chinese, "Long Live Chairman Mao!" The China Central Military Committee General Zhu set up a banquet treating Varlamov and offering him an award, the Minister of Culture Shen Yanbing spoke and issued Varlamov a commemorative badge, the footage of the Film Bureau Chief Yuan Muzhi's congratulating speech was fully included into *The Victory of the Chinese People* (Shan 2005; He 2009).

40 At the beginning of the Cultural Revolution in 1966, a French medical science delegation accepted an invitation to go to China and join a conference on cancer, this film documents the delegation's activities in China.

moments of that decade through this Super 8. Forty years ago we analyzed the scenes of those times through theme selection, adjusted the
camera angle and real color contrasts, and restored the living environment of the most important and vital time periods in modern Chinese
history.[41]

As the camera lens moves, we can see a traditional and ancient Chinese society that is yet fully revolutionary: the Summer Palace, the traditional small
courtyards, wooden stalls, the small retailers down the linked alleyways, the
imposing architecture in the Soviet style, large-character posters pasted on
the wall, the Red Guards entering Tian'anmen Gate. We can still get an experience of the political atmosphere of those times: the political pledges of
the Red Guards in the 1960s, army mobilizations, chaotic residential zones, the
destruction of Beijing's city walls, and so on. Such cinematic images observe
China from a Westerner's thoughts and perspectives, and for Westerners and
the Chinese gradually drifting far away from the old era, the cultural conflicts
and mental turbulence such documentary films reveal are unprecedented.
But, in that decade, the West's imagination of Red China unavoidably left an
imprint in the showing of the film.

   In 1971, Joris Ivens and Marceline Loridan spent 5 years shooting a large col-
lection of documentary films composed of 12 sections, entitled *How Yukong
Moved the Mountain Comment Yukong déplaça les montagnes* (Ivens and
Loriden 1976), the assistance and workers used in shooting the film came from
CCND. In the latter half of the 1980s, they spent a similar amount of time in
China shooting another documentary film entitled *The Tale of the Wind*, and
once again the work crew was comprised mainly of the creative cast from
CCND. In 1972, the Italian director Antonioni shot the film *Chung Kuo, Cina*,
which opened up Antonioni and his film to national criticism in China, but at
the beginning of the shooting, he was invited by Premier Zhou Enlai to shoot for

---

41   The documentary film *China*, 1966, directed by Maeva Aubert, produced in 1966. Currently
      only segments of this film are aired online at <https://vimeo.com/56706785>. This film is
      composed of a series of single extraordinary shorts. In one respect it shows a segment
      of the everyday life of Chinese people living through the historical tragedy of a violent
      background, and in another respect, this film is also the "travelogue film" of an amateur
      hobbyist. These two contradictory frames make up the contrasting juxtaposition of such
      dislocations in time and ideas. In front of the camera lens, they are the indirect product
      of a segment of history, man becomes a super spectator who both lives and observes, just
      like a never-ending play between the camera lens and representation, reality and illusion,
      outward appearance and screen. The producer hoped to use this film as the starting point
      and instrument for going to China to do investigative research, and to become the fore-
      runner of filming in a transitional medium.

22 days in China[42] using the core members of CCND. There were also other films like Lucy Jarvis' *China and the Forbidden City* (Jarvis 1972), Shirley MacLaine's *The Other Half of the Sky: A China Memoir* (MacLaine and Weill 1975),[43] Marcel Carrière's *Glimpses of China*, and Donald McWilliams' *Impressions of China* (McWilliams 1974).[44] Each of these was shot and sequenced under a bureaucratic arrangement. *The Fabled Forbidden City* for example filmed "the everyday life" of a Beijing family. The object of the film was the family of a student from Tsinghua University, Liu Zhijun. Afterward, Liu Zhijun had this recollection of the filming experience:

> One day in May, I was suddenly called out by the school's party politics office, and a serious-looking comrade representing the party committee handed me a document from the General Office of the State Council. The main idea was: the famous American female television producer Lucy Jarvis wanted to shoot a film based on a Beijing family, the documentary film [would be] fleshed out with several hundred years of history and entitled *A Fabled City*. She intended to reflect the great changes taking place after the founding of modern China, and hoped that this film could play a certain propaganda role in fostering Sino-American foreign relations and helping China enter the UN ... The Beijing Municipal Foreign Affairs Office went through strict examinations, and determined that my family, filled with children and grandchildren of upright red workers would be chosen from among many families to receive this 'political duty.'
>
> After I returned home, I found out that my parents' workplaces and the factories and schools where my two younger sisters and two younger brothers worked had been notified by their leaders respectively. Even though neither I nor my family members at the time knew whether mounting the silver screen was a good thing or a bad thing, there was enough faith to have no doubts: This was our honorable political duty that the party organization had handed to me, and I would certainly have to diligently complete the task. For caution's sake, the Assistant

---

42   At the time, China hoped to work with a famous western director more politically aligned with China to shoot a documentary about China and introduce modern China to the world. For Zhou Enlai, this was just like ping-pong diplomacy, it arose from the need for diplomatic policy.

43   Directed by Shirley MacLaine, Claudia Weill, produced in 1975, was nominated for an Oscar in the best documentary film category.

44   This is a short film edited from slide shows and super 8mm film materials shot by Canadian senior middle school student visiting China.

Director and Director General of Foreign Relations Department News, Zhang Ying, was entrusted by Premier Zhou Enlai to personally come to my house to make on-the-spot inquiries, to investigate my grandfather, parents, brothers and sisters, and the living situation in my family, then [Zhang] went to the local police station and resident committee to gain a deeper understanding to decide whether or not Americans should be allowed to come directly to my house.

At the very beginning of the filming process, Lucy, the director ran into a big problem, the entire family whether male or female, young or old, only wore three colors, black, blue and grey clothing, the men wore army green gym shoes and the women square mouthed side buckled black cloth shoes, three generations of people standing together like an army unit.

Liu said:

Because of this, my oldest younger sister borrowed red clothes from a new aunt who had just been wedded, the next oldest younger sister then went to the neighbor's house to borrow a dark purple jacket.

In *The Fabled City* there is a set of shots that were meant to show Chinese people's standard of living on the rise. We were just heading into Mid-Autumn Festival at the time, Guang'anmen food market suddenly put out all kinds of fresh vegetables, and you could get anything you wanted. In that decade, the people had to ration with stamps no matter what you bought, save that day which alone had no limit on the supply of meats and vegetables that you could buy without limit as long as you stood in line. My father's work unit specifically gave my family a 100 RMB bonus to make my family show the pride of Chinese people in front of the foreign traveler hotel. My mother clutched cash in her hand that amounted to three months of her own salary, delightedly squeezing into the crowd to buy vegetables ...

After the three months of shooting were over, Premier Zhou Enlai personally met Lucy's team, and expressed gratitude for their efforts in actively fostering Sino-American relations. But this event of my family participating in the shooting of *The Fabled City* was neither reported by the media nor spoken of by others, and even I myself didn't know what I looked like in the film in the end. It wasn't until a year later, in 1973, that I was accompanied by a politics teacher at Tsinghua who took me to the Sino-Soviet Friendship Society and finally saw this long English language documentary film, 57 minutes in length, entitled *The Fabled City*.

LIU 2012

A Canadian documentary film researcher pointed out that the relationship between these films and the subject being filmed is cold; they never successfully interact intimately with their subjects but only provide diary-like impressions of China shot by tourists (Shan 2002).

Travelogue style documenting; this is just like what Antonioni spoke about in a directorial biography: it is a travelogue, enriching one's life and perhaps also enriching other people's lives. The meaning of shooting the film and in directing one's own attempt to find a possibility first of all requires allowing oneself make sense of China. Because of this, in his footage, [paraphrasing him] in China, every morning from 5:30 to 7:30 the streets are dyed blue with thousands of blue-clothed people riding bikes to work, a never ending stream of bicycles occupying entire avenues, the entire city. That feeling was like having 8 million blue Chinese people passing before your eyes (Zhang 2008).

The director made the camera lens pan Wangfujing, the Western Quadrangle (xisi 西四), the drum tower and some unknown Beijing alleyways (hutong 胡同). The most complete segment shot was that of a Caesarian section surgery performed with acupunctural anesthesia. The director spared no film documenting the entire treatment in detail; he specially used several long lenses to establish the relationship between this traditional procedure of acupunctural anesthesia and the hospital environment with the one receiving the anesthesia. This is obviously no longer just the showing of a mysterious Asian medical practice, but rather connects this ancient medical practice to modern times and the lives of modern Chinese people.

He aims his lens at China's political center, Tian'anmen Gate, showing a young woman wearing simple attire, a spirit-at-ease elder doing Taijiquan, people resting on the side of Wangfujing road, the portrait of a student at the Great Wall, the Temple of Heaven teeming with tourists, the idle and easy everyday life of Beijing.

The people crowding in the Shanghai streets were drawn in by the director's camera, the facial expression of those facing the camera are curious and a bit afraid. This famous set of full-length footage documents pedestrians on streets, tea drinking at teahouses, and eating at small restaurants; Antonioni's camera follows the Yangzi River's water flowing calmly by, capturing the still life of boats and riverside families. At a Hui people's noodle restaurant in Suzhou, which allegedly was the best restaurant in the entire city, Antonioni's lens captures people eating noodles, wiping their mouths, smoking cigarettes, the old feeding the young, and in the commentary, he calmly says that their living conditions are so vastly different than ours that it makes "us" feel amazed (Zhang 2008).

With an excess of amazement, Antonioni tried to find a richly meaningful relationship for everything he saw in China, for example, tradition and modern reality, life and death, movement and rest. In the segment at the Shanghai Moat Temple, tea, tea houses, the elderly and all such elements symbolizing tradition were fully integrated with those elements filled with the feeling of the times like Mao Zedong portraits, propaganda posters, Beijing opera and music, creating a mysterious and yet not unpleasant atmosphere. Antonioni said of the rare and strange atmosphere there that, "The recollections of the past mingle with confidence in the present" (Zhang 2008).

The commentary in this segment spares words like gold, the background music is impassioned Beijing opera music, conveying a strong feeling of the times. The cinematic images themselves deeply transmit people's relation to the times (the relationship between humans and environment), and conveys that mystery and force implied under the still surface. Perhaps, this China that Antonioni filmed and understood was based on intuition and curiosity. He almost never drops any symbolically meaningful detail; he instinctively dodged bureaucratic plans and propaganda, and hoped to enter into the nooks behind the surface that became the most important point Chinese people would later take to heart.

For instance, Paula Rabinowitz suggested that documentary film is always the cinematic filming of history. Whether it is *The Fabled City* or *China* or those later films themed on the lives of common Chinese people, whether it is *China: Beyond the Clouds* (Agland 1994)[45] shot in 1994 by the widely influential British documentary directory Phil Agland, who spent three years in Yunnan filming it or it is Part I of BBC's *Wild China* (Chapman 2008), *The Heart of the Dragon*, all of them are understandings of China by means of Western thought. In their eyes, this China continuously hurrying in transformation obviously holds fable-like qualities.[46] Deepening thought, the many "documentations" in the everyday life of common Chinese people are all freeze-framed in this way

---

45   Phil Agland, from 1989 to 1994, took on the filming, directing and producing of this TV series shot in China with a total length of 7 hours, medium quality, VHS. It was co-produced for British, French Canal+ TV station and for viewing in the US, it has aired in over 60 countries. This film was coproduced with the China Film Coproduction Company. The prizes it has won include: The British Film Institute Prize (1995), best documentary film series and best picture. Three Emmy Awards: Best Picture, Best Original Music Score and Special Award. British Media Association Awards: best documentary series in 1995. Best independent film, 2 times: Best documentary film and best film grant. 1995 American Peabody Award. Royal Television Association Award for best education program. The Griersen Award in 1994 from the British Film Society.

46   Fables are born among common people and circulate among common people in the form of prose or rhymes, telling stories with satirical or exhortative implications. Later they are

by Western interpretations; furthermore, our "history" or our everyday survival conditions are also freeze-framed in this way.

The famous French film artist Marc Riboud has always been particularly fond of China. In an interview (Riboud 1997), he states that he has witnessed China rapidly hurrying from one world toward another, and that for a photographer, no other accelerating time than this constantly changing social scene could be more stimulating. He found new discoveries in every niche and frequently felt a visual shock. Such images shake pre-existing notions. He says that Asian society seems to be changing into an extremely Westernized society, and that the speed of its progression is far greater than anything Westerners have ever experienced. He states that photographing such a quickly changing China is difficult, as the images may come out unclear and may even be at odds with fact (Riboud 1997 [paraphrased]).[47]

For today's China, whether in fable or prophecy, the details in the footage are always recollections and a wealth worthy of treasuring. Under the projection of the Western lens, the origin of the cinematic images describing the look of socialist China were the details of everyday life; such details are easily overlooked by us due to over-familiarity. Expressing such cinematic images comes more out of artistic consciousness. Riboud argues that they do not represent any viewpoint or value judgment and even less provide evidence for the historical transformation of China. Carrying no implication of analysis and judgment, this is but the form of the documentary. This is the original intention of the director and photographer alike. It is only that the presentation of meaning becomes precisely the contrary through editing cuts, different viewership, and adding the main message to the film, repetitively and in an external fashion. Riboud explained at an exhibition that he roamed streets and villages

---

cited and recreated by literate scholars as means of arguing or debating points. The fables referred to in this paper mean using exhortative or satirical images to define China.

47   Marc Riboud was a French man who became freelance photographer in 1951. In 1952 he joined the Magnum Photo Society. In 1959, he was elected to be the associate Chair of the Magnum European Division, and again in 1975 and 1976 he was elected to be the chair of Magnum Europe. The characteristic of Riboud's works reflects some powerful and deeply meaningful content through miniscule details in life. He not only uses black and white to shoot journalistic photos, he also uses color to shoot, and these colored works of his are not only splendid, compositionally speaking, but are also elegant and refined. He has also published a massive quantity of photos in collections, among which are *Women of Japan* (1959), *Ghana* (1964), *The Face of North Vietnam* (1970), *Visions of China* (1981), *Train and Station* (1988). To China, he was by no means unfamiliar, since the 50s he visited China around 20 times, using the camera lens to document images of China. He consecutively published *Three Banners of China* (1966), *Marc Riboud in China, 40 Years of Photography* (1997), and *Shanghai Tomorrow*.

for long periods of time, but what he saw one day was usually different from what he saw in the next, and each often conflicted with the other. But he hoped that the surprising scenes he photographed when roaming about China would likewise surprise his viewers. While showing them he intentionally changed up the order of the works in terms of the times and regions. Jumping from one China to another he formed contrasts and through the differences captured the idea running through them. At the exhibition he said he was even fonder of China, so filled with life today, than any time before, and because of this he was warmly fond of Chinese people.[48]

From these shots that are continuously concerned with China taken by foreign documentary film directors we easily discover that China appears in the image of a whole nation, and not as single events and historical figures. In such shots and footage what comes through the camera is visual attention rather than deeper interpretation.

Ivens, for example, visited China once in the 1930s which kick-started his continuous appreciation for China over the long period of a half a century. The spirit of the Chinese people became the subject of his own personal documentary film creations. In 1958, Ivens again visited China, at which time the scenery of Chinese society extraordinarily excited him. Originally imitating the form of "the film report" he filmed a series of short films entitled *Letters to China*. Later, plans changed and he went to Inner Mongolia, Nanjing and Wuxi to shoot three short films expressing the building of socialism in northern China and the southern farmlands along with the people's enthusiasm in work and spirit. These were then edited tem into one film entitled *Early Spring* (original name *Snow*). You can see in the film:

> [footage] Some villages started to invest in farmland irrigation projects during the Spring Festival. The cooperatives, projecting a year of production, concentrated the one cow per household into one site. Last year, the cooperative produced on average 850 *jin* of rice on 1 *mu* of land, but this year they want to raise the quantity of production 100 percent. In Shanghai with Spring Festival soon to arrive, over 10,000 workers preparing to return home for New Year go to the train station to cancel their tickets and continue investing themselves at building sites. Shanghai's Steelworks Factory No. 6, and team B's steel workers drip with sweat while they forge a furnace of steel. On Nanjing Road, the first department

---

48   [Paraphrase] of extract from *Marc Riboud in China: 40 Years of Photography* (1997). This exhibition was hosted by the China Photographer Association and the French Embassy program in Culture and Science Cooperation in 1996.

store is thronging with people with business hours extended for an hour prior the Spring Festival. The second day of the New Year witnessed collective duty labor. In Beijing, at the bustling No. 13 cold water reserve worksite, cart pushers and shovel wielders form a lively scene of building socialism. Everyone gathers together to greet the new year, the work songs of over 27,000 rural laborers, officers and soldiers, cadres, and students resounded into the night for the 13 day long New Year celebration.

ZHANG 2006

From 1972–1975, Ivens filmed a big documentary series in China entitled *How Yukong Moved the Mountains*. The footprints of the film production crew crossed Daqing, and such places as Shanghai, Nanjing, Qingdao and Xinjiang, deeply connecting with China's workers, farmers, fishermen, professors, students, PLA soldiers, shop assistants, performers and handicraftsmen. Altogether, they shot 12 independent units of film: *The Daqing Oil Field*, *The Shanghai No. 3 Pharmacy*, *The Shanghai Steam Turbine Factory*, *A Woman-A House*, *A Fishing Village*, *A Military Camp*, *The Impression of a City*, *The Story of Balls*, *Professor Qin*, *Beijing Opera Team Rehearsal*, *The Training of the Beijing Circus*, and *Handicraftsmen*.

In the process of shooting, Ivens penetrated into the scenes of familiar life and the objects filmed, showing the life, labor and learning occurring in all strata of society in that stage of history. He very calmly describes the stability of Chinese people's lives and the social progress of this time period. At present the current number of reels of filmed source material is 12 hours' worth. Among them, the section describing education is *Professor Qin* with a film length of 12 minutes, and *The Story of Balls*, film length 19 minutes (after cutting and editing). Both of these films are small parts of the independent unit of the said series, the former primarily described a professor's life and work; the latter tells the story of a middle school in Beijing which stipulated that no one could kick balls after the class bell. One student, though, disobeyed well after the bell and narrowly missed injuring a teacher. The teacher confiscated all of the students' balls, and the students didn't cope with it well. Another teacher organized a class meeting to specifically discuss the affair, and finally both sides reflected on their own shortcomings.

In the camera lens, students and teachers scuffled over telling the filmmaker their own respective viewpoints on the argument that had just taken place between students and teachers. You can see that after Ivens' camera documented the event witnesses' summaries, he dives further into the event, and films the teachers' and students' analysis of it. The narration of the whole film is smooth, the rhythm never gets sluggish, and especially the calm and fair atmosphere in the film makes it hard for people to believe that this was filmed at a middle school during the Cultural Revolution.

The film presents a lot of footage that does not fit with Westerners' imagination of the history of the Cultural Revolution, which is also the main reason why Ivens faced a cold reception in the West for some time afterward. Loridan later recalled that when the Cultural Revolution had just begun, they were forbidden to come to China because they belonged to the "democratic party." In 1967, Ivens' wife went to China to shoot a film about the Vietnam War, but did not dare to visit the Chinese friends she had once been familiar with, and even didn't dare to knock on friends' doors when walking down the streets they lived on, for fear that it would bring her friends trouble.

At the end of the 1970s, increasingly more foreigners came to China to film documentaries. In their eyes, this China in continuous dramatic transformation obviously had a quality of "fable" in it. The film *China* in one respect, for example, showed the calm air of a spectator, which differed greatly from the looks of news documentary film in China at the time. This difference not only shows through in formal technique, but even more so shows through in the recognition of the function of documentary film. In another respect, criticism aimed at *China* also became the reflection of inner party struggles in the art world at the time, where misunderstandings were deep and hard to resolve.

In fact summarizing the director Antonioni's observations, we may discover the Chinese society behind the camera lens:

> [It] is a vast and yet barely understood nation, I can only observe it visually but cannot explain it on any deep level. I only know that this country was soaked in the unfairness of the feudal environment for a long period of time, and today I see a new fairness starting to emerge through everyday struggles. In the eyes of foreigners, such unfairness appears perhaps as slackness and poverty. But this poverty brought about the possibility of respecting survival, it revived a calm people even more humane than ourselves, and sometimes it approached the tranquility we have yearned for, a harmonious coexistence with nature, a close emotional connection between people, an obstinate creativity. This creativity solved the problem of the redistribution of wealth by simple means in a sphere often thought of as insatiable greed. I am not at all interested in Chinese people following the example of Westerners. I know they have the atomic bomb, but, it seems I am much more interested in showing you how they use a few simple materials to build factories, hospitals and childcare centers in a working environment of mutual respect. I want to tell you how much

pain and sweat such work costs and tell you that the category of joy—
different from us—can embrace everything over there, and basically that
that joy also belongs to us.

ZHANG 2008

This somewhat defensive summary obviously appeared overly abstruse and
unreasonable to Chinese people at the time. A worker at the Nanjing Big Bridge
Management Office, who participated in the film work at the time, recalled the
experience of filming this big bridge that made Chinese people at the time so
incomparably proud, and said:

> We introduced him to the situation, he was not impatient at all; he did
> not use the elevated frame we prepared for him. He took a steam boat
> for two spins on the river under the big bridge, but didn't film it, instead
> he demanded that the steamboat float downstream far away from the
> bridge, intentionally filming several shots from very bad angles, he filmed
> an impressive modernized bridge all crooked and shaky; even more
> base was how he inserted a shot of air-drying clothes under the bridge to
> vilify it.
>
> *Venomous Motive*, People's Daily 1974

The Red Flag Canal well-known outside of China was only scanned over in the
film, you can neither see the majestic bearing of "the man-made milky way"
nor see the flourishing scenery of the Linzhou Mountain rivers after rearrange-
ment, [and] the screen spares no effort to present [anything] but withered
land, lonely elders, exhausted animals and shoddy houses. The social commentary published in *People's Daily* on January 30, 1974, entitled *Venomous
Motive, A Base Trick*, attacks Antonioni with respect to his motives and artistic
techniques in the following way:

> In order to denigrate the Chinese revolution and attack China's socialist
> system, the film makes an intolerable vilification of the Chinese people's
> mentality, [the film director] describes the Chinese people as a popula-
> tion that is stupid and ignorant, isolated from the world, miserable, low
> in spirit, unhygienic, gluttonous, and simple-minded.

To achieve this goal, the article asserted that he resorted to extremely reaction-
ary and base filming techniques, "... in the choosing and processing of footage,
he never or rarely shot what is good, new and progressive, or at the time shoots

a little for appearances only, and finally cuts it out; while poor and backward scenes he captures every moment in grand and specific shots." Facing this "great industrialized city" of Shanghai, it continues, Antonioni tried to smear China's socialist industry,

> Fully knowing Shanghai has very many big modernized industries, the film producer goes to great lengths to ignore them completely, while going out of his way to gather shots of poor equipment and disorderly manual operations. Fully knowing the shipyards capable of making 10,000 ton boats towering along the shores of the Huangpu River, along with China's ocean-going ships anchored in the river, under Antonioni's lens, the big freighters in the Huangpu River all belong to foreign countries, while the small wooden boats are all Chinese. This is obviously a great achievement in fully denying and writing off all the battle lines of China's socialist project, it attempts to make people believe that today's new socialist China is no different from the old half-feudal/half-colonial Chinese state.

Well-versed in the demands of CCND's Chinese style film on content, today's people would have absolutely no doubts about Antonioni's artistic and creative motives at the time: Think of means and figure out methods to get to the true reality. The director is only using his perspective and means to observe China and show China, and that is all. Looking at *Chong Kuo, Cine* today, people now always feel grateful, grateful that this segment of film saves another perspective of documentation for the Chinese people of the time, allowing our later generations to peer into those times our past generation once lived through.

Overall, in contrast to CCND's creations, the cinematic images of China shot by Westerners focus on individualized things in the scene, they focus on the concrete description of everyday environments and all such details. In other words, the cinematic images enter history through the lens from a personal perspective. What is found in the cinematic image is all the details of personal life. It shows that there is a complicated interaction in the gap between the slogans and the system. Because of this, when viewing cinematic images of this period of China, we have no choice but to splice together two different gazes. That is, focus on the samples of grand narrative provided by CCND and then bring the gaze down a notch to look at those seemingly small and insignificant scenes of life. Just as the photographer Liu Xiangcheng said in the text *China after Mao 1976–1983*:

In the past many years I have established good and harmonious relations with my Chinese official counterparts, even though our aesthetic orientations differ greatly, moreover that we have a good many differences in terms of standards of a good cinematic work.

In August of 1979, the previous Vice President of the United States, Walter Mondale, visited the Beijing branch of *Shidai* magazine, during which time I visited a cloisonné factory in Beijing with Walter Mondale's wife and daughter. When I was preparing to take a photo of the mother and daughter buying souvenirs, a hand stretched into my viewfinder and re-arranged the position of an ashtray in the glass case in front of her. I turned my head around and saw a photo-journalist from Xinhua News Agency. Obviously this ashtray disrupted his aesthetic composition, making it ultimately unbearable for him not to reach in and move it. Afterward, he activated his Rolleiflex 120 flash and snapped the photo.

Just like this colleague of mine from Xinhua News Agency, many Chinese photographers believe they should take a photo the way they would handle a traditional Chinese landscape painting. Chinese photography is largely influenced by the idea of harmony between nature and man. This photojournalist from Xinhua News Agency must have believed the ashtray destroyed the balance of the picture, so he took it out.

LIU 2011, 45

We can easily discover from such a contrast two entirely different observational perspectives and compositions of the photographic image, and it is precisely this contrast, between instinct and reason, between observing and recording that furthermore helps us restore the principle and motive of CCND's documentary creation during this time period. Many years later, in *The Seventies*, published by Sanlian, a generation of intellectuals who were born and grew up in this era made the following recollection of the times:

I'm staring at it. It has long been difficult to accept that this is the 1970s in memory, but every image for me [I just have to] accept it; you are in a stream of people like ants. A gray stream of people. Everywhere there is vast poverty, [in the] city and countryside, because desolation was suddenly called spotless, straightforwardly beautiful. In a village in the north, what the camera captures is villagers struggling to flee, and at the same time turning back to look at the camera. I cannot find words to describe the expression in their eyes, because being far from the countryside for so long, by the 1990s I cannot avoid picking up the bad habit of other people's view that concentrates on this vast pre-modern state—the first half of my life. In the closing credits, a group of village elementary students assemble into lines on the playground to run a relay race, the big sun shining, poor and yet obstinate, like the crude tenacity of those stones and wild fruits in the barren mountain by my home. This scene actually captures the ignorance and vitality of an entire generation of people. *Chung Kuo, Cine* is the only cinematic image that truly records the 1970s, that I've seen up till today.

Depicting all the evils in peaceful times is easy, describing all the moments of joy in times of iniquity is very difficult and inappropriate. The taste of destitution, allow me to say straightforwardly, captures a pastoral mood, while the process of self-strengthening will always be explained as romantic in the future. The best time to endure hardships is in the time of youth, if you have the energy to strive and manage to compensate, you will get through with composure. Looking back on the hardships of the 1970s, personal events and political events overlap, the details of youth and the tragedy of the state enfold into one another to the point of making it hard to distinguish them.

BEI DAO and LI TUO 2009, 79

That is a sample of history, no one would have presaged that only several years would pass, and China would witness massive changes that would turn the world upside down, and that such changes would deeply impact the progression of human civilization.

3   Conclusion: the National Will of CCND's Cinematic Images

From the Yan'an Film Group of 1938 to the Beijing Film Studio of 1949, to the CCND organized in 1953 and then to the CCND after the transformations of the 1980s, this paper combed through the meaning of the CCND as China's only professional studio producing and making news documentary films in its historical development of reforms and its national cultural identity.

There is a vivid China in the *News Brief* that differs from that in paper documents. The introduction to and narration of this grand tale of education occurring at the early phase of socialism was continuously produced at the frequency of one issue per week with each segment lasting ten plus minutes. Through these rough and active documentary materials, I re-perceive this era in my imagination; the appearances of this era restored via these simple and full cinematic images have undoubtedly become the most immediate and clearest evidence. Even though we are separated from it by decades' worth of distance, the frame still preserved the discourse with an intense feeling of the times, and in the process of documenting history, *News Brief* itself became history—ultimately we rely on these infinitely plentiful and "accurate" images to return once again to the educational life that once belonged to a generation of people long ago.

The educational life found in documentary film is recorded in the activities, speech, thoughts and emotions of common people, composing the complex interactions of society in state institutions. In this age, as a director, one proceeded from the perspective of the state ideology when filming, keeping one's own personal identity concealed, and, while restoring the scene, one engages in documentary-style explanations of the content. Influenced by the length of the film, although the educational life could be restored in few words and scattered sentences, it is minimal, like one meter of sunlight, when what this history of educational life describes is a greater segment of truly existing history, and even more so the traces of everyone's lives. Considering the already gathered and sorted materials of the educational scenes restored to life by CCND's cinematic images, the documentary films that recorded the actual conditions of society and education through showing everyday details and the survival conditions of common students and teachers are not one of a kind, but they are certainly rare. In the majority of short news documentary films, what is shown is bumper crops, factories buzzing with machinery, and collectivism under strict organization. But in the limited cinematic images about China shot by Westerners, what we see is peasants in mud houses, sincere believers in temples, and especially the simple, bashful, terrified, curious and satirical Chinese gazes projected through close-up footage. Segment after segment of cinematic image connects, seemingly with no direct link to education, but truly composed by the context of state education in that era. These film segments and details naturally become indirect evidence restoring that segment of educational history, and moreover such evidence is obtained through the surface of the cinematic image while contemplating its "essential meaning."

Narrating events is originally an important discursive form in film, the story information transmitted by film makes up the source material of movies, and the narration of footage thus provides a practical possibility for such explanations. Formatted scenes of people, their thoughts, voices and experiences all converge together to constitute educational events awaiting our observation, and the fluidity of these events and their complex meaning often can only be expressed through the narrative form.

In addition, researching vast quantities of *News Brief*s requires decoding them by placing them in a much bigger context of the transformation of systems of visual culture. First of all, the original source materials of the *News Brief* are the products of the state ideology's visual culture, a shaping of the image of the state. Today, these films peacefully resting in the CCND archive show us a history that truly existed. In the footage that was a once a fresh and flourishing socialist state championing selfless sacrifice and hard struggle. These black and white images sometimes interspersed with color feel increasingly real as the sediment of time piles on. It tells the later generation: there is another dimension of knowing one's own nation's history, and at the same time it points out some social values that today's people find inconceivable. The China restored from these cinematic images shows that what is true is not the primordial state of life and society, but rather the mentality, environment and way of acting belonging to people living in a particular age (Zhang 2010). Second, current historical documentaries shot by re-cutting *News Brief* source materials make use of the historical and imagistic value of *News Brief* cinematic images, yet what is restored is the culture and values of today's society. The ironic force composed by such cinematic images is already hard to weigh in terms of artistic standards, and can only be "viewed" from the political and historical perspectives. The "witnessing" function it naturally forms after coming into being is much more meaningful with respect to the influence it brings to the entire current social culture along with its historical value. When researching these films, the key is interpreting different directors' focuses of concern. Is the creation itself leading the later generation's line of vision toward CCND's representation of the times or toward CCND itself?

In summary, in current research, the majority of scholars agree that *News Brief* undertakes the ideology of the nation-state. It is undeniable that this view is reasonable. However, this does not prove that all things revolve around the nation-state without any break whatsoever. In observing the cinematic images, I have discovered that the nation-state shown behind the cinematic image will preserve some warm memories, and the countless intentions between these memories are the substance of history.

Just as Arnold Joseph Toynbee pointed out, all of history cannot possibly be totally without fictional components. Simply choosing, arranging and showing facts is a method belonging to the scope of fiction, which likewise backs up the proposition that if all historians were not simultaneously great artists they would not have become great historians[49] (Ferro 2008, 151–190). Presenting

---

49   Investigating the truth is the essential problem of historiography, and cinematography, as
      a branch of historiography, similarly faces such questions. This research insists that truth
      vs. fiction is not only the substantial problem of documentary it is also one of the core
      problems discussed in cinematography.

and describing are two entirely different states; the former is only film material, while only the latter constitutes writing. Qian Mu insisted that writing history must have "meaning":

> Just like history, materials are infinite in number, and if the commander does not first determine a trajectory of meaning, [but] only focuses on methods and specifically uses a set of methods to steer these infinite materials, he will make historical research proceed endlessly, and even more so, meaninglessly. Yellow grass or white reeds as far as the eye can see, and although they are different materials, they make one unavoidably have a sense of more of the same old thing.
>
> QIAN 2001, 1

Therefore, history by no means completely exists in works of history, and what looks like a flood of masses of people in the cinematic image are similarly traces of history. What ultimately is the cinematic image? He Bingdi's answer perhaps might explain: "I'd rather forget it" (He 2005, 393). "Forget it"—although just two simple words—they are filled with a sincere scholar's deep meditation and inexplicable mood. It seems like recording whatever sparks interest more or less reflects the scene of those times as well as people's consciousness and emotions, and moreover [in this case] attempts to restore the likeness of a young Republic. Respectfully listening to the sound of history is a posture. Reflecting back on the past youth of the republic with honest eyes and respectful heart, this is an important principle of researching the CCND, and at the same time it is also a little bit of handing over history!

Filmography

Advancing in Step. 1955. Directed by Wang Chen. CCND Studio.

Black Mountain Northern Pass Elementary School Education Reform. 1960. Directed by He Zhongxin. CCND Studio.

Chairman Mao is the Red Sun in Our Hearts—Celebrating 17 Years of State Building. 1967. Directed by Anonymous. CCND Studio.

Child Party. 1957. Directed by Wang Chen. CCND studio.

China. 1965. Directed by Felix Greene. Society for Anglo-Chinese Understanding (SACU).

China: Beyond the Clouds. 1994. Directed by Phil Agland. Channel 4 UK.

China and the Forbidden City. 1972. Directed by Lucy Jarvis.

Chronicle of New China's Education. 2008. CCND studio.

Democratic Dongbei No. 13: Brief No. 13. 1949. Directed by Xu Xiaobing. CCND studio.

Early Spring. 1956. Directed by Ivens. CCND Studio.

Engineers of the Future. 1954. Directed by Chen Chunlie. CCND Studio.

Flying Beyond the Clouds. 1958. Directed by Wang Wei. CCND Studio.

Great Friendship. 1960. Directed by Wang Yonghong. CCND Studio.

Impressions of China. 1974. Directed by Donald McWilliams.

In the Summer Palace. 1956. Directed by Jiang Yi. CCND studio.

Liberated China. 1950. Directed by Sergei Gerasimov. CCND studio. Produced jointly by Beijing Film Studio and Moscow Gorky Film Studio.

Little Ones Can Do Big Things. 1960. Directed by Xiao Shuqin. CCND Studio.

My University: 1970–1976 the Worker, Farmer and Soldier University Student Memoir. 2010. Hong Kong Feng Huang Satellite TV.

Small Training Group. 1955. Directed by Duan Hong. CCND studio.

Student Life During Summer Break. 1950. Directed by Wang Xingming. CCND Studio.

Students Forge Steel. 1958. Directed by Wang Wei. CCND Studio.

Summer Camp. 1955. Directed by Tan Zhen. CCND Studio.

Sunday in Peking (Dimanche á Pekin). 1956. Directed by Chris Marker. Pavox Films.

The Little Trumpet. 1962. CCND studio.

The New Political Consultative Committee Preparatory Meeting is Established. 1949. Directed by Gao Weijin. CCND Studio.

The Other Half of the Sky: A China Memoir. 1975. Directed by Shirley MacLaine and Claudia Weill. Shirley MacLaine Productions.

The People's Commune is Good. 1958. Directed by Xiao Xiangyang. CCND Studio.

The University Under the Qilian Mountains. 1960. Directed by He Zhongxin. CCND Film Studio.

Two Summer Camps. 1957. Directed by Liu Caiyao. CCND studio.

Where Dreams Begin, My 1977. 2005. CCTV.

Work-Study Program. 1958. Directed by Xiao Xiangyang. CCND Studio.

References

Anderson, B.R. 1991. *Imagined Communities: Reflections on the Origin and Spread of Nationalism*. London: Verso.

Bei Dao and Li Tuo, eds. 2009. *The Seventies*. Shanghai: Sanlian Bookstore Press.

CCND Dept. of Film Materials. 2009. *News Brief China Science Education 1950–1987*. Shanghai: Shanghai Science and Technology Literature Publishing House.

CCND. 2009. *Diyipi quanguo tongyi jiaocai* 第一批全国统一教材 [The First National Set of Unified Teaching Materials], New China Firsts. Guangdong: Guangdong Education Publishing House.

CCND. 2009. *Diyisuo zonghe daxue: zhonguo renmin daxue* 第一所综合大学—中国人民大学 [The First Comprehensive University: China's Renmin University], New China Firsts. Guangdong: Guangdong Education Publishing House.

CCND. 2009. *Hanzi Jianhua fangan* 汉字简化方案 [The Character Simplification Project], New China Firsts. Guangdong: Guangdong Education Publishing House.

CCND. 2009. *New School for Cultivating Civil Servants: State Administration Institute*, New China Firsts. Guangdong: Guangdong Education Publishing House.

CCND. 2009. *Xinzhongguo diyidai liuxuesheng* 新中国第一代留学生 [The First Generation of Foreign Students in the New China], New China Firsts. Guangdong: Guangdong Education Publishing House.

Chai Wei. 2009. "Xin zhongguo jiaoyu jishi 新 中 国 教 育 纪 事 [Chronicle of New Chinese Education]." *The Strong Repercussions of Broadcasting*. 2009-11-24. *Zhongguo jiaoyu bao* 中 国 教 育 报 [Chinese Education Periodical].

Cheng Huangmei. 1989. *Contemporary Chinese Film* (Part II). Beijing: China Social Science Publishing.

Cheng Jihua. 1963. *Zhongguo dianying fazhanshi diyijuan* 中 国 电 影 发 展 史 第 一 卷 [The History of Development of Chinese Film], Vol. No. 1. Beijing: China Film Publishing House.

Di Sheng. 2005. "'Wenge' zhong de tingke, fuke yu zhaosheng '文革' 中的停课、复课与招生 [Suspending Classes, Resuming Classes and Enrolling Students in the 'Cultural Revolution']." *Over the Party History* (9).

Ding Gang. 2008. "Voice and Experience: Narrative Inquiry in Education." *Narrative Research Series in China's Education*, 1. Beijing: Educational Science Press.

"Editorial: Venomous Motive, A Base Trick." *People's Daily*, 1974-01-30.

Editorial Department of China Education Yearbook. 1984. *Zhongguo jiaoyu nianjian* 中国教育年鉴 [Chinese Education Almanac 1949–1981]. Beijing: Chinese Encyclopedia Publishing House.

Fang Fang. 2003. *Zhongguo dianying fazhanshi diyijuan* 中 国 电 影 发 展 史 第 一 卷 [The History of Development of Chinese Film], Vol. No. 1. Beijing: China Theater Publishing House.

Ferro, Mark. 2008. *Film and History*, trans. Peng Shuhui. Beijing: Beijing University Publishing House.

Fu Jianfeng. 2005. "60 wan daike jiaoshi gandong zhongguo 60 万代课教师感动中国 [600 Thousand Substitute Teachers Move China]." *Nanfang zhoumo* 南方周末 [Southern Weekend], 2005-12-26.

Gao Weijin. 2003. *Zhongguo xinwen jilu dianyingshi* 中国新闻记录电影史 [Cinematic History of Chinese News Documentaries]. Beijing: Central Literature Publishing House.

Gao Yubao. 1991. *Gao Yubao-Autobiographical Novel*. Beijing: PLA Literature and Art Publishing House.

Government Administration Council. 1954. "131st Meeting on the 24th of December 1953." *People's Daily*, January 12, 1954.

Gu Zheng. 2006. *Shijie sheyingshi* 世界摄影史 [Photographic History of the World]. Hangzhou: Zhejiang Photography Publishing House.

Guo Yanmei and Chen Jiaping. 2009. "Qianxi zhongguo jilupian fazhan guocheng-zhong de shijiao bianhua 浅析中国纪录片发展过程中的视角变化 [Superficially Analyzing Changes of Perspective in the Process of Chinese Documentary Film Development]." *Contemporary Television* (10).

He Bingdi. 2005. *Sixty Years of Reading History and Reading the World*. Guangxi Normal University Press, 393.

He Jimin, ed. 2009. *The Rise of the Sun in the East—The Most Wonderful Book of the Founding of China*. Beijing: Central Party History Press.

He Suliu. *Report on the Development of Chinese Documentary Film* (*zhongguo jilupian fazhan baogao* 中国纪录片发展报告). Beijing: Social Science Literature Publishing House.

How Yukong Moved the Mountains (*Comment Yukong déplaça les montagnes*). 1976. Directed by Joris Ivens and Marceline Loriden. Capi Films, Institut National de l'Audiovisuel (INA).

Inglis, David. 2005. *Culture and Everyday Life*. London and New York: Routledge.

Iwasaki Akira. 1931. *Film and Capitalism*. Tokyo: Sekaisha.

Li Lingge. 2008. *Jilupian xia de zhongguo: ershi shiji zhongguo jilupian de fazhan yu shehui bianqian* 纪录片下的中国：二十世纪中国纪录片的发展与社会变迁 [China in Documentary Film: The Development and Social Transformation of 20th Century Chinese Documentary Film]. Beijing: Tsinghua University Publishing House.

Li Yi. 1981. "Wenyi xinzuo Zhong fanying de zhongguo xianshi—Zhongguo xin xieshizhuyi wenyi zuopin xuan 文艺新作中反映的中国现实—中国新写实主义文艺作品选 [Chinese Reality Reflected in Artistic Creation—Selected Artistic Works of China's New Realism]." *Replacement Introduction,* Arts Research (1).

Liu Jie. 2007. *Jilupian de xugou—yizhong yingxiang de biaoyi* 纪录片的虚构——一种影像的表意 [The Fabrication of Documentary Film—An Idea of Film]. Beijing: Media University of China Publishing House.

Liu Xiangcheng. 2011. *China After Mao: 1976–1983*. Beijing: World Book Inc., 45.

Liu Zhijun. 2012. "Column: diary of Nixon's visit to China." CNTV, February 6, 2012, 19:58. <http://jishi.cntv.cn/nikesongfanghuariji/classpage/video/20120206/103981.shtml>.

Lu Xun. 1930. "Film and Capitalism." *Bud Monthly* 1 (No. 3).

New Child. 1950. Directed by Gong Lian. CCND Studio.

News Brief (1962–16). 1962. CCND Studio.

News Brief—China: the People 1961–1979. 2009. CCND Studio.

Qian Mu. 1949. "*Tuibian zhong de gucheng zhengzhi qingdiao* 蜕变中的古城政治情调 [The Political Sentiment of Ancient City in Metamorphosis]." *Beijing Daily*, 1949-01-24.

Qian Mu. 2001. *Zhongguo lishi yanjiu fa* 中国历史研究法 [Chinese History Research Methods]. Beijing: Living, Reading, New Knowledge Joint Publishing.

Riboud, Marc. 1997. *Marc Riboud in China: 40 Years of Photography*. New York: Abrams Press.

Shan Wanli. 2001. *Jilu dianying wenxian* 记录电影文献 [Documentary Film Literature] Beijing: China Film Publishing House.

Shan Wanli. 2002. "Waiguo jilupian li de bainian zhongguo 外国纪录片里的百年中国 [One Hundred Years of China in Foreign Documentary Film]." *Nanfang zhoumo* 南方周末 [Southern Weekend], 2002-08-29.

Shan Wanli. 2005 *Zhongguo jilupian dianyingshi* 中国纪录片电影史 [Cinematic History of Chinese Documentary Film]. Beijing: China Film Publishing House.

Shan Wanli. 2009. *The History of Documentary Film in China*. Beijing: China Central Party History Publishing House.

Shan Wanli. 2011. "Preface: *Documentary Storytelling*." In *Documentary Film Also Has to Tell a Story*, by Sheila Curran Bernard, 29. Beijing: World Books Publishing House.

"Strengthening the Determination of Film Production Work." *People's Daily*, 01-12-1954.

Tame, Chris R. 1983/1990. "Hypocrisy in The 'Peace' Movement: A Case Study." *Foreign Policy Perspectives* (No. 16).

"The Great Revolution and Grand Development of Our Education Enterprise." *People's Daily*, 1959-10-08.

Thomson, Paul. 1999. *Guoqu de shengyin* 过去的声音 [Sounds of the Past: Oral History]. Hong Kong: Oxford University Press.

van Sijll, Jennifer. 2007. *Cinematic Storytelling*. Studio City: Michael Wiese Productions.

Wang Wei. 2009. *Wo yu xinwen jianbao* 我与新闻简报 [News Brief and I]. [EB/OL]. [2013-03-06]. <http://www.cctv.com/endfilm/history/g8.asp>.

Weitz, Robin. 2000. *Who is Interpreting Whom: The Politics of Documentary Film*. Taipei: Taipei Yuanliu Chubanshi Stock Co. Ltd.

Wild China. 2008. Directed by Phil Chapman. BBC Natural History Unit and China Central Television (CCTV).

Williams, Raymond. 1991. *Culture and Society,* trans. Wu Songjiang and Zhang Wending. Beijing: Beijing University Press.

Xiao Tongqing. 2005. *Yingxiang shiji* 影像史记 [Recorded History of Film]. Guangzhou: Nanfang Daily Publishing House.

Yang Mingping and Fang Deyun. 2001. *Guochan jilipian fazhan zhengce shuli yu guanli chuangxin sikao* 国产纪录片发展政策疏离与管理创新思考) [Original Thought on the Sorting and Managing of Policies for the Development of Domestic Documentary Film].

Yang Xiufeng. 1959. "Woguo jiaoyu shiye de dageming he dafazhan 我国教育事业的大革命与大发展 [The Great Revolution and Grand Development of the Enterprise of Chinese Education]." *People's Daily*, 1959-10-08.

Zhang Lixian. 2006. *Mook* 0602. Beijing: New Star Publishing House.

Zhang Lixian. 2006. *Mook* 0701. Beijing: New Star Publishing House.

Zhang Lixian. 2006. *Mook* 0800. Beijing: New Star Publishing House.

Zhang Lixian. 2006. *Mook* 0801. Beijing: New Star Publishing House.

Zhang Lixian. 2006. *Mook* 0901. Beijing: New Star Publishing House.

Zhang Lixian. 2006. *Mook* 1001. Beijing: New Star Publishing House.

Zhang Lixian. 2006. "The commentary of the *Memories of the Year of Xu.*" Column in CCTV's *Witness: Portraits*, 264. Beijing: Xinxing Publishing House.

Zhang Lixian. 2007. *The Political Sentiment of an Ancient City in Metamorphosis.* Reader Archive 0705. Beijing: Xinxing Publishing House, 1.

Zhang Lixian. 2008. "Memories of the Year of Shen." Column in CCTV channel, *Witness: Portraits.* Mook 0800. Beijing: Xinxing Publishing House, 214.

Zhang Lixian. 2008 "Memories of the Year of Zi." Column in CCTV channel, *Witness Portraits*, Reading Library 0801. Beijing: Xinxing Publishing House, 242–317.

Zhang Lixian. 2009. "Memories of the Year of X." Column in CCTV's *Witness: Portraits.* Reading Library 0602. Beijing: Xinxing Publishing House, 269.

Zhang Lixian. 2008. "Commentary in *Memories of the Year of Zi.*" CCTV's *Witness Portraits* Column Reading Library 0801. Beijing: Xinxing Publishing House, 242–317.

Zhang Lixian. 2010. "Commentary in *Memories of the Year of Yin.*" in CCTV's *Witness Portraits*, Reading Library 1001. Beijing: Xinxing Publishing House, 230–317.

Zhou Xian. 2008. *Shijue wenhua de zhuanxiang* 视觉文化的转向 [The Turn to Visual Culture]. Beijing: Beijing University Publishing House.

Zhou Yang. 1951. "Carrying Out the Artistic Path of Mao Zedong." *Yibao* 艺 报 (4).

Zhou Yong. 2004. "The Theoretical Pursuit of Narrative Research in Education: ECNU Prof. Ding Gang Interview." *Research on Education Development* (09).

CHAPTER 5

Memory, History, and Role: Wang Lijuan and Her Schoolmates Who Graduated from Normal School

Zhao Jinpo
Translated by Chad Meyers

Abstract

With changes to policies related to the education of teachers, normal schools for cultivating primary school teachers have fallen away from people's sight and memories. As one of the melodies of the Chinese educational chorus, what does normal school offer for its graduates, and for fundamental education in rural China? How should we evaluate its benefits? All these questions are worthy of being taken into consideration.

This article focuses on the life trajectory of Wang Lijuan, who entered into a normal school in a certain province located in central China at the end of the 1980s; three years later, she held a teaching position as a primary school teacher in rural area. The author wants to explore the role of normal schools and their students in the development of rural basic education through investigating Wang and her schoolmates' memory of studying, working, marriage, and of their social relations.

1 Foreword[*,1]

1.1 *Presentation of the Issue*
On April 7, 2009, an online blog post titled "Teachers and Students at Xintai Middle School Present Lawsuit Against Government Education Bureau

---

* I would like to thank Professor Ding Gang for his guidance in this study and Professor Du Chengxian for his support with relevant documents and literature. The "Secondary Normal" group discussed in the article refers mainly to ordinary normal school students in secondary normal schools. All of the students have rural backgrounds. To respect and protect their personal privacy, "Wang Lijuan" and her fellow alumni have all been given pseudonyms.
1 This article was translated from its Chinese version, which was originally published in *China's Education: Research and Review*, 2009, volume 13, pp. 122–187.

© KONINKLIJKE BRILL NV, LEIDEN, 2019 | DOI:10.1163/9789004409606_006

Administration"[2] (Dream Blog, 2009) attracted the attention of many education workers, particularly among alumni of secondary normal schools. The subject of the post dealt with the case of a lawyer working as a teacher at a secondary normal school who took a group of secondary school graduates, his former students, and mounted a lawsuit at the local courtroom.

Memory is like a panoramic picture. In 1902, the famous industrialist and educator Zhang Jian founded the Tongzhou Normal School in Nantong. This was the first independent teachers' education school devoted to training elementary school teachers, and its founding also marked the beginning of secondary normal education in China (Gu Mingyuan 1998b, 1557).[3] In 1999,

---

2   See Dream Blog: "A Record of Xintai Teachers' and Students' Presentation of their Lawsuit Filed Against the Administration of the Government Education Bureau" (Dream Blog, 2009). On March 31, 2009, at Shandong Tai'an Intermediate Court, Beijing lawyer Zhang Gang, a former teacher at a secondary normal school, filed a lawsuit on behalf of his students of ten years' prior, totalling 63 graduates of the secondary normal school. The defendant was the government administration of the education bureau of his hometown, and the lawsuit, if successful, would require the defendant to arrange for resettlement employment for the plaintiffs according to the school's admission policy at the time the plaintiffs enrolled in the school. Case summary: ten years' prior, the plaintiffs passed the selection criteria for admission to the normal secondary school and completed their studies there three years later, after which they reported to the Xintai City Bureau of Education with a report card issued by the Provincial Department of Education and waited for their promised work assignments. However, they found that there was no employment option awaiting them, instead they would have to take an examination and only the most outstanding of the examinees would be selected for hiring. As graduates of normal secondary school, they took the examination together with the university graduates of that year, and the result was that less than one-tenth of the plaintiffs were given employment. Over the past 10 years, the plaintiffs filed many requests and appeals, all of which were denied and sent back. Many of the graduates were detained multiple times and three were sent to forced labor camps for reeducation. In the past 10 years, they have paid a high price in fighting for their rights, yet they never gave up their dream: to be primary school teachers in the poor rural areas in their hometown, to devote themselves to local education. After reading online about similar cases in Hainan Province, cases which the plaintiffs had won, and they began to consider using the law as their weapon. On April 2, 2008, 63 plaintiffs submitted an administrative indictment to the Intermediate People's Court of Tai'an City, sued the Xintai Municipal Government and the Education Bureau for failing to perform their administrative duties, and sued the Xintai Education Bureau for illegally making an administrative decision not to provide resettlement employment for the graduates. Since the case was submitted, in April 2008, various forces have been engaged in an intense contest. The court decided in January 2009 to formally file the case. The case of the normal secondary school graduates is offered here simply to call the reader's attention to the relevant social circumstances.

3   The *Education Dictionary* contains the following entry regarding Tongzhou Normal School: Tongzhou Normal School was established in May of the 28th year of Qing Emperor Guangxu (1902); the newly-named Minli Tongzhou Normal School soon became private. It later underwent multiple name changes and restructurings. In 1952 it became public, and the name was changed to Nantong Normal School of Jiangsu Province, offering a program of study

the *Opinions on the Adjustment of the Distribution Structure of Normal Colleges and Universities* issued by the Ministry of Education of the People's Republic of China stated that greater reforms must be made in teacher education nationwide in the coming century. The reorganization of teacher education resources has since been incorporated into the government's education plans. The structure of normal colleges and universities consists of three tiers for teacher training (undergraduate programs in higher education pedagogy, specialized programs in higher education pedagogy, and secondary education programs) and is transitioning to a two-tier structure (undergraduate programs in higher education pedagogy, specialized programs in higher education pedagogy). "Secondary normal schools" are set to become relics of the past.[4]

---

in elementary school education with specializations in general, early childhood, musical, and physical education. It recruited junior high school graduates, with two separate tracks of two-year and five-year courses of study. According to the entry on the "Tongzhou Normal School Conference" in *Zhang Jizi's Jiulu Education Record* (Volume 1), the conclusion was: "Normal schools have existed in China since the beginning of the 28th year of the Guangxu period. The non-governmental independently-run normal school began in Tongzhou." (Gu 1998, 1557).

The "Teacher Education" entry in the *Education Dictionary* contains the following content: China's teacher education began in the Shanghai Nanyang Public Normal School in the 23rd year of Qing Emperor Guangxu (1897). In the 28th year (1902), the opening of the Jingshi University Normal School marked the beginning of teacher education in higher education in China. In the 29th year (1903) the enactment of the "Guiding Regulations for Schools," the teacher education system became self-contained and was divided into two tracks, one for advanced the other for introductory teacher education. In 1912, the Ministry of Education promulgated the "Teacher Education Order," and the two-track normal school was split into two schools which were renamed the Higher Normal School and the Normal School. Six national normal teachers' schools were established in the six major regions for normal schools in the country, on a provincial basis. In 1938, independent and university-affiliated teachers' schools began to be founded. After the founding of New China, higher and secondary normal schools were founded independently of each other (ibid., 1397). See also: (Chen Nailin 1980, 109–110) and (Lu Wenwei 1981, 47–49).

4   Requirements laid out with the working objectives stated in *Several Opinions from the Ministry of Education on the Layout Adjustment of Teachers Colleges and Universities*: The adjustments to the hierarchical structure of teacher education in our country should be gradually extended from the urban to the rural and the coastal areas to the inland regions. The transition from three-tier teacher education (undergraduate programs in higher education pedagogy, specialized programs in higher education pedagogy, and secondary education programs) to a two-tier structure (undergraduate programs in higher education pedagogy, specialized programs in higher education pedagogy) should be carried out. By 2010 or so, the newly-added elementary and junior high school teachers-in-training will have more or less completed an undergraduate or training school level of education. The required goals for school layout adjustment are that the number of ordinary higher normal colleges, education colleges, and secondary normal schools will be reduced from 1,353 in 1997 to 1,000 or so by 2003, of which about 300 will be ordinary normal colleges and universities and around 500 of which will be secondary normal schools (He 2003, 241).

With the release of government documents, secondary normal schools have taken on a vanguard role in the reform of China's teacher education. As these schools are gradually withdrawn throughout the country, administrators in certain regions in central and western China, where the local economy and education conditions are still underdeveloped, have had to consider how to adjust their systems to condense local secondary normal schools. This has naturally given rise to a degree of anxiety among those who value a broader range in basic education (Hua Chen 2007). Although secondary normal education is set to disappear, to be replaced by higher normal education, this not only conforms to the state of teacher education worldwide but also to the reality of the development of teacher education in China. However, it will take a long time to complete this transition (around twenty years) (Bie Linye 2000). Many experts, based on the unbalanced economic development in some regions and the unbalanced development of education, proposed at the beginning of this century that the secondary normal schools should not be eliminated lightly, and that both the strengths and inadequacies of the secondary normal school training model should be carefully examined, calling for the preservation of the secondary normal school tradition so as to pass on its strengths (Gu 2003).

Did secondary normal education, as the main stage for training primary teachers in China complete its historical mission? Has the country's pre-ordained destiny for primary school teachers—especially those in rural areas—achieved its ultimate goal? Did the students who chose to undertake and graduated from secondary normal schools eventually fulfill the original "agreement" and make for the humble podiums of rural primary schools? What has secondary normal education contributed to China's primary education? What kind of life have secondary normal schools given to their graduates? At the same time as we turn through the pages of history, how can we continue to write more colorful music for the symphony of primary teacher education in our country? This is certainly a thought-provoking series of questions.

1.2   Research Ideas

History is rich in ideological and emotional content, and we need to enter history to perceive correctly and find understanding; from the perspective of educational history research, in addition to seeking "rules" and focusing on the ideas and systems produced by the elite, the activities and events pertaining to historical individuals of all backgrounds should also be the focus of research. To a certain extent, this approach can convey a deeper sense of the historical memories relevant to the education field and of their humanistic implications (Ding Gang 2009). Many books have been written on the historical study of teacher education in China (including secondary normal schools). Much of the thought and reflection offered in these works has benefited the development of China's secondary normal education in policy formulation, system implementation, teaching management, and related practices. In addition, there are also quite a number of articles that reflect the experience and feelings of front-line school workers in secondary schools or of primary school educators who graduated from secondary normal schools, regarding the teaching, management, and learning conditions in primary schools.[5]

To understand Chinese education, it is necessary to expose the true state of education in China. We must not simply rely on imagination or theory. We must first enter into China to gain a sense of the characters and events of the history of Chinese education, in particular details about the lived experience and feelings relevant to historical events (Ding Gang 2008a). The starting point and the end result of secondary normal education are both very clear, that is, to produce qualified primary school teachers. Therefore, a comprehensive study of the aspects of the life, learning, work, thoughts, romantic relationships, and emotions of secondary school graduates as primary school teachers not only offers a reflective perspective on the history of secondary normal education (policy programs, curriculum, teaching management, etc.), it also represents a reflection of the historical changes in Chinese primary education, pedagogy and teacher education. Examining the "background" of secondary normal graduates as a factor in this complex body of emotions, life experience, and changing roles also provides another means of understanding the real effects and influence of secondary normal education in history.

The reality contained in memory is only one aspect of history, and the history recorded in literature and historical materials likewise does not represent the reality of the past in its entirety. That representation is based on the intention of this study to both present historical realities as recounted by students at secondary normal schools and also to examine the archives and historical materials pertaining to secondary normal education in China since the 60th year of the founding of the People's Republic of China, and especially in the 30 years since the beginning of reform and opening up. Through the interlacing of personal memory and historical archives, we have attempted to depict an overall impression of the life trajectories of students who attended secondary normal schools and the role of secondary normal education for this set of individuals. The late 1980s and early 1990s was a watershed moment,

---

5 Many monographs and dissertations on this subject exist, such as: (Yang 1989), (Liu 1993), (National Education Committee, Secretary of Normal Education 1996), (Zhang 1984, 3–9), (Yu 1997, 35–41), (East China Normal University Teacher Training Institute 1996, 2–6), and (He Ming 2002).

representing the beginning of a fundamental change in the academic, intellectual, and cultural worlds of mainland China (Ge 2005, 2).[6] China's secondary normal education and the primary education with which it is so tightly bound bear the marks of that era without exception. Therefore, the period from 1989 to 2002 is the central focus of examination and description of the present article. The specific focus is the life trajectory of Wang Lijuan, a 1989 graduate of secondary normal school, along with the lived experience of other students and alumni of secondary normal schools. The purpose of the present study is to reveal and reflect on the historical role of primary school teachers, particularly those in rural areas, in an attempt to offer a true picture of the defining, withdrawal, appearance, interaction and reshaping of this role to explore possible answers to the problems presented herein.

1.3   *Research Methods*

This study attempts to introduce narrative research methods into educational history research. Specifically, concern with experience has been folded into the observation of daily pedagogical practice (Ding Gang 2008b, 55), through stories, oral reports, interviews, and literary analysis of writings on educational experiences (including the collection and use of relevant information in web blogs and BBS).[7] These represent the day-to-day educational and life experiences of secondary normal graduates working as rural elementary school teachers, taking a perspective focused on the practical pedagogical thoughts and work of these graduates both at the level of the individual (Wang Lijuan) and of the collective (secondary normal school alumni) to acquire an understanding of the reality of secondary normal education and the students who studied at these schools. The emphasis here is on revealing the past in its appropriate situational context and in its truest and most natural sense to search for answers on the basis of solid research, attaching importance to research based on process, context, and specificity rather than on

---

6   The 1990s was a new era for China, as social thought and philosophy thrived once again. "The fundamental changes in the academic, intellectual, and cultural worlds of mainland China began in the late 1980s and early 1990s. The 1980s and 1990s, was a watershed moment in history.... The '20th century' actually started in 1895 and ended in 1989" (Ge Zhaoguang 2005, 2).

7   In judging the authenticity and reliability of online resources, the author believes that one must look at posts made by internet users, at the "identity" of internet users, and finally at the authoritativeness of the information platform. When it comes to the topic of the feelings and inner experiences of "secondary normal students," the author has compared the content of online messages and telephone interviews. The author feels that the former possesses two special characteristics, namely that ideas are expressed quite directly, and there is often a large discrepancy among different replies in terms of the depth of content. Thus, the most relevant passages have been selected for inclusion in the present article.

conclusiveness, abstraction and generalization, which can also be considered an exercise in qualitative research methods (Chen 2000).

1.4   Presentation of Roles

"Lijuan is coming back to the village to be a teacher!" The villagers had crowded at the village entrance. In the courtyard of the Dawangmiao Village Elementary School, a welcome meeting for new teachers was underway.[8] Wang Lijuan's father, a man in his forties, was smoking under a eucalyptus tree not far from the school wall, staring toward the cornfield on the opposite side of the road, his tanned face bearing an irrepressible smile. All of their struggles over the past few years had not been in vain: his daughter had not only completed her schooling, she had even landed a government job.[9] After the school principal, his own daughter was now the second-ranking public employee in the village!

This scene took place on the morning of August 1992. That morning, Wang Lijuan, sitting on the rostrum at the primary school welcome meeting, was also very happy. Although the temporary rostrum lined with rugged old desks made her feel a bit uncomfortable, the 300 excited faces in front of her and the enthusiasm of the old principal as he shouted through the megaphone gave her the feeling that she, having just graduated from the provincial city normal school, had grown up. She even noticed two young boys in the student group giggling and saying to each other: "That's Miss Wang, the new teacher!"

For Wang Lijuan, 1992 was both an end and a beginning. When she returned to her hometown to work as a primary school teacher, she didn't seem to feel what her classmates had felt—suffering and confusion. Recalling that year, little had happened beyond the news reports about national leader Deng

---

8   "M" County, where Wang Lijuan's hometown is located, is a provincial special pilot county for reform, opening up and development. The hills rising in the distance and meadows produce wheat and corn, and specialties such as honeysuckle, garlic, and apricots. At the same time, there are rich mineral deposits and abundant resources in the area. The main deposits are coal, limestone, and bauxite, and the region is known as the "hometown of black gold." In 1994, M County was approved by the State Council for expansion and development to become a city, and its economic strength ranks first in the province. Wang Lijuan's is an ordinary village which was reclassified as a town in 1994 (Wang, 2009).

9   In November 1955, the State Council issued the "Regulations on the Urban-Rural Demarcation Standards" to determine the "agricultural population" and the "non-agricultural population" as demographic indicators. After 1963, the Ministry of Public Security used demographic statistics as a criterion for demarcating the type of household registration recorded in the population statistics. Urban zones that receive national grain supplies are classified as "non-agricultural populations," otherwise they are "agricultural populations." The dual structure composed of "urban" and "rural" areas in China thus took shape, and there are differences between the two types of household registrations (Hai Tian and Xiao Wei 2009, 11).

Xiaoping's visit to Shenzhen in the south and the propaganda about the arrival of a new era in China's socialist market economic system. However, no matter how society changed, Wang Lijuan's faint smile never faded, and life for her assumed a brilliant diversity as she eagerly looked forward to her life as a rural primary school teacher.

> Wang Lijuan: I am very content. It's good for a girl to work as a teacher. I wanted to be a teacher when I was a child. Now I am back in the village, close to my family, and I can help out a little. Besides, my little brother is still in the third grade at the village school!
>
> WANG 2009

The country's setting of the "rural elementary school teacher" as a social "role" is a matter of policy. As early as 1952, the State Education Commission promulgated the "Provisional Regulations for Normal Schools (Draft)," which clearly stipulated the policies for the treatment and services offered to students attending normal schools: they would receive scholarships and be assigned jobs.[10] Ensuring the quality of life of secondary normal school students and offering them a guaranteed future was a measure of national policy as China

---

10   The student-assisted scholarship system for normal school students was a system of academic funding for normal school students in China. After the founding of New China, Beijing Normal University took the lead in trials. In 1952, the Ministry of Education issued regulations for higher normal schools and normal schools (namely, "Provisions for Higher Normal Schools" and "Provisional Regulations for Normal Schools"), which stipulated that normal students should receive the "people's financial aid." In October 1978, the Ministry of Education reaffirmed that normal school students should all receive the people's financial aid, and divided these students into four levels: secondary, training school, undergraduate, and graduate students. In 1983, the system for the integration of financial assistance for scholarship students and merit scholarships was implemented. That is, a part of the people's financial aid was designated as a scholarship to reward outstanding students. In 1987, this was changed to a scholarship system for students majoring in teaching at normal schools. In addition, China began to set up the "university scholarship system" in 1932, divided into secondary normal scholarships and higher normal scholarships (including training school students, undergraduate and graduate students). This was discontinued in 1952. In 1983, a joint system of financial assistance and merit scholarships was implemented. In July 1987, higher normal colleges and universities changed the people's financial aid to scholarships for students majoring in teaching. In August of 1987, the State Education Commission required that the standards for secondary normal school financial aid grants should be raised in accordance with the standards for scholarships given to students majoring in teaching at higher normal schools. Refer to the two entries titled "Public Financial Assistance System for Normal School Students" and "Fellowship System for Normal College Students" in the *Education Dictionary* (Gu 1998, 1399).

sought to produce a larger base of teachers. Even in the early 1960s, when serious natural disasters occurred in China and production and living resources were scarce, the government still took every effort to ensure the full allocation of teacher training funds and expenditures.[11] It is precisely for this reason that the training of teachers for elementary education in China still made great developments during this difficult period.[12]

> As soon as students entered the normal school, their meals, housing and tuition were all covered by public funds. This was true from the Beiyang period (i.e. Beiyang government [1912–1928] refers to the central government of China, headed by Yuan Shikai in the early period of the Republic of China, which dominated the political structure of the late Qing Dynasty. It was also the first internationally recognized Chinese government after the collapse of the Qing Dynasty.) until the 1980s, implying a cultural tradition and career orientation that respected teachers and education. I went to university in 1978. At that time, 80% of the students at colleges and universities and 100% of the students at teachers' colleges received financial aid. Although the assistance only amounted to 19.5 yuan per month, students did not have to pay tuition and accommodation fees, and since food expenses were only 15 yuan per month, poor students were not only able to be self-sufficient; they could also save a few yuan a year to give to their parents. However, this tradition has been broken with the current national policy based on rejuvenating the country through science and education.
>
> DING DONG and XIE YONG 2008, 131

Why did Wang Lijuan go to secondary normal school? Wang Lijuan's parents and her third-grade head teacher understood it best: that only by going to school can one attain the greatest benefit.

---

11   1961 to 1963 was a period underscored by natural disasters in China. In the absence of food and clothing, the state adjusted the amount of financial aid given to students in secondary technical schools across the country, reducing it by 20% to 40%. However, the financial assistance given to students in secondary normal schools remained the same (He 1998a, 1206).

12   The number of students in secondary normal schools rose from 345,000 in 1952 to 839,000 in 1960, including intermediate normal schools and junior normal schools, the former of which recruited junior high school graduates or students with equivalent academic qualifications and the latter of which recruited elementary school graduates under the age of 25 or students with equivalent academic qualifications (ibid., 1099).

Wang Lijuan: Actually, when I was in junior high school, my academic performance was well-known at school. I had seventy or eighty *classmates* in *the same* class, and I was *always* among the top five. When I was about to graduate, the family asked me to take the test to get into secondary normal school. I didn't really know what secondary normal school was all about.[13] My parents did not understand, our head teacher told them that I was a good candidate for secondary normal school, and that going to secondary normal school was better than going to a regular high school, since you could start working earlier and would have a secure future. The daughter of my head teacher also went to study at secondary normal school one year earlier than me. It was even harder to pass the admission test into normal school in the provincial capital in 1989 than it was to get accepted to the local county high school (Wang 2009).[14]

For rural families, decisions regarding education in the family often viewed education as an investment, especially for poor rural families. Sending a child to secondary normal school was an investment in education with a high rate of return. What parents had to consider was how to get the most value out of their child's schooling, and at the lowest possible costs. By attending secondary normal school, their studies were subsidized by the state and they had a guaranteed job as well, so it was an attractive option for these families.

Moreover, in the late 1980s and early 1990s, the idea that "studying was of no practical value" became more and more pervasive and society began to place more emphasis on going into business. For families that were already not so well-off, earning enough money for children to attend high school and university only exacerbated their financial difficulties. Farmers were particularly reluctant to invest in their daughters' education. This was not only due to the traditional Chinese traditional idea that married daughters provide lower economic returns than sons, since after marriage daughters "belonged" to the family they married into; from the perspective of returns on investments in education, in developing countries such as China, the general idea is that girls

---

13   Meaning she did not fully understand what her studies would entail at this school in terms of their content, characteristics, and ultimate goals.

14   Due to various factors such as the varying education conditions across various counties and districts and the different selection processes for students specializing in teaching, it is difficult to assess the differences between the admission cut-off scores for secondary normal school admissions and the local high school admissions in the suburban counties of the Central Plains. However, in general, in 1989, the admission requirements in terms of test scores for secondary normal schools in provincial capitals and the scores for general normal school classes were basically the same as those of ordinary high schools in the suburban counties; the admission scores for programs for training specialized teachers in areas such as music, art, and special education were slightly lower, but there were additional requirements for these candidates in terms of interviews to assess their professional suitability and overall character.

who go to university don't enjoy the same prospects as their male counterparts, meaning that parents would also receive a lower return on their investment as they would return less to their parents than their sons. From this perspective, it was seen as more cost-effective to invest in educating sons (Sun Zhijun 2004, 134).

> Wang Lijuan: I think I've been more fortunate than my peers in the village. The difference is that our family only has two children, my brother and I, so my parents had less of a burden. Many girls in our village didn't continue studying after graduating from junior high school, not because their grades were low, but because they didn't see much of a point to it. They might as well start contributing to their families however they could. In addition, my dad was more open-minded [laughs].
>
> WANG LIJUAN April 15, 2009

> "Iron Drum": A mix of pride and feelings of inferiority was obviously one of the clearest markers of secondary normal students. All the secondary normal school students of that generation (the 1980s and the early 1990s) felt at least a moment of pride. As the ancient poem says, "My high horse proudly gallops with the gentle breeze of spring; in one day I see all the flowers of Chang'an and my heart sings!" In that era when a stable job meant a solid income, countless students with excellent academic performance opted to attend secondary normal school.
>
> "Iron Drum" June 6, 2009[15]

It was certainly worth it to send children to secondary normal school! It offered parents the opportunity to realize the great ideal of rural families: leaving the farm. Rural people regarded the acquisition of a registered permanent residence in an urban area as an important step in achieving a better life. This was the only thing these poor people knew to aspire to. As an important symbol in achieving this goal, having a non-agricultural permanent residence was a great comfort for ordinary rural people (Murphy 2009, 46). For the vast majority of farm children, state-assigned jobs meant a stable living that would allow them to eat "commodity grains," and their identity as farmers would disappear as they made the shift from a rural to an urban permanent residence. Attending normal school represented a kind of psychological satisfaction and

---

15   See "Iron Drum": *Secondary Normal Students: The Dreams and Grief of a Generation of Teachers* (Tianmen Primary School, Shimen Town, Tongxiang City, Zhejiang Province). The reflections of "Iron Drum" in this article are all derived from this source ("Iron Drum" 2009).

accomplishment for rural people, especially for the parents of normal school students.

As blogger "Yi An Shu Nv" writes in her blog, the decision to attend secondary normal school was the result of multiple factors:

> Yi An Shu Nv: Attending secondary normal school was a highly attractive option for children from poor rural families; it meant a shortcut, a way out. First of all, normal school students were given preferential treatment by the state, such as stipends for living expenses and easier means of moving from a rural to an urban permanent residence. Second, the number of students from a given school who passed the secondary normal exam became an indicator of the quality of education offered at that school. Also, the proportion of high school students who tested into university was extremely low at that time.
>
> YI AN SHU NV 2009[16]

In any case, sending children, especially girls, to secondary normal school, was probably the "best education investment model" for parents in rural China. Thus, 1989 marked the beginning of a "new era," and represented a turning point in Wang Lijuan's life.

However, for the vast majority of unknowing students who know little about their future, choosing to attend secondary normal school also meant deciding to give up the chance to attend university in order to devote one's life to carrying out the "glorious duties" of the primary school teacher behind the humble podium of a rural primary school classroom.[17] Wang Lijuan and her academy

---

16   See the blog of "Yi An Shu Nv": "I was a Secondary Normal School Student in the 1980s." The reflections of "Yi An Shu Nv" cited in this article all come from this source (Yi An Shu Nv 2009).

17   Regarding the future treatment of teacher training for primary education (including early childhood education), as early as 1952, the Ministry of Education promulgated the "Interim Regulations for Normal Schools (Draft)" covering stipulations for the four aspects of grants, job assignments, service and higher education opportunities. The main elements were: (1) Normal school students shall receive state financial aid; (2) Provincial, municipal or municipal and county education administrative agencies shall be responsible for assigning jobs to normal school graduates; (3) Normal school graduates shall serve at least three years in education (two years for graduates of normal training schools), and are not permitted to attend higher education or take on other work [before the end of that period]; (4) Normal school graduates with excellent academic performance in all subjects shall be guaranteed admission to normal college or academy for further education provided they report to the provincial and municipal education bureaus (graduates of normal training schools do not receive this preferential treatment). The number of students offered this guarantee shall not exceed 5% of the total number of graduates of the same year. This aspect of the 1956 "Normal School Regulations" also includes the

alumni were aware of this point when they decided to go to normal school. Only after a few years of work did Wang Lijuan develop a deeper understanding of the reality of her situation.

Of course, in the process of making an "agreement" with the state regarding their future by deciding to attend secondary normal school, many secondary normal students like Wang Lijuan did not have a very good idea of what "secondary normal school" was all about. Many students ended up there thanks to arrangements made by their parents, teachers, and even relatives and friends, entering these schools with varying degrees of joy and anxiety.

Wan Xiaoqin:[18] [*sighs*] In 1989, I went to secondary normal school for music teachers because of my older brother. At the time he was a teacher in the township and knew that I liked to sing. Maybe he thought I wasn't bad at it. (He) said that if I went to the special music teacher classes, I'd be able to be a junior high school teacher in the future, rather than going to teach at elementary school.[19] Everyone in the family did what he said, and so I started working hard, and that's how I got in.

WAN 2009

---

following stipulation regarding student transfers: generally, students may only transfer into normal schools; normal school graduates must fulfill at least three years of service as teachers and shall not attend higher education or change careers during this time (He Dongchang 1998a, 159–160, 589–592).

18   Wan Xiaoqin, a member of Wang Lijuan's graduating class, was enrolled in the first music class offered at the school. After graduating from secondary normal school in 1992, she returned to her hometown to work as a junior high school music teacher. Wan Xiaoqin herself said that she actually did not like music and had always loved reading literature, and that she wanted to try to write something. In 1995, she took part in the adult masters' program and went to the provincial college of education as a history major. In 1997, she took the entrance examination for higher education, going on to major in Chinese in a university undergraduate program, graduating in 1999, but because she did not learn English, she did not earn her degree. The following year, she stayed in the provincial capital. In July 2000, Wan Xiaoqin returned to her hometown in Z county, and has been working as a fourth grade language arts teacher ever since (Wan 2009).

19   In June 1989, the State Education Commission issued the "Circular on the Teaching Program for the Three-year Secondary Normal Schools (Trial)." Secondary normal schools (or classes) for training teachers of subjects such as arts, physical education, and foreign languages were allowed to be established, and an accompanying compulsory course system was set up. In order to strengthen their study of primary school textbooks and teaching methods for professional disciplines, students were required to focus on learning a certain specialty. At the same time, they were required to achieve average secondary normal school graduate levels in other areas such as ideology and politics, cultural knowledge, and education and teaching capabilities. In the same year, the State Education Commission issued the "Teaching Plan for Schools for Secondary Special Education (Trial)," and established or improved three-year or four-year training schools and classes

Yi An Shu Nv: At the age of 15, when I was still a child who didn't know anything, I also joined this team (referring to applying to secondary normal school) and became a secondary normal student. Three years later, some classmates whose grades in school were lower than mine in middle school were admitted to prestigious universities. As they happily entered the university campus to continue their education, I was 18 years old and I was already working as a teacher.

YI AN SHU NV 2009

A classmate of Wang Lijuan, Yu Qiang understood even less about what awaited him when he enrolled in secondary normal school. "When I took the test to get into secondary normal school, I didn't think about it too much, I didn't have the kind of awareness.[20] When my dad heard the teacher say it was 'pretty good,' he asked me to sign up for it. So I ended up going there" (Yu 2009).

However, of the 89 classmates in Wang Lijuan's class, not all of them were able to answer the call of their country or ultimately fulfill their "agreement" to go wherever they were required by national policy as she did.

Wang Lijuan: At that time, a lot of my classmates who graduated with me didn't work as primary school teachers after graduating, especially the male students. I feel like [*pauses*] around 70% were able to get jobs as teachers.

WANG 2009

One of the core values of teacher education is that when the nation and students elect to engage in teacher education, they have a common understanding. That is, teacher education is a very important task if the country wishes to cultivate talent. Therefore, the state must bear the cost of education. Accordingly, students also have to respond to the country's call. This is a tradition in China. The two sides did not have a contractual relationship. Their trust

---

for teachers in blind, deaf and mentally-disabled elementary education (He 1998b, 2867–2869, 2900).

   In the same year, Wang Lijuan's school began recruiting the first physical education, music, and art classes. In addition, special education classes were set up in schools. Each of these four classes had about 40 people per class, accounting for about one-third of the total number of students in the whole year (Wang 2009).

20   Referring to an awareness of the future path of actually returning to the village to work as a teacher. After graduating from secondary normal school in 1992, Yu Qiang worked for a while in a private elementary school before deciding to go into business (Yu Qiang April 15, 2009).

in each other is rooted in tradition and customs. Experience has shown that everyone can generally stick to their word (Ding Dong & Xie Bing 2008, 135).

The five-star red flag that waves on the elementary school campus has been a bright point in the village landscape, just like the youthful spirit of these young teachers. When you think of Wang Lijuan, you can't help but remember the lyrics of "Choice," her favorite song from that time: "You chose me. I chose you. This is our choice."

2   Departing from Assigned Roles

2.1   *Income and Status*

Not every student who attended secondary normal school was eventually placed on the stage of primary school education in accordance with the requirements of the "contract" they had made with their country, going on to carry out the designated role of "primary school teacher." A large number of secondary normal students either upon or after graduating changed their minds decided to cast off the role of "primary school teacher," jumping on lifeboats headed for other lands, and this was especially true for students of graduating classes after Wang Lijuan's year. There are many possible explanations for this, but the most direct and typical example is perhaps exemplified in the case of Yu Qiang. There is only one explanation for his transition: he was a young eighteen-year-old man, and he needed money!

> Author: Why didn't you return to your home town to get a teaching position after graduation?
> Yu Qiang: [*laughs*] I fell in love. Her family was in the city and I did not want to go back to the countryside. After graduation (June 1992), I tried to get my [employment] files sent to a private school in the city. We came from a public school and couldn't be admitted, and I didn't want to work at a private one. I only worked there for two months before I quit.
> Author: It seems that you really did not want to be a teacher.
> Yu Qiang: It was boring. A grown man leading a group of little kids! It was really boring. Besides, the pay was nothing ... we weren't even receiving the salary we were supposed to.
> Author: Did your girlfriend oppose your decision [to go into business] at the time?
> Yu Qiang: Oppose? When I was at the private school, we were almost broke. Her parents wanted to find a military official for her, someone with some political status. I didn't have money at the time ... what choice did I have but to go into business [*laughs*]?

Author: What about your files?

Yu Qiang: I gave up, I didn't care, I let it go, and that was it.

Author: Your parents, they didn't care?

Yu Qiang: Not really. At first, they tried to use their connections for me. They wanted me to go back to the county primary school. Later, when I insisted on staying in the city, they got angry and stopped trying to control [me]. Weren't they doing pretty well living with me in the city, anyway [*laughs*]?

YU 2009

On "Teacher's Day" in 1993, as Wang Lijuan was teaching in a rural classroom, leading the children as they read along with the textbook, her classmate Yu Qiang was engaged in finding work in the newly-introduced concept of the "futures" market. He found a training school in the provincial capital, diligently acquired new knowledge about stocks and thought about how to open a donkey meat restaurant—popular in the capital at the time—with some of his friends from the village.

In the early 1990s, in the new era when the socialist economic market was more open, young men who had graduated from secondary normal school faced greater pressure than their female counterparts. At that time, it was certainly a challenge for male teachers, especially for young people of Yu Qiang's era, to accept the reality of working as "rural elementary school teachers." In the eyes of most people in the society, men working as teachers, especially as rural primary school teachers, were seen as having few future prospects, and so it was hard for them to find wives. They felt embarrassed, confused, and uneasy amid a social atmosphere that valued "getting rich" above all else. In the Central Plains region at that time, many male teachers in rural areas and even primary and middle school teachers in towns and cities had given up careers as teachers in order to go into business. Giving up the stable career that had been so appealing to many parents and associates certainly demanded a great deal of confidence and courage.

In terms of wages, Wang Lijuan's monthly salary was 133.60 yuan, at a time when a bowl of noodles in an ordinary small restaurant on the street cost 4 to 4.5 yuan. After paying off debts and making some donations, her wages were in line with the income standards for "agricultural subsistence populations."[21] However, Wang Lijuan did not receive her first salary until November 1992.

---

21 According to statistics from national rural subsistence population regions (the fourteen provinces and autonomous regions of Inner Mongolia, Shanxi, Sichuan, Hubei, Hebei, Guangxi, Hunan, Xinjiang, Jiangxi, Jilin, Tibet, Hainan, Heilongjiang, and Fujian). In 1992, the per capita net annual income of farmers was a little over 700 yuan (Li 2000,

Wang Lijuan: When I first started working, I really did not expect that I wouldn't get paid, that I'd have to wait several months to receive my salary. Many teachers expressed criticism about this. Later, I wrote to my classmates and I discovered that the situation was the same in a lot of places, and some places were even worse off than us. I remember it was particularly annoying that even with our small salary we had to deduct a part of it every month, one day to "donate" to provide disaster relief, the next day to contribute to preparations for a festival.[22] It seemed like we never received our entire wages. Once, we even had to donate to the "Shaolin Wushu Festival" held in a neighboring county, because in order to get to the festival you had to pass through our area.

WANG 2009

In the early 1990s, education funds were used for other purposes in many parts of the country. Defaulting on teachers' wages was common—in 1993, the total wages owed to teachers across the country amounted to nearly 1.3 billion yuan (Yu 2000, 356–357). The lack of economic security led many teachers to change careers.[23] This had a significant impact on the thinking of newly graduated secondary normal students and their parents. In their eyes, they questioned the stable career they thought they could rely on by working as primary school teachers. Although the state had promptly promulgated a series of policy measures, it was true that the traditional idea that "children from well-to-do families do not become teachers" had seen something of a resurgence.[24] Teachers had no rights or status in society, and the basic conditions of rural schools and

---

125). According to this, Wang Lijuan's salary at that time, according to local price levels, belonged to the category of "agricultural subsistence populations" (Wang 2009).

22   Wang Lijuan's county was changed to a county-level city in 1994. The government took advantage of local resources to launch the biennial "four-carvings" art festival (stone, brick, wood, and jade carving) as a means of stimulating the local economy (Wang 2009).

23   According to a survey presented in Yu Yongde's *Rural Education Theory*, for example, in Kuancheng Manchu Autonomous County, Hebei Province, there were a total of 1,526 public school teachers. There were 70 people who applied for employment change in 1988. In 1989, 76 teachers submitted change of employment applications. In 1990, 87 applied for change of employment. In 1991, after the county party committee and county government imposed a "freeze" on change of employment for teachers, 86 applications were still submitted (Yu 2000, 355–357).

24   In 1993, the General Office of the State Council issued the "Circular on Effective Measures to Solve the Problem of Overdue Teacher Salaries," a "notice" which pointed out the following: In recent years, since 1992, the problem of overdue salaries for teachers in private and public schools has grown more prevalent in increasing areas of China. The problem has become rather serious. Arrears of teachers' salaries have seriously affected teachers' livelihoods, dampened their work enthusiasm and affected the employment stability of the teaching field. Teachers have responded very strongly.

teaching were especially poor. The social reality of low teacher wages made it impossible for secondary normal students not to feel disheartened when they compared their career horizons with other fields in society, leading many to abandon teaching to pursue other paths. This is the most important reason explaining why the base of teachers in rural China became so unstable—the inadequate distribution of teachers' salaries (ibid., 355–357).

> Yu Qiang: I dare to say that few people can really "love" this career from their heart. Especially boys. Very few are able to stick with it.
>
> YU 2009

Faced with great social change, even Wang Lijuan once distrusted her loyalty to her work:

> Wang Lijuan: At the time of graduation, there were not many boys who wanted to return to their hometowns to work as primary school teachers. If it were me, I would probably be the same. There are a lot of careers where you can earn more money than being a teacher.
>
> WANG 2009

This has become an object of great social concern. If the problem cannot be solved in time, it will not only seriously affect the nationwide implementation of nine-year compulsory education, it will inevitably affect the stability of society, causing a series of serious consequences. The "Notice" required that Government agencies at all levels must attach great importance to taking decisive and effective measures to quickly resolve the current problem of arrears of teachers' salaries and ensure that this kind of problem did not reoccur. The "Notice" also emphasized that the fiscal revenue of each township (town) was mainly to be used for the development of education. In areas where the arrears of teacher's salary was severe, no public money could be spent on constructing buildings or centers, or on vehicle purchases. If this stipulation was violated serious investigations would be carried out to find out which leaders are responsible. Acts of embezzlement, diversion, and misappropriation of educational funds were to be thoroughly investigated. In addition, in the same year, when the State Council issued the "Notice on Several Issues Concerning the Implementation of the Teachers' Law of the People's Republic of China," the document mentioned that in 1994, the "Teachers' Law of the People's Republic of China" would be published on January 1, requiring all localities and relevant departments to fully implement the stipulations of the Law through practical action. In order to implement the "Teacher's Law" in a timely manner, the notice said, it was imperative to ensure the total settlement of wages owed to teachers by the end of 1993, so that teachers could properly celebrate the Chinese New Year. At the same time, effective measures would have to be studied and formulated to ensure that new arrears did not arise in the future. For those who were in arrears after January 1, 1994, the responsibility of the relevant leaders was to be investigated according to law in order to effectively protect the legal rights of teachers (He 1998c, 3574–3575).

The impact of economic insecurity and the effect of general direction of social trends on rural elementary school teachers made Yu Qiang and others like him "give up." They instead chose to change careers (including going into business, transferring careers, taking other exams, etc.). For quality of life and personal dignity, they preferred to go south to Guangzhou and Shenzhen and be a "wage earner" to pursue greater aspirations rather than working in the humble position of a "male teacher in a rural primary school."

In fact, even after a decade or so, elementary school teachers in some rural areas in China are still struggling with government agencies, society, families, and all manner of systems to meet their basic survival necessities and earn their meager wages. In June 2008, "China Education News" published an article by a rural elementary school teacher—"Changes in Salary for a Rural Teacher Over a Ten-year Period." The article describes the changes in the author's wages in the ten years since graduating from normal school from 1998 to 2007, as well as the complex emotions that arose around these changes, as can be seen in the author's statement which contains a great deal of the following or similar words and ideas: painful, sent out once every three or four months, very inconsistent, never on time, forced fund-raising, mixed feelings, almost being laid-off, a performance-based wage system for rural teachers, deductions, petitions, 'smug intellectuals,' hopes and expectations, promises that teachers' wages will soon be increased," and so on.

As the article tells, monthly wages ranged from 248 to 1,153 yuan. It is not just the numbers that have changed, but more importantly, the sense of professional identity, belonging, and dignity felt by rural teachers (Wang 2008). How can rural primary school teachers be made to happily and securely remain at their post in service of basic rural education? Obviously, this is not a new issue—there is still a long way to go to achieve the exciting and hopeful goals expressed in the Teachers' Law issued 15 years ago.[25]

3   Family and Society

Compared to Yu Qiang, Wang Lijuan's older schoolmate Zhang Min (who graduated from secondary normal school in 1991) expresses a different kind of helplessness regarding the plight of "rural elementary school teachers."

---

25   Article 25 of Chapter 6 of the Teachers' Law of the People's Republic of China, which came into force on January 1, 1994, stipulates: "The average wage level of teachers should not be lower or higher than the average salary level of state civil servants and should be gradually increased" (He 1998c, 3571).

Zhang Min: After working for ten or so years, it was difficult to decide to resign [*sighs*]. But I didn't have a choice. The primary schools in mining areas were placed under the control of the local townships and towns, and teachers were re-assigned to rural primary schools by the towns and villages. I really felt I lost face, in those years it was so difficult to get out, and wouldn't people laugh at me for coming back? My child had just started elementary school and needed looking after. I didn't want him to lose too much. Besides, his father was doing business, he was busy and tired, and my family couldn't rely solely on my mother, so I had to "sacrifice." I don't mind teaching, but the professional and emotional hardships were another matter, I have really had enough these few years.[26] My family needs me more.

Around 1997, due to the related policies, a lot of small coal mines around the main mining area, which was the main recourse for my colleagues and miners, began to take off, and those privately-operated mines seriously damaged the state-owned mine, and as a consequence the main coal production and efficiency in our mining area declined rapidly, and life in the labor community around us was not nearly as good as in the past. Affiliated schools for children of these laborers started to experience erratic changes in their enrollment, as some students went to the city with their families, some went back to their hometown to study. During that time, teachers' thinking began to fluctuate dramatically.

In 2000, I think, something happened in the mining area which made our hearts sink: the parents of a student stole the corn of a local farming family and were caught. You can't imagine, ten years earlier, it could be the luckiest thing for one to work as a laborer in our main mining area.

---

26 The rural area where Zhang Min lived is the location of a subordinate mining area of the provincial capital bureau with a fairly good economy, the envy of people in surrounding areas, with its mining area, living communities with affiliated schools, hospitals, clubs, shops, post offices, and banks, etc. After graduating in 1990, Zhang Min was assigned to teach at the second junior high school in the area. Eventually she got married, and after some twists and turns, her working relations were transferred to the mining industry belonging to the city bureau system. Her work unit was also transferred to a primary school with relatively good conditions in the mine area. Around 1997, state-owned enterprises were reformed throughout the country, and the mining bureau was changed to an enterprise-owned coal group, leading to fluctuations in the employees in the mining areas. In 2003, the subordinate mines in the area where Zhang Min was working were facing bankruptcy, and upper management decided that the workers' children's schools in the mining area were to be taken over by the local township school district (Zhang 2009).

In 2001, our son Benben was born, and [then] his father and his colleagues were suspended from work. Everyone said that the (coal) mines were facing bankruptcy, and the children's schools were facing restructuring. The teachers were really uneasy. They didn't know if they would be taken over by the local government. For years a few of teachers of our school had been becoming students who had been admitted to graduate schools, in fact, it turned out that there were even a few young teachers of the middle school of the township who had passed the exam to be county civil servants during that years ... I couldn't take the daily feelings of anxiety. [Teachers] were faced with the danger of being laid off, many people went to the principal for help, tried to use their connections, fearing they might lose their jobs, and relationships [among the teachers] became nuanced and uncomfortable ...

When Benben was a year old, because I had to work, I sent him to his grandmother's. My parents were not in good health. They lived close to me but couldn't help me out, and the two of us had such an awkward time managing because of work [pause]. I went to my mother-in-law to see my son once a week. Every time I left, he cried and my eyes would fill with tears.... Returning to work, as soon as I thought about how I might return to the rural school I was originally at, I felt overwhelmed with emotion [sigh].

ZHANG 2009

In 2002, Zhang Min's partner completely left behind his original job—he was laid off—to start a business. In 2005, Zhang Min resigned in order to devote herself to her family and bring up her son. Eventually, her colleague told her that an administrator had already sent out a notice that the school of the mine district was to be placed under the management of the township where the local county was located, but that the transition would happen in stages.

Zhang Min: I thought Benben and his father were doing pretty well, our business was doing all right, I didn't think about whether or not it was worth it. I only quit because our family didn't have the security at the time ... I don't really think about it anymore. I was a teacher for over ten years, but I didn't get much out of it, I wasn't rich or poor, and it was a pretty uncomfortable situation.... There are many people who are not teachers, what is there to regret [laughs]? When I had just quit, I was often in contact with my old classmates and colleagues. Now I'm only in touch with one or two of them. My good friends are all teachers [laughs].

ZHANG 2009

Owen Goffman writes in *The Presentation of Self in Everyday Life*: "When an actor assumes an established social role, he usually finds that a specific front stage has been set up" (Goffman 1989, 27). There are too many unpredictable factors that are quietly affecting secondary normal school graduates' life stages, whether they be recent graduates or are already working, to the extent that they cannot "solidify" their "stage role," they can't "watch their own wheat fields"! And for those among them like Zhang Min, the burden of caring for a family is also a reason that cannot be ignored. Abandoning the stable jobs pursued by the older generations over the course of many years, backing out on the initial "contract" with the country and, along with it, on the ardent call from the rural primary education industry, many secondary normal graduates decided to follow the rising trend of the times.

All of these choices and divergences were rooted in pure necessity!

Even so, according to the author, among the 1992 graduates, there are still many students who have returned to their hometowns to serve as rural primary school teachers (or junior high school teachers) like Wang Lijuan. Some of them still work in their original positions. Most of them are female. They are duty-minded, kind-hearted, and quietly working away at their posts. Like their parents, they don't have many luxuries in life, and some are just living "ordinary" lives.

At the beginning, most of their parents seriously helped them choose this life path as a teacher. After being confirmed and selected by the National Secondary Normal School, they chose to go along with the economic tide in a quiet way. The rural primary and secondary school teachers became a troop of leaders, most of them serving in primary and secondary schools in the places where their childhood dreams took shape. After graduation, they still returned to the "place where dreams began" and weaved future dreams for the children of the village ...

4   The Front and Back Stages of the Performance

In August of 1992, Wang Lijuan started serving as a primary school teacher and began to faithfully fulfill the role of "educator." Due to her teaching methods and generally good teaching results, she soon became one of the most popular teachers in the primary school, coming out on top in the "Language Arts Open Class" competition in the 1993 Chunxiang School District and laying a foundation for the future backbone teaching staff of the school district.

Wang Lijuan: Isn't that what working in rural primary schools is like? You have to do a little of everything! In the first few years of working, I taught almost all the courses for the first to fifth grades, I really became something of an "all-in-one" educator [smiles]. This is what going to normal school prepares you for. Frankly speaking, when I was a primary school teacher, I realized that I had really learned quite a lot of things at secondary normal school.

> WANG 2009

Why would secondary normal school graduates serving at rural primary schools become "idols" that primary school students like and even look up to? In their three or four years at secondary normal school, what kind of education do the majority of students receive?

Wang Lijuan: As soon as we entered school we began military training, which lasted nearly two months.[27] It was extremely rigorous, but I really got a lot out of it. In the three years at secondary normal school, we had to fold up our blankets so they looked like blocks of tofu. We had to take many courses on all kinds of subjects, [including] a lot of language arts classes. Every evening during the self-study period the students would take turns going to the podium to read from the newspaper. It seems like we didn't go into other subjects like mathematics, physics and chemistry as deeply as students at regular high schools do. Of course, we definitely spent more time taking physical education, music, and art courses than they [high school students] did, and we had a good time [smiles].

> WANG 2009

Iron Drum: I think that the excellence of this group of people must have left a deep impression on the teachers at secondary school. The junior high examinations weren't so terrible at the time, and the ones who tested into secondary normal schools were generally highly gifted and determined students. In some sense, though, secondary normal school was a kind of Garden of Eden for these outstanding students, as artistic and aesthetic subjects were given greater importance than mathematics, physics, and chemistry. Whatever the subject or activity, there was always

---

27 All levels of schools across the country attach great importance to the ideological and political education of young students. Wang Lijuan said that the military training in her year of enrollment lasted about one month longer than the previous year (Wang 2009).

a group of students who devoted themselves completely to excelling at it. One group was obsessed with sports and fitness. I still recall how thrilling it was to see a boy named Yan Yongquan from the class that entered in '86 who constantly challenged himself to break the high jump record which he himself had set. There was a group of people who were obsessed with art, and they'd really stand out at every kind of calligraphy and painting exhibition. The entire student body would go crazy at the annual competition to judge the top ten singers in the school; there was a group who devoted themselves to the art of eloquence, from giving speeches to telling stories. How can students at current so-called famous schools compare? I can still remember the outstanding improvised speech made by a girl named Yang Lan; then there was a group of literature lovers, and from one day to the next they had formed a literature club. Many students could already write impressive essays.... but they hadn't had time to fully perfect their abilities, to completely develop themselves, when this group of vibrant seeds was scattered across the barren countryside.

"Iron Drum" 2009

As early as 1963, the Ministry of Education issued the "Draft Plan for Three-Year Normal Schools (Consultation Draft)," which clearly defined the training objectives of secondary normal schools: producing qualified primary school teachers with a cultural level equivalent to high school levels and who possessed an understanding of the party's educational principles and policies, a basic knowledge of education science and the requisite ability to handle the work of primary education. The document clarified that normal school students were to teach at elementary schools in the future, especially in rural primary schools. Adjustments were made to the specific courses in the curriculum, and requirements were set regarding the basic skills-training approach for secondary normal students.[28]

---

28   The 1963 Ministry of Education document was primarily meant to address the inadequacies of the previous secondary normal school curriculum (mainly the overemphasis on the subject of pedagogy and the insufficient courses dedicated to cultural knowledge in the pre-1958 curriculum, and the insufficient number of courses on the subject of pedagogy in the post-1958 curriculum). The adjustments introduced in 1963 were as follows: 7% of the curriculum was to be devoted to politics, 64% to cultural courses, around 4% to courses on pedagogy, and 15% to physical education and art courses. The areas of political studies, language arts, pedagogy, and mathematics in the curriculum were strengthened, especially language arts and mathematics. In particular, the total number of teaching hours devoted to language arts occupied around 24% of the total hours in the curriculum language arts courses, 96 more hours than the new high school teaching plan (draft); besides requiring tangible increases in the requirements for reading and writing skills in

In 1980, after the reform and opening up, the Ministry of Education issued the *Notice on Printing and Distributing the Trial Draft of the Teaching Plan for Secondary Normal Schools and the Trial Draft of the Teaching Plan for Preschool Teachers' Schools* (He 1998a, 1207). The document introduced new adjustments to the teaching calendar and curriculum for secondary normal schools in China. The new arrangement specified the required and optional courses for the curriculum and fully addressed the requirements for basic courses, pedagogy courses, and placed emphasis on preparing secondary normal students to teach primary school students' three favorite subjects—sports, music and art.[29]

---

line with high school levels, content related to developing oral expression skills was also given greater emphasis and more attention was to be given to learning how to correct student essays. In the area of basic skills, the following aspects were emphasized: students must solidify their grasp of skills such as writing on the blackboard, pen and brush writing, being able to correctly and skillfully grasp the form, sound, and meaning of Chinese pinyin and common characters, as well as being capable of speaking Mandarin, reading aloud, and so on. In addition, secondary normal students were to receive more focused instruction on pronunciation, writing, grammar, rhetoric and children's literature than high school students. The document stated that secondary normal students were to be guaranteed sufficient training in applying teaching methods utilizing teaching materials for primary school language arts and arithmetic. Students were also required to acquire a broad knowledge base and possess necessary musical and artistic knowledge and abilities. The document also mentioned that no foreign language training was to be provided (He 1998a, 1208–1209).

29　This was an important document which played a positive role in the historical development of secondary normal education in China, designed as it was to correct many problematic issues, establish a normal teaching program and improve the quality of teaching. The document established three-year and four-year programs of study for secondary normal schools and the recruitment of junior high school graduates and youth with equivalent academic qualifications (private primary school teacher training usually lasted two years). The curriculum was set as follows: required courses in political theory, language arts, mathematics, physics, science, chemistry, biology, physiology, history, geography, foreign languages, psychology, education, teaching methods for primary school language arts and arithmetic education, sports and physical education teaching methods, etc., and arrangements for music and art teaching methods as well as the teaching of common knowledge relating to natural science for primary school students were to be established according to the particular conditions in each region.

In addition, the Normal School for Minorities began to offer courses in minority languages. Specifically, language arts classes were subdivided into text selection and writing, basic knowledge of language arts and basic language skills, teaching methods utilizing primary school language arts teaching materials and other courses. Moreover, training in basic skills such as listening comprehension, speaking, reading, and writing as well as abilities relating to Mandarin language, pinyin, characters, essay correction and oral expression was strictly and solidly emphasized to prepare students to teach primary school language arts. In addition, a certain amount of self-study time was required to be allotted each week, and students were to be guided in learning how to write Chinese

For example, for teaching music classes, secondary normal students were to be given basic training in music theory, teaching basic musical concepts, reading sheet music, singing, playing keyboard instruments, etc. Classes on music, art, and relevant teaching methods could be required or optional courses, according to local conditions. These requirements laid a good foundation for the training of primary school teachers in China.

Thereafter, in 1986, the *Notice of the State Education Commission on Adjusting the Teaching Plan for Secondary Normal Schools* was released, introducing adjustments to the teaching content laid out in the 1980 *Notice on Printing and Distributing the Trial Draft of the Teaching Plan for Secondary Normal Schools and the Trial Draft of the Teaching Plan for Preschool Teachers' Schools* in order to better meet the practical needs of the time, adjusting the teaching plan for cultivating secondary normal students and strictly delineating standards for teaching hours and course subject classification. Among them, foreign languages, preliminary computer knowledge, and basic education technology were included as elective courses. Reforms in secondary normal school curriculum closely followed the pace of the times and the needs of social development—Wang Lijuan's elective curriculum at that time included "Education Technology" and "Computing Basics" as two new courses not contained in the previous year's curriculum.[30]

---

characters. Psychology classes were included to integrate the overall needs of primary education, starting with ordinary psychology, focusing on acquiring a basic understanding of children's and educational psychology. Pedagogy courses focused mainly on education theory, education policy, primary education, teaching work, and basic principles and methods of school management (He 1998b, 1862–1863).

However, the "Notice" also clearly states: Four-year teacher training programs can conditionally offer foreign language classes; three-year programs will not offer foreign language training. This stipulation created an obstacle for many normal school students who wished to pursue other work besides primary school teaching.

30   For example: for three-year programs, weekly class hours devoted to biology, geography, second-year mathematics, and third-year physics classes were each respectively reduced by one hour, with a total reduction of 30 class hours per subject; greater emphasis was placed on the teaching of Mandarin, writing, and other foundational skills in language arts classes. This kind of training in basic skills was to be begun from the moment students began studying at the school, in coordination with the cultivation of organizational management, oral presentation and writing skills as well as other various subjects and activities. A basic "pass/fail" standard for basic skills such as Mandarin and writing was to be set, and training was to be carried out in stages over students' years of schooling. The *Notice* also proposed the integrated teaching of education technology and physics as well as an increase in weekly political course hours from one hour weekly to two; adjustments were made to the elective course system—courses on music, music teaching methods, fine arts, and fine arts teaching methods could either be compulsory, or compulsory for the first two years and elective for third-year students, as determined according to local

Wang Lijuan: At that time, we were in the second year of the "Education Technology" course, learning to make slides, using projectors, it was really good training. Oh, there was also a course in basic computing. It was a pretty confusing subject for me to study. I just remember how careful everybody was whenever we went to the school physics building with the teacher. The computers were covered with cloth, like they were very expensive [*laughs*]. Although I only learned a little bit of *all this* [knowledge from the course], I thought it might be important in the future, so I couldn't bring myself to get rid of some of the books from the secondary normal teaching materials, even for quite a few years [after graduation]!

WANG 2009

In 1989, the State Education Commission issued the *Three-Year Secondary Normal School Teaching Program (Trial)*, calling for further planning and step-by-step, deepened, reform to meet the needs of local economic and cultural development and of nine-year compulsory education requirements for primary school teachers. Reform requirements emphasized cultivating the three "loves" and the two "preparations" in secondary normal students;[31] the teaching plan was to be based on the actual national conditions, emphasizing the implementation of the "four integrations principle,"[32] and ideological education was to be given greater stress, so that ideological, political, moral

---

circumstances. At the same time, foreign language, basic computing, and education technology could also be considered for inclusion into the elective course offerings. For pedagogy, psychology, and teaching methodology courses, the *Notice* called for the gradual resolution of the problems of combining theory with practice, with a more focused orientation toward the practical work of teaching in primary, and stipulated that students who did not pass their internships could not graduate (He 1998b: 2487).

31   Three "loves": Loving the socialist motherland, loving the Chinese Communist Party, and loving primary education. Two "preparations": prepared with a good sense of social morality and professional teaching ethics and prepared with a spirit of hard work and innovation (ibid., 2868).

32   That is: the integrations of unity and flexibility, of compulsory and elective courses, of in-class and extra-curricular activities, and of school education and social practice, leading to the overall integration of compulsory courses, elective courses, extra-curricular activities, and social practice in the education and teaching activities of secondary normal schools (ibid., 2868). In May 1998, the Department of Normal Education of the Ministry of Education issued the *Three-Year Secondary Normal School Curriculum Program (Trial)*. The secondary normal curriculum was established as a combination of four elements: compulsory courses, elective courses, activity courses and student teaching practice (He 2003, 91). Secondary normal curriculum has always changed along with the needs of the society and has continued to grow in this direction.

education (especially teaching morals) and psychological cultivation would be included throughout the learning process.[33]

The diversity in the content and forms of the school curriculum made the learning process easy and enjoyable for students like Wang Lijuan and her schoolmates, and so they were able to assume their roles as rural primary school teachers with a great deal of enthusiasm and good cheer.

In the school, even in the whole school district, Wang Lijuan was well-known for her mastery of the "five basic skills."[34]

> Wang Lijuan: I even taught music lessons at secondary normal school for a while, taught them how to read music and sing. A lot of teachers envied me, some of them even asked me to teach them, which was something I wasn't expecting [*grins*]. I always liked to sing, but I didn't sign up for the music teachers' group, I just took this course because I don't really like to move, I'm kind of fat and no good at dancing [*laughs*]. As soon as I started at normal school, the teacher in charge of the class reminded us that although we had our specific specializations we should try to become well-rounded individuals, and we should try to learn other skills based on our interests and strengths. I think this was the best part about how they taught at secondary normal school. Then there were many extra-curricular activities, which were also very good. My family said that after going to secondary normal school, I became more active and lively than when I was in junior high school. I think we were all like this, unlike our

---

33   Emphasis on ideological and political education and professional ethics has always been a part of secondary normal education. The 1989 *Three-Year Secondary Normal School Teaching Plan* (*Trial*) fully reflects this point. In June of that year, *China Education News* published the article "Rethinking the Greatest Mistakes and Strengthening Ideological Education," citing Deng Xiaoping's "The Greatest Mistake in Ten Years was in Education ..." and proposing that all levels of schools and teachers should focus on the cultivation of the "four virtues" (as a new socialist generation, students were equipped with lofty ideals and moral integrity, were well-educated and had a strong sense of discipline) with an ardent spirit, looking to sincerely teach and educate to uplift and make it a priority to guide students firmly in the correct political direction (Commentators, 1989).

The Teacher's Division of the Ministry of Education issued the *Moral Education Curriculum for Secondary Normal Schools* (*Trial*) and the *Code of Conduct for Students in Secondary Normal Schools* (*Trial*) in 1990 (He 1998b, 3065) and 1998 (He 2003, 93), respectively. These were important guiding documents for student management in secondary normal schools across the country.

34   The five basic skills include: the "three calligraphies"—chalk, brush and pen—as well as stick figure drawings and Mandarin language. Schools of different regions set different requirements for basic skills.

old junior high school classmates who went to high school, they were boring ...

WANG 2009

"Yi An Shu Nv" wrote in her blog that her time at secondary normal school was a sort of "ideological baptism" for her and gave her resilience for facing life's challenges. Whether it was due to the richness of life there, or out of a desire to find the meaning of life, years spent at secondary normal school seem to be worth remembering and recalling.

> "Yi An Shu Nv": Secondary normal school is the most beautiful time of one's life. I remember the first day there, I saw the most prominent plaque in front of the conference room at the school entrance that read, "Loyalty to the Party's Educational Cause." At the opening ceremony, the school leader offered some profound thoughts on this idea. Through all the activities organized by the school and even after I started my job as a teacher, I understood the profound meaning of this sentence in more depth and understood the extent of my own responsibility.
>
> Life at secondary normal school was rigorous. Military training taught us to follow rules, to fold our blankets so that they resembled "blocks of tofu," and whether we were sitting, standing, walking, everything had its proper posture, and your room had to be immaculate, if you didn't do it right you'd be called out and criticized. They checked once a day, and every Monday they'd do a thorough inspection. The "Student Union" was the most authoritative student organization. In the morning they'd inspect morning exercise, in the evening they'd inspect the self-study rooms, they'd check that the lights were out. They'd check which dormitory had lights on, they'd listen to hear if there was any talking in the dormitories, [and] if they caught you they'd teach you a lesson. You might even find your name on the blacklist on the bulletin board the next day. Everything was quantified, everything was judged, all militarized management. Also, from the first day of school, the school required teachers and students to speak Mandarin at all times. It was hard for some people to adapt to this at first, their Mandarin sounded really terrible, but precisely because the school really stressed this aspect of promoting its use, I was later able to speak smooth and fluent Mandarin.[35]

---

35   "Yi An Shu Nv" recalls a story: After the lights were turned off at night, the students had the habit of talking in bed. They weren't allowed to speak their local dialects during the day, which made them feel uncomfortable, so bedtime was a good opportunity to speak

I took a lot away from my years at secondary normal school. Life there was rich and colorful. Secondary normal students stand out for their well-rounded skill set. The school valued each course in the curriculum, all the disciplines, from major to minor subjects, went hand in hand. Besides language arts, mathematics, and classes on cultural knowledge like that there were classes such as music, art, sports and physical fitness, and calligraphy. You had to pass in every subject. Every class had its examination that had to be passed. We had to take more than a dozen classes with their accompanying exams each semester. With my wide range of interests this was not too difficult for me; I often averaged around 90% or more (on a scale of 100%) and was the top student in the class. I was also given a "city-level" rating in the "pentathlon" of quick calculation, stick figure drawing, musical instruments, calligraphy, and checking the dictionary. In the three years at normal school, I not only learned to read and play music and other forms of fine arts, I also became completely proficient at calligraphy with brush, pen, and chalk. In addition to imparting knowledge from books, we learned about teaching methods, practiced how to teach, how to be a model for others, how to teach through our actions.

This kind of training occurred in many forms, such as making speeches in the ten minutes before class, speech-training exercises for children, tongue-twisters in physical education class ..., these basic skills are seemingly simple, but very important, and mastering them was conducive to the overall growth and development of secondary normal students.

Life at secondary normal school was meaningful. The most meaningful thing I learned was how to do good things for others, how to serve other people. Each class was divided into group units, and we would go out into the community and help the needy, the widowed elderly, military veterans, and others with their housework, cleaning, laundry ... the night before graduation, we handed over the area we were responsible for to the next group of students in the year behind us. This kind of

---

freely in whatever dialect they wanted. One night, everyone was chatting excitedly when I suddenly heard a voice outside: "Open the door! Open the door! You're not asleep yet? Who's not speaking Mandarin?" One of the teachers was doing the nightly rounds. The next morning we found our dormitory was blacklisted. At the time, those of us from that dormitory were so ashamed, we wanted to bury our heads in the ground. After that, when we'd go to sleep, we'd always jokingly remind each other: "You have to dream in Mandarin, otherwise you might end up on the blacklist!" (Yi An Shu Nv 2009).

continuous transmission from one year of students to the next taught me
how to care for others and how to perceive society correctly. The political
and ideological education at that time wasn't simply empty talk, it
involved concrete action.

   Life at secondary normal school was pleasant. The most memorable
recollection is of us all getting together to see a movie. At the time, seeing
films was the most fashionable, most popular, and most interesting form
of entertainment. At that time, getting together to go see a film was a
novel thing. We dressed up neat in our school uniforms, lined up in long
queues, and walked proudly through the streets, the locals looking at us
with envy as we talked and laughed, we were as excited as if it were
Chinese New Year. There were countless joys in secondary normal school
life, as well as many lifelong regrets. The biggest regret is the failure to
embrace English as a subject of study. At the time, secondary normal
school did not offer English classes; so many students who were interested in learning English lost the opportunity to continue their studies.

   YI AN SHU NV 2009[36]

It was this series of revamped and improved primary school teacher training
policies that made it possible for Wang Lijuan, "Yi An Shu Nv," and their fellow
secondary normal school alumni to grow into "all-in-one-package" primary
school educators; it is also through planned, purposeful, organized extracurricular activities and educational practices that mobilized the enthusiasm and
initiative of secondary normal students and cultivated their ability to be self-
sufficient, autodidactic, and self-managing such that these young students have
grown into model servants at the forefront of primary education. Secondary
normal education focused on the needs of future primary school teachers,
especially the ability to handle multi-disciplinary teaching after graduation.
The demands of practical teaching work informed how secondary normal students were educated, with special attention given to the principles governing
the physical and mental development of secondary normal students, the cultivation of their interests and strengths, and their overall development into
lively, active, and well-rounded individuals. These practices have deep implications for today's primary school teachers. The period of secondary education
is a time in which the various talents of students are brought out and fully

---

36   This Internet text has been slightly modified.

developed. Diversifying the curriculum structure, further focusing on teaching content and preparing students for professional life should be the goals of any reform (International 21st Century Education Commission 1996, 118–119). Looking at the development trends of the secondary normal curriculum, to some extent secondary normal schools can be said to have achieved this.

4.1   *The Joys and Worries of Teaching Primary School*

The reality of life and work at rural primary schools, however, is not as colorful as life at secondary normal school. The differences between pre-work and post-work life is sometimes difficult for graduates to accept, and the work is certainly full of challenges.

> Wang Lijuan: Teaching and studying are different! When I first started working time moved very fast, everything was fresh and exciting. The environment in the little village was okay, I didn't have many co-workers, I couldn't really date or anything [*laughs*], there wasn't much to choose from, nobody organized any activities, there wasn't anyone besides the students, if I wasn't teaching class I was correcting my students' homework, there was a while when I really missed my classmates and friends and everyone from my secondary normal school days ...
>   WANG 2009

Tian Tian, a 1999 graduate of secondary normal school, expressed how she stuck with her work along with her feelings of helplessness about her situation.

> Tian Tian: At normal school the campus was beautiful. After coming to this elementary school, [I discovered] the school was very old ... after a storm, the whole class was buried in mud, even the tables were buried.... At the time I just felt like crying, one reason was that after leaving my hometown, and after studying all those years, I always thought things would get better and better in the future, I didn't expect to end up here; another reason was that I felt guilty—what would become of these children? In the rest of the world, things are already quite developed, but hardly anything has changed here in decades.
>   I don't feel spiritually deprived at all, but materially I do feel extremely deprived. Spiritually I feel okay because I get along quite well with the other teachers, and the students are very kind to me, they are very willing to talk to me, once I get to know them over time it's really hard to leave them. So I didn't want to leave last year, I thought I would see this group

of students off and then I'd figure out a plan for myself.... A lot of times when I don't have water, the students know I can't carry it [the water] myself, and they'll help me out ... so I often go home and talk with my parents and cry. I tell them about how the living conditions aren't good, we often have no water, public security isn't good, and they tell me to go ahead and try to transfer somewhere else.[37]

The learning atmosphere in our school is very good and the achievement levels are also very good, so the school's rankings are among the best in the district.... Because they are young teachers, they accept new things faster, and they'll put new ideas into practice. There's a custom at our school, at the beginning of the school year there is a plan, first there's the school plan, then each teacher has their own plan.... The school teachers usually live together and only go home on weekends, so they usually talk about education when they are chatting, not just at Wednesday night conferences.

... At first, I was quite happy with the learning atmosphere at the school. The students worked hard and learned well. There was no need to think about going to schools with better conditions. There might not be these kinds of opportunities to discuss my teaching at schools with better conditions, everyone would just be thinking about their own problems, and that would be really monotonous. Sometimes we really don't have enough time to share our evaluations of our classes. Everyone is talking. There are many opinions, just like at a debate.

I said to the leader when I had arrived at the school, I hope the school can give me space to let me do my own teaching experiments and study some of my own teaching methods. The leader said yes. But my first experiment was a failure, because I didn't understand what first grade children really wanted. I was groping forward on my own at the time ... children these days aren't the same as they used to be—just doing

---

37   Tian Tian's school was under construction and the surrounding wall had been demolished, with only a net serving as a barrier, to no avail. In the evenings local youth would enter the school grounds to make trouble. When the principal tried to stop them they called him an old man and said it was their territory, and challenged him to a fight. They would drink and break bottles [on the grounds]. The teachers were understandably frightened and felt very uncomfortable. After all, they were working so hard in such miserable conditions, yet they were treated as if they were worthless. On one occasion, Tian Tian's mobile phone and 800 yuan were stolen from her room, the room had been turned over, which was a big blow to her. Similar incidents have happened to her colleagues. After intervention by the local village committee, the situation improved, but only for a while (Tian Tian and Zhang 2003).

whatever the teacher says. [Now] They have their own ideas. Teachers have to be a little childlike, if not, you won't be a good educator because you won't understand children, you won't know what the children want. Love is also very important, if a teacher is loving, students will have a sense of security, they will respect the teacher very much, they don't need to criticize, the teacher can just tell them the truth as they see it and it will move them.... These years I've mainly relied on listening in on classes, I'm still groping my way forward, and the curriculum reform is really new for me, ... the leader said that I have such a deep emotional connection with my students, so why hadn't I written anything about that? So later I wrote something, and I sent it out, and I got a letter back saying they needed [me to pay a] 200-yuan publication fee. I haven't written anything since then [*laughs*].

... I feel that being a village teacher can give me a space, certain material conditions, and allow me to do my own research, and I don't want for anything.... When it comes to wages, though, I'd rather not bring it up. When I first started working I needed to buy a lot of things. I thought since I was already working, I was independent; I could earn money to support myself. But in the end I didn't get paid for a whole year. Later, they made up the difference, 300 yuan a month, but they still owe me a few months' pay.

TIAN TIAN and ZHANG WENZHI 2003

Although Tiantian's experience cannot fully represent the lives of secondary normal school students after graduation, the experiences she has lived through reflect the voices and realities of the majority of rural primary school educators. In particular, by adopting the perspective of new teachers just beginning to work we can better understand the complex emotions contained in the title of "rural primary school teacher."

Life is diverse, and there is likewise a diversity of accompanying troubles. Chen Xingchuan and "Iron Drum" express their experience of another kind of life after graduating from normal school.

Chen Xingchuan: When I first became a teacher, I was so proud to think that I could live as a teacher for three years. When I found out more about my work environment, I felt more and more depressed, I began to doubt myself, doubt other teachers around me. The beautiful image I originally had of what a "teacher" was slowly collapsed, replaced by an image of common vulgarity. I unintentionally began to see things in a really gloomy way. But I respected how things were, I respected my own discovery: our teachers have been lying to us the whole time.... "Time is more precious than gold," the teacher teaches students to cherish time, to work hard in school and criticize other kids who waste all their time playing. But what had teachers been doing as they recited famous sayings like that to their students? ... Playing mahjong all night, drinking at parties, watching TV, ... some teachers never seriously read a book after graduating from normal school, they would just teach students the few pitiful things they managed to learn at normal school ... they can't raise their spirits on their own, so they anesthetize themselves with entertainment and distractions, and the spirit becomes more and more empty, the mind more and more numb, and how can a numb teacher nourish a child's heart? I often find that some teachers ask students to band together in solidarity, while at the same time encouraging students to be "secret agents" for the so-called maintenance of class discipline, they ask students to tell on each other if discipline is violated. They use every kind of method to get students to keep tabs on each other in order to achieve the goal of maintaining class order. The purpose may have been reached, but the young mind has learned to split into factions and parties, to hate one's peers. Teaching the rules of the games of the adult world to children is the easiest mistake for a teacher to make.... I often see teachers usually saying over and over to their students: you can't look at your classmates' work when doing homework. When the final exam comes, to keep up the hypocrisy, students who perform well are called on to "look after" of students with poor grades, filling the innocent minds of children with confusing ideas. I don't know how teachers can get away with contradicting themselves and going back on their word so much. A teacher can preach about morality all they want, but it's nothing if they don't show it through their actions. Education should be able to purify the human soul, and as a teacher, we should first purify ourselves.

CHEN 2003

"Iron Drum": As soon as they graduated from secondary normal school, students were split into different destinies: some people with the right backgrounds entered official circles, many people quickly moved up in their jobs, occupying top positions before anyone else could, and an extremely small proportion of people went straight from secondary normal school to normal training schools or normal universities. (In our year, only one or two graduates got into normal universities), most people were scattered across the countryside—it was difficult to get to live in a city at that time, you had to have a very solid background. How many people have considered the fates of these secondary normal students who are adrift in the countryside? Who understands their emotional struggles, the loneliness of their situations?

"Iron Drum" 2009

Chen Xingchuan's story is a portrayal of the post-graduation life of many secondary normal school students. It is a kind of hidden "pain" and "struggle," reflecting how young primary school teachers have tortured themselves as they grapple with professional ethics and personal growth in their careers. The helplessness expressed by "Iron Drum" is also an attempt to understand the cause of these teachers' suffering. In the real world, these distresses are not temporary, and they lead to inner contradictions that are often related not only to the lack of diversity in the education system and the tedious working environment, but also to the motivation and positioning behind the work. Wang Lijuan has experienced similar distress, but she seems more optimistic.

> Wang Lijuan: I feel like I'm living the same day over and over again.... I imagine others feel the same. It's a bad feeling to find oneself becoming so listless! Later, I communicated with other classmates from other places, and I felt better after talking with them. I started to consider what my job was all about. I began to try to learn more myself, to continue my learning. If you don't keep going forward there's really nothing to feel motivated about!
>
> WANG 2009

When young teachers become a part of a school's faculty, their sense of responsibility can change in two directions: positive change (seeing it as their own responsibility to revitalize education) or negative change (a lack of enthusiasm for their own professional responsibility). After the 1990s, with the advent of the information society and the development of the social economy, young teachers need two or three years longer for this positive change to take place, sometimes even more time, and it is a very unstable process.[38]

---

38 The observed period for the two changes, according to the initial test made before 1987, was one to two years, the positive rate of change was 60.2%; after 1988, the observed period for negative change was one to six months, or even less, and the rate of negative change was 80.16% (Yu 2000, 355).

In addition, a report on the situation of rural primary and secondary school teachers on their school life also shows that there is a very limited range of activities for rural teachers to engage in in their spare time, they have to live in small spaces, and they have a very limited vantage point on society. All of these findings have a direct impact on the lives of secondary normal students after graduation.[39]

After secondary normal students begin teaching, they tend to exhibit negative psychological tendencies due to the influence of the working environment. The mental status and work attitude of their colleagues, especially the school leaders, directly affects these relatively simple young minds. A primary school teacher talked about the leader at the school:

> At the beginning of the school year, when the teachers were being assigned teaching tasks, the [principal] "confided in" the teachers: "This year, I won't teach the main subjects, I want to teach 'Thought and Morality' on a full-time basis. Two classes of fourth grade mathematics will be taught by such-and-such a teacher. To be frank, now that I'm principal shouldn't I take it easy a little? You all have seen it, we ask for money and there's no money, the income of the school is collected by the government; you try to earn some authority but you have no power, if officials want to do an inspection they just go ahead with it, if they want to criticize they'll criticize. So I want to take it easier, it's exhausting teaching all the time." The dozen or so teachers present remained silent. We also remained silent whenever he came to work after 9:00 in the morning and went home by 3:00 in the afternoon, as he sometimes did.
>
> QI FEN 2003

As secondary normal graduates just beginning their teaching career, they often disapprove of or aren't used to this kind of leadership. In time, however, they grow accustomed to it, and resign themselves to following along with the

---

39 A study of 7 primary schools and 3 middle schools across the country showed that teachers' leisure activities mainly include: chatting, basketball (men), mahjong, surfing the Internet (in areas with Internet access), poker, or no leisure activities; their main concerns are: wages, curriculum reform, layoffs and personnel allocation issues. The study also covered rural teachers' training methods: mainly on-the-job training and self-study, specifically including on-the-job continuing education, self-study exams, correspondence studies, out-of-office training, school-based training, and assignment learning (Education Online 2003).

"thinking" of the leader as a way to "adapt." That is to say, at present, there are still many problems in building a solid base of rural primary school teachers, but the "leadership effect" remains a key factor in solving the problem.

In their actual work, the topic of job promotions is a painful one for secondary normal graduates working as rural primary school teachers. They feel a great deal of pressure working with graduates of normal universities or training schools. Some of the reason for this has to do with policy, but it also depends on individual efforts. It is difficult to make generalizations about this.

> "Oriental Mangosteen":[40] So why do secondary normal students [in terms of job titles] often end up feeling so uncomfortable in their work? First, it is a local policy issue. For example, the title promotion document in my region stipulates that the basic conditions for promotion to first-year secondary teachers are seven years of working experience for graduates of normal universities or training schools, thirteen years of working experience [fifteen years, prior to 1998] for secondary normal school graduates, so I put my nose the grindstone and was finally promoted to first-year secondary teacher after 13 years of work. I am now a senior-ranking secondary school teacher. However, among my secondary normal school classmates, there are still some that have not earned this promotion. One important reason for this is that their original academic qualifications are low, so they are at a disadvantage when the "points" are tallied up to decide who gets promoted. There have even been some surprising cases where students whom they have taught went on to graduate from university and have been promoted before them! Second, I am a high school teacher. Most of my teachers are college graduates or above. Thinking back on the path I've taken, I suppose I've also had some kind of foresight—as early as the second year after I began to work [1986], I took some correspondence classes, studied hard for 6 Spring and Autumn semesters, and when I received my undergraduate diploma in 1992, I had even been named an "outstanding student." In work, I don't dare to relax. I hope that putting in more I'll eventually get more in return. Hard work

---

40   On March 22, 2006, in the "Educational Teaching Forum—Hongxia Online" section of the "K-12 Education Forum" network, a 1985 secondary normal school graduate with the user name "Oriental Mangosteen" initiated a forum discussion titled "Secondary normal school students, who can remember you?" There were 18 former teachers and students who participated in the discussion, with 49 total replies. See "K-12 Education Forum: (Discussion) Secondary normal school students, who can remember you?" ("K-12 Education Forum" 2009).

pays off. I have received many awards which are the envy of my peers! So I have made up for the shortcomings of my original academic qualifications, so I could "stand out" in my work, laying a solid foundation for future promotions!

"K-12 Education Forum" 2009

5   Transitioning Roles

5.1   *Continuing Education and Further Training*

In 1995, 21-year-old Wang Lijuan was married. Her husband is a physics teacher in the township's middle school. He also graduated from secondary normal school two years before she did. Shortly after their marriage, the school district, taking into account her individual needs, arranged for Wang Lijuan to be a full-time language arts teacher in the township's central primary school, which is closer to the middle school. This is a model school for primary education in the township. Among the fifteen teachers, there are five primary school teachers from different backgrounds. Apart from the principal, all of the public school teachers are women, and there are five private school teachers who were transferred to public schools, two of whom are men.[41]

---

41   In September 1986, the State Education Commission issued the *Trial Measures for the Certification Examination for Primary and Secondary School Teachers*. The purpose of the teacher assessment certificate system is to build a qualified base of primary school teachers to more effectively meet the needs of the nine-year compulsory education system and its future development, and improve basic education services, which are applicable to primary and secondary school teachers at non-nationally qualified schools (He 1998b, 2491–2492). In 1992, the National Education Commission promulgated the *National Ten-Year Plan for the Education Field and the Essentials of the Eighth Five-Year Plan*, stating that by 1993 most primary school teachers should have met the nationally required academic standards or have obtained a professional assessment certificate (He 1998c, 3258–3263).

Many rural private school teachers have made "positive shifts" in their career by obtaining assessment certificates. According to statistics, in 1993 the national distribution of academic qualifications among full-time primary school teachers was as follows: 0.18% had university undergraduate degrees or above, 3.57% held specialized university training program degrees, and 60.72% were graduates of vocational schools. In 1994, the number of qualified primary school teachers in the country had increased from 49.8% in 1980 to 86.6%. At the same time, the proportion of private primary school teachers in the country fell from 61.4% of all primary school teachers in 1980 to 32.4% (Yu 2000, 349). From this point of view, Wang Lijuan had not yet met the standard requirements for central primary school teacher qualifications.

In the two years after graduation, Wang Lijuan felt that she had progressed rapidly, thanks to taking advantage of the continuing education programs offered by the teacher training school in the county.[42] Her title changed from "third-tier primary school teacher" to "second-tier primary school teacher." After serving as a full-time teacher, she also served as the class teacher of the fifth grade class and the school's Young Pioneer team counselor. Since her teaching achievement results have consistently been at the top of the township rankings, the township education management office also listed her as one of the township's "backbone" teachers.

---

42   In 1991, the State Education Commission issued the *Opinions on the Continuing Education of Primary School Teachers*. The continuing education of primary school teachers includes in-service training of teachers who have obtained requisite teacher qualifications with the main goal of improving their background in political thought, teacher morality, education theory, and education as well as their overall teaching ability. The main levels are divided into new teacher apprenticeship training, teacher job training and key teacher training.

   The *Opinions* mainly cover the following points: (1) The training of key teachers and new teachers should be made a priority. The forms and methods that continuing teacher education assumes should be determined according to teachers' geographical and professional circumstances as well as the specific content of the training programs. Training should be largely independent and short-term in nature and take place mostly in teachers' spare time. (2) Changes should be made to teacher training to better fit the special nature of continuing education and according to the regularity of in-service training. The "closed-off" style of administration should be replaced by an open, forthcoming, and engaged style; on-campus and off-campus activities should be integrated as a means of pursuing a new approach to in-service teacher training. (3) The building of training organizations requires the formation of four levels of training networks at the provincial, county, township and school levels, with an emphasis on basic training at vocational schools for continuing education for primary school teachers. (4) Principals should recognize the importance of this work and actively organize and guide teachers in their political and professional learning in consideration of their practical circumstances. Principals should also provide a diverse range of elements in continuing education activities, such as senior teachers sharing their experience with younger ones, going over how to prepare for classes and plan lessons, learning through observation, discussing pedagogical research, holding lectures on specialized topics, guiding the way of self-directed learning, etc. These are the most basic, most frequent and most commonly used elements for teacher training. Only by fully capitalizing on this fundamental link with teacher training can we truly reap the tangible benefits of continuing education. (5) The teacher training departments of normal schools and training schools are an important base for teachers' continuing education. Teachers' achievements in continuing education should

Wang Lijuan: Having a "specialized degree" is one of the township education management office's clear requirements for central primary school teachers. Before I transferred to the central school, I signed up to enroll in a "satellite television education" normal training school.[43] My partner had already passed the exam and enrolled in an undergraduate program. We are also preparing to have a child, not getting one [a college or training school diploma] would make things difficult for us in the future.

WANG LIJUAN May 8, 2009

Wang Lijuan, while completing her teaching tasks and at her partner's encouragement, would continue her studies on her own, taking advantage of winter and summer vacations to attend course lectures and take final exams at the provincial education college. In April 1997, she completed 12 courses and got a college diploma in October. At that time, her child had just been born. When it comes to academic education, she seems to have a lot of ideas.

---

be made an important part of teacher assessment. In the *Opinions* it was also pointed out that all school offices must offer their teachers systemic and economic guarantees and recognize the importance and urgency of this work. Schools must understand the imbalances extant in the development of primary education and teacher training in the country, as this kind of training will not be implemented and developed in a unified way throughout the country. Measures will first be tested at pilot centers, and from there gradually extended (He 1998c, 3243–3244).

43 In 1993, the State Education Commission issued the *Opinions on Strengthening Communication between Higher Normal School Correspondence Education, Satellite TV Education, and Self-study Examinations for Pedagogical and Managerial Training for Middle School Teachers*. In order for middle school teachers to be able to more quickly earn academic certifications, all provinces, autonomous regions, and municipalities directly under the Central Government established a new model for training primary and middle school teachers which facilitates communication between higher normal school correspondence education, satellite TV education, and self-study examinations in accordance with the views expressed in the State Education Commission's [1992] Document No. 5 (*Opinions on Accelerating Academic Qualification Training for Middle School Teachers*). This kind of training, commonly known as "three communications" training, offered 12 majors corresponding to primary and middle school subjects such as Chinese language and literature (Ibid., 3539).

Wang Lijuan: After I graduated from normal school, the school began to offer college classes. [Students] could also learn foreign languages, how wonderful![44] However, ours [referring to the program she attended] wasn't bad either, right [laughs]? It had both theory and practice.

WANG 2009

---

44 The "Specialization Classes for Normal Schools" were pilot classes for the school system reform in China's secondary normal schools with the purpose of training primary school and kindergarten teachers with university-level specialized preparation. The program was proposed in 1983 after a survey of the East China region. In 1984, it was first offered at Nantong Normal School in Jiangsu Province. In the fall of 1985, these classes began to be offered separately at Beijing No. 3 Normal School, Shanghai Fourth Normal and Preschool Normal School, Nanjing Xiaozhuang Normal School, and Wuxi and Guangzhou Normal Schools (Gu 1998, 1399). In 1992, the State Education Commission issued the *Notice on the Approval of Pilot Work for Training Specialized Primary School Teachers in Some Provinces (Autonomous Regions)* which clarified the need for researching and exploring training and administrative models for these classes according to the specific needs of primary education. Cooperation was to be strengthened between secondary normal schools and higher normal colleges, so that they could give full play to their respective advantages to ensure that primary school teachers are prepared with the best of both normal school and training school curriculum models. Trials were conducted on two types of systems: a three- and two-stage system (for graduates of secondary normal schools) and a five-year system (for junior high school graduates and above). For students who graduated from training schools and who intended to teach in primary schools, job assignations were evaluated according to the relevant regulations in *Trial Regulations for Primary School Teachers* and were integrated with the specific circumstances in pilot provinces and municipalities. The *Notice* approved training programs for producing specialist-level elementary school teachers in Beijing, Tianjin, Shanghai and 29 secondary normal schools (or teachers' colleges) in 14 provinces including Jiangsu, 14 in the three- and two-stage system and 15 in the five-year system, 15 of which were included in the 1992 Enrollment Plan, with a total of 1,310 enrolled students (He 1998c, 3316–3318). In the same year, the National Education Commission's *Key Points of the National Education Ten-Year Plan and the Eighth Five-Year Plan* put forth the main goals for the development of education in the 1990s: every effort would be made to complete the long term standardization of administrative conditions in normal colleges and universities within five years (scheduled for 1997) or a little longer, and trials would be conducted to establish five-year elementary normal schools in large cities and economically developed regions with adequate conditions. University graduates from non-teaching colleges would be encouraged to pursue work as teachers in primary and secondary schools. Corresponding policy mechanisms were to be established to improve the employment rate of graduates (Ibid., 3258–3264).

    The introduction of the above two documents marked a new step in the nationwide strengthening of the reform of the secondary normal schools. Wang Lijuan's alma mater implemented a five-year college program, which was jointly run with the provincial education college. The trial enrollment was set at 60 students in two classes. Enrollment began in 1993.

5.2   *Educational Background and Diplomas*

The implementation of continuing education for primary school teachers is a way for the state to improve the overall quality of primary education teachers. However, continuing education training itself cannot solve the problems centering on primary school teachers' academic qualifications. The state has put forward higher requirements for teacher education, especially with the advent of the information society and the coexistence of a diversity of cultural values. Since it is already difficult to coordinate primary school teachers' qualifications in terms of overall knowledge base, ideas, and methods with the process of education modernization, the state's constant raising of the academic qualification requirements for primary school teachers is inevitable. However, the means and methods for offering secondary normal school graduates opportunities to raise their level of academic qualification, as well as the actual results brought to these graduates remains a problem. Like Wang Lijuan, many secondary normal graduates have earned further qualifications through satellite television correspondence courses or by taking independent study examinations. They already lost the chance to go to university when they accepted the "agreed upon" role of "primary school teacher," and now, even by studying on their own, it seems impossible to make up for the lack of formal higher education.

> Wang Lijuan: I am doing all right. I've learned a lot on my own, but I've never really gotten over something. After all, I have never really gone to college. Nowadays, there are more and more primary school teachers who graduated from normal colleges or normal universities. They are better prepared than us [*sighs*]. At least they can choose where they want to work, but what choice do we have [*smiles wryly*]?
>
> WANG LIJUAN May 8, 2009[45]

Wang Lijuan has strong feelings regarding her normal school's failure to offer English (or other foreign language) classes. She feels that this not only neglected the students' futures, but was also a waste of their time spent studying English in primary and middle school. This is the consensus of many secondary normal students, especially those who had the opportunity to go to college or graduate school.

45   Although Wang Lijuan is a cheerful person and a primary school leader, one still senses a heaviness in her speech, as if, after all the excitement and joy, the confusion and distress brought about through 17 or 18 years of work, what remains is a kind of exhaustion. With the continuous deepening of education reform, primary school teacher jobs generally require academic qualifications above the training school level, while most of those with secondary school-level qualifications are older, experienced teachers whose capacity for innovation is often inferior to that of young teachers. This, coupled with the growing pressure to obtain higher academic qualifications has led to a serious degree of occupational

In the real world, the value of a diploma is reflected in jobs, income, the kinds of positions and the number of opportunities it makes available. The original diploma of secondary normal school graduates is highly limited in this regard. For many, its value cannot even be compared with a regular high school diploma. The futures of many secondary normal graduates seem closely tied to their original diplomas, making Wang Lijuan and her fellow secondary normal school alumni feel a kind of helplessness about their prospects.

> Yi An Shu Nv: Although I became one of the core members of the teaching staff, my students liked me and my parents were satisfied, although I also took the self-study exam and obtained a university [undergraduate] diploma, whenever I am asked for my original qualifications, I often don't want to talk about it. When I am alone at night, I often feel so sad! Now employers first want to see "full-time undergraduate student" on the first line of the academic resume, which completely excludes secondary normal school graduates like us. How can we make up for this basic gap in our qualifications? This is the saddest part of being a secondary normal graduate.
>
> YI AN SHU NV 2009

> Lin Yiming:[46] I didn't care about it at the time, and I went ahead anyway to get my undergraduate degree, which took me two years. After graduating, many people in the undergraduate class had a second opportunity to choose their careers, but I didn't have a chance, because people didn't want graduates of secondary normal schools. [The starting point] was at least training college level; even if I found a place that would hire me, it would be hard for me to leave since my original employer hardly ever let anyone go. There had been other cases like that there.
>
> LIN YIMING 2009

---

burnout among teachers with this background (Xin Xing, 2006). Wang Lijuan's feelings of helplessness are almost certainly an expression of this burnout and stress.

46   Lin Yiming is a fellow alumnus from the same year as Wang Lijuan who graduated from the "satellite TV" teacher training course in 1995, taking part in the undergraduate examination in 1996. In September of the same year, he entered the provincial university undergraduate pedagogy program. In July 1998, he obtained a diploma in adult higher education. From August 1992 to December 1998, Lin's archives had been kept in the local office of education in his hometown. In 1999, Lin Yiming began working at the "M" City Teacher Training School. In 2001, he was admitted to Capital Normal University to pursue graduate studies. Now, he teaches at an institution in Beijing, teaching students political thought and ideology (Lin 2009).

"Iron Drum": We were some of the best and most promising individuals, and some of us have reluctantly gone on to strive for higher levels of success. But most have had their wings broken, so they could no longer aspire to greater career heights. The first wing is the diploma, and the second is English. By the time we secondary normal graduates finally earned our undergraduate diplomas through countless (mainly financial) struggles, many urban school recruitment conditions required that "The first degree should be undergraduate ..." When I went to teach at the high school, in a meeting the principal somewhat scornfully referred to "second-degree undergraduate diploma holders ..." Although the comment wasn't directed specifically at me, I still felt deeply humiliated. Teacher training academies and correspondence degree programs are the highest level of education that most secondary normal graduates can achieve, and getting into graduate school is practically impossible for us because our school didn't offer English classes. This three-year gap is an insurmountable obstacle for most secondary normal school graduates, reducing us to the level of common uneducated people. To this day I detest anyone who has studied a foreign language.

> "Iron Drum" 2009

"Academic qualification discrimination" is an important problem facing graduates of secondary normal schools. Many are very outstanding candidates in aspects such as pedagogical skills and basic literacy and they are well-liked by their students. However, because of their "original qualifications," they are subject to discrimination when it comes to promotions, evaluations or granting titles. Some scholars believe that new forms of academic discrimination centered on educational background and qualifications will continue to increase. This represents a loss of power for graduates of secondary normal schools and it is also a disguised affirmation of exam-based education (Ding Dong and Xie Yong 2008, 123). Feelings of embarrassment about their education background have made many elementary school teachers who graduated from secondary normal school see their academic background as a sort of "wound." Many cannot escape their secondary normal backgrounds, so they cannot seek other kinds of employment. Many of those who have succeeded in breaking free from their secondary normal background have done so because they were the most successful teachers in their schools, earning their students' love and admiration. However, it seems that a large number of these individuals were later reluctant to discuss their secondary normal school background in their future work, as if it were an "unspeakable" background.

Transforming one's "role" is a process of growth. Although Wang Lijuan values her academic qualifications, her own contributions in her work are really of greater value. Thanks to her diligence and dedication, especially in the work of implementing the "Pujiu" (nationwide nine-year compulsory education system), she has won wide acclaim from leaders, colleagues and students alike, giving her an increased sense of self-worth.[47]

> Wang Lijuan: The days when "Pujiu" was first announced were intense times. All of our central schools set to work building libraries, restoring archives, filling in materials, meeting with students' families in their homes. Every task had really strict requirements.[48] I was responsible for the work at the school library. In the fall of 1995, our school and the central primary schools in the neighboring towns engaged in mutual inspections. Everyone pointed out little flaws wherever they could.
>
> WANG 2009

Many fresh graduates of secondary normal school have witnessed the struggles of rural primary schools as they worked to earn the provincially granted title of "Recognized Nine-Year Compulsory Education County" and to meet the requirements laid out by superiors. In order to build a school library, Wang Lijuan moved her own books to the school; in order to fill in gaps in the teaching files, many school teachers made up previously-assigned "homework"; in order to convince some parents to throw away the idea that "going to school is useless," children who dropped out of school were permitted to go back to school. Teachers went door-to-door, going to great trouble for their work.

> Wang Lijuan: Regardless of how you put it, although the "Pujiu" inspections were really exhausting, a lot of achievements came out of them. At the very least, the teachers got their salary on time, and the leadership

---

47   In 1992, the State Education Commission's *Essentials of the National Ten-Year Plan for Education and the "Eighth Five-Year Plan"* proposed that the main goal of education development in the 1990s was to basically achieve the nationwide implementation of the nine-year model (primary through middle school) for compulsory education by 2000 (He 1998c, 3258, 3705).

48   In 1994, the State Education Commission issued the *Interim Measures for the Evaluation and Acceptance of Compulsory Education*. According to the requirements of the evaluation items and indicators, the primary school teaching equipment books, and materials should meet the provincial-level classification and standard requirements to meet the basic needs of teaching. The "Pujiu" acceptance criteria required that schools keep the annual student dropout rate below 3% (Ibid., 3705).

was quite supportive of teachers continuing their studies. Of course, the school environment also became much more beautiful than it had been.

WANG 2009[49]

The task of implementing "Pujiu" policy measures was a true test for secondary normal school graduates. Thanks to this "educational movement" they developed a deeper understanding of Chinese primary education. In the spring of 1998, Wang Lijuan took the job of a primary school leader and became the director of a rural primary school, achieving an important conversion of her role as an educator. Due to the outstanding "Pujiu" work done by many graduates of secondary normal school, they should be considered a core force in the primary education ranks.

5.3   Zhao Xia's Story

Zhao Xia narrates the story of her own growth and development in her online post titled "Pursuing the Dream of a Secondary Normal School Student."[50]

> As the eldest daughter in the family, faced with the economic pressure of having three younger siblings to send to school, I chose to attend secondary normal school 12 years ago. At the age of 17, during the second year of secondary normal school, we who were still children broke free of the restraints posed by our families, free from the pressure of having to prepare for the entrance exam. We were at a playful stage of our lives, lost in singing, dancing, playing musical instruments and practicing sports. I too nearly let myself go amid this flurry of enjoyable activity, but I still felt somehow reluctant to do so. Thus, in 1996 I became one of the first two students in the class to sign up for independent study exams.[51]

---

49   The State Education Commission's *Notice on Issuing the Interim Measures for the Evaluation and Acceptance of Nationwide Compulsory Education* stipulated the following regulations for education expenses: Salaries of faculty and staff (including policy subsidies issued by governments at all levels) are to be paid on time and in full (Ibid., 3705). Wang Lijuan said that the salary was paid "uncharacteristically regularly" for a while.

50   See Zhao Xia: "Pursuing the Dream of a Secondary Normal School Student" (Online post on web page "Renmin Wang"). All of the quotations pertaining to Zhao Xia are derived from this source (Zhao Xia 2009).

51   At that time, Zhao Xia's normal school did not allow students to apply for outside examinations while they were studying at normal school, so she could have had to work in secret: after the lights were turned off and the person in charge of nightly inspections had gone, she would carefully sneak into the hallway to study under the dim lighting. She used the term "going under" to describe secondary normal students' use of extracurricular time for independent study in music, sports and other courses. She shows her different views

I stuck to my pursuits in this way, knowing I was treading on thin ice. How many times before and after dinner, watching the cheerful figures of the students on the playground, did I shake my head and dismiss my desire to forget my ambitions and let myself have some fun? How many weekends, as my roommates returned to the dormitory after whiling away their time shopping and eating in town, did I have to force myself to calmly continue studying? After two years of hard work, in 1998, half a year after graduating from secondary normal school, I received my hard-won Chinese language specialist diploma.

I began working as a rural primary school teacher. With seven lessons a day, plus having to prepare lessons and correct homework, I didn't even have time to catch my breath. There was no way for me to finish all of my work during the day, and most of the time in the evening I would normally use for self-study I now had to dedicate to finishing whatever teaching-related tasks remained. I was so overwhelmed, I felt I had failed. But I knew I couldn't stop moving forward, even if other teachers thought I was somewhat mentally abnormal for studying like that every day. Whenever I heard somebody make a comment, I would just smile and set myself to working even harder. I made a strict plan regarding my work and rest schedule according to the constraints of my situation.[52] After working for three years, I finally held my undergraduate diploma in my hand, tears streaming down my face ...

After getting my diploma I felt confused for some time—I didn't know what my next goal was. From what I could tell, in the future anyone who didn't know how to use a computer would certainly fall behind the times. So I set myself to learning about computers. At secondary normal school, I once represented the school in the first provincial computer skills

---

on the secondary normal school curriculum, expressing her feeling that taking these courses was a waste of their youth.

52   At secondary normal school, Zhao Xia made full use of the best times for memorizing—early morning and dusk—and compiled the key knowledge points she had learned into a little booklet. There was a cemetery behind the school which she chose as her main place for studying due to its tranquility, determining to pursue her own dreams no matter what other people might say or how strange they might find her. Once, while she was studying at the cemetery around dusk, when someone approached her and asked with great concern whether she had some problem she couldn't get over, and said that she had been watching her for several afternoons.

For those around her, Zhao Xia was seen as "abnormal," "outrageous" and "weird." The kind of hard work she displayed was not only an expression of her personality, but also clearly shows how secondary normal students had to go beyond the efforts of ordinary people if they wished to achieve the same degree of educational and career achievement.

competition for secondary normal students, but since I didn't have a computer after graduating, I forgot nearly everything I had learned. After earning my degree, it was time to pick it up again. At that time, my salary was only 500 yuan a month, and buying a computer was no small expense. I started to save everything I possibly could, and I found I could keep my monthly living expenses to within 60 yuan. After half a year of hard work plus the original savings I had accumulated, I became the first person in the school to buy a computer. Of course, I had no idea how to work it. I had no teacher, no training, no help—just a book, a computer, and willingness to dedicate intensive study to the subject.

One year later, I transferred to the experimental primary school in the city. I remember how surprised the new teachers were when they saw me use multimedia computer programs as teaching aids in my first class. None of the other teachers who had come from countryside villages knew how to use computer programs except for me. Naturally, I was chosen to teach the school's experimental class. The courseware I have designed has won multiple awards—at the annual meeting of the "National Four Integrations" last year, my courseware was awarded the first prize and for a time was even the focus of news reports.

... With the encouragement of my colleagues and husband, I picked up my English book and started a new stage in my voyage: preparing to take the graduate school entrance examination.

ZHAO XIA 2009

5.4   *Lin Yiming's Story*

During an extracurricular activity in the early summer of 1992, Lin Yiming and his schoolmates sat together on the lawn of the sports field of the provincial secondary normal school discussing where they would be headed after two months and their future plans. His mind was in the same state as when he made that decision [to attend secondary normal school] three years prior—confused and at a loss. In that year, the big wall to the left of the school entrance was covered by a large poster of national leader Deng Xiaoping giving a speech in Shenzhen as part of his tour of southern China; the poster was sharply defined and conveyed a sense of enthusiasm. "Going into business" was the hottest topic of discussion among staff members of every organization, the most inspiring and tempting social concept, and it was what the students at secondary normal school talked about most.

Many secondary normal graduates who went on to become primary school teachers ended up following a similar career development trajectory, beginning by throwing themselves headlong into their teaching work while at the same time continuing to strengthen their capabilities and overall character. Through their dedicated work they soon became core members of the teaching staff and took on a more important position. Lin Yiming's change of role came about in another way.

> Lin Yi Ming: In May 1992, I took the qualifying examination for the provincial university organized by the school, and I was fortunate enough to be selected. However, due to "some special internal reasons" relating to the school, after taking the qualifying exam I ended up returning to my hometown to work as a teacher in the central primary school, where the only male staff members besides myself were the principal and the director. Out of the total sixteen teachers, seven were public teachers, three were private teachers who had been recruited, and the rest were secondary normal school graduates who had graduated ahead of me. The south and north sides of the small square grounds were the two blocks of classrooms which stood facing each other, a total of twelve classrooms in two stories, with four faculty dormitories on each of the east and west sides of the grounds. In the middle of the school grounds was the flagpole, there was a well in the southeast corner, a men's and women's toilet in the southwest corner, and the main entrance was the central corridor of the southern block.
>
> At that time, the title of "primary school teacher" grated on my ears. I couldn't bear to face the peers I'd spent my childhood with. Many people are snobbish—when I was first admitted to normal school, everyone in the village envied me, but when they heard I would return to the village to teach at the primary school they thought I "didn't have much of a future." Many of my male classmates from normal school either changed careers after graduating or immediately went into business to start making money. I wanted to do the same, but I didn't have a choice. I was living at school at the time. It was a quiet life, and all I wanted was to work hard, keep learning and hopefully one day I would be able to leave the village and fulfill my dream of going to university. I thought I wouldn't stay in that school for too long ... [and] honestly, a lingering fear would arise in me whenever I thought about the few teachers who had been teaching at that school for decades.
>
> The school leaders, including school district leaders, took good care of me. When I graduated, I enrolled in the "satellite TV" specialized teacher training course—I may have been the first of my classmates to do so— and the school supported me. Later, I participated in the township's primary school teaching skill competition and won the first prize. I then

participated in the county-level competition as a representative of the township and took home the second prize. Even with all of this, I still couldn't stand my situation. I didn't like the feeling of having no hope of finding a romantic partner. My hope was to be able to teach in the junior high school.

In March 1995, I really couldn't stand it anymore. I felt like a trapped animal. I wrote a letter to the director of the township education office, asking the leader to transfer me to a higher level unit: either to the "township office" or to the middle school. I had just finished taking the independent study teacher-training specialization course. In the letter I wrote, "I don't want to waste my youth away in this tiny square school like a blind mule!" Later, the director of the education office came to our school for an investigation and talked to me, telling me that the education office team was in need of a younger member. After looking into it, he agreed that I could start work at the education office after summer vacation. I was overjoyed. At the end of July, I rode my bike to the education office and asked when I should check in. The head of reception assumed a displeased expression and asked, "Who told you to come here? How come I haven't heard anything about you transferring here? We have already brought somebody new in to work."

I was beyond angry. I felt that I had been played. I went directly to the director who had spoken with me. He was nowhere to be found. I didn't give up. Later on I went several times to look for him, but I never saw him ... Afterward, a friend told me that the one that had been brought in to work at the education office had graduated from secondary normal school a year after me. He had been teaching in the town middle school, and his dad was the village party secretary! At the time I really wanted to quit. I wanted to forget about teaching and go look for work in the south. What is this place, I thought? Finally, my family consoled me by saying that I was still young, nothing was as simple as we wanted it to be. All of this business made me start to hate the school work environment here, I always felt that I didn't belong here, and that I couldn't belong here!

Later, I started working at the town middle school, my alma mater. I got in contact with the principal, a good man who had been my physics teacher. I began teaching first-year middle school language arts. The school assigned me two language arts classes, with more than 70 students per class, and I was the head teacher of one class. Every week there was one big essay assignment to be formally revised as well as one short essay assignment (which the school required that we read over). This was a really big workload, but I didn't say anything, I accepted it all. Every morning I got up at 5:30 and supervised the students' morning exercises, and at 10:30 PM I was still correcting homework and would spend some time studying English. I had found a burst of motivation! At the end of the term, the two classes I taught ranked first and second among the eight classes in the four middle schools. That year I felt I had really made some great achievements, and I was really happy. My students liked me very much; one time when I was not feeling well, dozens of students rode their bikes to my house to check on me, scaring the whole village.

On Teacher's Day in 1996, I was named one of the town's "Excellent Teachers." That year I passed the college entrance examination and entered the provincial university. The school principal "warned" me that I could not break the school regulations, if I wanted to enroll in university I would have to leave, and my files [related to work assignment] would have to stay. I didn't care, I was going to university!

In July 1998, I completed my undergraduate studies and graduated. I thought of going to another region, but in the end I returned to this middle school, because I couldn't go anywhere because of my files and my original educational background and qualifications. When I returned, everyone looked at me coldly, and many asked me: "So you ended up coming back after all?" I continued teaching language arts. I didn't want to interact with anyone apart from my students, I would teach, I would study English—all I wanted was to take the graduate school entrance exam! I had already taken it in January 1998, and I knew the only thing I could do was to keep going forward.

Six months after returning to the middle school, that is, in January 1999, the County Education Bureau and the principal of the teacher training school came to our school to coordinate with the "teaching office." They wanted to transfer me to teach in the county teacher training school, and in view of my situation, I was exempted from paying the 20,000 yuan "city entry fee," but with the condition that I could only take the graduate school entrance exam after working for one year. I only had to consider it a little while before agreeing to it, because if I quit my job to go to school I wouldn't have any income, and all my savings would be gone. I would be completely broke, and I had to live after all.

Going to work at the teacher training school was also a crucial step in my life. What made me most happy was when my files were finally released. When that happened, the world around me brightened; whenever relatives, old friends and colleagues mentioned me it was always with a positive connotation.

I made great progress in the teacher training school. I felt that the school leaders and I were on the same page; they supported my using my spare time to continue my studies, even giving me the "green light" for me to go to the provincial capital to sit in on tutoring classes for preparing for the graduate school entrance examination. In September 2001, I was admitted to graduate school, and I took all of my files with me to Beijing Normal University.

LIN YIMING 2009

Lin Yiming's story offers another picture of the transformation of secondary normal students' life roles. In the countryside, primary school teachers with a specialized secondary education background, no matter how much they love their profession and students, are subject to the demands of their personal growth that require too much sacrifice and effort. Moreover, harmful elements of the education system environment such as the emphasis on seniority, the way officials tend to protect each other's interests, the prevalence of social climbing, and the catering to those in power to advance one's own career, have condemned earnest young teachers whenever they are judged, appraised, or considered for promotion. Their enterprising spirit and enthusiasm are impaired, the realization of their personal ambitions and the satisfaction derived from a sense of accomplishment are out of balance, and their passion for devoting themselves to the cause of education is gradually extinguished. Cases like those of Lin Yiming who are able to enter the university classroom, and who make it to the big city, are few and far between. With their background as "secondary normal school graduates," these teachers are continuously engaged in a game with the social reality around them as they struggle to earn the respect of society, to "enjoy" the same right to attend university that their peers who attended high school have enjoyed, and to change the discrimination they have faced as a result of their particular educational background and qualifications. In the process of surviving amid the social reality, they have learned to adjust for and distinguish the circumstances and value of their own existence.

Indeed, compared with the average graduate of secondary normal school, those like Lin Yiming are more active and ambitious individuals. Some of the doctors and university teachers I know personally were once secondary normal school students, and it could be said that all of them were able to escape the preordained "life script" for secondary normal students and to pursue a situation that would truly allow them to fulfill their own sense of life purpose solely thanks to their unremitting efforts. If they seem to have more talent and character than their fellow secondary normal school graduates, it would be more apt to say that they have been given a richer and deeper set of life experiences thanks to their premature employment and to the complexity of the social environment.

It is based on a deep understanding of the reality of rural primary education and the life of teachers that Lin Yiming cherishes each change in role he has experienced. He often feels that he is a relatively lucky person. He feels that the fact that he was able to go from a rural school to a county teacher training school is not due to his having taken advantage of his days off to work as a substitute teacher at that school, nor was it because he possessed the necessary education qualifications or because he was selected by his leaders due to his outstanding teaching abilities, but rather, he gratefully attributes his good fortune to the "wisdom" of his superiors. Now Lin Yiming is working at a university in Beijing. He said that he once considered taking the civil servant test in Beijing, but he was never able to successfully register, the cause of which he surmises is the far-reaching discrimination against graduates of secondary normal school. Lin Yiming said that every "transmutation" in his development is the beginning of a new "contract," and through this constant process of "transmutation" he has gradually come to discover and recognize himself.

Considering the stories of growth and maturation shared by Wang Lijuan, Zhao Xia and Lin Yiming, we can feel the pressure posed by different forces. However, they all have something in common, that is, as Zhao Xia said: "We want our own stage, and we can't wait any longer! Our dreams may be far away from reality, very far away, but as long as we hold a dream in our heart and don't give up on it, life can blossom into beautiful flowers." After all, one's life path is ultimately under our own control.

6   The Role of Rural and Urban Spaces in Social Connections

Most rural school teachers would be satisfied and content knowing that one day they might become "teachers in the city." It seems that the old saying that "People make for higher ground, while water flows to the lowest ground" holds a grain of truth. Who among the secondary normal school graduates working in rural schools doesn't dream of working as a teacher in the city, of becoming an urban dweller? In speaking of the secondary normal school graduates of those years, Wang Lijuan does not deny the fact that the majority of rural teachers dream of going to teach in the city.

Wang Lijuan: Who doesn't want to move to the city [to work as a teacher]? No matter how you put it, it's always better to work in the city than the countryside. If the opportunity fell into my lap, I'd take it too. This is how life works, isn't it?

WANG 2009

Although both are teaching roles, the difference between teaching in the city and teaching in the countryside apparently requires little explanation.

Wang Lijuan: First of all, the feeling and quality of life are completely different. In the eyes of rural people, people in the city seem so full of spirit. This point alone makes it a goal worth fighting for. Second, how is the education and teaching environment in the countryside? Can you compare them with the city? The most beautiful primary schools in the county are in the city. Parents and cars line up to pick up the children after school. How can you compare the sense of achievement felt by urban teachers with how rural teachers feel? Finally, in terms of teaching, how can you compare the cutting-edge methods, tools, and training as well as the opportunities for growth afforded to teachers in the city with the conditions rural teachers have to deal with?

WANG 2009

Even after Wang Lijuan's graduation over a decade ago, the gap between urban and rural education and teaching is still huge.

Wang Lijuan: You often hear about "sending teachers to the countryside," right? Do you think this has another kind of connotation? Have you ever thought about why they send them to the countryside? This is nothing more than conveying another implication: the city is on a superior level to the countryside, and so this "sending" of teachers is done as a kind of "gift" from the city to the country, a noble act of extraordinary charity which fills rural teachers with both trepidation and gratitude. We rural teachers are not only discriminated against in the city, we are also sub- ject to our own discrimination against ourselves. If we really are capable teachers, why can't we say, "We don't want your charity!" Why can't we say "You city folk need to learn from us who are closest to humanity and nature." Why can't we "send teachers to the city!" Currently most of the curriculum reform efforts are concentrated in the city, and do you know why? This is an expression of the way in which our country fundamentally looks down on rural education. It is reasonable to say that the country-side is the main front of curriculum reform. Because there are so many students in the country, curriculum reform operates under the slogan "for the development of all students," but I think it should be changed to "for the development of students in the city," which would be in line with the status quo of our curriculum reform. The teachers in the countryside dedicate their time and energy to attending classes, but what do they learn there? How can rural teachers learn language arts, the violin, political theory, and how to use courseware? Yet rural teachers stand in awe of what goes on in urban schools, constantly discussing how great students in the city are and how hopeless their own students are. They don't learn the breakthroughs in the curriculum reform, they simply feel ashamed of their self-perceived inferiority.

Teachers in the countryside, if you think about it, teach students who are rejected by the city. We are teaching students whose overall quality and character is basically poor. It's difficult enough for us to get them to stay in school for three years, and both our expectations and our gains are far lower than those of teachers in the city. How can we not compare to the teachers in the city [if the present era is really about spiritual values]?

We have been the objects of entirely too much discrimination, we can't avoid it. You see, if a school in the city is worse than one in the countryside, then most of the education funds that should have been destined for rural schools are funneled instead to improving the city school. Thinking about it again, hasn't the proportion of awards given to rural schools fallen even lower? We can no longer discriminate against ourselves.[53]

ANONYMOUS 2009

Going to the city to work as a teacher is naturally the dream of most rural primary school teachers, and Li Huili, a secondary normal school graduate, is no exception.[54] After all, despite the fact that it is still a primary school teaching

---

[53]   Quoted from an anonymously written article in *China Rural Education Online* titled "Essays on Teaching: Rural Teachers Raise Their Heads (Anonymous 2009)." The "voice of the heart" expressed in this article was written during the implementation period of the *Opinions of the Ministry of Education on Promoting Urban Teachers' Support for Rural Education* (document dated February 26, 2006). The article reveals the psychological gap felt by rural teachers, and the reason for this gap is thought-provoking.

[54]   Li Huili comes from the same hometown as Wan Xiaoqin. She graduated from secondary normal school in 1991 and is now a teacher at the third elementary school in Z County. (Li 2009).

role, teaching in the city primary school offers a more compelling stage for one's career.

6.1   *Li Huili's Story*

The day after she turned eighteen, August 22, 1991, Li Huili officially became a teacher at Lijiatang Primary School in Dali Town. She was the second daughter in her family, after her elder sister, and she had two younger brothers who were in school, one in junior high school, the other in elementary school. It was rare to find a family of four siblings in the Central Plains during the 1990s. Her sister had married in 1991, and Li Huili's work allowed her parents to breathe a sigh of relief, after all they now had a new helper. Li Huili is a beautiful, gentle and competitive girl. In her secondary normal school class, she was a quiet student who studied hard and always ranked among the top students in her class. She also took the qualification examination for normal university, but she gave up during the second round because her family needed her assistance.

Li Huili felt all right as a primary school teacher, but she could never reconcile herself to her role as a rural teacher. Some people say that happiness comes out of comparisons with others of the same kind. Her classmate Wen Mei was quite average in all aspects when they were at secondary normal school, but because her father had a connection in one of the county bureaus, she was able to work in the county's number one kindergarten!

Li Huili's school was not far from the town government building, and a short time after she began working her colleagues introduced her to Kong Dongdong, a town government employee Although Kong Dongdong was a fairly average person, he was basically an honest man, especially considering that his father was both the head of the village and the accounting director of Wanggang Village, the wealthiest village in the town. After getting to know each other over a period of time they found they got along rather well—Kong Dongdong's parents, in particular, took a liking to Li Huili for her gentle and generous nature as well as her strong work ethic.

In the spring of 1993, Kong Dongdong transferred to the county's technical supervision bureau. In May of the same year, he and Li Huili were married in Wanggang village, and getting the daughter-in-law "into the city" became the Kong family's most important task. The cost of entering the city was not a problem for the family in itself, but the process of actually making the payment and the question of whom to pay proved problematic. In those years, anyone who went to the city to work had to pay the "urban expansion fee," which in Li Huili's county was 25,000 yuan. However, Li Huili herself was already a very competitive person, and on Teacher's Day of October 1993 she was awarded the annual title of "excellent rookie teacher" for her teaching achievements, a very timely event.

After many twists and turns, in the spring of 1994, Li Huili's name appeared on the list of new teachers in the county's new third elementary school. By autumn of the same year, she had finally begun working as a teacher in the city (Li 2009). Li Huili's successful entry into the city was due to various reasons, but she certainly couldn't rely solely on her honorary title of "excellent rookie teacher" since each year there were at least ten of these excellent candidates in the town, most of whom were middle and primary school teachers who had been working for no more than three years, and there were thirteen towns in the county. A similar case is that of Wang Yuhong, a fellow classmate of Wang Lijuan from the same year, who is now the deputy director of "M" city's number one kindergarten. In the eyes of Wang Lijuan, social connections are key for secondary normal school graduates to successfully transform their role in society.

> Wang Lijuan: She [Wang Yuhong] is 3 years older than me. She was one of the older students in our secondary normal school class and she was much more mature than [the rest of] us. She served as a secretary of the Youth League branch for 3 years and even worked as a cadre of the academic committee. Before she graduated from the school in 1992 (when she was 21 years old), she and her family honored the wishes of an old friend of her father. After graduating, she first taught in the rural primary school for more than a year, and got married. Everyone knew that her father-in-law had helped her transfer to the experimental primary school in M City. Primary school leaders have always valued her.[55] I rather admire her. She's always done things with a clear vision. But then again," if they say you're good, then you're good even if you aren't good; if they say you're not good, then even if you are good you're still not good." That's how it works now, right [*laughs*]?
>
> WANG 2009

In Chinese society, it cannot be denied that the use of relationships is still one of the main channels to personal success. Relationships through marriage also play an undeniable role in the restructuring of roles, and this is a very real part of our lives. Li Huili's entry into the city is not a problem, as she was qualified to do so; neither is Wang Yuhong's case a problem, given the fact that she truly was one of the most outstanding students in her school. What these

---

55   He was the director of a certain town's grain management office, and his son worked at a company in M city.

two have in common is that they were both born in rural villages, and such a background posed an inherent obstacle to the advancement of their careers. Everyone should have the opportunity to realize oneself, but when it comes to succeeding in life one cannot wait silently for the ideal conditions to be produced. It is necessary to actively create these conditions, to adapt to society's needs. The fact is that Li Huili is still a well-loved teacher among her students, and that Wang Yuhong does have the required talents for his own educational work. In this regard, the role of social connections does not represent much of a problem. The concept that "each individual should make the most of their talents and capabilities" indeed poses a challenge to the teacher management system itself, and to a certain extent this is also an indirect manifestation of equity in education.

Jin Xiaosheng, another secondary normal graduate, took another kind of "indirect" path to becoming a teacher in the city.[56]

> Wan Xiaoqin: When he (referring to Jin Xiaosheng) went to the city, he really did it on his own. When he had just graduated, he didn't want to go back to the countryside, but he didn't have any options. He spent more than half a year teaching in a run-down primary school before leaving, he didn't even bother with his files and such, [*pauses*] but he may have worked something out with the village education office, to take an unpaid leave—to work in the city to make some money. I think he was helping one of his cousins working in the steel industry or something, anyway, after a while he had made some money. All of the teachers here, even the leaders of the village education office, admired him, we all thought he was pretty talented and capable, but none of us had expected that he would end up teaching at a private primary school in the city. That was probably 1997 or 1998. I heard that his cousin's business was losing money, [and] around that time they were getting started with all kinds of enterprise reforms. We didn't understand what it was all about. Anyway, he ended up following his own advice, that working as a teacher was a stable career, but he absolutely would not teach at a rural primary school, so later he found a position at a private school. I think he bought shares in the school, and even ended up being one of the people in charge there. Think about it, in this world it's really difficult to land a legitimate position in the city, and how can we make that fair? Now, besides teaching at

---

56   A hometown acquaintance of Wan Xiaoqin, who is currently teaching at the number two primary school in Z county.

the number two primary school in the city, I think he's still somewhat in charge, but I'm not exactly sure in what capacity. Oh, and he was really good at calligraphy, when we were in school he was really well-known for that ...

WAN 2009

In order to find a better space for personal development in the city, many of Wang Lijuan's secondary normal school alumni have joined the ranks of private primary school teachers in the city, where they have had to rely on their continuous efforts to reshape their original roles in society.

> Wang Lijuan: Around 1992, there were a lot of private schools in our county. At that time, some of them were run by teachers from the city who had decided to go into business for themselves. Some even began by running training classes and expanding from there to offer training courses in electronic keyboard and musical instruments, computer training classes, etc., and later on they increased the scale of their centers until they had become primary schools. Many of the students in my year who were in the art class would go into the city to teach classes as substitute teachers at these schools, both to make money and gain experience; many of the students who studied music also went to the city to find a second career, they were all more capable than us "regular normal school" students. Some of my classmates were constantly using these channels to form connections with the outside world and they ended up leaving to work elsewhere. One girl in the music class a year behind me who was teaching these classes in the city on the weekends met a teacher from the city and began to learn vocal performance from her, and she took a recruitment test for adults, and even went to Beijing Central Conservatory of Music, she's still there working as a tutor in an arts center.
>
> WANG 2009

Of course, as primary school teachers who graduated from secondary normal school transition from rural areas to urban centers, who might look back at the children who remain on the primary school campuses? Who is likely to sign up again for the humble stage of the rural primary school classroom? Wang Lijuan once said that right after graduating, many Chinese teachers and students, including those who graduated from five-year college class programs, cared more about their own personal development than their salary or income, since they were all quite young, only seventeen or eighteen years old, or in their early twenties at most. What young person doesn't have dreams? Are they more worried about how long they will remain as teachers in rural primary schools? Do they want to continue on indefinitely in an environment like that found in rural primary schools? Where does their future path lie?

> Wang Lijuan: In fact, to be honest, rural schools still can't keep graduates around [even in] these years. Few of them willing to stay. Once the graduates of secondary normal schools became the backbone of the schools; or they made some achievements, and one by one they all "flew" away. In the past few years, the township teaching office has recruited teachers from other walks of society, but they are of varying and uneven quality. On the whole, they lack the sound character and dedication to the profession that the previous graduates of secondary normal school had.[57] There are only a handful of good ones, all of our leaders are worried, because they don't know when a teacher might decide to "fly" away.
>
> WANG 2009

It seems that what the teachers who graduated from secondary normal school and who "flew" away left behind is a great deal of regret and food for contemplation. Since time and energy are limited, this study has failed to investigate and gather statistics on the rates of employment and turnover (including changing careers and leaving the ranks of rural primary education teachers) for graduates of secondary normal schools who have returned to the countryside to teach in rural primary schools. Judging by the information offered by Wang Lijuan and her fellow alumni, however, there should be many such cases. Therefore, solely in terms of the actual situation of rural primary education, it is hard to say that the country's original "agreement" with "rural primary school teachers" achieved its goals within the planned period. Far too many social reports and data indicate that the current lack of qualified rural primary school teachers remains an unavoidable problem of basic education in the Chinese countryside, especially in poorer rural areas.

6.2   *Considerations of Roles in History*
History can often be deceptive. In the 10 years after Wang Lijuan graduated, many secondary normal school students weren't dealing with feelings of "reluctance" about beginning their work, they simply did not have the opportunity

---

57   As both a school leader and a graduate of a secondary normal school, Wang Lijuan clearly feels herself to be in a contradictory position. She deals with both concerns about the development of the school as well as anxiety about the personal growth of the younger generation of teachers.

to play the role that should have been theirs—that of the rural primary school teacher.

In the autobiographical online novel titled, "The Ardent Years of Secondary Normal School Students," the protagonist Wen Lin is a graduate from the last three-year (1998–2001) program at Taiyao Normal School.[58] The year he graduated, he was already psychologically prepared to look for a job (the school stopped assigning jobs in 2000). Upon graduating in 2001, Wen Lin was recommended by the school to teach classes as a substitute teacher at the Taiyao Sub-district Office Primary School, earning 200 yuan a month. His original intention in choosing to substitute teach was to gain further training and experience in public schools, looking to strengthen his skills for use in future recruitment examinations. However, even with everything he has gained through his hard work and effort, society and even friends and relatives continue to mock and sneer at him.

> Younger sister (with a look of disdain): "You can't even manage your own affairs, and you're trying to tell me what to do? You call what you do 'work'? Don't you feel pathetic?"
>
> Dad (coming over): "Linlin, your sister is right, are you managing your own affairs? Find a legitimate job and then we'll talk! How are you going to survive on two hundred yuan a month?"
>
> Dad: "Come out here, you waste of space! Don't think I wouldn't hit you!"
>
> Mr. Huang, a colleague: "The school pays too little, a young man can earn more than this just by working a little!"
>
> YI JING TI XIAN 2009

This kind of existence is chilling to consider. After the original teacher returned to the school, Wen Lin was "laid off." While "idling" at home for more than half a year, he was asked to work as a substitute teacher but his father wouldn't let him. Besides working on the land at home, helping his parents do some small-scale farming, he would go out and look for work when he had time. As soon as potential employers learned he had graduated from a teacher's school,

---

58   Wen Lin is the protagonist of the "Tian Ya Community" online novel titled "The Ardent Years of Secondary Normal School Students." The author of the novel uses the name "Yi Jing Ti Xian." This autobiographical novel rather vividly records the personal experiences of secondary normal school students in the last class to graduate from the three-year program (Yi Jing Ti Xian 2009).

however, they would think there was something wrong with him: if he's not working as a teacher what is he doing looking for work here?

He explained that he was not assigned a teaching job, and others felt that he hadn't been assigned one because he had been a bad student (normal schools had only just stopped assigning jobs, which people were perhaps unaware of); other employers felt that graduates of normal schools couldn't do anything besides teaching, and were unwilling to hire them. After failing to find employment in this way, Wen Lin once again chose to work as a substitute teacher in the summer of the year after graduation.

> Principal Cen: I heard that you did a good job in the sub-district primary school. I hope you will do as good of a job here. Conditions here are very poor. Let me explain. First, you won't be teaching here with us, you'll be going to a simple affiliate primary school of the district to teach, your salary is paid by our office here, and it won't be very much, around what you were originally being paid. You must be mentally prepared. If you're unwilling to do the job you should let us know.
>
> ....
>
> Wen Lin was shocked when he came to the simple elementary school the next day. How could this kind of school still exist in the 21st century? He couldn't help but think of a scene from the movie Not One Less. Things were pretty much the same here as in the movie, but the movie was set in the west! The house was quite run-down, no water or electricity, and there was only one old teacher. And the village was only ten miles away from the city, the village entrance was a public road, transportation was very convenient, and on the face of it the village didn't look poor. The low-lying classrooms were in stark contrast to the surrounding residential groups of tall concrete tile houses. A group of gray-faced rural children looked at him curiously.
>
> Principal Cen: You've seen what things are like, it'll be a little harder work. There's only one class of students here, that is, all the courses in this class are taught by you, you don't need to teach the minor subjects if you don't want to, but the language arts and mathematics have to be taught. If you feel hesitant, you can let me know, I respect your opinions.
>
> Teacher Yu: The village is certainly not poor. The ordinary people can get by all right. I don't know why they haven't done any renovation or reconstruction here, every year the education committee has funds for renovating the old school buildings (built in the 1970s). They must think that it is after all a simple elementary school. Just two and a half rooms, two classrooms and two grades, this half of the room is our office. When

the children reach the third grade they go over to where the school principal teaches. How far is your home from here? Is it easy for you to get to work?

Wen Lin: It's a little over nine miles away, and it's not too bad to get here.

Teacher Yu: Do your best. It is a pity that students like you weren't assigned jobs. It is really a contradictory situation, they say for that there are more graduates from normal schools or colleges than before, *graduates* will no longer be assigned jobs working in schools. But the fact is: all rural schools are lacking teachers *nowadays*, in rich towns, in poor towns, wherever. In many places students are taught by older teachers who used to be unqualified ones paid by local village committee and later became regular teachers after passing the teacher qualification examination of the country. (Yi Jing Ti Xian 2009)

"Yi Jing Yi Xian's" novel offers a vividly profound portrayal of the lack of teachers in rural basic education and the uncomfortable position of secondary normal school graduates in being unable to find teaching positions even in rural society.[59] This contradiction represents an irreversible trend in social development, and it can pose a difficult struggle for any individual who has to deal with this contradictory state of affairs in their own lives.

It is undeniable that at the beginning of the 21st century graduates of normal schools are facing serious employment problems due to the continuous strengthening of teacher education reform measures in various districts of China as well as the large number of graduates of higher normal colleges or holding equivalent qualifications (through obtaining teacher's qualification certificates) who have joined the ranks of primary school teachers. It could be said that the potential for personal development is extremely limited in the face of "policies" of every sort.

On New Year's Eve in 2003, Wang Lijuan and several of her old classmates from her 1989 secondary normal school year met in a restaurant near the provincial higher college to celebrate the ten years since their graduation. One of the classmate's three-year-old daughter was knocking a small spoon excitedly against the table ... over ten years ago this area had been filled with lush celery

---

59   According to the Ministry of Education's *Statistical Bulletin on the Development of National Education in 2001*, in 2001, there were 637,790 primary school faculty members, a decrease of 75,200 from the previous year. Among them, 579,700 were full-time teachers, a decrease of 62,600 from the previous year. The primary school student-to-teacher ratio is 21.64:1, somewhat lower than the previous year's 22.21:1 (He 2003, 1232).

fields.[60] The campus opposite the restaurant had been their alma mater. At that time its sign read "Z City Normal School" and was a significant landmark in the suburban zone. Now, their former alma mater was drowned amid a bustling market and noisy crowds.

> Wang Lijuan: Everyone had an inexpressible sadness in their hearts, and the atmosphere was very depressed. We had originally talked about going in together and taking a look around, but after we ate everyone went their separate ways. I went in [but] I really felt a sense of loss. Oh, the time is gone, we're old [pauses]. I suppose this is also the inevitable process of social development. Who can stop it? Just do what you need to do as best you can [*laughs*]!
>
> WANG 2009

Wang Xinru:[61] On the National Day holiday, I went back to my hometown and visited my normal school alma mater which I hadn't seen in many years—and which had already been converted into an ordinary high school. The alma mater I remember had already been changed beyond recognition, the marble school sign, standing alone amid the holly bushes outside the school entrance, serving as the only reminder of how the school used to be. Most of the teachers from those years are struggling with post-reform college entrance examination training. I heard that on the morning when the last batch of secondary normal students graduated, all the teachers and students of the teachers' college burst into tears and that it's a memory too sad to recall.

Since then, I have been a person without an alma mater. From then on, we have often been afraid to mention our true origins—secondary normal school. Today, most of us have gone through various forms of continuing education, obtaining specialized certificates, undergraduate or even higher degrees, I myself came only half a step away from earning a doctoral degree. However, anyone without a hometown to return to is always a wanderer, and the depression felt by a student who can't proudly say where they spent their school years is something that cannot be

---

60   Wang Lijuan's alma mater was upgraded to "Z Higher Normal Training College" in 2002 after merging with "Z City Education Academy." By the end of the year, five normal schools in the country independently upgraded to higher normal training colleges and three schools which were primarily normal schools were upgraded to higher normal training colleges after merging with education academies (See *China Education Yearbook* 2003).

61   See Wang Xinru: "The Last Secondary Normal School Student" (*Education Online* 2009).

dispelled by any title. Secondary normal school will always be my personal spiritual home; on every occasion, I obsessively tell everyone that I
am a secondary normal school student!

WANG XINRU May 10, 2009

What a giant leap to go from "Z Normal School" to "Z Higher Normal Training
College!" With the gradual historical retreat of the secondary normal schools,
the concept of "secondary normal student" will also become history.[62]

However, is there really no shortage of "specialized normal school graduates"
among rural primary school teachers? Do we really no longer need "secondary
normal school graduates?" What does the story of Wen Lin, the "last graduate
of secondary normal school," explain?

"Iron Drum": I have never known how to evaluate this group of people.
Speaking from another angle, it is precisely because of this group of
people that China's basic education is not as bad as it could be. It is this
group of people who have challenged the status quo of basic education
in China, especially regarding the burden of offering quality primary

62   With the further development of nine-year compulsory education and the full implemen-
      tation of quality education, the new curriculum reform of basic education has higher
      and higher requirements for the education level and knowledge base of primary school
      teachers. The existing administrative standards and teaching models of secondary nor-
      mal schools are obviously unable to meet the current needs for cultivating primary school
      teachers. To this end, on January 13, 1998, the State Council approved the Ministry of
      Education's *Action Plan for Education Revitalization for the 21st Century*, requiring that by
      around 2010, qualified regions should strive to have upgraded the requisite qualifications
      for full-time primary school teachers to the specialist level. In order to ensure the realiza-
      tion of this goal, in March 1999, the Ministry of Education's *Opinions on the Adjustment
      of the Layout of Normal Colleges and Universities* put forth the requirement that the goal
      of the transition of normal colleges is to move from a three-tier to a two-tier structure.
      In June 1999, the *Decision of the Central Committee of the Communist Party of China and
      the State Council on Deepening Educational Reform to Promote Quality Education in an All-
      round Way* also called for "strengthening and reforming teacher education and vigorously
      improving the quality of teacher training." Under the guidance of these requirements,
      the nationwide structural adjustments to teacher training schools have opened the cur-
      tain of reform in many transitional modes such as "removal and reorganization of higher
      vocational colleges, independent promotion, affiliation with undergraduate colleges, and
      conversion into teacher training institutions" (He Ming 2002, 2).
          The general situation of China's secondary normal education development from 2001
      to 2005 is shown in Figure 1–Figure 3 (data compiled according to the *China Education
      Yearbook* [2001–2006]). (Ministry of Education of the People's Republic of China 2009).

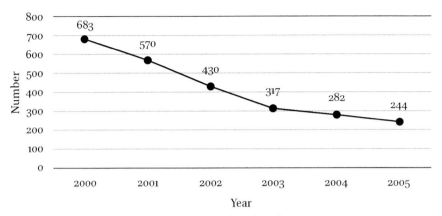

FIGURE 1   Number of secondary normal schools in China from 2000–2005
MINISTRY OF EDUCATION OF THE PEOPLE'S REPUBLIC OF CHINA JULY 1,
2009

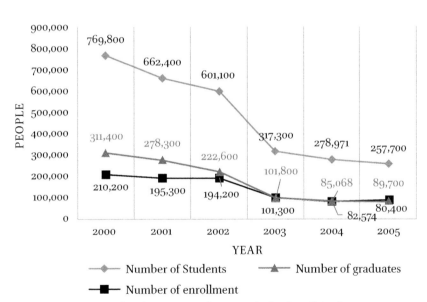

FIGURE 2   Situation of students in secondary normal schools in China from 2000–2005
MINISTRY OF EDUCATION OF THE PEOPLE'S REPUBLIC OF CHINA JULY 1,
2009

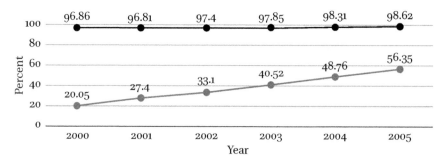

FIGURE 3   Education level of primary school teachers throughout China from 2000–2005
            Supplementary Explanation: Those taking on primary school teaching positions in
            towns, rural areas and cities throughout the country in 2005 with institute of high-
            er learning education levels or higher were respectively 78.01% (cities), 67.17%
            (towns) and 47.49% (rural areas).
            MINISTRY OF EDUCATION OF THE PEOPLE'S REPUBLIC OF CHINA JULY 1,
            2009.

education in rural areas. They basically represent the core force of the
basic education sector in rural areas. It is the existence of this group of
people that allows many students to retain vivid images of at least a few
teachers in their memories after many years. Numerous examples around
me prove that I am not at all being arrogant in describing secondary normal students the way I do.
    "Iron Drum" June 6, 2009

The role of secondary normal education and secondary normal school students in the history of Chinese teacher education and in the long history of
education in China in general will all take time to verify. In the early 1990s,
there were many graduates of secondary normal school who left behind their
roles as elementary school teachers to follow the trend of going into business,
while rural primary schools continued to need qualified teachers. In 2000,
experts announced that "The task of getting rural primary school teachers to
achieve the statutory teacher qualifications remains quite formidable" (Bie
2000). Today, in 2009, due to the widening gap between rich and poor, and the
social and economic downturn, the survival status of the "left-behind teachers"
who comprise a portion of the rural education faculty, and thoughts expressed
in texts like "What should we Dongan-based secondary normal students do
now (Hong Wang [Hunan] "People's Voices" section May 16, 2009)?" have once

again triggered social attention and concern about the issue of rural primary education teachers.[63,64]

The "historical facts" described here and the reality conveyed by personal narratives of secondary normal school graduates reveals only a microcosm of the history of the development of teacher education in China and the complex journey of rural primary education. The gap between the ideal goal and the actual situation of teacher education in China's primary education system prompts us to think constantly about the experience of Wang Lijuan and her fellow secondary normal school graduates, exploring ways to fill this gap. As former secondary normal school student Wang Lijuan said: "Do what you need to do as best you can!" This means we must never stop working hard!

---

63   See Qu Mingzhi's *A Record of the Unfortunate State of Survival of "left-behind teachers" in rural China*. The article analyzes the two main reasons for the existence of "left-behind teachers:" first, if either the husband or wife in a family is a teacher, the other partner must seek work in other places to earn enough to support the family; second, factors such as school layout adjustment and urban-rural teacher mobility (the author found that most mobile teachers are male teachers; in rural schools they are especially common, and especially in small villages, where in some cases 40% or more are mobile teachers) are an important influence. The article expresses that in rural areas, when teachers receive wages it should be equivalent to the income of a stable job, at least enough to support a family, but the reality is that the spouse must generally find outside work to earn a living, so these "left-behind teachers" are often looked down on by others and have to deal with other kinds of social pressure. Due to the many troubling factors given above, these "left-behind teachers" have undergone spiritual and psychological changes leading to any number of emotional problems such as feelings of loneliness and inferiority and the desire to give up on oneself, or even to give up working as a teacher (Qu 2009).

64   Please refer to: (*Hong Wang* [Hunan] "People's Voices" section May 16, 2009). The issue began in 1998, when more than 50 junior high school graduates from Dong'an participated in the unified examination organized by the Hunan Provincial Department of Education in accordance with national requirements to gain admission to Yongzhou Normal School (Qiyang Normal and Lingling Normal School) as regular full-time normal students. However, three years later, in 2001, when these students graduated and returned to Dong'an to assume their assigned jobs as per national policy, the Dongan County Education Bureau refused to arrange work for these students on the grounds that there were too many primary school teachers. Over the years, these students have spoken out in response to this treatment. The article poses the question: "Since we are already concerned about aging primary school teachers, why are we not making use of the legitimate, young, and energetic secondary normal school students who have been trained in regular full-time normal teacher classes? Why are we so restricted from applying for teacher recruitment exams by the primary school teacher recruitment requirements?"

References

Bie Linye. 2000. "The Adjustment of the Layout of the Middle School and the Gradual Opening of the Teacher Education System—Policy Suggestion on the Reform of the Teacher Education System in China." *Educational Research* (7): 55–59.

Chen Nailin. 1980. "Tongzhou Normal University is the First Normal School in China." *Journal of Xuzhou Normal University (Philosophy and Social Science Edition)* (4): 109–110.

Chen Xiangming. 2000. *Qualitative Research Methods and Social Science Research*. Beijing: Education Science Press.

Chen Xingchuan. 2002. "Teachers' Lies." In *Tomorrow Education Forum*. Edited by Huang Xu. Fuzhou: Fujian Education Press.

Commentators. 1989. "Rethinking the Biggest Mistakes and Strengthening Ideological Education." *China Education News*, 1989-06-24 (1).

Ding Gang. 2008a. "The Narrative Shift in Educational Research." *Modern University Education* (1): 10–16.

Ding Gang. 2008b. *Voices and Experience: Educational Narrative Exploration*. Beijing: Education Science Press.

Ding Gang. 2009. "Narrative Paradigm and Historical Perception: A Method Dimension of Educational History Research." *Educational Research* (5): 37–41.

Ding Dong and Xie Yong. 2008. *A Record of Thoughts on Education*. Fuzhou: Fujian Education Press.

East China Normal University Teacher Training Institute. 1996. "Normal Education in China: 1981–1996." *Journal of East China Normal University* (3): 2–6.

Ge Zhaoguang. 2005. *Lectures on the History of Thought*. Beijing: Life, Reading, and New Knowledge Sanlian Bookstore.

Goffman, Owen. 1989. *Self-presentation in Daily Life*. Translated by Huang Aihua and Feng Gang. Hangzhou: Zhejiang People's Publishing House.

Gu Mingyuan. 1998. *Educational Dictionary* (Additional Compilation). Shanghai: Shanghai Education Press.

Gu Mingyuan. 2003. "The Tradition and Change of Normal Education." *Higher Normal Education Research* (5): 1–6.

International 21st Century Education Committee. 1996. *Education—Wealth is Hidden Within*. Chinese Department of UNESCO Headquarters, translated. Beijing: Education Science Press.

Hai Tian and Xiao Wei. 2009. *My University 1970–1976: Workers, Peasants, Soldiers, and University Students*. Beijing: China Friendship Publishing Company.

He Dongchang. 1998a. *Important Education Documents of the People's Republic of China (1949–1975)*. Haikou: Hainan Publishing House.

He Dongchang. 1998b. *Important Education Documents of the People's Republic of China* (*1976–1990*). Haikou: Hainan Publishing House.

He Dongchang. 1998c. *Important Education Documents of the People's Republic of China* (*1991–1997*). Haikou: Hainan Publishing House.

He Dongchang. 2003. *Important Education Documents of the People's Republic of China* (*1998–2002*). Haikou: Hainan Publishing House.

He Ming. 2002. *Where is the Secondary Normal Education Going—Also on the Reform and Exploration of Jiujiang Normal School in Jiangxi Province.* Dissertation, Huazhong Normal University.

Hua, Chen. 2007. "Thinking about Trends in Secondary Normal Education in China." *Education Frontier* (2): 70–72.

Online Education. 2003. "A Survey of Rural Education." (Jiangsu, Zhejiang, Sichuan, etc.) In *Tomorrow Education Forum.* Edited by Huang Xu. Fuzhou: Fujian Education Press.

Li Shaoyuan. 2000. *Rural Education Theory.* Nanjing: Jiangsu Education Press.

Liu Wenxiu, ed. 1993. *Contemporary Teacher Education in China.* Beijing: Educational Science Press.

Lu Wenwei. 1981. "China's First Normal University, Nantong Normal School." *Jiangsu Education* (1): 46–47.

Murphy, Rachel. 2009. *How Migrant Labor is Changing Rural China.* Translated by Huang Tao and Wang Jing. Hangzhou: Zhejiang People's Publishing House.

National Education Committee, Secretary of Normal Education. 1996. *Fifteen Years of Normal Education in China.* Changchun: Northeast Normal University Press.

Qi Fen. 2002. "My Rural Education Experience." In *Tomorrow Education Forum.* Edited by Huang Xu. Fuzhou: Fujian Education Press.

Qu Mingzhi. 2009. "The Sad State of Survival of Left-behind Rural Teachers." *China Education News*, 2009-06-11 (4).

Sun Zhijun. 2004. *Education Costs, Benefits and Family Education Decisions in Rural China: A Study Based on Gansu Province.* Beijing: Beijing Normal University Press.

Tian Tian and Zhang Wenzhi. 2003. "Rural Female Teachers: Persistence and Helplessness." In *Tomorrow Education Forum.* Edited by Huang Xu. Fuzhou: Fujian Education Press.

Wang Junping. 2008. "Changes in Salary for a Rural Teacher Over a Ten-year Period." *China Education News*, 2008-06-16 (8).

Xin Xing. 2006. "Investigation and Thinking on the Status Quo of Primary School Teachers' Job Burnout in Shanghai." *Chinese Education: Research and Review* (10).

Yang Zhiling. 1989. *Teacher Education in China.* Beijing Normal University Press.

Yu Benfa. 1997. "A Century of Normal Education in China." *Education Research and Experiments* (1): 35–41.

Yu Yongde. 2000. *Rural Education Theory*. Beijing: People's Education Press.

Zhang Anmin. 1984. "A Review and Outlook of Normal Education Since the Founding of the People's Republic of China." *Xi'an: Journal of Shaanxi Normal University*: 3–9.

Websites

Anonymous. 2009. "Teaching Essays: Rural Teachers, Raise Your Heads!" [2009-06-02]. <http://ncjy.cersp.com/sXcjs/sCzzj/200710/246.html>.

China Education Yearbook of the Ministry of Education (2001–2006). 2009. [2009-06-03] <http://www.moe.edu.cn/edoas/website18/top_nianjian.jsp>.

Dream Blog. 2009. "A Record of Xintai Teachers' and Students' Presentation of their Lawsuit Filed Against the Administration of the Government Education Bureau." [2009-04-09] <http://blog.sina.com.cn/s/blog_5b4a8f210100ct02.html>.

Hong Wang (Hunan). 2009. "Voices of the People" column. [2009-05-16] <http://people .red-Net.cn/peopleshow.asp?ID=326042>.

"Iron Drum." 2009. "Secondary Normal School Students: the Dreams and Sorrows of a Generation of Teachers." [2009-06-06] <http://www.smxx.cn/article/showarticle .asp?articleID=710>.

K-12 Education Forum. 2009. "(Discussion) Secondary Normal Students, Who Can Remember You?" [2009-03-12 22: 52] <http://sq.K12.com.cn/disc/viewthread.php?t id=249897&start=0&rid=639857>.

Ministry of Education of the People's Republic of China. 2009. "The China Education Yearbook (2001–2006)." [2009-07-01] <http://www.moe.gov.cn/jyb_sjzl/moe_364/ moe_369/>.

Wang Xinru. 2009. "The Last Secondary Normal School Students." [2009-05-10] <http:// bbs.eduol.cn/post_15_120909_0.html>.

Yi An Shu Nv. 2009. "I Was a Secondary Normal Student in the 1980s." [2009-04-16] <http://blog.sina.com.cn/s/blog_52fb4aab0100a0ki.html>.

Yi Jing Xiu Xian. 2009. "The Ardent Years of Secondary Normal School Students." [2009-04-28] <http://www.tianya.cn/pub-license/content/culture/1/305493.html>.

Zhao Xia. 2009. "The Pursuit of a Secondary Normal School Student's Dream." [2009-05-12] <http://politics.people.com.cn/GB/8198/74182/74183/5135449.html>.

CHAPTER 6

Educational Beliefs: Educational Inquiry from a Female Teacher

Geng Juanjuan
Translated by Arthur Wan

Abstract

This is a narrative research into the stories of a female teacher of Chinese language that aims to summarize the routine in her teaching, to discover her educational beliefs behind her behaviors by analyzing her narration of her growth in her career, and to understand the formation of her personal educational beliefs relative to a broader vision by understanding her personal stories. This essay attempts to focus on life narratives to observe personal professional development, concepts about teaching, and the ideals and pursuits of representative teachers in the Chinese cultural context, so as to facilitate our understanding of educational beliefs.

1 Introduction[1]

1.1 *Research Background and Methodology*

As the largest institution of education studies in English-speaking countries, the American Educational Research Association (AERA) has published three editions of *Handbook of Research on Teaching* (1963, 1973, 1986) that include thorough research on teaching and directly or indirectly raise the idea of logical positivism in teaching. For example, in the edition edited by Gage (1963) much light is shed on logical positivism. In the chapter by Getzels and Jackson, special attention is paid to teachers' personalities. The chapter by Medley and Mitzel successfully heralds the appearance of the "Classroom Observation Study," specifically "Process—Result Research" in the 1970s. In the *Handbook of Research on Teaching, Second Edition* by Travers (1973), attention given to classroom observation research and the tradition of logical positivism was

---

1 This article was translated from its Chinese version, which was originally published in *China's Education: Research and Review*, 2002, volume 2, pp. 181–232.

also employed. In 1986, the *Handbook of Research on Teaching, Third Edition* (Wittrock) indicated scholars' interests turning to "Qualitative Methods" and research on teachers' thinking. Meanwhile, qualitative research and research on teachers' thinking have developed by leaps and bounds. Teaching is now viewed as the "practice of teaching"; pedagogical theories have become "theories about practice" and teaching research has changed to research-in-context.

In China, there is a tradition of qualitative research studies focusing on teaching, and there are two accepted ways to conduct teaching research based on practice. One depends on teachers' "stories," offered in lectures, open classes, auto-biographies, shared personal experiences and exchanged views with colleagues. These recognized teachers are active in teaching and research activities focusing on different subjects at various schools and they play a significant role in promoting teaching among their peers. Another way to conduct research on teaching is to summarize and theorize effective methods. Rather than logical positivism and deduction, this is actually a method of qualitative research that promotes understanding via interpretation. As an example, teachers represent their classroom experiences through recording, narrating and disseminating their personal "stories." Such attempts are continuous efforts that have become a tradition, as exemplified by the *Selected Writings of Wei Shusheng* published in recent years.[2] Wei's works abound in insights, vividly typified by experiential classroom activities, which cannot be found in theoretical works. In recent decades, reforms in "Education Science" put such "story"-oriented empirical narratives to the test. The "scientificity" and "objectivity" of those narratives have been questioned, making them less popular than they once were; however, the "empirical" nature of such research has regained academic attention because the question still remains: "Why are teachers still not good at teaching, even after learning educational psychology?" In this essay, research into this topic is based upon anthropology, hermeneutics and modern psychology while taking into consideration Chinese traditions in teaching and learning as well as the latest Western research.

The focal subject of this study is a teacher of Chinese language at a secondary school in Guangxi Province for whom the pseudonym Li Qun will be used.

---

2 Mr. Wei Shusheng 魏书生 has been invited to give speeches and lectures all over China so as to orally share his "personal stories" about teaching and education. His stories have also been published in books including *Yuwen jiaoxue tansuo* 语文教学探索 [Exploration of Chinese Teaching] in 1990 and *Wei Shusheng wenxuan* 魏书生文选 [Selected Writings of Wei Shusheng] (Vol. 1 and 2) in 1995.

Other subjects are teachers and students, and, in the interest of protecting their privacy, their real names will also not be used.

Two things need to be made clear. Firstly, Li Qun was chosen for this study because she is on good terms with the author's friend "L." This offered convenience to the research since, due to the personal connection, Li Qun was willing to share her thoughts and reflections. Moreover, L and Li Qun have been colleagues for years and have become close friends supporting and understanding each other. L also understands this project's research plan and has provided much valuable background information about the life and thoughts of Li Qun. Secondly, the research subjects are not limited to Li Qun and her students, and this study's narrative will use an "integral" method to take advantage of various references.

Special research subjects need special material collection methods to ensure that the aimed objective will be achieved. For instance, classroom observation can be employed to assess teaching skills. However, the professional knowledge and belief systems of teachers cannot be sufficiently assessed only by classroom observation. Likewise, if a paper-and-pencil assessment is utilized to gauge teachers' professional knowledge and belief system, how can we know the position of such knowledge and beliefs in practice? Taking all factors into consideration and with continuous reflections and revisions, this study combines interviews, observations and access to material collections to obtain the final data. As an example, before a class, the teacher is interviewed in order to learn about her teaching plan, objectives, classroom imagination, and her reasons for such an arrangement. What follows is classroom observation focusing on classroom activities, the teacher's classroom routine, potential or unexpected situations, the teacher's reactions, and so forth. After class, we ask the teacher about her understanding of the classroom situation that was observed. The practices mentioned above have been designed, reviewed, and readjusted in the process of the research.

The data was collected from June 1998 to February 1999 in the following ways:

1. On-the-spot observation of 42 Chinese language classes. 12 classes were given to Class A by Li Qun and 22 to Class B, for whom Li Qun served as the class mentor. The additional 8 classes were given to Class C, in the same grade level, by a new Chinese language teacher who had only been at that school for 2 years. The case of the other teacher is used for comparative study.

2. Interviews with the subject teachers. The interviews with Li Qun were held mainly in the office, or in classrooms, corridors, playgrounds, her apartment, her friends' apartments, streets, and so on. Face-to-face

interviews and telephone interviews were also utilized. Topics included the classroom imagination[3] of Li Qun, her understanding of classroom behaviors, her views about the subject she teaches, her comments on students, her ideal classroom situation, her professional experience, her life, her outlook on life, her family stories, and so forth.

3.   Interviews with other relevant people, including friends, colleagues, and students of Li Qun. Topics vary from their views about the teaching, classroom activities and life stories of Li Qun.

4.   Records of significant events outside the classroom, including events on campus and Li Qun's gatherings with friends.

5.   Collection of materials about Li Qun, including her work reports, syllabus, resume, photos, academic essays and her revisions of student diaries and writings.

Adhering to the field visits and records, I will tell "a story of Li Qun." The accuracy of this story depends on facts and Li Qun's support. All narratives were approved and revised by Li Qun. While this general story may not be able to fully reflect the educational beliefs of Li Qun, it is hoped that through depicting the teaching, learning, and life of Li Qun and her students, her educational beliefs based in a Chinese cultural context would be sufficiently illustrated.

1.2   *Basic Viewpoint*

Much research on teaching shows that students' performance is closely related to their teachers' idiosyncrasies. In the past, most research focused on teachers' behavior. For instance, Graham (1991) believes that students' success or failure is influenced by their teachers. But in recent years, some scholars have begun to explore the educational beliefs of teachers—certainly a very challenging mission, for it is a field involving people's will, attitude and view of life, and its theory is based on a specific and concrete system of values, hypotheses,

---

3   Classroom imagination is the teacher's imagination about all possible situations in the class, including the knowledge to be taught, students' potential reactions and participation, possible confusions and how to avoid or clarify them. The term "Classroom Imagination" was coined by Greta Morine-Dershimer (1978–1979) who thought that teachers' classroom imagination is their predication of whatever may happen in the class and that such imagination plays an exceptionally significant role in handling what actually will happen in the class. Through teachers' imagination, their educational beliefs and professional knowledge will be summarized (Elbaz and Clandinin 1983, 1986). Leinhardt (1993) depicts "teachers' agendas" as follows: a. Activities of both teachers and students are included; b. Students' behavior will be predicted; c. Quizzes and examinations would be regularly proposed and used as an assessment instrument; d. The position of a particular class session in the syllabus would be specified; e. A particular teaching principle, be it concrete, abstract or consistent, would be included, such as "This concept will be very helpful to us in understanding the next concept."

preferences and expectations. Actually, a completely objective capturing of teachers' educational beliefs is almost "mission impossible." From the perspective of logical positivism, teachers' educational beliefs usually depend on "biased" hypotheses, which are definitely not perfect; however, their use is highly valuable as part of hermeneutic theory.

Generally speaking, the large amount of research on teachers' educational beliefs by foreign scholars can be categorized into the following two groups. First, those who recognize that teachers' belief systems have very strong effects on their teaching activities: Harvey, Prather, White, Alter, and Hoffmeister (1966); Harvey, White, and Hoffmeister (1968); Gallup (1970); Munby (1984); Nespor (1987); Brickhouse (1989); Behar and Pajares (1994); Behar, Pajares, and George, (1995); Borko, Hilda, and Putnam (1996). Second, some scholars consider that there are remarkable differences between teachers' self-claimed beliefs and those that they actually practice in teaching: Aguirre and Speer (1996); Borko and Putnam (1996); Calderhead (1996); Ernest (1989); Pajares (1992); Schoenfeld (1996); Thompson (1992).

In China, "educational concept" is a term similar to educational belief. Most "educational concepts" are continuities of traditional methods of education research and tend to reveal the content of ideas and emphasize actual effects. In recent years, Chinese educators and the public have paid much attention to the reform and development of primary and secondary education. How might we educate a new generation so that they can devote their talents to the socialist modernization cause in China in the new era? This is a popular topic reflecting the tenor of our age. People have offered different answers from their own perspectives. Some say we should reduce students' burden; some propose examination reforms; some prioritize reforming managerial system at schools; and some attach great importance to building strong teacher teams.

This essay intends to survey the career trajectory of a teacher living in China through telling a vivid story about her. It will explore an ordinary teacher's ideals and pursuits, and her reflections of her job. This may contribute to a better understanding of teachers' personal educational beliefs.

1.3   *Two Basic Hypotheses*

The conceptual framework of this essay is based on two basic hypotheses. Firstly, personal educational beliefs are complex personal concept systems whose actual existence hinges on a particular context. Secondly, an appropriate contextualization of a personal educational belief mirrors the perspective and pattern of cultural anthropological studies. Only under the condition that cultural background and effective documents are preserved as fully as possible, can the personal educational beliefs of a teacher be properly understood and described. The peculiarity of the perspective of a cultural anthropology of education belief lies in that it exists in all kinds of specific educational activities. A teacher's educational beliefs determine his or her tendencies in thinking and understanding, in conceiving of what is possible and proper, in what objectives he or she will set, in what knowledge will be used, what actions will be taken, and so forth. It will demonstrate that the teacher's educational beliefs are not a unified and stable internal system, but full of conflicts. In different contexts, different beliefs will compete with each other and a sequential order of priorities will thus be formed. Therefore, the ethnographic method is used in data collecting, and "story-telling" is employed in narrating the teacher's personal educational beliefs. "Stories" give a meaning to the experience gained in teaching and learning, which will also help conceptualize and examine such experience. In other words, experience that is not distilled in "stories," no matter how impressive, is not real reliable experience that can be objectified. Only when translated into written words, can experience gain its meaning. If we want to change complex perplexities in the classroom into rich educational experiences in reality, we need to find "story" models that can express the content and meaning of such experiences. Meanwhile, this research concentrates on "individuals" rather than on "groups." For this reason, this research will center on specific persons, instead of "representative" teachers, and observe their particular activities. A widely applicable model is definitely important, but a model can only be built through observing individuals whose activities comprise that model. Thus, this research may not be able to summarize a reliable "prototype," especially not a "prototypical teacher." Nonetheless, there will be the educational beliefs of a teacher born in a certain era, living in her social and educational contexts, and having her particular life and career experiences.

1.4   *My Understanding of "Exploration"*

By "exploration," I mean the process of discovering personal educational beliefs.

The exploration includes dimensions A, B and C. Dimension A discovers the pattern in the teacher's daily life and thus delves into the conceptual system behind daily behaviors. Dimension B divides the teacher's educational beliefs into different themes and then places different beliefs in different positions according to the value system linked with each theme. Dimension C situates the teacher's personal educational belief in her personal history and explores the formative factors. Dimension A reveals the teacher's personal educational belief. Dimension B discloses what kind of value the educational belief holds in our eyes, and Dimension C illustrates "Why it is so."

In terms of the procedure, the first step is a survey that tries to build a set of data as inclusive as possible through ethnographic methods like observation, interviews and material collections. The second step is reproduction which constructs "stories" or "episodes" on the basis of factual materials. Step three is abstraction that discovers and summarizes behavioral "routines" of the teacher from stories and episodes. Step four is inference that deduces the personal educational belief behind the teacher's behaviors through her various routines. The last step is attribution which investigates the formative factors of her personal educational belief.

1.5   *A Teacher's Personal Beliefs about Education*

Terms like "belief," "creed" and "conviction"[4] are used to refer to a spiritual phenomenon developed in human's social and spiritual activities. This phenomenon represents the believing in and observation of a certain notional system by humans as social creatures and usually crystallizes in concepts.

When talking about religious belief, Engels pointed out that "Even the most ridiculous superstition reflects the eternal nature of humanity" (Marx and Engels 2002, 65). This indicates that human beings need various kinds of faiths including superstitions because they are based on eternal human nature. A person may choose to believe in one or another belief but it is impossible that he has no belief, for that would deprive him or her of existential value in this world. This is true of beliefs relevant to the universe, society, other human beings, and any specific field. For instance, in *What I Believe*, Bertrand Russell expounds his beliefs in "Nature and Man," "The Good Life," "Moral Rules," "Salvation: Individual and Social," and "Science and Happiness," while in *My Pedagogic Creed*, John Dewey elaborates upon his creeds about "What Education Is," "What the School Is," "The Subject-Matter of Education,"

---

4   I find the definitions of belief, creed and conviction in different reference books. A) Belief: A view about which one is sure of. Creed: A norm to stick to. See *Xiandai hanyu cidian* 现代 汉语词典 [Contemporary Chinese Dictionary] edited by the Dictionary Editing Office at Institute of Linguistics in Chinese Academy of Social Sciences and published by Shangwu yinshuguan in 1979. B) Creed: A deep belief in respect to a religion or doctrine used as guiding principle for behaviors. See *Cihai* 辞海 edited by the *Cihai* Editorial Committee and published by Shanghai cishu chubanshe in 1979. C) Conviction: A person's firm faith in the rules and ideals he or she should follow in life. The faith is deep-rooted and ideal-centered. Due to the faith-holder's active attitude vis-à-vis reality, well-grounded reflection upon his or her knowledge and a strong sense of responsibility and duty, the conviction gradually comes into being. The conviction is usually mixed with the believer's emotion and will, externalized in his or her standpoint in life, and dominating the believer's behaviors. See *Xinlixue cidian* 心理学词典 [Psychology Dictionary] edited by the *Psychology Dictionary* Editorial Committee of Eight Universities and published by Guangxi renmin chubanshe in 1985.

"The Nature of Method," and "The School and Social Progress." Similarly, each teacher has his or her own belief or creed about themselves, the nature of intelligence and talent, the nature of the subjects taught, about learning, students as individuals and as a group, and about their working environment. A teacher may know if he or she is good at teaching a certain subject; some teachers believe intelligence is innate, while some others think it is acquired.

In this essay, "teacher's personal educational belief" refers to the doctrine a teacher practices in teaching. For a better analysis of the cases, this concept will be clarified from several aspects as follows. Firstly, in terms of function, a belief can be categorized as the belief as it is proclaimed and the belief as it is practiced. The former exists in the teacher's personal conceptual system as objective knowledge and it is easily recognized and represented by the teacher. It can also be easily affected by new external situations, but it cannot exert a direct impact upon teaching. On the other hand, the belief as it is practiced is knowledge internalized. It is not only rationally accepted, but also includes irrational factors including personal will, emotions and attitudes. A belief practiced can help develop a habit that will have direct influence on teaching activities; however, it might not be easily recognized by the teacher and will not be easily affected by new settings. On the contrary, it is under considerable influence of culture and habits. This essay will focus on belief as it is practiced.

Secondly, in terms of background, the personal educational beliefs of a teacher usually have a unique background. Different backgrounds produce beliefs different in intensity, and contradictory beliefs will fight against each other for "priority." Educational theories, diverse teaching regulations, and rules (textualized or not) do not directly govern teachers' behaviors but do stipulate a series of activities required to meet standards, and therefore provide a framework for the teacher's "improvisational performance"[5] "on the spot."

Thirdly, in terms of origin, a teacher's educational beliefs stem from personal experiences that include the teacher's experiences as "a child of parents" and "as a student in the classroom," as well as his or her experiences of receiving education at a school for teachers, and the actual teaching practices, interpersonal relationships, academic research, and the influences of other people.

Fourthly, in terms of its content, a teacher's educational beliefs could be inclusive, mainly including his or her belief in the nature of teaching, in teachers' roles, in the process of learning and teaching, and in students. Lastly, it is

---

5   "Improvisational performance" derives from Symbolic Interactionism as noted by the sociologist Herbert George Blumer and it suggests that people act a certain way towards things based on the meaning those things already have, and these meanings are derived from social interaction and modified through interpretation. See Ding 1997.

worth mentioning that when we say a teacher has a specific set of educational beliefs, we actually mean his or her various behaviors bespeak his or her particular beliefs about education.

2   Stories about Li Qun's Teaching

These stories are based on our field observations in and outside the classroom, on interviews with Li Qun, her students, colleagues and friends, on material collections, and so forth. But the stories are not simply the original records; instead, they are formed by the organic integration of episodes collected at different times and in different places. Li Qun, the researcher, and all participating teachers reviewed and revised the stories and tried to reach an agreement before finalizing them. As for places where disagreement lies, different views will be presented to the readers who will make their own judgment.

2.1   *Classroom Imagination (Story 1)*[6]

On a Sunday evening, Li Qun takes her daughter, Xiaoyu, to the Children's Palace for piano lessons. It is near nine o'clock when they return. Li Qun reminds Xiaoyu to do her homework and then she starts to think about what she should prepare for her class the next day.

Although very familiar with the routine and the textbooks used in each class, and though she could proceed smoothly without any preparation, Li Qun still finds some time to prepare, adding new knowledge and inspiration, planning how to start, how to arrange activities for students, and how to link different parts; namely, to mentally "rehearse" the whole class, a habit formed in the past years.

Li Qun reviews the instructions on how to use the Chinese textbook for junior high school students, which state that Book Four aims at developing students' critical thinking. Tomorrow, Li Qun will teach a unit on argumentation and she hopes, through several classes, her students will find and practice an effective way to make arguments.

In the first class for the unit on argumentation, Li Qun goes straight to the point: "We have learned narrative writing, expository writing, and persuasive writing. Today, we will learn a specific type of persuasive writing— argumentative writing. Argumentative writing usually consists of a position on a topic, critique of the topic and a conclusion [these are written on the blackboard]. Now let's turn to our textbook to see what the position, the

---

6   This story is from an interview on classroom imagination with Li Qun on June 2, 1998.

critique, and the conclusion are." In this class, the basic structure and techniques in writing an argumentative piece are introduced to the students.

In the following day, there will be the third class for the same unit on persuasive writing and it will focus on "Two Examples of Argumentative Writing." For this class, Li Qun has a very clear objective: to continue strengthening students' knowledge about the structure and techniques for argumentative writing, so as to lay a foundation for future study. She is also mindful of the steps to be taken.

Step One: To review what is learned in the last class, with three questions being raised—What is the structure of argumentative writing? (To establish a position, to present a critique, and to draw a conclusion) What are the two types of argumentative writing? (Direct argumentation and indirect argumentation) What are the major methods to make an argument? (To argue against the topic, to argue against the evidence, and to argue against the conclusion) Then Li Qun will come to the focus of this class—"Today let's study two examples of argumentative writing, to see how to establish a position, and how to argue against a given opinion."

Step Two: Students will be asked to read the text silently and quickly and find out what position is established, and how the author argues against the topic. Then Li Qun will go around the classroom to see students' reading speed and note-making (which is a habit developed in grade one of secondary school). A few minutes later, Li Qun will comment on students' performance in reading and ask questions like: What position is established in the first piece and in the second piece respectively? Questions will be written on the blackboard. After that, Li Qun will emphasize that the foremost thing in an argumentative writing is to establish a position by finding and arguing against the given topic and then she will guide the students so that they can have a thorough understanding of the topic.

Step Three: Ask students in the mini-seminars (four students around two tables, which has become a classroom routine) to discuss what methods the authors use in the two pieces; then ask them to raise their questions, share their understandings, and make comparisons of different methods; finally, conclude what argumentative methods have been taught until now and list them on the blackboard.

Step Four: Ask students to read the conclusion of the first piece together and then summarize that this way to conclude an argument is called "citing famous sayings." Then ask them to read the conclusion in the second piece together and observe how to make a conclusion.

From Step Two to Step Four, the analysis of the given writings would be done and educational guidance would be provided to students to let them think what kind of person they want to be and what is the right attitude toward life.

Step Five: Give the students a topic, and ask them to spend several minutes thinking about it before inviting them to share views about how to use the structure and methods they have learned to argue against the given opinion. This is actually a small step in writing training. Li Qun hopes her students will not only know this framework for argumentative writing but also apply it in their writings. In the next class, she will ask students to spend several minutes writing a passage, and in the class after the next one, there would be formal and complete guidance for argumentative writing.

Li Qun is always very serious about her teaching. Even if it is a very familiar subject, she will not just improvise; instead, she will make a plan that includes the psychological and knowledge assessments of the students. In her classroom imagination, there is a clear "plot," which means she is keen to stress the formula in writing. For instance, in the unit for argumentative writing, the formula is "to establish a position, to argue for the topic, to argue against the topic, and to make a conclusion."

2.2   *Strict Discipline (Story 2)*[7]

At 7:35 AM on Monday, Li Qun goes to Class B to see students reading in the morning. She is the mentor of the class and checks to see if the students have covered their desks with a tablecloth as required. All students have come to class on time. The homework for different subjects is placed on the first desk in the first row, and the teachers' student assistants of those subjects will collect the homework later. In Li Qun's class, there are detailed rules for everything. Today, Li Qun is pleased to see all the desks covered with blue tablecloths. This is actually a requirement of the school, but in the past many classes did not fulfill the requirement and were criticized for that. If a class is criticized, that means the loss of the class mentor's face. What is more, Li Qun thinks that this responsibility will help the students form good habits that will benefit them in the future. The other two class mentors in the same grade do not seem to take it seriously, however, as they only require students to cover the desks but never check to see that it has been done.

For example, Z is the class mentor of Class D. In the last class of the day, many students fidget anxiously and start to collect their things prior to leaving. Seeing that, Z says angrily, "Why you are in such a hurry? No one is allowed to leave until 12 o'clock!" The whole class quiets down immediately; then the school bell rings (at 11:40). Pausing for a moment, Z continues to give students homework assignment and finally says, "Class is dismissed." At that point,

---

7   This story comes from an observation (1998-06-03, N1) of Li Qun's classroom, and an observation (1998-06-15) of teacher Z who apprenticed with her.

there are still 16 minutes until 12. That being the case, how can a teacher ensure his or her instructions will be followed next time? More interestingly, two students in the back row whisper while collecting their things. One says, "When shall we hand in our homework? I didn't hear what our teacher said." The other replies, "No hurry. Although the teacher says it is the day after tomorrow, there is no need to worry because every time he asks us to do the exercises in the Extracurricular Workbook, teacher Z doesn't check every one, but only just asks some students in next class to see if they have done it."

Usually, this would not happen in the classes taught by Li Qun because she is very familiar with the students' "ability" to judge each teacher's style and whether the teacher is serious. "To be honest, I like students who take the initiative to do things as required, but that is idealistic, so strict discipline is needed." Therefore, Li Qun will act cautiously so that there will be no loophole to be exploited. With strict discipline and rules, everything is in order in her classes.

2.3   *Preset Orbit for Students (Story 3)*[8]

The first class of the day is Chinese language for Class B. Everything goes smoothly just as Li Qun imagines, and there are usually very few unexpected situations, for she is always able to have the class under control. After explaining the text, she is satisfied because from the students' answers she sees that they have understood the basic format and techniques in writing an argumentative piece. Then Li Qun turns to a specific case, saying, "Consider the opinion, 'What is the use of good school performance if graduation means the beginning of unemployment, and people studying atomic bombs even earn less than those selling tea eggs ...'" Then she asks students to think over this case, spend three minutes discussing it, and tell how they would argue against such an opinion. Although critical thinking had been repeatedly emphasized in class, some students still adhere to their old way of thinking by offering answers such as, "This is wrong because people with poor education will find it hard to get a job." Obviously, students do not follow the orbit preset by Li Qun. To address this problem, Li Qun provides further guidance: "The first step is to identify your target, so please tell me, what your target is. Then let me know how you will argue against it. Will you address the given thesis first or the proofs first? Will you disprove the given thesis directly or use your proofs to disprove the thesis? From what perspectives will you argue?" She hopes her students will bear in mind the framework for argumentative writing in practice. Li Qun

---

8 This story comes from an on-site observation (1998-06-12), a classroom observation (1998-06-03, N1), and an after-class interview (1998-06-03).

usually has a preset orbit for her class and can make the class follow the orbit step by step.

2.4 *The Relation between Classes (Story 4)*[9]

After students finish the reading in the morning, Li Qun talks in the corridor with the English teacher who says the recent test result shows that it is six of one and half a dozen of the other for Class A and Class B. The English teacher also says that only a few students get high marks, and several students do not treat their homework seriously, so it might be better if the class mentor could address those issues.

The second class is Chinese language for Class A. Li Qun feels somewhat depressed even though the same topic will be taught in the class. She feels confused, for comparatively, she thinks students in Class B are cooperative, lively and responsive, and she is also more spirited in the class, while in Class A students are joyless and even the top students are pretty unresponsive. On the surface, Class A is less competent than Class B; however, Class A gets better results in exams than Class B does. They are all her students, but Li Qun feels a greater responsibility toward Class B and spends more effort on it since she is the class mentor, hoping Class B can outdo Class A.

As usual, Li Qun feels depressed and spiritless that day; the students are also silent. When asked "What can we learn through the conclusion drawn by citing the saying," two students just say "I don't know." Li Qun is angered and she knocks the desk with the chalk and says, "You don't know the answer to such a simple a question? Is that what you have learned?" Actually, the first student she asked in Class B also did not answer this same question, but the second one answered it after getting a slight reminder. Seemingly, what angers Li Qun is not just their failure to give the right answer in Class A, but also their silence and their uncooperative attitude. The atmosphere in Class A is not improved after the teacher loses her temper, and that lasts until the end of the class. Li Qun proceeds with the lesson, yet with less vigor than in Class B.

Two days prior, in another Chinese language class, students were quite active due to the fact that their class mentor Y sits in the back of the classroom marking their homework. It seems that the students treat their mentor and other teachers differently, but Li Qun does not agree with that, believing "All teachers would feel low-spirited in that class and the main reason lies in the temperament of the students." However, the students have their own reason: "Ms. Li is too strict!" "Ms. Li just hopes her own class (Class B) will outdo us!"

---

9   This story comes from a classroom observation (1998-06-10), an on-site interview (1998-06-02, 1998-06-10, 1998-06-17), and an interview with students (1998-06-24).

Li Qun feels wronged. Although admitting that she wishes for better performance from her class, Li Qun still thinks it is merely human nature, and she believes as a teacher, she will not reveal a biased feeling like that, and she has actually treated the two classes equally.

> Before me, another teacher taught Chinese language to Class A in which the competition between Class A and Class B is already quite fierce. This is because Class A gets a lot of awards, ranking first in many activities, and has become the envy of many classes. Once, in the school's 100-meter race, a student of our class (Class B) was a shoulder ahead of the student in Class A. A girl in our class saw that and requested the song "Soft-hearted" on the School Radio Station. She said, 'This song is played for XX (from Class B) because we hope he will not be soft-hearted and will beat his rival!' That made me angry and I asked them to bring back their tape because friendship is also important in competition, and her behavior would undermine the friendship between classes. Nevertheless, students in Class A always attribute competition between students to the teachers, so much so that one student, in his writing, even asks me why I always instigate Class B to bully Class A. He also claims his class will 'overpower' Class B.

It is possible that Li Qun externalizes her expectations, which have been captured by sensitive students. Or it may be that those students are still teenagers who cannot form a mature attitude to those things, and they also fail to see that their teachers are also human beings.

Comparing one class to another seems to be the most frequently used "model" in the teachers' daily narrative. For example, when they are discussing their teaching work or the students' performances, they always say "Class A is such and such, and Class B is such and such." A class is a basic unit of a school, so comparing classes is a common phenomenon that influences teachers, students, and the relation between them. After some time, a stable dynamic of teacher-student-relation is formed in the teaching, but with considerable difference between Class A and Class B.

2.5   Criticism (Story 5)[10]

During a mid-morning exercise, Li Qun does not stand beside her class to supervise as usual. Instead, she stays in a distant corner, where she can observe

---

10   This story is from a classroom observation (1998-09-21), an on-site interview (1998-09-21), and an interview with students (1998-09-21).

the students but where the students will not easily see her, hoping to see her students do as well as if she is there. She is disappointed to find that the class monitor does not do his duty to gather the whole class together, and does not comment on the day's exercise before dismissing them, so that the students in the class just scatter like little sparrows. Li Qun has spent much time on the monitor and trusts him, and she thinks she cannot turn a blind eye to this and that discipline needs to be emphasized. Therefore, when the monitor is on his way back to the classroom, Li Qun waits before the door in the corridor and stops him. With mixed feelings of disappointment and desperation, Li Qun sort of loses control of her temper,

> "Why did you dismiss them before gathering together? You thought I didn't see you? I just want to see what you would do without me being there. You are a good student and should do the same good job no matter if I am there or not!" Knowing he has done wrong, the monitor hangs his head in silence. Another student behind Li Qun pokes his tongue out at the monitor. Believing the criticism will work its effect, Li Qun softens her voice and says: "All right, be careful next time; just go back to the classroom."
>
> We all hope the students can depend on 'autonomy' rather than on 'heteronomy,' but reality is always disappointing. A colleague once told me, she always gives priority to nurturance and seems to find that it works, for one student has done exceptionally well. However, when that student visited her after graduating from university, she wondered, 'Is this the same student I taught in the past?' To me, autonomy is indeed a great challenge for the students.

2.6   Teaching Writing (Story 6)[11]

In the third and fourth periods, Li Qun goes back to her office to mark students' writings from the last week.

...

On the third day, Li Qun leads the students in analyzing "Reading the *Biography of Meng Chang Jun*" in Section Four of the unit on argumentative writing. Because it is a classical piece, they start from the vocabulary, the meaning of the sentences, and then move to textual analysis following the clues of the structure and style of argumentative writing. Finally, students are asked to

---

11   This story is from a classroom observation (1998-06-11) and an on-site interview (1998-06-12).

write a short passage under the title "Why I am against the idea that 'school education is useless.'"

The fourth day is for writing a complete piece and the topic is "Why I am against the idea that 'reading is useless.'"

As before, the first half of the two writing sessions is used to comment on students' writings and provide proper guidance, while the second half is for students to write.

In a recent inspection, Li Qun was criticized by the local Education Bureau, who believes she does not give enough comments on students' writings and that this is not good for students. However, Li Qun thinks that analyzing writings in class is more important and effective than detailed comments on the writing of each student. Li Qun's opinion is not accepted by the inspectors and she feels wronged, but she believes in her long-term experiences and adheres to the old practice.

That day, they deal with an argumentative text titled "Modesty Helps a Person Make Progress." Li Qun asks students to recall the features of argumentative writing, namely the writing techniques. A boy provides a relatively complete answer: "There are three parts. The first part raises the main argument and specifies what it is. The second part uses sub-arguments to support the main argument and explains why it is so. The third part draws a conclusion." Li Qun writes this answer on the blackboard. Then she reads the writings of two students and asks the class to discuss the strengths and weaknesses in the writings. Li Qun chooses the more representative writings to read instead of the best ones. Students are very active in the discussion. One writing uses two students in the class as examples and that evokes great interest and debate. A girl comments: "The first piece displays skillful techniques and a complete structure, but the sub-arguments are not clear enough." Li Qun agrees by saying: "Well-said. Are there any other comments?" Another girl answers: "Using students in our class as an example is not very proper because they are not representative of factual evidence and thus not convincing." "Exactly, factual evidence should not only be real but also representative," Li Qun continues her comment by saying: "The key issue for this topic is how to arrange the sub-arguments. Many students have two sub-arguments which do not seem to differ from each other." After pointing out the main problem, Li Qun also says: "There are two ways to approach the topic 'Modesty Helps a Person Make Progress.' One is to prove 'Modesty will let us see the merits of other people,' and the other is 'Modesty will let a person see his/her own demerits.'" No doubt that Li Qun's comment makes sense, which gives it credit. Finally, she concludes her comment by saying "There should be different types of evidence. Famous sayings, like 'Conceit is the enemy of progress,' could be employed in the argument to form a contrast."

After that, Li Qun reviews the structure of argumentative writing with the students and provides further guidance for writing.

First, she produces a detailed framework as follows and copies it on the blackboard while explaining it.

Framework for Argumentative Writing

Beginning: The First Paragraph—Introducing the target (Identifying the opinion to be criticized)—The argument and evidence to be criticized

Body: Criticizing the fallacies in the writing targeted—Criticizing its arguments and evidences.
            The Second Paragraph—Criticizing the fallacy from the first perspective (Sub-argument + theoretical evidence + facts + summary)
            The Third Paragraph—Criticizing the second fallacy from the second perspective (Sub-argument + theoretical evidence + facts + summary)

Ending: The Fourth Paragraph—Concluding the essay, reiterating your view, proposing a solution, and calling for action …

Then Li Qun offers specific guidance for writing on the given topic. She spends only a little time on the argument to be criticized because all students have the same one. She explains that the difficulty lies in the method of criticism and the angles from which the argument should be formed. In order to answer the questions, she asks students to discuss the paragraphs they wrote the day before. The first student says, "In the target argument, the gauge for whether reading is useful or not is how much money can be made …" This answer reflects the sharpness of a debater, for he reveals the logical problem of the target argument by addressing the norm of "useful" or "useless," which is actually a good start. "Unemployment of some college graduates is just a problem caused in a developing society and it will not last long," says another student. This opinion will trigger the observation and discussion of a series of social phenomena, and a lot of factual evidence can be used to argue from a historical point of view. It can be said that there are brilliant sparkles reflecting the students' wisdom in the answers. Nonetheless, Li Qun thinks that,

"The answers of the two students merely touch upon the superficial phenomena and could hardly penetrate the problem. We actually have discussed this topic with colleagues teaching Chinese language." She reviews students' intellectual efforts and comments on the first student's view by saying "This is a discussion of the purpose of reading."

She also tries to lead the students' intellectual activities to her orbit by commenting on the view of the second student: "Yes, in the long run, reading is useful." Then Li Qun uses several examples to illustrate, including the example of a well-educated American scientist charging 10,000 American dollars for drawing a line [in a design], or Midea Group offering a high salary for employees with a PhD, and so forth. Subjectively, these vivid stories and the former comments on the students' views reflect that Li Qun "hopes to guide the students to argue from the two perspectives and be more insightful," while objectively, Li Qun states her preset orbit and even provides a standard answer. According to this answer, the view "school education is useless" can be criticized from two aspects. From one aspect, students should figure out what is the purpose of school education for individuals. From another, they should ask what benefits education can bring to the nation in terms of advancing science and technology and encouraging a more courteous society.

Li Qun views this as a primary course, namely an introductory course for argumentative writing, which should help students master the basic structure of this kind of writing so that they can proceed with the theme and the literary grace of the writing, "but the training for literary grace is very challenging, and so far I haven't found any effective method," Li Qun admits.

2.7   Choice of the Objective (Story 7)[12]
The course module on argumentative writing comes to an end. Recently, Li Qun has been reflecting upon the changes and features of the unified examination. In the previous year's examination, particular emphasis was placed on the relation between reality and the course of Chinese language and how to use knowledge comprehensively. Li Qun ponders the events of this year that might be used in the exam. In retrospection of the newspapers of the past year, she finds that the biggest news is the construction of the "Beijing-Kowloon Railway," which she thinks is just the topic for one task in the writing. This year, there have also been news reports of flood control and relief, over which the whole country is highly concerned. Li Qun thinks this topic is bound to appear in the paper. Therefore, she decides to ask students to give speeches in the

---

12   This story is from an interview (1998-06-18).

first five minutes of the class, guiding their attention to this hot news and getting them prepared for relevant questions. As the syllabus also requires speech
training during the three years in the junior high school, these two things can
be achieved at one stroke.

With those thoughts in mind, Li Qun starts to mark students' homework,
which includes a regular exercise—students hand-copy the vocabulary in the
present class or unit. They have to copy each word while previewing the class,
and copy them again while reviewing the class. Actually, Li Qun thinks it is
nothing more than repetitive labor and sometimes suspects its effect. The copy
seems to be a little unnecessary and useless, but according to her experiences
in past years, if teachers do not ask students to copy, a fair number of students
will lose points in the exams, even though most grade-two students feel there
is no problem with their dictionary. Eventually, she still chooses to ask students
to copy.

As a teacher, Li Qun often has to adjust her teaching according to various
factors. Sometimes, there are dilemmas. She eventually chooses to play safe.

2.8   *Expectation (Story 8)*[13]

The graduating classes return to school two weeks earlier than other classes,
so they have their first class in the burning-hot middle of August. In that
class they learn the journalistic text "A million PLA soldiers cross the Yangtze
River." The humming noise of the ceiling fans drowns out the teacher's voice.
Looking at the students, Li Qun feels a little anxious, so, on the first day of
the new semester, she summarizes the situation of last year's senior high
school entrance examination. Then she tells her students they will face a more
challenging situation because it is more difficult to get into a key senior
high school than to get into a key university. That means the offer from a
key high school almost equals the offer of a university. Li Qun hopes her students will always remember their own goals and the fierce competition. Even
though she feels tired in such weather, she still raises her voice to reiterate the
issue so that students distracted by the weather and the summer holidays may
focus on their own business.

Li Qun asks students to review the structure of journalistic writing they
learned in grade one and analyze the present piece so that they will know how
many major points are included. The first student asked stands up but says
nothing, so Li Qun lets her sit down. The second one hangs his head and fixes
his eyes on the textbook. After a short hesitation, he says: "I did not finish (the
whole piece)." Li Qun becomes a little worried and is aware that they cannot

---

13   This story is from a classroom observation (1998-08-17), (1998-08-18).

provide the right answer because they have not read carefully; otherwise, simple questions like these could not have made them frustrated, not to mention that the two students asked are among "the top" in the class.

Giving further tips, Li Qun hopes some students can provide the right answer. Guiding the students until they can do what she expects is usually what Li Qun does in situations like this. This time, however, the students' performance is not very encouraging, so she asks: "Is it so?" In fact, she does not mean to ask the student to answer this question because she tells the student, "Please sit down," before an answer is given. She asks another student and expects the right answer. She hopes to use this way to spur meditation among the students, but she is disappointed. Feeling somewhat depressed, Li Qun does not want to linger on this question due to the schedule to be followed, so she just tells them the answer.

2.9 *Teaching Framework (Story 9)*[14]

At the end of the class, Li Qun asks them to prepare for the "5-minute speech practice" after class. There are reports about the flood on CCTV channel every day and Li Qun asks the students to pay close attention and do a presentation in the next class. "This is a specific training on a given topic," explains Li Qun. She also gives detailed guidance for the speech: "You shall make your speech articulate and consistent while giving the speech before the whole class." She asks two students to "rehearse" on the platform.

...

The speaking training on the topic of "Flood Control and Relief" lasts more than one month. In Class A and B, where Li Qun teaches Chinese Language, it goes smoothly. Students take turns to give a speech on the platform and the audience students listen quietly, but the speakers' clothes, their expressions, and their manner of speech occasionally give rise to ridicule and discussions among the listeners, which quickly calm down if their strict teacher, Li Qun, looks at them. In Class B, which is usually livelier, Li Qun finds an interesting phenomenon that there is no one applauding for the speakers. Li Qun then advises they applaud before and after each speech, for that will show the responsiveness of the audience and encourage the speakers. This advice is implemented very well. Li Qun explains, "I would say that is pretty unusual because normally other students would take the initiative to applaud while another student is giving a speech. This is what they are trained to do in the Chinese Language course. Perhaps they refrained because they pay too much attention to discipline and mistakenly believed that applause is not allowed."

---

14   This story is from a classroom observation (1998-08-9).

Class A, which is more inactive and quiet, surprises Li Qun this time, for they give applause when they hear interesting opinions. However, compared to Class B, Class A seems to be more prudent.

All comments are made by Li Qun and they usually cover three aspects: articulation, the journalistic style, and accuracy. There is an interesting anecdote during the comments. The speech by a girl in Class B is about the Financial Crisis in Asia and the status of the RMB. The girl is natural, relaxed, articulate, and clear-headed. In terms of the speech, she does a good job. Li Qun also positively comments on the speech by another student, saying the topic is good. Then she keeps analyzing the former girl's speech by referring to the statement "Japan has changed its Prime Minister and the government does not want to spend money curbing the financial crisis," so as to emphasize the superiority of socialism, but she does not give a further comment on the girl's performance. Li Qun usually will not spare praise on the good job done by students, but this time, it is training on a specific content and a given goal. Although the student does not quite follow the goal, Li Qun still discovers worthwhile factors for ideological education in her presentation. Li Qun does not pay much attention to other aspects that are beyond her framework.

Li Qun cares about whether the goal is achieved, and she is always ready to inculcate ideological education, so she will consciously neglect factors beyond the set goal.

2.10   *Free Time (Story 10)*[15]

Teacher Z, the young apprentice of Li Qun, attends her first class on the unit of journalism. Before that, Li Qun reviews his teaching plan and gives him some advice. In the school, there is such a tradition that all teachers with less than three years' teaching experience should be apprenticed to a mentor. Every semester, the apprentice teacher should give an open class, which will be attended and assessed by all other teachers and recorded in his/her archive. The assessment will determine if he/she can "finish the apprenticeship" by the end of the third year.

In the second session in the morning, Z teaches Chinese Language to Class C, where he also has the 5-minute speech practice module inspired by Li Qun but with the addition of his own innovations in form and content. In the first place, he tells his students that it is a practice of "Commenting on the news," which raises great interest among students because images of famous CCTV anchors like Shui Junyi and Jing Yidan come to mind. Secondly, they have

---

15   This story is from a classroom observation (1998-08-9).

a broader range of choice in topics, not only focusing on the flood but also including other events.

Students fidget in their seats, so it is not very quiet in the classroom. The previous semester, students in Class C also felt unrestrained while many teachers were attending the "Open Class."

There are three students giving speeches in the beginning, one being a volunteer and the other two are decided by taking turns. Students in the audience will comment on the speeches first and the teacher then gives a concluding or complementary comment. Like the other two classes, Class C does not have many students volunteering for questions, but from their expressions and body language, it can be noted that they want to give it a try. Therefore, teacher Z says, "Hi Mr. / Miss XX, I know you have something to say ..."

Today, when the first student ascends the platform, the whole class becomes brisk, expressing their excitement by all kinds of means except for loud acclaim. Applause is common even without the teacher's reminders. Some boys even extend their arms towards the speaker and clap their hands vehemently. Some speakers comment on the topic of flood relief; some pretend to be a sports commentator, giving long and vivid description of recent sports matches. After the speech, two boys are asked to comment on the speech and teacher Z says "Let's see who will be the next commentator." As he hesitates, the boys start to bargain and one boy says: "It is the girls' turn, for boys have already been asked." Teacher Z listens with a smile when this boy is echoed by other boys. The girls pout at the boys, but their teacher finally adopts the boy's advice and says, "OK. Now let's invite a girl," which makes the boys very happy. In the meantime, some students lose their self-control and start fidgeting and whispering. Z feels that it is a little too much, so he pulls a face, criticizes them, and takes away things like the pencils with which they play. Quiet returns to the class, yet the students deprived of their toys are not upset and two boys in the back row murmur, "Don't worry, he will simile soon."

As predicted, Z gets back to business and reveals a childish smile. He also adopts the textual analysis used by Li Qun, and no student says "No" when asked a question. Their answers may be wrong or far-fetched, but they are all thoughtful. In the class, Z often pays attention to the students' thoughts and reasoning skills according to their answers, always thinking "Why it is so?" in an attempt to find the unreasonable parts and provide proper guidance. In his class, students study the teacher's intention, and vice versa. Students thus can express their understanding, right or wrong, with considerable freedom. Sometime, this method will backfire because students may get distracted and the situation gets out of control, at which point the teacher will interfere. Sometimes, it is so embarrassing that the teacher's plan will get nowhere.

Here is an example. At the end of this class, Z gives the assignment, asking each student to do a week-long day-by-day report on a certain on-going activity. Immediately, students take their opportunities to ask questions: "Haven't we done the same thing in the past?" "We are at school every day, so how do we know what has been done?" "Too much homework!" Those questions and complaints make Z feel that the assignment might indeed be a little excessive, so he just defends himself slightly, and the students reckon that as a compromise.

Viewed from the general requirements for teaching, this homework is problematic because it fails to consider continuity and gradualness. It is true that there are the units on journalistic writing for students in both Grade one and Grade Three, but Z does not give enough attention to the different requirements and key points for different grades. Experienced teachers like Li Qun will not have such a problem, so students will not challenge her teaching plans. For example, both Li Qun and Z ask students to write a report on the people involved in the flood relief, but Z does not specify if it should be "one person" or "several persons," while Li Qun not only clearly says the "people" should be "PLA soldiers" but also reminds them that the report should reflect "what role the PLA have played in the flood control and relief." Li Qun knows that "students have been trained to write on one person in Grade one, and it will be a new thing to write on a group of people by referring to the text "Who are the dearest people?" Besides, Li Qun intends to guide students to have an integrative analysis of the materials in the newspaper.

Compared to Z, Li Qun does not give full play to students' expression of ideas, but she can control the situation very well.

3 Rules in Li Qun's Teaching

3.1 Rule One: Well-Prepared Outline for Teaching

The well-prepared outline by Li Qun is typified by her careful preparation before the class. It can be seen from Li Qun's class imagination in Story 1 that she treats her teaching very seriously. Years of teaching make her very familiar with each text, yet instead of relying on experience and improvisation, she always conscientiously prepares and plans for the class.

We also find Li Qun forms her own teaching skills, with the most particular being "integrating reading with writing." From Story 1, we can see her "special way" to analyze the texts is to summarize the structure of the texts and use it as a norm to better students' understanding and training. As an example, in the unit on argumentative writing, the structure is "identifying the target—direct argumentation, indirect argumentation—conclusion." In the whole process of teaching this unit, the clue of "integrating reading with writing" is very clear. In the first class on the unit of argumentative writing, she clearly introduces the structure of this type of writing and keeps emphasizing it in subsequent classes. Training students to write is a step-by-step process. The first step is to give an example topic. Then students will be asked to think on the topic and say how they will criticize the given view according to the structure of argumentative writing. Thirdly, students will spend several minutes writing a passage, after which the teacher gives formal guidance and then students write a complete piece. Lastly, the teacher comments on the writings and sees if students have used the skills taught (Story 1, Story 3 and Story 6).

The skill of "integrating reading with writing" typifies Li Qun's professional standards in teaching. It is personal rather than official, and it is a practical rather than textual or purely conceptual teaching goal. The firm and personally-fulfilled objective in teaching will make a rigid teaching plan possible. On the contrary, a class with no fixed aim is usually connected with an indecisive teacher.

In addition, we also see that Li Qun adheres to her objective in the class. She gradually leads students to her preset "traps" (Story 3 and Story 6). Meanwhile, as for the unexpected performances of the students, Li Qun will correct the wrong ones and neglect the irrelevant ones, letting them disappear and not affecting the class (Story 6, Story 8 and Story 9).

3.2   Rule Two: Intensive Training on Basic Knowledge and Skills

It is obvious that Li Qun gives top priority to basic knowledge and skills in her teaching. One example is her requirement of students in grade two to copy new words (Story 7). A more typical instance is the style of "Personal Writing" that integrates reading and writing. Although her teaching covers the understanding of the theme, analysis of the author's tone and emotion, and appreciation of the graceful diction and genre, she still believes structure is the foremost thing. Actually, this is the basic training of students' writing skills. The training in basic knowledge and skills takes effect in the senior high school entrance examination.[16] However, there are also adverse effects. For example, in terms of literary talent and unique theme and content, these students "fail to do a good job," as Li Qun puts it.

---

16   In the senior high school entrance examination in 1999, Li Qun's classes performed better
        in Chinese Language than other classes.

3.3   *Rule Three: Teacher's Authority and Manners in the Classroom*

Like other teachers, Li Qun establishes a special relation with her students through interactive teaching. Due to various reasons, the relation with Class A is not as desirable as with Class B (Story 4). Nonetheless, for Li Qun, there is no room for compromise in teaching and students could not find fault with her scrupulous plans. As a matter of fact, this kind of teacher-student relationship is characterized by the teachers' dignity and authority and subsequent respect by students. This relation is full of tension, which also reflects the authority established by Li Qun. For example, students in Class A are quieter (Story 4), and in Story 9, Class B is more cooperative and always listens to Li Qun. Class A is less cooperative and tends to take its own initiative even if in small things like applause. In Story 5, we can also see that although students in Class B are used to Li Qun's rigidity, they still fail to follow the rules in her absence. From students' point of view, Ms. Li is not very approachable. It is apparent that Li Qun's near-perfect teaching plan and exceptional control of the class help build such a teacher-student relationship which establishes her undisputed authority in the class.

The authority of a teacher is mirrored by the lack of flexibility in classroom behaviors, which is typified by the handling of "difficult" students in Story 3 and Story 6. This is also obvious if we compare teacher Z with Li Qun, in whose class students have less "unauthorized" rights and less opportunities to express their thoughts freely (Story 10). In contrast, we also see that Li Qun's good control of the class is based on her proper handling of the knowledge and her impressive prediction of students' behaviors (Story 10).

3.4   *Rule Four: Reconciling Different Tasks*

As a teacher, Li Qun has to readjust her plan according to various situations. We can take Story 7 as an example. Li Qun makes a teaching plan for the unit on journalistic writing according to the following factors: the requirements for the unified examination by the local Education Bureau, Li Qun's review of the past exams, and her understanding of the syllabus and textbooks. Additionally, Li Qun faces pressure due to the school's assessment (Story 2), the assessment by the local Education Bureau, examinations (Story 7 and 8), the competition between different classes (Story 4), and so forth.

It is apparent that Li Qun has the ability to reconcile various tasks and adopt a methodology and teaching materials (Story 7) by taking different factors into account. Sometimes it is hard to make a choice, but as a conscientious teacher, she usually makes decisions conducive to students' rate of admission into higher schools, which plays a decisive role in the children's future.

4   Li Qun's Narrative about Her Professional Career[17]

I am grateful for my college years when I lay a solid foundation in Chinese language studies. It was only in the internship during the last year when I really started to learn to be a teacher. At that time, my mentor told me that classes have to be consistent, so that a teaching plan is indispensable. Teaching is just like story-telling that has a clear uniting storyline as well as suspense through telling the audience, "Please wait until the next session." "One session, one gain" was proposed then. The "gain" is actually a key point. Some teachers want to grasp all the important things in a class, but that is counter-productive and ends in students' grasping no key point. A teacher needs a focus in the teaching plan, and I attach great importance to the focus aspect of making a teaching plan because of the influence of that mentor. However, the teaching plan then is only for a single text rather than an entire unit. In trying to make a perfect plan, teachers might neglect basic knowledge. In making the plan, teachers are also led by their own intentions and usually will not consider students' specific situations in terms of their knowledge and thinking ability.

After graduation, I was assigned to a teaching position in a school affiliated with a state-owned corporation. In order to learn from other teachers, I often went to attend their classes in the first semester. Once in a Chinese language class for grade one taught by a middle-aged teacher, I did not pay much attention to the fact that she copied all the new Chinese characters on the blackboard. I even showed some contempt. However, in a later test, I found that students in my class did a bad job in the character part and their scores were also undesirable. That sounded the alarm for me and reminded me of my sitting in that teacher's class. Since then, I started to pay attention to basic knowledge, which quickly took effect and my work was also recognized and praised by the school leadership.

Our school was not well-known and we were eager to learn from others. If any teacher from other schools came to give a lecture, or if there was an open class, we would even cancel our classes to attend.

In the second half of the 1980s, there was an unprecedented reform in Chinese language teaching. For example, in Guilin, the place where our school was located, there was a series of open class contests titled "Autumn along the Li River" and "Spring in Guilin" which attracted a lot

---

17   This part comes from interviews with Li Qun and has been approved and revised by Li Qun.

of participants. There were also a lot of famous expert teachers of Chinese language coming to our city to give lectures.

Once, discussions were held on "Ability Building" and it is then that I attended the lectures by Mr. Wei Shusheng. Though deeply impressed by Mr. Wei, I was aware that it would not be easy to copy or imitate him. However, he gave top priority to the ability building of students, especially their ability of self-education, and that was very inspirational to me.

Later, I attended the class by Mr. Qian Menglong. I clearly remember that he had just given an open class to teachers from Shandong Province that morning in which he analyzed the text "March toward the Desert." In that class, I noticed the efforts made to improve students' oral language skills. Stick figures were used in the class to give vivid illustration about how to cultivate a forest shelter, and then students were asked to describe it orally, which was pretty satisfactory to me. At noon, I went to the Auditorium at the Army Academy. I held seats for teachers from Shandong because they lived quite far away, yet I was blamed by someone who did not know the reason. Mr. Qian proposed the "Three M" idea, namely "teachers as the main guidance, students as the main focus and training as the main method," which had a great influence on me. In that session, Mr. Qian analyzed the text "The Dead Sea is not Dead," and impressed deeply on me in two aspects. One was that students were taught the right way to learn. The other was Mr. Qin taught students to "Learn by Morpheme," that is, to learn by guessing the meaning of each Chinese character in a phrase. In this way, even without a dictionary, students would know the meaning of the phrase. Another thing is teaching students to think independently. The last sentence in the text is: "The Dead Sea is indeed going to die." Mr. Qian asked students to discuss "Will the Dead Sea really die?" Finally, he used "Chemical Equilibrium" to make a conclusion: The Dead Sea will not die. After the class, I consulted a chemistry teacher who told me it is true, which made me admire Mr. Qian very much.

We also attended classes given on units. Those were experimental classes offered by several teachers in Guilin. At that time, there was usually no so-called "unit" in the textbooks and teachers just put relevant texts together.

From that background, I formed my own special methodology. In 1988, I took part in the "Contest of Reformed Teaching" as the representative of my school and got the second place award. The Director of the Education Bureau highly praised me and mentioned me as an example several times in his speech. Later, a member of the Assessment Committee told me I took 5 minutes to review what was learned in the last class. Some Committee members thought that was too long; otherwise I would have gotten the first place award.

Then I got married and had a child …

In 1992, I went to Liuzhou with my colleagues to attend the observation classes given by excellent teachers from the greater city area. I learned the method of "Integration of Reading and Writing" but hadn't yet tried it in teaching writing. After attending the demo class by a teacher from Luchuan County, I truly understood what "Integration of Reading and Writing" was. I bought the book *Personal Style Writing* by that teacher and studied it closely. He advocated summarizing with an outline by referring to famous works and using them as guidance for students' writing. After returning from Liuzhou, I started an experiment in a grade one class. After a period of time, I found it improved their writing quickly, so I kept using that method in my class. In the beginning, I merely followed suit, but I gradually put my own ideas into it and that has worked more effectively.

In 1993, I was transferred to work in a key school in the same city. There I studied the concept of "How to Write Faster" by Mr. Yang Chuchun of Hunan Province. It introduced how to efficiently read a topic, to decide a theme and content, to produce a framework, and so forth. With the help of such a concept, a teacher may teach as much in one class session as can typically be covered in two. I tried it and it works. In my class, there were even students who could finish a piece in 20 minutes. I also tried to combine it with the technique of "Personal Style Writing" and the unit-oriented methods, and they also worked well together.

Later, there were not as many opportunities for exchange as before. Nowadays, it seems there are a lot of new terms and concepts popping up, aren't there? My colleague attended a training project and offered a lecture on "Constructivism" after returning to our school. I was among the audience of the lecture, and afterward I realized it is almost the same as "Link the old and the new knowledge," a concept we talked about in the past. Afterwards, I discussed "Constructivism" with another colleague in that project and obtained a deeper understanding of it. For example, a teacher points out the weakness in the students' present knowledge system and asks them to search for it online. After becoming familiar with some new concepts, students will again be asked to see what weakness there is and do further research. This procedure is quite complicated and cannot be easily represented in one class session.

In the spring of 1993, Ms. Yu Yi came to our city and advocated the idea that "a teacher should be like a director." Her class on "Ode to a Tea Flower" was very impressive. Unlike other teachers, she did not write the title of the text on the blackboard. She wrote "flower" while talking about "flower," "tea" while elaborating on "tea," and did not write "ode" until finishing the whole text. She started from "flower," then moved to "tea flower," and finally finished with "Ode to a Tea Flower." As for her "director" theory, I couldn't agree more, and that is also what I want to achieve in teaching.

5   The Personal Educational Belief of Li Qun

If there is a guiding theory behind each behavior, then according to the anecdotes and routines in Li Qun's teaching, we can infer that her personal educational belief is her guide. In the meantime, Li Qun's narrative of her career growth is a recollection and reexamination of her profession.

5.1   *The Nature of the Process of Learning*

Li Qun prepares her teaching plans conscientiously and prioritizes the training in basic knowledge and skills. What philosophy does each of those things reflect?

In the first place, the conscientious teaching plan specifies the content of teaching, that is to say, the content is made easily available and included in the teaching, the textbooks, and reference books. Students just need to digest and internalize it. According to Li Qun, learning is a process of reception.[18]

Secondly, classes should be arranged systematically according to students' knowledge and the content for learning. For instance, in teaching the unit on argumentative writing, the first class elaborates on the most inclusive rule of the whole unit—the structure of argumentative writing. In the following class, this rule will be reiterated. Meanwhile, new knowledge will be added by illustrating concepts like positive argument, negative argument, and concluding

---

18   D.P. Ausubel believes reception learning differs from discovery learning in that, in the former, learning of new knowledge relies on what is already known and does not include any discovery by students. They only need to absorb what is taught, that is to say, they need to integrate it into their present cognitive structure, so that it may reappear and may be used for a certain purpose in the future. The basic feature of discovery learning is that students do not learn what is given to them. Instead, before absorbing any knowledge, they have to take the initiative to discover it. The only difference between discovery learning and reception learning is the former has one more step—discovery. See Shi 1994, 232–233.

with a famous saying. In doing so, consideration should be given to both the logical consistency of the information and connection between students' old and new knowledge. Usually, in the training on writing, Li Qun first leads students to learn the structure of argumentative writing through reading. Then she asks students to orally describe the framework and write a short passage on paper. Finally, complete guidance is provided and students are asked to finish an essay on a given topic in a fixed period of time. Those steps form a "training in writing trilogy" that gives sufficient consideration to students' cognitive structure. In this sense, Li Qun views this kind of learning as a process of meaningful learning.[19]

According to Ausubel's Assimilation Learning Theory, it seems that Li Qun deems learning as a meaningful reception process. Nonetheless, this does not seem to provide a satisfactory explanation for her teaching. For example, Li Qun designs her teaching in a way that abides with the principle of meaningful reception learning and she believes she could pass knowledge to her students this way. Meanwhile, she also needs a way to assess how much knowledge is received by her students. How does she know whether the students have really absorbed what she has taught?

Perhaps she has to wait to see if the knowledge "may be used for a certain purpose in the future" (Shi 1994, 232–233). But the "recognition of the past knowledge" and to "use it for a certain purpose" are two levels of intellectual activities, and we want to know which is the goal Li Qun wants to achieve. These questions shed light on other features of Li Qun's teaching.

First of all, in Li Qun's class, there is an objective and definite answer for every question, including the prepared questions and the open questions. For instance, in the writing class, Li Qun asks her students to "discuss how to argue against 'school education is useless,'" which is actually an open question, but later questions are guided so that students can give "standard answers" preset by Li Qun. From Li Qun's point of view, this is the preliminary stage in argumentative writing and needs basic training so that students can develop the ability to form a basic structure. Of course, such a structure is a primary norm that is not negotiable.

---

19   D.P. Ausubel believes there are two preconditions for meaningful learning. "Firstly, students show the tendency to engage in meaningful learning, namely the tendency to establish a connection between what is newly learned and what is known. Secondly, what will be learned is potentially meaningful to the students and enables them to connect their present knowledge ... Any learning with the above two features is meaningful learning." See Shi 1994, 232–233.

In the second place, Li Qun's objective standard for the learning proficiency of students is to see if they give the right answers according to the rules. "Rule" is an essential concept in Li Qun's teaching. There are "rules" for writing, for textual analysis, and for answering questions. Although we know those "rules" cannot cover everything, if any of the students' work (oral or written) has no "rule" to follow, it will prove they have not made enough effort. Like learning writing, Chinese language learning is also based on "imitation." Therefore, the gauge for the efficacy in learning is to see if "the imitation is careful enough," namely, to see if students can use a certain body of "knowledge" to provide a standard answer to a certain question.

Thirdly, students' personal understanding and interpretation of questions in class is considered undesirable. We can see from the former stories that students' "correct" or "incorrect" oral and written work reflects their personal interpretation systems. Such a system usually floats under the mechanism of teaching constructed by the teacher, resurfacing and disappearing in turn. Sitting in Li Qun's class, we feel that she is connecting new information with the old, attempting to promote students' understanding of topics that are becoming increasingly complicated, and that she is also improvising new situations for student practice. However, in handling "new settings," the authority of the teacher and the lack of flexibility in the design usually prevent most students from giving full play to their intellectual potential. Consequently, a learning process characterized by "Concentration—Doing the Assigned Work—Memorizing" is formed, and learning turns out to be a process of accepting the known rather than understanding.[20]

---

20   "Teaching for Understanding" is a project created by Harvard Graduate School of Education to help teachers in the Boston, MA region. The project aims at establishing schools based on constructivism. According to the "Educational Issues Series," Constructivism posits that there are two typical values in assessing the learning process: to deem learning as a process of obtaining facts, and to view it as a process reliant on thinking and understanding. They differ from each other in that when a student "knows" (viewing knowledge as a fact) something, he can represent what he knows as required, namely show the knowledge or a certain skill, while understanding is a higher level of intellectual activity based on "knowing." According to the consensus reached in contemporary cognitive science, understanding means the ability to have various thinking activities about a given subject, such as explaining, finding evidence and examples, summarizing, applying knowledge and skills, analogizing, and expressing the same subject in a new way ... In brief, understanding means the ability to use all kinds of ways to represent knowledge and to further develop it. What is stressed here is the application of knowledge and skills in new settings. If students can only repeat what they have been told or what they have read in books, then it is not possible to tell if they have really understood the subject. If the teacher views learning as a process of obtaining facts, and the learning process

In short, Li Qun's belief in the learning process can be summarized as follows: Learning is a process of meaningfully accepting the known.

5.2   *The Nature of the Teacher's Role*

What kind of teacher's image has Li Qun created?

First, a teacher is the authority in knowledge. While assessing other teachers, Li Qun's first standard is to see the professional knowledge displayed in their teaching. In preparing for her own classes, she also tries to have a thorough understanding of the contents in the textbooks from an academic perspective. Before each class, she spends much time studying the textbook, never allowing the existence of any question which she cannot answer. Teachers who attend her class usually comment on her by saying "Li Qun's analysis is thorough and profound."

Second, a teacher should give top priority to laying a basic knowledge structure for students. Li Qun's classes are well-organized, with the teacher like a director and students like actors acting plays made by the former. The interest and attention of students should center on the plays which aim at helping students form their basic knowledge structure. However, those plays do very little to promote students' independent or critical thinking. They also ignore the teacher's personality characteristics (such as her enthusiasm and creativity) and her profound learning.

Thirdly, a teacher plays the role of modeling positive behavior in the classroom. Li Qun always tries to live out the traditional belief that a teacher should be "a paragon of virtue and learning," both at and out of school. For example, she can resist materialism and is self-disciplined. In Li Qun, we feel the morality of Confucianism, namely the ideal of being a person of virtue. Teaching is imparting knowledge and educating people, so Li Qun tries to be a commendable model for her students.

---

is summarized as "Concentration—Doing the Assigned Work—Memorizing," then the learning outcome is only measured by whether specific questions can be answered. On the contrary, if the teacher thinks learning is a process of understanding, connecting old and new knowledge and comprehending an increasingly complicated knowledge base and information system, then the teacher will make an effort to ignite students and listen to the understanding (based on what they know) of the questions by students with different backgrounds, and to understand students' conceptual systems on the given subject or topic. The teacher can also design a teaching method to help students update and develop their current knowledge structure, so as to connect and reconcile the new and old knowledge. The assessment also focuses on testing to assess if students can flexibly use their knowledge in new settings. See Harvard Graduate School of Education 1999.

Fourthly, a teacher should be a person of dignity and authority revered by students. In Li Qun's classes, a teacher is the authority of knowledge and order. All explanations made by the teacher are right, factual, and incontestable truth. Students should accept the knowledge according to the teacher's teaching. Morally, a teacher is almost a "saint" exhibiting no grief, no elation, and no selfishness. In the role of a teacher, she is admirable but not amicable, respectable but not approachable.

Therefore, Li Qun's belief in the role of a teacher can be summarized as that of "a scholar psychologist."[21] Actually, we can identify the features of Li Qun

---

21   From 1988 to 1992, Christine Bennett, a professor at Indiana University, completed
      research about how teachers view their role and found seven teaching perspective types
      at two levels. The first three perspectives are just like primary colors while the other four
      are like the secondary and tertiary colors made by mixing the primary colors. This essay
      will use the seven perspectives to explore Li Qun's understanding of a teacher's role and
      the nature of teaching. Perspective One: Teachers as the "Inculcators." Inculcators view
      the passing of theoretical knowledge as their primary task in teaching and do not refer
      to factors like the nature of the learners, subject matter relevance, teacher personality
      characteristics (such as their enthusiasm and creativity). The focus of their teaching is
      control and discipline. Perspective Two: Teachers as "Empowerers." Empowerers describe
      teaching as utilizing a power able to shape the society and give more emphasis to the self-
      actualization, rights, independence, and self-control of children. They add a social action
      dimension to teaching, hoping to use policies, cultural pluralism, and tolerance of various
      views to affect students. Perspective Three: Teachers as "Friendly Pedagogues." Friendly
      Pedagogues define education as a function of class preparation and teacher personality
      (organization and enthusiasm). Their eclectic goals and values in education mean a dislike
      of preaching and monotonous work; instead, they advocate questioning and discussion.
      They also put emphasis on a well-prepared syllabus and students' feedback. Perspective
      Four: Teachers as "Facilitators of Thinking." They believe the foremost goal in teaching is
      thinking and life-long learning. Although they are versatile, they de-emphasize academic
      content and stress critical thinking, problem-solving, and self-learning, such that they
      resemble Empowerers. They attach more importance to the cognitive rather than social
      dimension of education. Perspective Five: Teachers as "Nurturers." Nurturers perceive
      teaching as an interaction with students. They think good teachers are open, responsible,
      flexible, and attainable (respectable but unapproachable). They emphasize the progress
      of the learners, and care about their future, just like the Empowerers. Because they do not
      prioritize academic content, they also resemble the Friendly Pedagogues. Perspective Six:
      Teachers as "Friendly Nurturers." Friendly Nurturers also stress academic content, and
      like Friendly Pedagogues, they emphasize teachers' personality characteristics like enthu-
      siasm, humor, and approachability. They want to maintain a balance between knowledge
      acquisition and students' interest. Perspective Seven: Teachers as "Scholar Psychologists."
      Scholar Psychologists stay at the center of all opinions and their content area empha-
      sizes knowledge of the discipline as a greater integration of those opinions. There are
      many teachers in this category but it is hard to define them accurately. They emphasize
      academic knowledge and prioritize connecting different areas like the Friendly Scholars.

as a teacher, but it is not easy to classify them. She prioritizes transmission of knowledge, emphasizes the basic structure of knowledge, stresses the relevance of different kinds of knowledge, and makes meticulous teaching plans for the classes. In addition, she gives priority to the connection between the future of students rather than their present life, understands the nature of adolescent growth from a psychologist's view and maintains an appropriate distance from her students. She does not believe a teacher should be open, responsive, flexible, unadmirable but unapproachable. She does not think a teacher should give up the central role in knowledge transmission, nor does she think cooperative learning would be more efficient. Also, she does not believe the teacher-student-relationship and personal characteristics of the teacher have any considerable influence on learning outcomes.

6   Stories about Li Qun's Life

We have analyzed stories about Li Qun's teaching, her narrative about her professional career, and our understanding of her teaching and educational beliefs. It seems we now need to draw a conclusion, so why should we tell her life stories? Our reasoning is that, from our point of view, her teaching is not just an educational issue, and this research does not aim to find a kind of norm for teaching, important as that may be. Instead, we want to examine those behaviors and narratives in order to make more profound discoveries. Knowing her life stories, understanding the environment she grew up and works in and her interaction with the greater environment will greatly benefit our analysis and interpretation of her teaching stories.

6.1   *Courtyard*

In the years of its planned economy, China's ministries, like the Railway Ministry, Ministry of Transport, Ministry of Coal Industry, Ministry of Petroleum and Chemical Industries, and Ministry of Construction, all had their own enterprises and institutions which were organized in a pyramid structure all over China. In urban areas at that time, housing, pensions, and many other benefits were administered by "work units," and only "jobless" people went to the

---

Meanwhile, they make meticulous teaching plans like the Friendly Pedagogues and are responsive and approachable like the Nurturers. In short, they emphasize the connection between knowledge and students' futures rather than the present life, describe students in psychological language, and understand the nature of adolescent growth. Seeing themselves as the counselors of students, they are willing to listen to their questions while keeping a proper distance from them.

non-governmental "Neighborhood Committee" for any possible benefits. In such a system, enterprises affiliated with the central ministries were relatively independent, building their own residential areas, usually at the outskirts of cities and towns, implementing policies related to their own industries, and sometimes speaking dialects different from those of the local people.[22] They also had their own "courtyard culture" that differed from the local culture. After retiring from military service, Li Qun's father went to work for a business like this.

According to the needs expressed in the "Third Front Movement," oil storage facilities for air defense were constructed in a mountain valley near a city. Li Qun was 8 years old then and moved there with her parents and other college graduates from Beijing, Sichuan, Wuhan, and other places. Though it was a remote village, the bright bulbs at night created an awe inspiring and even frightening atmosphere. It is possible to imagine what kind of reverence and pride the young Li Qun felt.

There was little cultural life in the mountainous village, but in the common courtyard there were occasionally events like the "Propaganda Performances." Deeply affected by such an environment, Li Qun felt strongly attached to the Chinese Communist Party, to her motherland, and to socialism. Therefore, in 1976, when three state leaders passed away, she was greatly saddened and felt as if heaven would fall, though her sentiment would not have been understood by a child outside the courtyard. Life in the courtyard laid the foundation for her future thoughts, which is reflected by her introducing ideological education in her classes. Nevertheless, children today can hardly understand stories like "The Seven Matches," [a story about Chinese Red Army in the Long March (1934.8–1936.10)] and a "generation gap" is thus formed in teaching.

After the "Lin Biao Incident," the work project was canceled and all people like her parents are transferred to work in the city. In 1974, Li Qun went to a secondary school near her home in that city. There was no positive learning environment at that time, and even today, local people still consider that school to be a kind of two-bit school. Yet Li Qun met several respectable teachers there. It was said that the father of her teacher of Chinese language had been a General in the Kuomintang Army. For that reason, this teacher had been exiled to Guangxi with her father, even though he was a graduate of

---

22   As an example, people working for the Liuzhou Railway Bureau developed a phonetic system called "Liuzhou Railway Dialect," which was a mixture of the local Liuzhou dialect with various others spoken by the railway staff from all over the country. Like the "Yishan dialect," it is an independent branch in the broad Liuzhou phonetic system. Offspring of the "Liuzhou Railway People" naturally inherited this dialect.

Yenching University. Another teacher graduated from a missionary high school in Shanghai. While the backgrounds of those teachers have not been verified, it is true that they were capable of teaching different subjects and they were all very good at English. Li Qun respected their exceptional learning and a career as a "teacher" thus formed a concrete and wonderful image in her mind.

As a result, she chose an educational institution for her college entrance examination in 1979. There were, of course, other reasons. Besides math, in which she got a very low mark, her scores in all other subjects were quite good. It was not that she did not study hard. It is just that she thought she did not have any talent in math at all. Her math teacher encouraged her by saying "Li Qun, you are good at other subjects and that means you are a smart girl. You also work hard. Therefore, I just want to say it's my fault and I am sorry ..." Li Qun was aware she had to face the college entrance examination—that her scores from four subjects had to compete with other students' scores from five subjects. In truth, she only got a little more than 10 in math, but her total score still met the undergraduate admission requirement. She also thought her personality characteristics would make her a good teacher.

As for what school and major to choose, Li Qun's parents gave her complete autonomy and respected her choice of an educational school. Her father's opinion was that "Teachers depend on their knowledge to make a living and they won't be ordered around all the time." This was obviously the career guidance of a father who had been involved in ideological and political work, and who had experienced a special period in Chinese history.

6.2   *Going to the Platform*

Li Qun was grateful for the four years she spent at the university where she laid a solid foundation in professional expertise. In the Chinese Department of her normal university, Li Qun was an obscure student with no exceptional talent and she was not very enthusiastic about social activities. Her academic outcome was also not impressive. However, in the internship undertaken in her last year, she performed unexpectedly well, and she says that she "found the feeling of being a teacher all of a sudden."

Wuzhou No. 1 High School was where Li Qun first formally ascended the platform in a classroom. She made full preparation for the first class, while the team leader and students were not optimistic about her because she had never made an appearance in public and lacked the experience of addressing a large audience. To prepare, she watched the video of "The Man in a Case" [a short story by Anton Chekhov] very carefully. Her first thought was to have a thorough understanding of the content, so she prepared for it conscientiously and produced a detailed teaching plan. She also wanted to make her teaching as appealing as that of Ms. Yu and did not want to follow tradition by writing the title on the blackboard, saying "The name of today's text is ...," and introducing the author and his background. Instead, she wanted to use a picture as the lead-in so as to interest the students. When that day arrived, however, she was quite nervous. The teacher in charge of that subject read Li Qun's plan and thought it was nice. When he told her he would not attend the class, Li Qun felt more relaxed.

On her way to the classroom, her heart pounded violently, and the students walking with her suggested they sing a song. Campus folk songs were popular then, so they sang "Walking on the Country Road," which brought much peace to Li Qun. However, all her efforts to calm down were futile the second she reached the door of the classroom. She doesn't recall how she ascended the platform or how she started the class, but once in front of the class, she concentrated on the content and gradually her nervousness dispersed. She became passionate and finally found the very feeling of being a teacher. After class, Li Qun found out that the above-mentioned teacher had been listening to her, sitting just outside the classroom. His compliments, encouragement and consideration deeply moved Li Qun and made her believe she had "found the feeling of being a teacher all of a sudden." Looking back to early stories like this, Li Qun believes that "to be a teacher is my fate."

6.3   School for Children of Employees

After graduation, Li Qun worked for 9 years in the school for children of the enterprise where her father worked. Like other schools not run by the Communist Party, schools for children of enterprise employees were also run by non-government sectors. They were in the managerial system headed by the local educational authorities, but they were actually affiliates of the enterprise. Culturally, they had a close relationship with the enterprises and possessed their own unique features. From the view of public schools, they were not mainstream and were different in many aspects.

Employees of the enterprises were divided into three types: the frontline staff—people working on-site, the secondary staff—people working in the office, and the third-rate staff—people working in the property management division. The first type was responsible for an enterprise's profit and they were usually viewed as the bread-winners for the other types of employees. In such a system, school stall fell into the third type; thus, the annual bonus of teachers depended on the profitability of the enterprise. If the enterprise declined, the school would also decline, and the latter was responsible to the former.

Almost all students at Li Qun's school were children of the staff of the enterprise, and they varied in their academic performance. Their fathers usually worked in the frontline of the enterprise, often only remaining at home for two months of every year and having almost no time to care about their children's education. Mothers were at home, but most were housewives or ordinary workers with little formal education. Meanwhile, the frontline staff members had a strong sense of superiority, due to which they had little reason to be objective. They could say what they wanted to the school and seldom viewed education as a professional field. They also showed no respect for the opinions and practices of professionals. Sometimes, parents complained to the general manager of the enterprise and the manager would immediately interfere by calling the headmaster of the school.

Li Qun encountered such a case not long after she started to work at the school. The monitor in her class was a bright boy with good grades. Li Qun liked him and believed he had a promising future. Though Li Qun was not active when she was a student, she still thought the comprehensive ability of a person was very important to his or her life. Therefore, she purposefully asked the bright student to participate in activities, like making the blackboard newspaper, to build his abilities. To Li Qun's surprise, the boy's mother told her, "You give too much homework to my son; otherwise he could have had better grades." Li Qun explained to her the significance of taking part in some extra-curricular activities, but it did not seem to have an effect because one day the headmaster asked Li Qun, "Is it true that you have asked your students to participate in too many non-academic activities?"

Li Qun also encountered an unpleasant incident during the first quiz she gave. She designed the paper and the weight of the points assigned to each area. Then she had the papers printed. She told the students the date and the scope of the test beforehand. After the test, she marked and graded the papers carefully. The highest mark was over 80, but most students get marks between 60 and 80, and a few failed. That is a normal score distribution. However, there were disturbances after students got their grades. Several parents came to school to complain, "My kid always got more than 90 in the past. How come he got just a little more than 70 this time?" Afterward, the leader of the school asked to speak with Li Qun and said that their investigation showed that the quiz section on ancient Chinese, which happened to be the students' weakness, was granted too much weight in the overall score; in addition, he said that the papers had been graded too strictly. After that, school leaders would come to observe her classes without any notice.

Later, in fulfilling a writing assignment, a student wrote a letter to Li Qun that allowed her to understand a lot of things. In the letter, the student said something to the following effect: Ms. Li, in the past, in the afternoon on the day before a test, we sit in the classroom, waiting for our teacher to guide us in a review. If we are not too lazy, we will usually get nice scores. All teachers do that, but why didn't you? Li Qun wrote a long comment in reply. She explained that if she were to do that, they might get better scores, but what would they do for the senior high school entrance examination? From our point of view, Li Qun explained her reasoning to the student and also gained a better understanding of herself. It might be possible that from this she began to understand it is not enough to develop teaching skills only according to her personal preference. A good teacher not only has to consider what is good for him- or herself, but also has to give account to the views of the school and parents.

Thus, she began to observe and adopt practices widely acceptable in the school. Understandably, those practices typified the value of that school. At that school, it was not rare for a student to be called out from the rest students and blamed in public, for example at school-level assemblies, in classrooms, in corridors, on the playground, or on other occasions. Almost all the teachers took similar actions when they spotted the "misbehavior" of a student. Usually, younger teachers stayed closer to students in the beginning. Some even buddied up with the students and mixed with them. But they soon found the drawbacks this brought to teaching. Some students would turn a blind eye to the teacher's instructions in the class, using grins to resist and disarm the teacher. As a consequence, those "fresh and young" teachers would change within a year and would distance themselves from students. Most teachers became quite strict. In turn, students would elect the "witch class mentor teacher" in private.

In the first year, Li Qun was also on close terms with the students, acting as if they were her classmates. Some students ran to her in the distance and would come up to hang their arms around her neck. Some encouraged her before the open class by saying "Don't be afraid, Ms. Li, we will be cooperative." And after the class, they would ask "How was it? We did a good job, didn't we?" But Li Qun felt the problem in the classroom, for "in a class session, you even can't finish a simple topic on a spring outing."

Gradually, her image of being "respectable but not approachable" came into being, which also reminds us of the "teacher-student relationship characteristic of maintaining teachers' dignity and authority that is respected by students."

One cultural practice popular in that school was closely related to "examination-orientation." The school was responsible to the enterprise and to parents, and the rate of admission into higher schools was the only gauge of success. According to the school's policies, bonuses for teachers depended on the enterprise's profit, and each teacher's bonus depended on students' scores in the subject taught by the teacher. For example, in the unified examination, if the average score of all students in a teacher's class was one mark higher than the average in the city, the teacher would get a certain amount of bonus pay, calculated by multiplying the average score in the city and the extra score earned by the teacher's class. On the one hand, this spurred teachers to set their own goals and try to find more effective methods of teaching, some focusing on numerous grade-oriented practices and some eager to predict questions that would be on the exam papers. On the other hand, it caused interpersonal tension between teachers. This was not tension between two specific teachers or among several teachers; it was between teachers teaching different subjects to the same class of students who would argue with each other over those students' schedules. If they were not teaching the same student class, there would be no fight. Teachers in charge of the same subject for different grades would teach the same subject to the same students throughout three years and then start another cycle by teaching a new set of students. In this case, teachers of the same subjects, whether teaching the same grade or not, would also compete with each other in terms of their students' scores, and they would not share their experience and references with each other. Generally, personal relations would have some effect on the tension. For instance, teachers who had fun together were on better terms. One day, however, when other colleagues had left the office, Li Qun saw that the new teacher L was still there, so Li Qun shared some of her hard-won references with L. L was deeply moved and they became close friends. This story reveals the pressure on teachers produced by the score-oriented tradition.

However, it was still an open-minded school where people thought it was essential to learn from others. Therefore, during the 9 years she spent there, Li Qun attended various seminars, observations, and trainings. Through contact and exchanges with the outside world, she accumulated experience and gradually formed her own effective teaching method.

By the end of the 1990s, China went deeper into reform, a move that affected schools operating for children of enterprise employees as ministry-affiliated enterprises became localized. Also, due to housing issues, Li Qun was transferred to work in the present key school in the city.

6.4   *Key School*

At the new site, Li Qun wanted to be recognized by the school as soon as possible, so she worked even harder. At the end of the first semester, she won the First Principal Award, the only one among teachers of Chinese language. In the unified examination, her classes' average score in Chinese language ranks first in her city.

Returning to teach grade one for the second time, she had a colleague studying in an MA Program. Seeing he had a book on psychology, she borrowed it and read it carefully. Afterward, she let "praise" play a dominant role in the classroom. In her memory, she almost never criticized students in that whole year. For example, after each examination, she just asked students to recall what kind of good job they had done. It worked smoothly in the beginning, but "gradually problems started to appear." "Showered with heartening words from the teacher, students still made many mistakes," "and it got worse in grade two …" Li Qun reflects, "Moreover, I also experienced frustration in achieving higher academic titles. I don't think it was fair play, if I think about some teachers who made it. So during that period of time I felt lost because my achievements were not recognized." Due to all those factors, Li Qun decided to stop the "Praise Policy." Instead, she shared a story from a magazine with her students in which a teacher does not interfere when a student experiences "puppy love." The student appreciates that understanding teacher. However, that student later drops out and blames the teacher by saying 'Why didn't she criticize me when I was not sensible?'"

Li Qun is strict to both students and herself.

Her daughter, Xiaoyu, loved singing and listening to music when she was a little girl. At age four, her daughter heard her uncle play seven notes on an electronic organ. Surprisingly, Xiaoyu remembered all of them and could play them on the organ as well. Since then, Xiaoyu displayed an exceptional interest in musical instruments, and Li Qun felt her daughter had a talent for music and she wanted to buy a piano for her. But Li Qun did not have enough money for it, so she felt guilty.

Nonetheless, Li Qun declined when a friend wanted to recommend her for a part-time teaching position at the night school of the Culture Palace, saying she needed more time with her daughter. That friend said, "This is nothing but an excuse. Even if you don't do it, you will not spend more time with your daughter." Li Qun thought about her friend's reply and said nothing, but she knew the real reason was that she was afraid such an activity might undermine her image. "How can a teacher do a part-time job?" She actually had two concerns. One was that doing a part-time job would be considered moonlighting, and that is against the professional ethics of being a teacher. The other concern was that if a teacher went to work part-time for another institution, the school might think she was distracted from her duty and would not tolerate it. Another time, another friend recommended her for a family tutoring position. She agreed to do it but refused to accept any money, saying she was happy to help the student but unhappy to accept money. The friend and parents were embarrassed and they said, "You have worked hard but you do not take money. You really put us in an awkward situation." Li Qun just replied, "What will other people say if they know I take money?" Actually, what worried Li Qun was not only that accepting the money "might invite gossip," but also that her part-time teaching "would invite gossip." Faced with similar situations later, she always reminded herself that she was a teacher who was supposed to be a noble, diligent, devoted and non-mercenary figure. Another situation that made Li Qun feel proud was that she tutored a student from another class in writing for free. The student wrote an essay and planned to submit it to *Guilin Daily*. Years later, part-time tutoring would become a common thing among school teachers and Li Qun felt the strong demand from students and parents, so she gradually accepted the idea of "receiving reasonable pay for one's work." But again, Li Qun did not accept much money, only whatever was given by the parents, or the minimum pay accepted by her colleagues.

In fact, Li Qun threw all her energy into teaching. She kept an eye on all kinds of details. She had to supervise students to see if they had done their duty, so it was usually around 7 PM when she arrived home after work. More often than not, in the whole office building, she was the last to have her supper. Even being so conscientious, there were still several incidents in the previous semester. One is that 6 students were absent from the music class, including the class monitors, and high, average and low performing students. Then a boy in the class was beaten by young adults outside of the school. A girl lent two porn comic books to her classmates and did not think it was wrong, arguing, "If there are places renting the books, then I can rent them." Another student mistakenly handed in his diary as the summer vacation homework. Those incidents exerted great pressure on Li Qun. A colleague and friend of Li Qun said, "Actually, similar things also happen in other classes, but Li Qun always think it is her fault. I have tried many times to persuade her into seeing the point that our school and teachers are not perfect, and that she is not the only person who should be responsible. I don't want her to take these kinds of things too seriously. There are many things that will make people feel helpless, so why not let them be?" But Li Qun worried that the leadership and other people would attribute the incidents in a given class to the incompetency of the class mentor, a judgment she found difficult to face. She worked to improve classroom management, gave admonitory speeches to students, increased contacts with parents, and asked them to provide more supervision. Her anxiety and concerns for her students were more than obvious.

One day, an article titled "How can any teacher take it anymore?" echoed Li Qun's thoughts. "Sometimes, there is really little we can do in education. As teachers, we surely have our professional ethics, but it is also a livelihood, and teachers are also ordinary human beings!" says Li Qun. She quit being the class mentor after that.

This reminds us of the Chinese tradition of viewing teachers as "sages." Even to this day, Chinese teachers are still not viewed as ordinary people.

6.5   *Family*

History left a deep imprint on Li Qun's family. Staff members in the enterprise where Li Qun's father worked fell into three groups: professionals, non-professionals, and others. Li Qun's father was a veteran and was thus naturally connected with the non-professionals. Retiring from the army, he worked on party affairs in the local authority and reached the section chief rank. In the 1960s and 70s, everything went smoothly for her father, but after the 1980s, intellectuals regained attention. For this and other reasons, her father was marginalized and neglected, eventually being transferred from an important position to work for the school; finally he retired as a section chief rank cadre. Actually, her father was crestfallen for a long time as he neared his retirement.

When her father was transferred to work as Secretary of the Party Branch at the school, Li Qun had just started her teaching career there, so she was still under the protective "umbrella" of her father. That is only one factor of their relationship. Additionally, her father has had a significant influence on her in other aspects, especially in his understanding of life, social milieu and in inter-personal relations. Many times, he has reminded her "to master professional expertise and never do administrative work." Li Qun has a younger brother, but she is the one who better understands and fulfills their father's expectation. As the oldest child in the family, she is also expected to be the first in the family to achieve social recognition. Therefore, she is eager to excel and works very hard. As a reward, she has become one of the "top teachers" in her school after only a few years. That, along with the report about her tutoring writing students for free, brings great comfort to her father.

Li Qun's mother had a bad family background that was not progressive in politics, and thus she did not qualify to join the Communist Youth League. She became an analyst at a local cement plant. As Li Qun recalls, her mother did all the housework without a single complaint. She also asked her children to take their father as a role model so as to pursue progress. We can imagine the sense of loss and the wishes in the inner heart of Li Qun's mother, as well as how she felt when Li Qun joined the Communist Youth League in grade two of second-ary school. She shared with Li Qun all her thoughts and feelings.

Later, Li Qun had her own family. After graduating from university, she was introduced to the man who would become her husband. "We met once and then I thought he was not bad." Indeed, he is a kind and faithful husband who brought Li Qun a peaceful and stable family life after marriage. Of course, after marriage, Li Qun became the actual spiritual and financial leader in the family.

Her daughter, Xiaoyu, has been her spiritual pillar.

Xiaoyu is now 8 years old. She is quiet, sensible and considerate. One day, Li Qun's colleague came with her 4-year-old daughter. The two adults went out and asked Xiaoyu to stay at home with the little girl. For over one hour, Xiaoyu tried to cater to the various wishes of the little girl by sharing all her toys, hoping she would be happy, but when their parents returned, they saw two joyless kids, with the little girl unhappy and Xiaoyu feeling wronged. A similar case had happened between this little girl and another 10-year-old girl. That time, the elder child neglected the younger one, leaving her crying loudly. Li Qun believes that it is important to develop her daughter's social skills to prepare her for future life; therefore, she taught her to be courteous, considerate and helpful when she was a very little girl. Now, whenever there is a dinner party, Xiaoyu knows is very courteous. In the case above, Xiaoyu did not do a very good job in taking care of that little girl, but she tried very hard to put up with her demands.

As a teacher, Li Qun gives her daughter little help in her learning. She does not send her to any tutorial classes; nor does she give her daughter any extra homework. Many parents buy reference books and pay for tutors. Those things are not difficult for Li Qun. However, what she does is merely remind her daughter by asking, "Have you finished your homework?" Usually, Xiaoyu takes the initiative to finish her homework, but a child is a child, so during holidays, she needs her mother to remind her "Finish your homework and then you can play." That is all Li Qun does to help her daughter, which differs from her attitude toward her students. In fact, Xiaoyu is a very clever, gentle and obedient child. Li Qun hopes she will have a happy childhood and she believes her own "inactivity" will help foster initiative in Xiaoyu.

If there are conflicts between Li Qun's school work and family affairs, she will definitely choose the former over the latter, even if it means sacrificing Xiaoyu's time to learn to play piano.

6.6   *Friends*

Most of Li Qun's friends are in the circle of education and they are usually kind and honest. A former colleague is a very important friend to her. Actually, she was once her best friend. Years ago, this friend resigned and went to Zhuhai, where she bought a piece of property and registered for local permanent residency two years later. Upon coming back to visit her family, this friend had a completely different mood and appearance, and she gave a lesson to her old friend Li Qun. Li Qun was kind of touched and also considered changing her job.

Later, there was an opportunity for Li Qun to work in an administrative position, but she ultimately did not choose it because of her father's influence. The vicissitudes in his life and fickleness of interpersonal relations made her father strongly opposed to her taking any administrative position. He hoped his daughter would "depend on her expertise to make a living" and avoid complex interpersonal relations. She listened to her father in that instance, but now she still feels a little regretful. She has also thought about doing business, but there has been no good opportunity and she doubts her capacity in business. When the above-mentioned friend returned to Guilin again, Li Qun finally gave up all those ideas. Different from the previous time, that friend is now not so proud and confident because she has experienced the colorful world out there that sometimes also makes people feel helpless. Now she feels her problem is that "she does not have much confidence in any other career than in teaching."

Li Qun has a typical feminine hobby of shopping for all kinds of accessories and souvenirs. In the past, there were various things like that in her not-so-spacious home. Those kinds of clay figurines, beautiful paper bags, and potted landscapes reflect the owner's taste in life. Without going there to see, you might not believe a teacher like Li Qun would have a house like that. She usually dresses plainly and seems strict and inflexible to her students, but it is another thing when it comes to her relationships with colleagues. Before spring festival and important holidays, Li Qun has been known to buy pretty clothes and gifts for the children of her friend, L. To spend her leisure time, Li Qun and her daughter go window-shopping, sight-seeing, and watch TV. When possible, Li Qun also travels to other places during her long breaks. She has been doing that for years. We also hear that in her audio-visual classes, she sometimes uses some TV programs she has come across and that sounds quite interesting.

In a visit to the new apartment building funded by the school, we find that Li Qun's apartment is spacious and each detail reflects her efforts. For example, the tiny night light in the corner and the delicate patterns on the hooks on which to hang things make us marvel at her perfectionist attitude and beauty-loving nature. Nevertheless, we also hear students complain, "To prepare for the school sporting event, we have to tailor-make uniform sportswear. We all prefer black T-shirts and white trousers because black is the fashion and it is beautiful, but Ms. Li asks us to buy deep blue trousers. When we march in the sports event, we don't feel a sense of pride." Li Qun does not understand and says "The sportswear is chosen by class monitors and I am just responsible for helping pay for it and bringing it back. Students in my class wear the deep-blue trousers and white Banilu T-shirts which were the most fashionable clothes for students." As a matter of fact, both the teacher and students have a beauty-loving heart, but their different roles, ages, and experiences give rise to problems in communication.

7   Contributory Factors to Li Qun's Educational Belief

From stories about Li Qun's life, we can feel the impacts on her present educational belief left by her career and daily life. For example, Li Qun's concept of a teacher originates from her junior high school life, when she admired the knowledgeable and conscientious teachers. Another influence is from her father, whose belief that a person should rely on his or her own expertise and professional dedication has become the gauge of a good teacher for Li Qun. Her first teaching experience as an intern also played an influential role, as her efforts were recognized by the mentoring teacher and that strengthened her belief in the importance of a thorough understanding of knowledge as a teacher. In the past 36 years, numerous factors have affected Li Qun's educational belief system, but we will just try to identify the stable and significant ones, and present them as follows.

7.1   Social Influence
In terms of education, society has its will fulfilled by teachers via educational authorities, schools, and academic research. Li Qun's educational belief is subject to social influence typified by the guidance of local education authorities. For instance, the Education Bureau requests schools to implement documents and seminars aiming for ideological and political education. Through an incentive system, teachers are guided in a certain direction so that schools can successfully implement society's will in areas such as selecting those who are talented.

7.2   School Culture
At a school, its culture plays a leading role. School culture is an invisible force consisting of the norms, values, beliefs, conventions, and rituals formed when people working together face challenges and solve problems. The culture of a school can provide support to teachers trying to improve their teaching and can also exclude teachers unwilling to identify themselves with such a group. It can inspire teachers to work for the same goal and may also penalize a teacher seeking individual benefit. It may encourage teachers to set a high

standard for students and may also indicate that one should "not expect better performance from those kids." In this way, school culture gradually exerts a subtle shaping effect on teachers' educational beliefs. The contents of school culture include the attitudes and beliefs of the school's staff and the neighbors around the school, its criteria of culture, and the interpersonal relations inside the school. In a school, those factors are usually quite stable and play their roles in the development of the school in the long term, but they may also become a hindrance when there should be some changes. How about the culture in the school where Li Qun has worked for 9 years?[23] In the matrix containing school, parents and educational authorities, school is usually the party taking the most blame for problems. However, those people who interfere with teaching affairs at school rarely understand education and show little respect for teachers' opinions. The only way to try to persuade them is to tell them that educators can help children take advantage of opportunities to further their education and reduce the number of "destructive delinquents" in the schoolyard. To those blamers, the hard-working parents give the guardianship of the children to the school, so they consider it to be the school's fault if the kids end up "good for nothing" or suffer any accident. They only care about the result. There is no collaboration, but just "giving orders" and "taking orders." While talking about students, teachers often say "I warned that so-and-so, and I am surprised to find that he/she is actually ..." and "That so-and-so is really slow, for he still does not understand me even if I have explained three times." From the teachers' point of view, students are juveniles who should be subject to strict discipline.

In terms of interpersonal relations, the incentive system aiming to improve the rate of admission into higher schools incurs tension between teachers while some teachers are on better terms because they often go out together having fun. As for this part of school culture, Li Qun is influenced by it on the one hand and also refuses to be part of it on the other hand. What she accepts is the emphasis on the admission rate. Although some teachers claim that test scores are not the only way to assess a student, they are still pessimistic about some students' futures because the school provides very few opportunities for students to give play to their other talents and potentials. The part Li Qun does not accept is that she does not join the entertainment-oriented

---

23 We have conceived an interview about school culture asks the following questions: What are the conventions and rituals at your school? Who are the role models? Are there any typical stories at your school? How do you think of students' learning outcomes? How is the relationship between colleagues? How is the relationship between students and teachers?

teachers because she intuitively believes "solid expertise" is the trump card. What impresses Li Qun deeply at the enterprise-affiliated school is how parents are highly influential in all school affairs. This kind of school has a subtle relationship with the enterprise, which culturally determines that the nature of such a relationship is one between the superior and the subordinate.

7.3   *Personal Life Philosophy*

The primary life philosophy for Li Qun is: To make a living through "solid expertise" and to be the master of your life. Factors like Li Qun's father, her strong personality, and her "boss status" at home all have had formative influence on her life philosophy. In the meantime, her life philosophy also exerts direct influence on her education philosophy, her concept of a teacher, and her attitude toward students.

In short, Li Qun's personal educational belief is formed in practice under the joint influence of social forces, school culture, and her personal life philosophy.

8   Afterword

In a recent meeting with Li Qun, she asks when I will come to her school again. At the beginning of this research, Li Qun was intuitively conservative about our observation, so, consciously or unconsciously, she just talked about "positive" things and avoided what she thinks to be "negative." However, we just need the truth, be it "positive" or "negative." We want "yes" or "no," "why" and "why not." When we tell her our research will come to an end, Li Qun feels as though bereft of something because she is used to the attention we pay to her. She wishes this kind of "attention" could last, for she is able to experience a different self while being exposed to the "attention" of others.

Suddenly, she asks me how to apply for an MA program. That is outside of my expectation, because at the outset, I had advised her to further her education so as to distance herself from the environment where she has lived over a decade, as a way to reexamine her life from a different angle. At the time, she thought otherwise. Yet now, she is preparing for the coming MA entrance exam to be held this year.

I cannot make a prediction for Li Qun's teaching career in the future, but I have already seen her willingness to make a change. I sincerely hope she will become a more autonomous new individual, so that one day, when she looks back at her career as an educator, she will see a life path leading to a higher level of "autonomy."

References

Chinese-Language Sources

Cihai Editorial Committee. 1979. *Cihai* 辞海 [Encyclopedia of Mandarin Chinese]. Shanghai: Shanghai cishu chubanshe.

Dictionary Editing Office at Institute of Linguistics in Chinese Academy of Social Sciences. 1979. *Xiandai hanyu cidian* 现代汉语词典 [Contemporary Chinese Dictionary]. Beijing: Shangwu yinshuguan.

Ding, Jiongxiao. 1997. Ketang jilv de shehuixue fenxi: yixiang gean yanjiu 课堂纪律的社会学分析：一项个案研究 [A Sociological Analysis of Classroom Rules: A Case Study]. MA Degree Thesis. Shanghai: East China Normal University.

Marx, Karl and Friedrich Engels. 2002. *Makesi enkesi quanji diyijuan* 马克思恩格斯全集第一卷 [Marx Engels Collected Works, Volume 1]. Beijing: Renmin chubanshe.

Psychology Dictionary Editorial Committee of Eight Universities. 1985. *Xinlixue cidian* 心理学词典 [Psychology Dictionary]. Nanning: Guangxi renmin chubanshe.

Shi, Liangfang 施良方. 1994. *Xuexi lun* 学习论 [Learning Theories]. Beijing: Renmin jiaoyu chubanshe.

Strauss, Anselm, and Juliet Corbin. 1997. *Basics of Qualitative Research* 质性研究概论, trans. Xu Zongguo 徐宗国. Taipei: Juliu Tu Shu Gong Si.

Wei, Shusheng 魏书. 1995. *Wei Shusheng wenxuan* 魏书生文选 [Selected Writings of Wei Shusheng] (Vols. 1 and 2). Guilin: Lijiang chubanshe.

Wei, Shusheng 魏书. 1990. *Yuwen jiaoxue tansuo* 语文教学探索 [Exploration of Chinese Teaching]. Kaifeng: Henan daxue chubanshe.

Non-Chinese-Language Sources

Abelson, Robert. 1979. "Differences Between Belief Systems and Knowledge Systems." *Cognitive Science* 3: 355–366.

Aguirre, Julia, and Natasha Speer. 1996. "Examining the Relationship Between Beliefs and Goals in Teacher Practice." Paper presented at the annual meeting of the American Educational Research Association, New York.

Behar, Linda S., and Frank Pajares. 1994. "The Effect of Teachers' Beliefs on Students' Academic Performance During Curriculum Innovation." Paper presented at the annual meeting of the Midwestern Educational Research Association, Chicago.

Behar, Linda S., Frank Pajares, and P.S. George. 1995. "Making or Breaking Curriculum Innovation: The Effect of Teachers' Beliefs on Students' Academic Performance." Paper presented at the annual meeting of the American Educational Research Association, San Francisco.

Borko, Hilda, and Ralph Putnam. 1996. "Learning to Teach." In *Handbook of Educational Psychology*. Edited by David C. Berliner and Robert C. Calfee, 673–708. New York: Macmillan.

Brickhouse, N.W. 1989. "Teachers' Beliefs about the Nature of Science and their Relationship to Classroom Practice." *Journal of Teacher Education* 41(3): 53–62.

Calderhead, James. 1996. "Teachers: Beliefs and knowledge." In *Handbook of Educational Psychology*. Edited by David C. Berliner and Robert C. Calfee, 709–725. New York: Macmillan.

Calderhead, James. 1998. "The Development of Knowledge Structures in Learning to Teach." In *Teachers' Professional Learning*. Edited by James Calderhead, 51–64. London: Falmer.

Chekhov, Anton. 1898. "The Man in a Case." In *Three Stories: The Grasshopper, The Man in a Case, The Darling*. Bristol: Bristol Classical Press.

Connelly, F. Michael, and D. Jean Clandinin. 1985. "Personal Practical Knowledge and the Modes of Knowing: Relevance for Teaching and Learning." In *Learning and Teaching the Ways of Knowing*. Edited by Elliot Eisner, 174–198. Chicago: University of Chicago Press.

Ernest, Paul. 1989. "The Knowledge, Beliefs and Attitudes of the Mathematics Teacher: A Model." *Journal of Education for Teaching* 15: 13–34.

Gallup, R.S. 1970. "A Cross-Sectional Developmental Study of the Relationship Between Female Elementary Teachers' Beliefs, Academic Preparation and Experience in Teaching." PhD. Diss., University of Florida.

Gudmundsdotir, Sigrun. 1991. "Culture Dimensions of the Good Teacher." ISATT (International Study Association of Teacher Thinking). University of Surrey.

Gudmundsdotir, Sigrun. "Narratives on Teaching." *The Fourth Handbook for Research on Teaching*. <http://www.jpt.unit.no/~jsg/sigrun/publikasjoner/NARRPR.tml> (Accessed April 20, 1998).

Harvard Graduate School of Education. 1999. "Educational Issues Series (1999), Teaching for Understanding: Educating Students for Performance." <http://www.weac.org/onweac/under.html> (Accessed January 29, 1999).

Harvey, O.J. 1986. "Belief Systems and Attitudes Toward the Death Penalty and Other Punishments." *Journal of Psychology* 54: 143–159.

Harvey, O.J., M.S. Prather, B.J. White, and J.K. Hoffmerister. 1968. "Teachers' Beliefs, Classroom Atmosphere and Student Behavior." *American Educational Research Journal* 5: 151–166.

Harvey, O.J., M.S. Prather, B.J. White, R.D. Alter, and J.K. Hoffmerister. 1996. "Teachers' Belief Systems and Preschool Atmospheres." *Journal of Educational Psychology* 57: 373–381.

Munby, Hugh. 1984. "A Qualitative Approach to the Study of a Teacher's Beliefs." *Journal of Research in Science Teaching* 21: 27–38.

Munby, Hugh, and Tom Russell. 1996. "Theory Follows Practice in Learning to Teach and in Research on Teaching." Paper presented at the annual meeting of the American Educational Research Association, New York.

Nespor, Jan. 1987. "The Role of Beliefs in the Practice of Teaching." *Journal of Curriculum Studies* 19: 317–328.

Nilssen, Vivl, Lsvang akole, Trondheirn, and Sigrun Gudmundsdotir. 1998. "Unexpected Answers: Case Study of a Student Teacher Dealing in a Math Lesson." Paper presented at the annual meeting of the American Education Research Association, San Francisco.

Schoenfeld, Alan H. 1996. "Elements of a Model of Teaching." Paper presented at The Annual Meeting of the American Educational Research Association. New York.

Thompson, Alba. 1992. "Teachers' Beliefs and Conceptions: A Synthesis of the Research." In *Handbook of Research on Mathematics Teaching and Learning.* Edited by D. Grouws, 127–146. New York: Macmillan.

Index